Analog and Digital Electronic Circuit

Analog and Digital Electronic Circuit

Ankit Tiwari

RANDOM

RANDOM PUBLICATIONS

NEW DELHI (INDIA)

Analog and Digital Electronic Circuit

ISBN 978-93-5111-232-7

Published in 2014 in India by

RANDOM PUBLICATIONS

4376-A/4B, Gali Murari Lal, Ansari Road
New Delhi-110 002
Phone : +91-11-43580356, +91-11-23289044
e-mail: randomexports@gmail.com, sales@randompublications.com, info@randompublications.com

Reprinted 2022

Type Setting by : Keystoneprintads, Delhi-110051
Digitally Printed at : Replika Press Pvt. Ltd.

Preface

Analog devices and systems process signals whose voltages or other quantities vary in a continuous manner. They can take on any value across a continuous range of voltage, current, or other metric. The analog signals can have an infinite number of values. Analog systems can be called wave systems. They have a value that changes steadily over time and can have any one of an infinite set of values in a range.

Analog signals represent some physical quantity and they can be a model of the real quantity. Most of the time, the variations corresponds to that of the non-electric (original) signal. The quantities that are to be measured, monitored, recorded, processed and controlled are analog and digital, depending on the type of system used. It is important when dealing with various quantities that we be able to represent their values efficiently and accurately.

There are basically two ways of representing the numerical value of quantities, analog and digital. Digital circuits are circuits dealing with signals restricted to the extreme limits of zero and some full amount. This stands in contrast to analog circuits, in which signals are free to vary continuously between the limits imposed by power supply voltage and circuit resistances. These circuits find use in "true/false" logical operations and digital computation.

Digital circuits are made from analog components. The design must assure that the analog nature of the components doesn't dominate the desired digital behaviour. Digital systems must manage noise and timing margins, parasitic inductances and capacitances, and filter power connections. Bad designs have intermittent problems such as "glitches", vanishingly-fast pulses that may trigger some logic but not others, "runt pulses" that do not reach valid "threshold" voltages, or unexpected ("undecoded") combinations of logic states. This book is designed for advanced undergraduates and graduate students with background knowledge in basic electronics including biasing, modeling, circuit, analysis, and frequency response.

I thank all members of my team who have helped in the preparation of the book. My special thanks go to "Random Publications" who have published the book.

– ***Ankit Tiwari***

Contents

Preface .... *v-vi*

1. **Introduction** **1**

Digital and Analog Signals 1
Design Issues in Digital Circuits 4
Digital Circuits 11
Analog Representation 11
Digital Number System 13
Digital System 15
Code Conversions 18
Numbers Versus Numeration 21
Binary Codes Systems 26

2. **Different Operating Conditions of a Transistor** **29**

Introduction 29
Transistor Configurations or Connections 35
Common-base (CB) Configuration 36
Charcterstics of CB Configurations 36
Common-emitter (CE) Configuration 37
Common Collector (CC) Configuration 38
Comparison of Three Configurations 39
Operating Point (Quiescent, Q or Silent Point) 40
Different Point on the Characterstics 40
Types of BJT'S 41
Transistor Terminals 43
Transistor Action 44
Transistor Biasing 46
Need for Biasing a Transistor 47
What Happens if a Transistor Is Not Biased 48

3. **Digital Binary Numbers and Codes** **50**

Digital Binary Numbers 50
Signed Binary Numbers 53
Representation of Unsigned Binary Fractions 59
Digital Binary Codes 59

Decimal To Binary 64
Information of Hamming Codes 67
Error Detecting 71
Theory of Error-correcting Codes 72

4. Digital Electronic Circuits 81

Introduction 81
Digital Integrated Circuits 82
Digital Electronics 84
Cleaning and Etching of Wafers 90

5. Design of Biasing Circuits 94

Voltage Or Potential Divider Biasing 97
Two Battery Bias Stabilisation 98
Thermal Resistance 101
Determine of Operating Point In Presence of Self Heating 102
Bias Compensation 103
Base Resistor/Fixed Bias Circuit 103
Biasing With a Feedback Resistor 104
Emitter Resistance Biasing (Or Self Bias) 107

6. Equivalent Circuits of Transistor Amplifier 108

Voltage and Power Gains 111
Alternative Ac Equivalent Circuits for the Amplifier 112
Relationship Between Input and Output of a Transistor Amplifier 113
Analysis of Transistor Amplifier 115
circuit of Common Emitter Amplifier 118
effect on an emitter bypass Capacitor 124
Frequency response 126
Common Source Amplifier At High Frequencies 128
Biasing in MOS amplifier Circuits 130

7. Semiconductor Diode 137

Introduction 137
Rectifiers 139
Characteristics of Diode 141
Half Wave Rectifier 142
Semi Conductor Memories 144
Decoders 148
principle of Varactor or Tuning Diodes 151

8. Combinational Circuits Design 155

Logic Circuits and Design procedure 155
Combinational Analysis procedure 156
arithmetic Circuit 157
Arithmetic Logic Uni 162
Multiplexes Circuit 164
circuits Decoders 167
Function of Magnitude Comparator 171

Technique of Binary multiplier 172
subtractor of Binary adder 173

9. Analysis of Sequential Circuits 176

Circuit Analysis 176
Sequential Circuits 179
Design of Sequential Circuits 180
Analysis of Clocked sequential Circuits 180
State reduction 182
States Assignment 183
single binary bit of Flip flops 184
Circuit Elements of Latches 198

10. Digital Signals and Gates 205

Introduction 205
variations of the Exclusive and OR gate 208
implementation of NAND and NOR gate 210
The Exclusive-NOR gate 214
TTL NAND Gates 215
Multiple Logic Input Gates 221
The inverter and "Buffer" Gate 228
Single-transistor Inverter Circuit of the NOT Gate 230
logic of Output Gates 239

11. Binary System 253

Basic Rules of Binary System 253
Binary Numbers 254
Octal Number System 257
Hexadecimal Number System 259
Integer Number 265
addition of large bit Binary Numbere 267
Numbers Versus Numeration 269
Negative Binary Numbers 270
Subtraction of Large Bit Binary Numbers 273
Binary Multiplication 278
Decimal to Binary Notation 279

***Index* 285**

1

Introduction

DIGITAL AND ANALOG SIGNALS

Signals carry information and are defined as any physical quantity that varies with time, space, or any other independent variable. For example, a sine wave whose amplitude varies with respect to time or the motion of a particle with respect to space can be considered as signals. A system can be defined as a physical device that performs an operation on a signal. For example, an amplifier is used to amplify the input signal amplitude. In this case, the amplifier performs some operations on the signal, which has the effect of increasing the amplitude of the desired information-bearing signal. Signals can be categorised in various ways; for example discrete and continuous time domains. Discrete-time signals are defined only on a discrete set of times. Continuous-time signals are often referred to as continuous signals even when the signal functions are not continuous; an example is a square-wave signal.

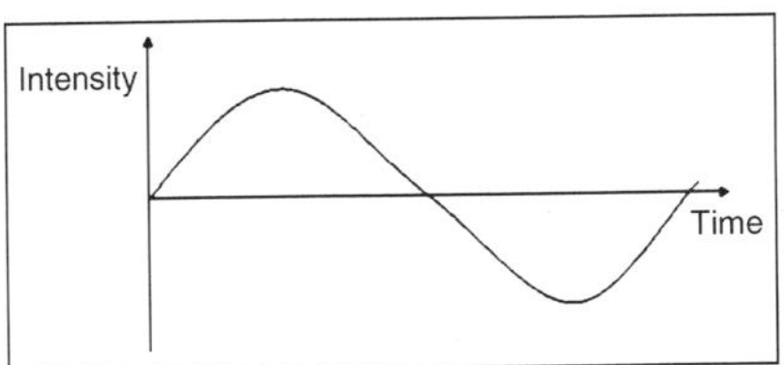

Fig. Analog Signal

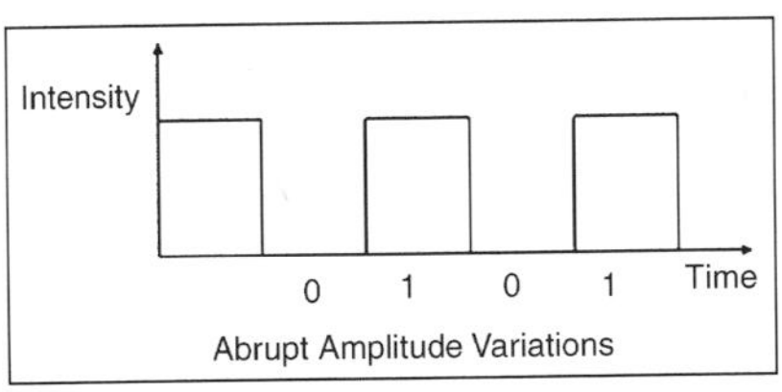

Fig. Digital Signal

Another category of signals is discrete-valued and continuous-valued or otherwise known as digital and analog signals. Digital signals are discrete-valued and analog signals are continuous electrical signals that vary in time as shown in Figures. Analog devices and systems process signals whose voltages or other quantities vary in a continuous manner. They can take on any value across a continuous range of voltage, current, or other metric. The analog signals can have an infinite number of values. Analog systems can be called wave systems.

They have a value that changes steadily over time and can have any one of an infinite set of values in a range. Analog signals represent some physical quantity and they can be a model of the real quantity. Most of the time, the variations corresponds to that of the non-electric (original) signal. For example, the telephone transmitter converts the sounds into an electrical voltage signal. The intensity of the voice causes electric current variations. Therefore, the two are analogous hence the name analog. At the receiving end, the signal is reproduced in the same proportion.

Hence the electric current is a model and is an electrical representation of one's voice. Not all analog signals vary as smoothly as the waveform shown in Figure. Digital signals are non-continuous, they change in individual steps. They consist of pulses or digits with discrete levels or values. The value of each pulse is constant, but there is an abrupt change from one digit to the next. Digital signals have two amplitude levels. The value of which are specified as one of two possibilities such as 1 or 0, HIGH or LOW, TRUE or FALSE and so on. In reality, the values are anywhere within specific ranges and we define values within a given range.

A digital system is the one that handles only discrete values or signals. Any set that is restricted to a finite number of elements contains discrete information. The word digital describes any system based on discontinuous data or events. Digital is the method of storing, processing and transmitting information through the use of distinct electronic pulses that represent the binary digits 0 and 1. Examples of discrete sets are the 10 decimal digits, the 26 letters of the alphabet, etc. A digital system would be to flick the light switch on and off. There's no 'in between' values.

ADVANTAGES OF DIGITAL SIGNALS

The usual advantages of digital circuits when compared to analog circuits are:

- *Noise Margin (resistance to noise/robustness):* Digital circuits are less affected by noise. If the noise is below a certain level (the noise margin), a digital circuit behaves as if there was no noise at all. The stream of bits can be reconstructed into a perfect replica of the original source. However, if the noise exceeds this level, the digital circuit cannot give correct results.
- *Error Correction and Detection:* Digital signals can be regenerated to achieve lossless data transmission, within certain limits. Analog signal transmission and processing, by contrast, always introduces noise.

- *Easily Programmable:* Digital systems interface well with computers and are easy to control with software. It is often possible to add new features to a digital system without changing hardware, and to do this remotely, just by uploading new software. Design errors or bugs can be worked-around with a software upgrade, after the product is in customer hands. A digital system is often preferred because of (re-)programmability and ease of upgrading without requiring hardware changes.
- Cheap Electronic Circuits: More digital circuitry can be fabricated per square millimeter of integrated-circuit material. Information storage can be much easier in digital systems than in analog ones. In particular, the great noise-immunity of digital systems makes it possible to store data and retrieve it later without degradation. In an analog system, aging and wear and tear will degrade the information in storage, but in a digital system, as long as the wear and tear is below a certain level, the information can be recovered perfectly. Theoretically, there is no data-loss when copying digital data. This is a great advantage over analog systems, which faithfully reproduce every bit of noise that makes its way into the signal.

DISADVANTAGES

The world in which we live is analog, and signals from this world such as light, temperature, sound, electrical conductivity, electric and magnetic fields, and phenomena such as the flow of time, are for most practical purposes continuous and thus analog quantities rather than discrete digital ones. For a digital system to do useful things in the real world, translation from the continuous realm to the discrete digital realm must occur, resulting in quantisation errors. This problem can usually be mitigated by designing the system to store enough digital data to represent the signal to the desired degree of fidelity. The Nyquist-Shannon sampling theorem provides an important guideline as to how much digital data is needed to accurately portray a given analog signal.

Digital systems can be fragile, in that if a single piece of digital data is lost or misinterpreted, the meaning of large blocks of related data can completely change. This problem can be diminished by designing the digital system for robustness. For example, a parity bit or other error-detecting or error-correcting code can be inserted into the signal path so that minor data corruptions can be detected and possibly corrected. Digital circuits use more energy than analog circuits to accomplish the same calculations and signal processing tasks, thus producing more heat as well. In portable or battery-powered systems this can be a major limiting factor. Digital circuits are made from analog components, and care has to be taken to all noise and timing margins, to parasitic inductances and capacitances, to proper filtering of power and ground connections, to electromagnetic coupling amongst data lines. Inattention to these can cause problems such as "glitches", pulses do not reach valid switching (threshold) voltages, or unexpected ("undecoded") combinations of logic states. A corollary of the fact that digital circuits are made from analog components is the fact that digital circuits are slower to perform calculations than analog circuits that occupy a similar amount of physical space and consume the same amount of power. However, the digital circuit will perform the calculation with much better repeatability, due to the high noise immunity of digital circuitry.

DESIGN ISSUES IN DIGITAL CIRCUITS

Digital circuits are made from analog components. The design must assure that the analog nature of the components doesn't dominate the desired digital behaviour. Digital systems must manage noise and timing margins, parasitic inductances and capacitances, and filter power connections. Bad designs have intermittent problems such as "glitches", vanishingly-fast pulses that may trigger some logic but not others, "runt pulses" that do not reach valid "threshold" voltages, or unexpected ("undecoded") combinations of logic states. Additionally, where clocked digital systems interface to analog systems or systems that are driven from a different clock, the digital system can be subject to metastability where a change to the input violates the set-up time for a digital input latch. This situation will self-resolve, but will take a random time, and while it persists can result in invalid signals being propagated within the digital system for a short time.

Since digital circuits are made from analog components, digital circuits calculate more slowly than low-precision analog circuits that use a similar amount of space and power. However, the digital circuit will calculate more repeatably, because of its high noise immunity. On the other hand, in the high-precision domain (for example, where 14 or more bits of precision are needed), analog circuits require much more power and area than digital equivalents.

CONSTRUCTION

A digital circuit is often constructed from small electronic circuits called logic gates that can be used to create combinational logic. Each logic gate represents a function of boolean logic. A logic gate is an arrangement of electrically controlled switches, better known as transistors. Each logic symbol is represented by a different shape. The actual set of shapes was introduced in 1984 under IEEE\ANSI standard 91-1984. "The logic symbol given under this standard are being increasingly used now and have even started appearing in the literature published by manufacturers of digital integrated circuits." The output of a logic gate is an electrical flow or voltage, that can, in turn, control more logic gates. Logic gates often use the fewest number of transistors in order to reduce their size, power consumption and cost, and increase their reliability. Integrated circuits are the least expensive way to make logic gates in large volumes. Integrated circuits are usually designed by engineers using electronic design automation software.

Another form of digital circuit is constructed from lookup tables, (many sold as "programmable logic devices", though other kinds of PLDs exist). Lookup tables can perform the same functions as machines based on logic gates, but can be easily reprogrammed without changing the wiring. This means that a designer can often repair design errors without changing the arrangement of wires. Therefore, in small volume products, programmable logic devices are often the preferred solution. They are usually designed by engineers using electronic design automation software. When the volumes are medium to large, and the logic can be slow, or involves complex algorithms or sequences, often a small microcontroller is programmed to make an embedded system. These are usually programmed by software engineers.

When only one digital circuit is needed, and its design is totally customised, as for a factory production line controller, the conventional solution is a programmable logic controller, or PLC. These are usually programmed by electricians, using ladder logic.

STRUCTURE OF DIGITAL SYSTEMS

Engineers use many methods to minimize logic functions, in order to reduce the circuit's complexity. When the complexity is less, the circuit also has fewer errors and less electronics, and is therefore less expensive. The most widely used simplification is a minimization algorithm like the Espresso heuristic logic minimizer within a CAD system, although historically, binary decision diagrams, an automatedQuine–McCluskey algorithm, truth tables, Karnaugh maps, and Boolean algebra have been used.

Representations are crucial to an engineer's design of digital circuits. Some analysis methods only work with particular representations. The classical way to represent a digital circuit is with an equivalent set of logic gates. Another way, often with the least electronics, is to construct an equivalent system of electronic switches (usually transistors). One of the easiest ways is to simply have a memory containing a truth table. The inputs are fed into the address of the memory, and the data outputs of the memory become the outputs.

For automated analysis, these representations have digital file formats that can be processed by computer programmes. Most digital engineers are very careful to select computer programmes ("tools") with compatible file formats. To choose representations, engineers consider types of digital systems. Most digital systems divide into "combinational systems" and "sequential systems." A combinational system always presents the same output when given the same inputs. It is basically a representation of a set of logic functions. A sequential system is a combinational system with some of the outputs fed back as inputs. This makes the digital machine perform a "sequence" of operations. The simplest sequential system is probably a flip flop, a mechanism that represents a binary digit or "bit". Sequential systems are often designed as state machines. In this way, engineers can design a system's gross behaviour, and even test it in a simulation, without considering all the details of the logic functions. Sequential systems divide into two further subcategories. "Synchronous" sequential systems change state all at once, when a "clock" signal changes state. "Asynchronous" sequential systemspropagate changes whenever inputs change. Synchronous sequential systems are made of well-characterised asynchronous circuits such as flip-flops, that change only when the clock changes, and which have carefully designed timing margins.

The usual way to implement a synchronous sequential state machine is to divide it into a piece of combinational logic and a set of flip flops called a "state register." Each time a clock signal ticks, the state register captures the feedback generated from the previous state of the combinational logic, and feeds it back as an unchanging input to the combinational part of the state machine. The fastest rate of the clock is set by the most time-consuming logic calculation in the combinational logic. The state register is just a representation of a binary number. If the states in the state machine are numbered (easy to arrange), the logic function is some combinational logic that produces the number of the next state.

In comparison, asynchronous systems are very hard to design because all possible states, in all possible timings must be considered. The usual method is to construct a table of the minimum and maximum time that each such state can exist, and then adjust the circuit to minimize the number of such states, and force the circuit to periodically wait for all of its parts to enter a compatible state (this is called "self-resynchronisation"). Without such careful design, it is easy to accidentally produce asynchronous logic that is "unstable", that is, real electronics will have unpredictable results because of the cumulative delays caused by small variations in the values of the electronic components. Certain circuits (such as the synchroniser flip-flops, switchdebouncers, arbiters, and the like which allow external unsynchronised signals to enter synchronous logic circuits) are inherently asynchronous in their design and must be analysed as such.

As of 2005, almost all digital machines are synchronous designs because it is much easier to create and verify a synchronous design—the software currently used to simulate digital machines does not yet handle asynchronous designs. However, asynchronous logic is thought to be superior, if it can be made to work, because its speed is not constrained by an arbitrary clock; instead, it runs at the maximum speed of its logic gates. Building an asynchronous circuit using faster parts makes the circuit faster. Many digital systems are data flow machines. These are usually designed using synchronous register transfer logic, using hardware description languages such as VHDL or Verilog. In register transfer logic, binary numbers are stored in groups of flip flops called registers. The outputs of each register are a bundle of wires called a "bus" that carries that number to other calculations. A calculation is simply a piece of combinational logic. Each calculation also has an output bus, and these may be connected to the inputs of several registers. Sometimes a register will have a multiplexer on its input, so that it can store a number from any one of several buses. Alternatively, the outputs of several items may be connected to a bus through buffers that can turn off the output of all of the devices except one. A sequential state machine controls when each register accepts new data from its input. In the 1980s, some researchers discovered that almost all synchronous register-transfer machines could be converted to asynchronous designs by using first-in-first-out synchronisation logic. In this scheme, the digital machine is characterised as a set of data flows. In each step of the flow, an asynchronous "synchronisation circuit" determines when the outputs of that step are valid, and presents a signal that says, "grab the data" to the stages that use that stage's inputs. It turns out that just a few relatively simple synchronisation circuits are needed.

The most general-purpose register-transfer logic machine is a computer. This is basically an automatic binary abacus. The control unit of a computer is usually designed as a microprogram run by a microsequencer. A microprogram is much like a player-piano roll. Each table entry or "word" of the microprogram commands the state of every bit that controls the computer. The sequencer then counts, and the count addresses the memory or combinational logic machine that contains the microprogram. The bits from the microprogram control the arithmetic logic unit, memory and other parts of the computer, including the microsequencer itself. In this way, the complex task of designing the controls of a computer is reduced to a simpler task of programming a collection of much simpler logic machines.

Computer architecture is a specialised engineering activity that tries to arrange the registers, calculation logic, buses and other parts of the computer in the best way for some purpose. Computer architects have applied large amounts of ingenuity to computer design to reduce the cost and increase the speed and immunity to programming errors of computers. An increasingly common goal is to reduce the power used in a battery-powered computer system, such as a cell-phone. Many computer architects serve an extended apprenticeship as microprogrammers. "Specialised computers" are usually a conventional computer with a special-purpose microprogram.

AUTOMATED DESIGN TOOLS

To save costly engineering effort, much of the effort of designing large logic machines has been automated. The computer programmes are called "electronic design automation tools" or just "EDA." Simple truth table-style descriptions of logic are often optimised with EDA that automatically produces reduced systems of logic gates or smaller lookup tables that still produce the desired outputs. The most common example of this kind of software is the Espresso heuristic logic minimizer. Most practical algorithms for optimising large logic systems use algebraic manipulations or binary decision diagrams, and there are promising experiments with genetic algorithms and annealing optimisations.

To automate costly engineering processes, some EDA can take state tables that describe state machines and automatically produce a truth table or a function table for the combinational logic of a state machine. The state table is a piece of text that lists each state, together with the conditions controlling the transitions between them and the belonging output signals. It is common for the function tables of such computer-generated state-machines to be optimised with logic-minimization software such as Minilog. Often, real logic systems are designed as a series of sub-projects, which are combined using a "tool flow."

The tool flow is usually a "script," a simplified computer language that can invoke the software design tools in the right order. Tool flows for large logic systems such as microprocessors can be thousands of commands long, and combine the work of hundreds of engineers. Writing and debugging tool flows is an established engineering specialty in companies that produce digital designs. The tool flow usually terminates in a detailed computer file or set of files that describe how to physically construct the logic. Often it consists of instructions to draw the transistors and wires on an integrated circuit or a printed circuit board.

Parts of tool flows are "debugged" by verifying the outputs of simulated logic against expected inputs. The test tools take computer files with sets of inputs and outputs, and highlight discrepancies between the simulated behaviour and the expected behaviour. Once the input data is believed correct, the design itself must still be verified for correctness. Some tool flows verify designs by first producing a design, and then scanning the design to produce compatible input data for the tool flow. If the scanned data matches the input data, then the tool flow has probably not introduced errors. The functional verification data are usually called "test vectors." The functional test vectors may be preserved and used in the factory to test that newly constructed logic works correctly.

However, functional test patterns don't discover common fabrication faults. Production tests are often designed by software tools called "test pattern generators". These generate test vectors by examining the structure of the logic and systematically generating tests for particular faults. This way the fault coverage can closely approach 100 per cent, provided the design is properly made testable. Once a design exists, and is verified and testable, it often needs to be processed to be manufacturable as well. Modern integrated circuits have features smaller than the wavelength of the light used to expose the photoresist. Manufacturability software adds interference patterns to the exposure masks to eliminate open-circuits, and enhance the masks' contrast.

DESIGN FOR TESTABILITY

There are several reasons for testing a logic circuit. When the circuit is first developed, it is necessary to verify that the design circuit meets the required functional and timing specifications. When multiple copies of a correctly designed circuit are being manufactured, it is essential to test each copy to ensure that the manufacturing process has not introduced any flaws. A large logic machine (say, with more than a hundred logical variables) can have an astronomical number of possible states. Obviously, in the factory, testing every state is impractical if testing each state takes a microsecond, and there are more states than the number of microseconds since the universe began. Unfortunately, this ridiculous-sounding case is typical. Fortunately, large logic machines are almost always designed as assemblies of smaller logic machines. To save time, the smaller sub-machines are isolated by permanently-installed "design for test" circuitry, and are tested independently. One common test scheme known as "scan design" moves test bits serially (one after another) from external test equipment through one or more serial shift registers known as "scan chains". Serial scans have only one or two wires to carry the data, and minimize the physical size and expense of the infrequently-used test logic. After all the test data bits are in place, the design is reconfigured to be in "normal mode" and one or more clock pulses are applied, to test for faults (*e.g.*, stuck-at low or stuck-at high) and capture the test result into flip-flops and/or latches in the scan shift register(s). Finally, the result of the test is shifted out to the block boundary and compared against the predicted "good machine" result.

In a board-test environment, serial to parallel testing has been formalised with a standard called "JTAG" (named after the "Joint Test Action Group" that proposed it). Another common testing scheme provides a test mode that forces some part of the logic machine to enter a "test cycle." The test cycle usually exercises large independent parts of the machine.

TRADE-OFFS

Several numbers determine the practicality of a system of digital logic: cost, reliability, fanout and speed. Engineers explored numerous electronic devices to get an ideal combination of these traits.

Cost

The cost of a logic gate is crucial. In the 1930s, the earliest digital logic systems were constructed from telephone relays because these were inexpensive and relatively reliable. After that, engineers always used the cheapest available electronic switches that could still fulfill the requirements.

The earliest integrated circuits were a happy accident. They were constructed not to save money, but to save weight, and permit the Apollo Guidance Computer to control an inertial guidance system for a spacecraft. The first integrated circuit logic gates cost nearly $50 (in 1960 dollars, when an engineer earned $10,000/year). To everyone's surprise, by the time the circuits were mass-produced, they had become the least-expensive method of constructing digital logic. Improvements in this technology have driven all subsequent improvements in cost.

With the rise of integrated circuits, reducing the absolute number of chips used represented another way to save costs. The goal of a designer is not just to make the simplest circuit, but to keep the component count down. Sometimes this results in slightly more complicated designs with respect to the underlying digital logic but nevertheless reduces the number of components, board size, and even power consumption. For example, in some logic families, NAND gates are the simplest digital gate to build. All other logical operations can be implemented by NAND gates. If a circuit already required a single NAND gate, and a single chip normally carried four NAND gates, then the remaining gates could be used to implement other logical operations like logical and. This could eliminate the need for a separate chip containing those different types of gates.

Reliability

The "reliability" of a logic gate describes its mean time between failure (MTBF). Digital machines often have millions of logic gates. Also, most digital machines are "optimised" to reduce their cost. The result is that often, the failure of a single logic gate will cause a digital machine to stop working. Digital machines first became useful when the MTBF for a switch got above a few hundred hours. Even so, many of these machines had complex, well-rehearsed repair procedures, and would be non-functional for hours because a tube burned-out, or a moth got stuck in a relay. Modern transistorised integrated circuit logic gates have MTBFs greater than 82 billion hours (8.2×10^{10}) hours, and need them because they have so many logic gates.

Fanout

Fanout describes how many logic inputs can be controlled by a single logic output without exceeding the current ratings of the gate.[6] The minimum practical fanout is about five. Modern electronic logic using CMOS transistors for switches have fanouts near fifty, and can sometimes go much higher.

Speed

The "switching speed" describes how many times per second an inverter (an electronic representation of a "logical not" function) can change from true to false and back. Faster logic can accomplish more operations in less time.

Digital logic first became useful when switching speeds got above fifty hertz, because that was faster than a team of humans operating mechanical calculators. Modern electronic digital logic routinely switches at five gigahertz (5×10^9 hertz), and some laboratory systems switch at more than a terahertz (1×10^{12} hertz).

Logic Families

Design started with relays. Relay logic was relatively inexpensive and reliable, but slow. Occasionally a mechanical failure would occur. Fanouts were typically about ten, limited by the resistance of the coils and arcing on the contacts from high voltages. Later, vacuum tubes were used. These were very fast, but generated heat, and were unreliable because the filaments would burn out. Fanouts were typically five to seven, limited by the heating from the tubes' current. In the 1950s, special "computer tubes" were developed with filaments that omitted volatile elements like silicon. These ran for hundreds of thousands of hours. The first semiconductor logic family was resistor-transistor logic. This was a thousand times more reliable than tubes, ran cooler, and used less power, but had a very low fan-in of three. Diode-transistor logic improved the fanout up to about seven, and reduced the power. Some DTL designs used two power-supplies with alternating layers of NPN and PNP transistors to increase the fanout. Transistor transistor logic (TTL) was a great improvement over these. In early devices, fanout improved to ten, and later variations reliably achieved twenty. TTL was also fast, with some variations achieving switching times as low as twenty nanoseconds. TTL is still used in some designs. Emitter coupled logic is very fast but uses a lot of power. It was extensively used for high-performance computers made up of many medium-scale components (such as the Illiac IV). By far, the most common digital integrated circuits built today use CMOS logic, which is fast, offers high circuit density and low-power per gate. This is used even in large, fast computers, such as the IBM System z.

DIGITAL CIRCUITS

The quantities that are to be measured, monitored, recorded, processed and controlled are analog and digital, depending on the type of system used. It is important when dealing with various quantities that we be able to represent their values efficiently and accurately. There are basically two ways of representing the numerical value of quantities, analog and digital.

ANALOG REPRESENTATION

Systems which are capable of processing a continuous range of values varying with respect to time are called analog systems. In analog representation a quantity is represented by a voltage, current, or meter movement that is proportional to the value of that quantity. Analog quantities such as those cited above have an important characteristic: They can vary over a continuous range of values.

Analog Voltage vs Time

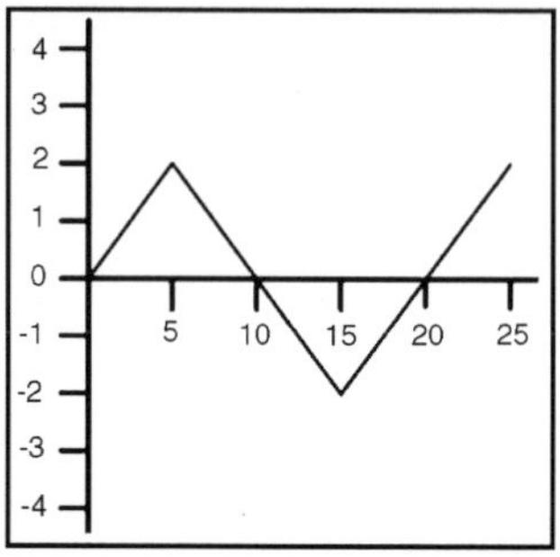

DIGITAL REPRESENTATION

Systems which process discrete values are called digital systems. In digital representation the quantities are represented not by proportional quantities but by symbols called digits. As an example, consider the digital watch, which provides the time of the day in the form of decimal digits representing hours and minutes (and sometimes seconds). As we know, time of day changes continuously, but the digital watch reading does not change continuously; rather, it changes in steps of one per minute (or per second). In other words, time of day digital representation changes in discrete steps, as compared to the representation of time provided by an analog watch, where the dial reading changes continuously. *Below is a diagram of digital voltage vs time*: Here input voltage changes from +4 Volts to -4 Volts; it can be converted to digital form by Analog to Digital converters (ADC). An ADC converts continuous signals into samples per second. Well, this is an entirely different theory.

Digital Voltage vs Time

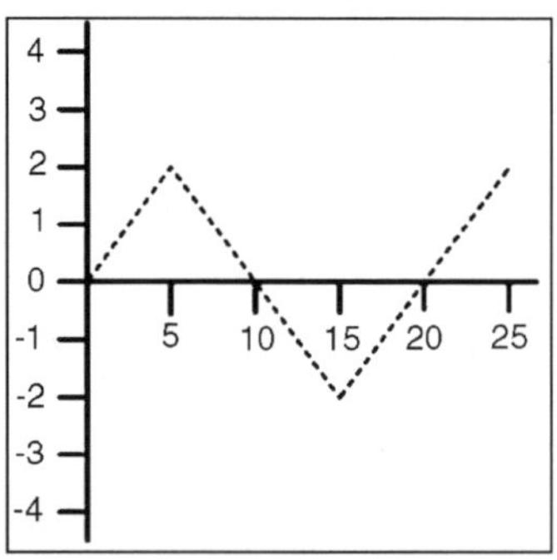

The major difference between analog and digital quantities, then, can be stated simply as follows:

- Analog = Continuous
- Digital = Discrete (step by step)

ADVANTAGES OF DIGITAL TECHNIQUES

- Easier to design. Exact values of voltage or current are not important, only the range (HIGH or LOW) in which they fall.
- Information storage is easy.
- Accuracy and precision are greater.
- Operations can be programmed. Analog systems can also be programmed, but the available operations variety and complexity is severely limited.
- Digital circuits are less affected by noise, as long as the noise is not large enough to prevent us from distinguishing HIGH from LOW (we discuss this in detail in an advanced digital tutorial section).
- More digital circuitry can be fabricated on IC chips.

LIMITATIONS OF DIGITAL TECHNIQUES

- Most physical quantities in real world are analog in nature, and these quantities are often the inputs and outputs that are being monitored, operated on, and controlled by a system. Thus conversion to digital format and re-conversion to analog format is needed.

DIGITAL NUMBER SYSTEM

Many number systems are in use in digital technology. The most common are the decimal, binary, octal, and hexadecimal systems. The decimal system is clearly the most familiar to us because it is a tool that we use every day. Examining some of its characteristics will help us to better understand the other systems. In the next few pages we shall introduce four numerical representation systems that are used in the digital system. There are other systems, which we will look at briefly.

- Decimal
- Binary
- Octal
- Hexadecimal

BINARY COUNTING

Table. Binary Counting Sequence

2^3	2^2	2^1	2^0	Decimal
0	0	0	0	0
0	0	0	1	1
0	0	1	0	2
0	0	1	1	3
0	1	0	0	4
0	1	0	1	5
0	1	1	0	6

0	1	1	1	7
1	0	0	0	8
1	0	0	1	9
1	0	1	0	10
1	0	1	1	11
1	1	0	0	12
1	1	0	1	13
1	1	1	0	14
1	1	1	1	15

Representing Binary Quantities

In digital systems the information that is being processed is usually presented in binary form. Binary quantities can be represented by any device that has only two operating states or possible conditions. *E.g.*. a switch is only open or closed. We arbitrarily (as we define them) let an open switch represent binary 0 and a closed switch represent binary 1. Thus we can represent any binary number by using series of switches.

Typical Voltage Assignment

Binary 1: Any voltage between 2V to 5V

Binary 0: Any voltage between 0V to 0.8V

Not used: Voltage between 0.8V to 2V in 5 Volt CMOS and TTL Logic, this may cause error in a digital circuit. Today's digital circuits works at 1.8 volts, so this statement may not hold true for all logic circuits.

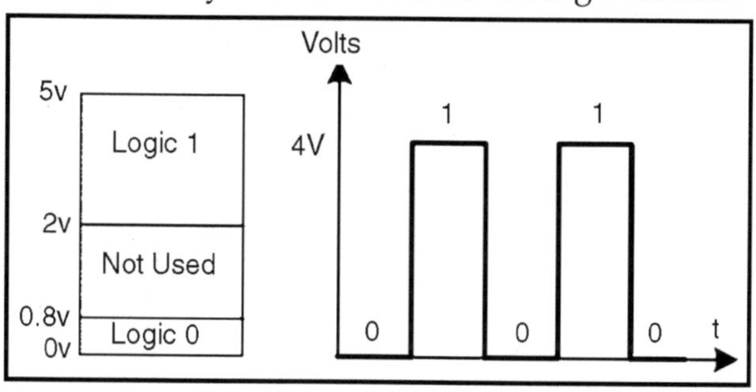

We can see another significant difference between digital and analog systems. In digital systems, the exact voltage value is not important; eg, a voltage of 3.6V means the same as a voltage of 4.3V. In analog systems, the exact voltage value is important. The binary number system is the most important one in digital systems, but several others are also important. The decimal system is important because it is universally used to represent quantities outside a digital system. This means that there will be situations where decimal values have to be converted to binary values before they are entered into the digital system. In additional to binary and decimal, two other number systems find wide-spread applications in digital systems. The octal (base-8) and hexadecimal (base-16) number systems are both used for the same purpose- to provide an efficient means for representing large binary system.

DIGITAL SYSTEM

While the binary numeration system is an interesting mathematical abstraction, we haven't yet seen its practical application to electronics. What makes binary numeration so important to the application of digital electronics is the ease in which bits may be represented in physical terms.

Because a binary bit can only have one of two different values, either 0 or 1, any physical medium capable of switching between two saturated states may be used to represent a bit. Consequently, any physical system capable of representing binary bits is able to represent numerical quantities, and potentially has the ability to manipulate those numbers. Electronic circuits are physical systems that lend themselves well to the representation of binary numbers. Transistors, when operated at their bias limits, may be in one of two different states: either cutoff.

If a transistor circuit is designed to maximize the probability of falling into either one of these states (and not operating in the linear, or active, mode), it can serve as a physical representation of a binary bit. A voltage signal measured at the output of such a circuit may also serve as a representation of a single bit, a low voltage representing a binary "0" and a (relatively) high voltage representing a binary "1." Consider the following transistor circuit:

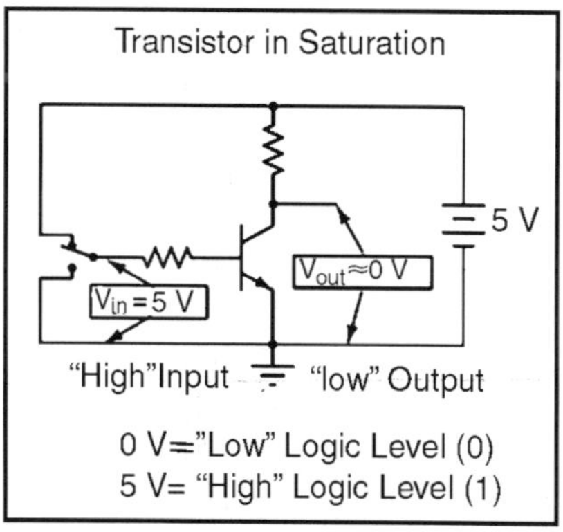

In this circuit, the transistor is in a state of saturation by virtue of the applied input voltage (5 volts) through the two-position switch. Because it's saturated, the transistor drops very little voltage between collector and emitter, resulting in an output voltage of (practically) 0 volts. If we were using this circuit to represent binary bits, we would say that the input signal is a binary "1" and that the output signal is a binary "0." Any voltage close to full supply voltage (measured in reference to ground, of course) is considered a "1" and a lack of voltage is considered a "0." Alternative terms for these voltage levels are high (same as a binary "1") and low (same as a binary "0"). A general term for the representation of a binary bit by a circuit voltage is logic level. Moving the switch to the other position, we apply a binary "0" to the input and receive a binary "1" at the output:

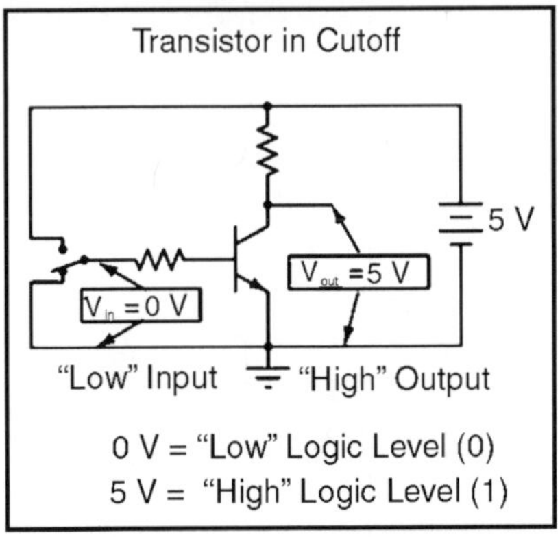

What we've created here with a single transistor is a circuit generally known as a logic gate, or simply gate. A gate is a special type of amplifier circuit designed to accept and generate voltage signals corresponding to binary 1's and 0's. As such, gates are not intended to be used for amplifying analog signals (voltage signals between 0 and full voltage). Used together, multiple gates may be applied to the task of binary number storage (memory circuits) or manipulation (computing circuits), each gate's output representing one bit of a multi-bit binary number.

The gate shown here with the single transistor is known as an inverter, or NOT gate, because it outputs the exact opposite digital signal as what is input. For convenience, gate circuits are generally represented by their own symbols rather than by their constituent transistors and resistors.

The following is the symbol for an inverter:

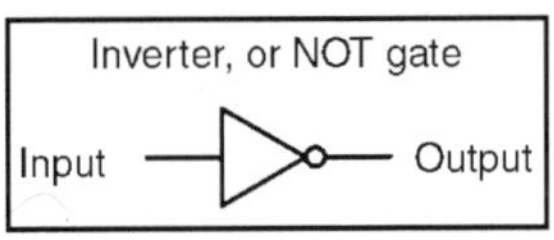

An alternative symbol for an inverter is shown here:

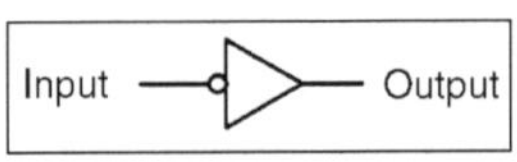

Notice the triangular shape of the gate symbol, much like that of an operational amplifier. As was stated before, gate circuits actually are amplifiers. The small circle, or "bubble" shown on either the input or output terminal is standard for representing the inversion function. As you might suspect, if we were to remove the bubble from the gate symbol, leaving only a triangle, the resulting symbol would no longer indicate inversion, but merely direct amplification. Such a symbol and such a gate actually do exist, and it is called a buffer, the subject of the next section. Like an operational amplifier symbol, input and output connections are shown as single wires, the implied reference point for each voltage signal being "ground." In digital gate circuits, ground is almost always the negative connection of a single voltage source (power supply).

Dual, or "split," power supplies are seldom used in gate circuitry. Because gate circuits are amplifiers, they require a source of power to operate. Like operational amplifiers, the power supply connections for digital gates are often omitted from the symbol for simplicity's sake. If we were to show all the necessary connections needed for operating this gate, the schematic would look something like this:

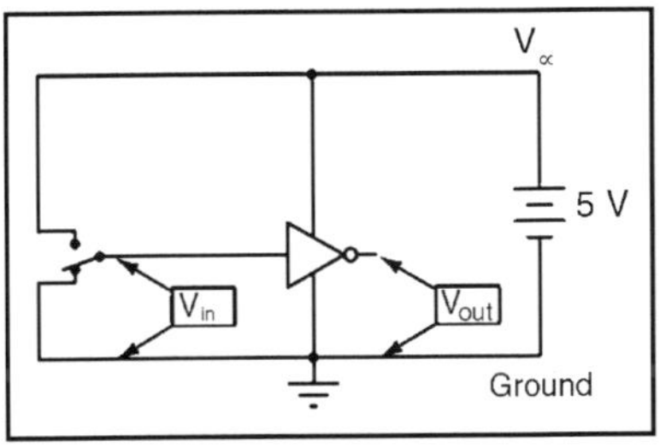

Power supply conductors are rarely shown in gate circuit schematics, even if the power supply connections at each gate are. Minimizing lines in our schematic, we get this:

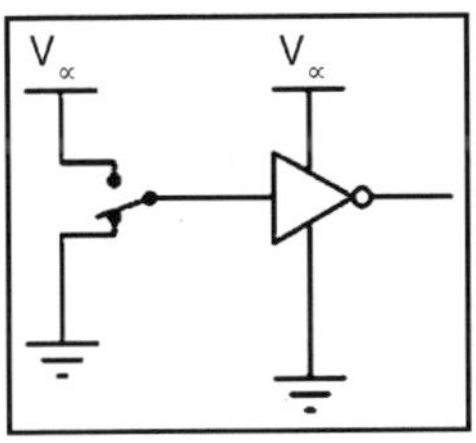

"V_{cc}" stands for the constant voltage supplied to the collector of a bipolar junction transistor circuit, in reference to ground. Those points in a gate circuit marked by the label "V_{cc}" are all connected to the same point, and that point is the positive terminal of a DC voltage source, usually 5 volts. As we will see in other sections of this chapter, there are quite a few different types of logic gates, most of which have multiple input terminals for accepting more than one signal. The output of any gate is dependent on the state of its input(s) and its logical function.

One common way to express the particular function of a gate circuit is called a truth table. Truth tables show all combinations of input conditions in terms of logic level states (either "high" or "low," "1" or "0," for each input terminal of the gate), along with the corresponding output logic level, either "high" or "low." For the inverter, or NOT, circuit just illustrated, the truth table is very simple indeed:

NOT Gate Truth Table

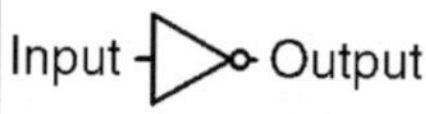

Input	Output
0	1
1	0

Truth tables for more complex gates are, of course, larger than the one shown for the NOT gate. A gate's truth table must have as many rows as there are possibilities for unique input combinations. For a single-input gate like the NOT gate, there are only two possibilities, 0 and 1. For a two input gate, there are four possibilities (00, 01, 10, and 11), and thus four rows to the corresponding truth table. For a three-input gate, there are eight possibilities (000, 001, 010, 011, 100, 101, 110, and 111), and thus a truth table with eight rows are needed. The mathematically inclined will realise that the number of truth table rows needed for a gate is equal to 2 raised to the power of the number of input terminals.

CODE CONVERSIONS

Converting from one code form to another code form is called code conversion, like converting from binary to decimal or converting from hexadecimal to decimal.

BINARY-TO-DECIMAL CONVERSION

Any binary number can be converted to its decimal equivalent simply by summing together the weights of the various positions in the binary number which contain a 1.

Binary	Decimal
11011_2	
$2^4+2^3+0^1+2^1+2^0$	$=16+8+0+2+1$
Result	27_{10}
	and
10110101_2	
$2^7+0^6+2^5+2^4+0^3+2^2+0^1+2^0$	$=128+0+32+16+0+4+0+1$
Result	181_{10}

You should have noticed that the method is to find the weights (*i.e.*, powers of 2) for each bit position that contains a 1, and then to add them up.

DECIMAL-TO-BINARY CONVERSION

There are 2 Methods

- Reverse of Binary-To-Decimal Method
- Repeat Division

Reverse of Binary-To-Decimal Method

	Decimal	Binary
	45_{10}	$=32 + 0 + 8 + 4 + 0 + 1$
		$=2^5+0+2^3+2^2+0+2^0$
	Result	$=101101_2$

Repeat Division-Convert Decimal to Binary

This method uses repeated division by 2.
Convert 25_{10} to binary.

Division	Remainder	Binary
25/2	= 12+ remainder of 1	1 (Least Significant Bit)
12/2	= 6 + remainder of 0	0
6/2	= 3 + remainder of 0	0
3/2	= 1 + remainder of 1	1
1/2	= 0 + remainder of 1	1 (Most Significant Bit)
Result	25_{10}	$= 11001_2$

The Flow chart for repeated-division method is as follows:

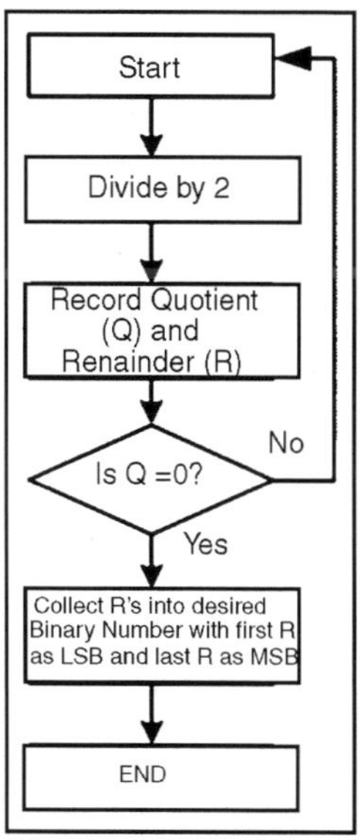

BINARY-TO-OCTAL/OCTAL-TO-BINARY CONVERSION

Octal Digit	0	1	2	3	4	5	6	7
Binary Equivalent	000	001	010	011	100	101	110	111

Each Octal digit is represented by three binary digits.
Example:
$100\ 111\ 010_2 = (100)\ (111)\ (010)_2 = 4\ 7\ 2_8$

Repeat Division-Convert Decimal to Octal

This method uses repeated division by 8.
Example: Convert 177_{10} to octal and binary

Division	Result	Binary
177/8	= 22+ remainder of 1	1 (Least Significant Bit)
22/8	= 2 + remainder of 6	6
2/8	= 0 + remainder of 2	2 (Most Significant Bit)
Result	177_{10}	$= 261_8$
Binary		010110001_2

HEXADECIMAL TO DECIMAL/DECIMAL TO HEXADECIMAL CONVERSION

Example:
$2AF_{16} = 2 \times (16^2) + 10 \times (16^1) + 15 \times (16^0) = 687_{10}$

Repeat Division- Convert Decimal to Hexadecimal

This method uses repeated division by 16.
Example: convert 378_{10} to hexadecimal and binary:

Division	Result	Hexadecimal
378/16	= 23+ remainder of 10	A (Least Significant Bit)23
23/16	= 1 + remainder of 7	7
1/16	= 0 + remainder of 1	1 (Most Significant Bit)
Result	378_{10}	$= 17A_{16}$
Binary		$= 0001\ 0111\ 1010_2$

BINARY-TO-HEXADECIMAL/HEXADECIMAL -TO-BINARY CONVERSION

Hexadecimal Digit	0	1	2	3	4	5	6	7
Binary Equivalent	0000	0001	0010	0011	0100	0101	0110	0111

Hexadecimal Digit	8	9	A	B	C	D	E	F
Binary Equivalent	1000	1001	1010	1011	1100	1101	1110	1111

Each Hexadecimal digit is represented by four bits of binary digit.

Example:

$1011\ 0010\ 1111_2 = (1011)\ (0010)\ (1111)_2 = B\ 2\ F_{16}$

OCTAL-TO-HEXADECIMAL HEXADECIMAL-TO-OCTAL CONVERSION

- Convert Octal (Hexadecimal) to Binary first.
- Regroup the binary number by three bits per group starting from LSB if Octal is required.
- Regroup the binary number by four bits per group starting from LSB if Hexadecimal is required.

Example: Convert $5A8_{16}$ to Octal.

Hexadecimal	Binary/Octal
5A816	= 0101 1010 1000 (Binary)
	= 010 110 101 000 (Binary Result = 2650 (Octal)

NUMBERS VERSUS NUMERATION

It is imperative to understand that the type of numeration system used to represent numbers has no impact upon the outcome of any arithmetical function (addition, subtraction, multiplication, division, roots, powers, or logarithms). A number is a number is a number; one plus one will always equal two (so long as we're dealing with real numbers), no matter how you symbolize one, one, and two. A prime number in decimal form is still prime if it's shown in binary form, or octal, or hexadecimal? is still the ratio between the circumference and diameter of a circle, no matter what symbol(s) you use to denote its value. The essential functions and interrelations of mathematics are unaffected by the particular system of symbols we might choose to represent quantities. This distinction between numbers and systems of numeration is critical to understand.

The essential distinction between the two is much like that between an object and the spoken word(s) we associate with it. A house is still a house regardless of whether we call it by its English name house or its Spanish name casa. The first is the actual thing, while the second is merely the symbol for the thing. That being said, performing a simple arithmetic operation such as addition (longhand) in binary form can be confusing to a person accustomed to working with decimal numeration only. In this lesson, we'll explore the techniques used to perform simple arithmetic functions on binary numbers, since these techniques will be employed in the design of electronic circuits to do the same. You might take longhand addition and subtraction for granted, having used a calculator for so long, but deep inside that calculator's circuitry all those operations are performed"longhand," using binary numeration. To understand how that's accomplished, we need to review to the basics of arithmetic.

BINARY ADDITION

Adding binary numbers is a very simple task, and very similar to the longhand addition of decimal numbers. As with decimal numbers, you start by adding the bits (digits) one column, or place weight, at a time, from right to left. Unlike decimal addition, there is little to memorize in the way of rules for the addition of binary bits:

0 + 0 = 0
1 + 0 = 1
0 + 1 = 1
1 + 1 = 10
1 + 1 + 1 = 11

Just as with decimal addition, when the sum in one column is a two-bit (two-digit) number, the least significant figure is written as part of the total sum and the most significant figure is "carried" to the next left column. Consider the following examples:

- 11 1← Carry bits → 11
- 1001101 1001001 1000111
- + 0010010 + 0011001 + 0010110
- ———— ———— ————
- 1011111 1100010 1011101

The addition problem on the left did not require any bits to be carried, since the sum of bits in each column was either 1 or 0, not 10 or 11. In the other two problems, there definitely were bits to be carried, but the process of addition is still quite simple. As we'll see, there are ways that electronic circuits can be built to perform this very task of addition, by representing each bit of each binary number as a voltage signal (either "high," for a 1; or "low" for a 0). This is the very foundation of all the arithmetic which modern digital computers perform.

NEGATIVE BINARY NUMBERS

With addition being easily accomplished, we can perform the operation of subtraction with the same technique simply by making one of the numbers negative. For example, the subtraction problem of 7 – 5 is essentially the same as the addition problem 7 + (–5). Since we already know how to represent positive numbers in binary, all we need to know now is how to represent their negative counterparts and we'll be able to subtract.

Usually we represent a negative decimal number by placing a minus sign directly to the left of the most significant digit, just as in the example above, with -5. However, the whole purpose of using binary notation is for constructing on/off circuits that can represent bit values in terms of voltage (2 alternative values: either "high" or "low"). In this context, we don't have the luxury of a third symbol such as a "minus" sign, since these circuits can only be on or off (two possible states). One solution is to reserve a bit (circuit) that does nothing but represent the mathematical sign:

- $101_2 = 5_{10}$ (positive)
- Extra bit, representing sign (0=positive, 1=negative)
- |
- $0101_2 = 5_{10}$ (positive)
- Extra bit, representing sign (0=positive, 1=negative)
- |
- $1101_2 = -5_{10}$ (negative)

As you can see, we have to be careful when we start using bits for any purpose other than standard place-weighted values. Otherwise, 1101_2 could be misinterpreted as the number thirteen when in fact we mean to represent negative five. To keep things straight here, we must first decide how many bits are going to be needed to represent the largest numbers we'll be dealing with, and then be sure not to exceed that bit field length in our arithmetic operations.

For the above example, I've limited myself to the representation of numbers from negative seven (1111_2) to positive seven (0111_2), and no more, by making the fourth bit the "sign" bit. Only by first establishing these limits can I avoid confusion of a negative number with a larger, positive number. Representing negative five as 1101_2 is an example of the *sign-magnitude* system of negative binary numeration. By using the leftmost bit as a sign indicator and not a place-weighted value, I am sacrificing the "pure" form of binary notation for something that gives me a practical advantage: the representation of negative numbers.

The leftmost bit is read as the sign, either positive or negative, and the remaining bits are interpreted according to the standard binary notation: left to right, place weights in multiples of two. As simple as the sign-magnitude approach is, it is not very practical for arithmetic purposes. For instance, how do I add a negative five (1101_2) to any other number, using the standard technique for binary addition?

I'd have to invent a new way of doing addition in order for it to work, and if I do that, I might as well just do the job with longhand subtraction; there's no arithmetical advantage to using negative numbers to perform subtraction through addition if we have to do it with sign-magnitude numeration, and that was our goal!

There's another method for representing negative numbers which works with our familiar technique of longhand addition, and also happens to make more sense from a place-weighted numeration point of view, called *complementation*. With this strategy, we assign the leftmost bit to serve a special purpose, just as we did with the sign-magnitude approach, defining our number limits just as before. However, this time, the leftmost bit is more than just a sign bit; rather, it possesses a negative place-weight value.

For example, a value of negative five would be represented as such:
Extra bit, place weight = negative eight:

- |
- $1011_2 = 5_{10}$ (negative)
- $(1 \times -8_{10}) + (0 \times 4_{10}) + (1 \times 2_{10}) + (1 \times 1_{10}) = -5_{10}$

With the right three bits being able to represent a magnitude from zero through seven, and the leftmost bit representing either zero or negative eight, we can successfully represent any integer number from negative seven, ($1001_2 = -8_{10} + 7_{10} = -1_{10}$) to positive seven ($0111_2 = 0_{10} + 7_{10} = 7_{10}$).

Representing positive numbers in this scheme (with the fourth bit designated as the negative weight) is no different from that of ordinary binary notation.

However, representing negative numbers is not quite as straightforward:

Zero	0000	Negative one	1111
Positive one	0001	Negative two	1110
Positive two	0010	Negative three	1101
Positive three	0011	Negative four	1100
Positive four	0100	Negative five	1011
Positive five	0101	Negative six	1010
Positive six	0110	Negative seven	1001
Positive seven	0111	Negative eight	1000

Note that the negative binary numbers in the right column, being the sum of the right three bits' total plus the negative eight of the leftmost bit, don't "count" in the same progression as the positive binary numbers in the left column. Rather, the right three bits have to be set at the proper value to equal the desired (negative) total when summed with the negative eight place value of the leftmost bit. Those right three bits are referred to as the *two's complement* of the corresponding positive number.

Consider the following comparison:

Positive Number	Two's Complement
001	111
010	110
011	101
100	100
101	011
110	010
111	001

In this case, with the negative weight bit being the fourth bit (place value of negative eight), the two's complement for any positive number will be wthatever value is needed to add to negative eight to make that positive value's negative equivalent. Thankfully, there's an easy way to figure out the two's complement for any binary number: simply invert all the bits of that number, changing all 1's to 0's and visa-versa (to arrive at what is called the *one's complement*) and then add one! For example, to obtain the two's complement of five (101_2), we would first invert all the bits to obtain 010_2 (the "one's complement"), then add one to obtain 011_2, or -5_{10} in three-bit, two's complement form. Interestingly enough, generating the two's complement of a binary number works the same if you manipulate *all* the bits, including the leftmost (sign) bit at the same time as the magnitude bits. Let's try this with the former example, converting a positive five to a negative five, but performing the complementation process on all four bits. We must be sure to include the 0 (positive) sign bit on the original number, five (0101_2). First, inverting all bits to obtain the one's complement: 1010_2.

Then, adding one, we obtain the final answer: 1011_2, or -5_{10} expressed in four-bit, two's complement form. It is critically important to remember that the place of the negative-weight bit must be already determined before any two's complement conversions can be done. If our binary numeration field were such that the eighth bit was designated as the negative-weight bit (10000000_2), we'd have to determine the two's complement based on all seven of the other bits. Here, the two's complement of five (0000101_2) would be 1111011_2. A positive five in this system would be represented as 00000101_2, and a negative five as 11111011_2.

SUBTRACTION

We can subtract one binary number from another by using the standard techniques adapted for decimal numbers (subtraction of each bit pair, right to left, "borrowing" as needed from bits to the left). However, if we can leverage the already familiar (and easier) technique of binary addition to subtract, that would be better. As we just learned, we can represent negative binary numbers by using the "two's complement" method and a negative place-weight bit. Here, we'll use those negative binary numbers to subtract through addition.

Here's a sample problem:

Subtraction: $7_{10} - 5_{10}$ *Addition equivalent*: $7_{10} + (-5_{10})$

If all we need to do is represent seven and negative five in binary (two's complemented) form, all we need is three bits plus the negative-weight bit:

Positive seven = 0111_2

Negative five = 1011_2

Now, let's add them together:

```
         111  <— Carry bits
         0111
 +       1011
 —————
        10010
 |
```

Discard extra bit.

Answer = 0010_2

Since we've already defined our number bit field as three bits plus the negative-weight bit, the fifth bit in the answer (1) will be discarded to give us a result of 0010_2, or positive two, which is the correct answer. Another way to understand why we discard that extra bit is to remember that the leftmost bit of the lower number possesses a negative weight, in this case equal to negative eight. When we add these two binary numbers together, what we're actually doing with the MSBs is subtracting the lower number's MSB from the upper number's MSB. In subtraction, one never "carries" a digit or bit on to the next left place-weight.

Let's try another example, this time with larger numbers. If we want to add -25_{10} to 18_{10}, we must first decide how large our binary bit field must be. To represent the largest (absolute value) number in our problem, which is twenty-five, we need at least five bits, plus a sixth bit for the negative-weight bit. Let's start by representing positive twenty-five, then finding the two's complement and putting it all together into one numeration:

$+25_{10} = 011001_2$ (showing all six bits)

One's complement of $11001_2 = 100110_2$

One's complement + 1 = two's complement = 100111_2

$-25_{10} = 100111_2$

Essentially, we're representing negative twenty-five by using the negative-weight (sixth) bit with a value of negative thirty-two, plus positive seven (binary 111_2).

Now, let's represent positive eighteen in binary form, showing all six bits:

$18_{10} = 010010_2$.

Now, let's add them together and see what we get:.

11 <— Carry bits

100111

+ 010010

— — — —

111001

Since there were no "extra" bits on the left, there are no bits to discard. The leftmost bit on the answer is a 1, which means that the answer is negative, in two's complement form, as it should be. Converting the answer to decimal form by summing all the bits times their respective weight values, we get:

$(1 \times -32_{10}) + (1 \times 16_{10}) + (1 \times 8_{10}) + (1 \times 1_{10}) = -7_{10}$

Indeed -7_{10} is the proper sum of -25_{10} and 18_{10}.

BINARY CODES SYSTEMS

Binary codes are codes which are represented in binary system with modification from the original ones.

Below we will be seeing the following:

- Weighted Binary Systems
- Non Weighted Codes

WEIGHTED BINARY SYSTEMS

Weighted binary codes are those which obey the positional weighting principles, each position of the number represents a specific weight. The binary counting sequence is an example.

Decimal	8421	2421	5211	Excess-3
0	0000	0000	0000	0011
1	0001	0001	0001	0100
2	0010	0010	0011	0101
3	0011	0011	0101	0110
4	0100	0100	0111	0111
5	0101	1011	1000	1000
6	0110	1100	1010	1001
7	0111	1101	1100	1010
8	1000	1110	1110	1011
9	1001	1111	1111	1100

8421 Code/BCD Code

The BCD (Binary Coded Decimal) is a straight assignment of the binary equivalent. It is possible to assign weights to the binary bits according to their positions. The weights in the BCD code are 8,4,2,1.

Example: The bit assignment 1001, can be seen by its weights to represent the decimal 9 because.

$$1 \times 8 + 0 \times 4 + 0 \times 2 + 1 \times 1 = 9$$

2421 Code

This is a weighted code, its weights are 2, 4, 2 and 1. A decimal number is represented in 4-bit form and the total four bits weight is $2 + 4 + 2 + 1 = 9$. Hence the 2421 code represents the decimal numbers from 0 to 9.

5211 Code

This is a weighted code, its weights are 5, 2, 1 and 1. A decimal number is represented in 4-bit form and the total four bits weight is $5 + 2 + 1 + 1 = 9$. Hence the 5211 code represents the decimal numbers from 0 to 9.

Reflective Code

A code is said to be reflective when code for 9 is complement for the code for 0, and so is for 8 and 1 codes, 7 and 2, 6 and 3, 5 and 4. Codes 2421, 5211, and excess-3 are reflective, whereas the 8421 code is not.

Sequential Codes

A code is said to be sequential when two subsequent codes, seen as numbers in binary representation, differ by one. This greatly aids mathematical manipulation of data. The 8421 and Excess-3 codes are sequential, whereas the 2421 and 5211 codes are not.

NON WEIGHTED CODES

Non weighted codes are codes that are not positionally weighted. That is, each position within the binary number is not assigned a fixed value.

Excess-3 Code

Excess-3 is a non weighted code used to express decimal numbers. The code derives its name from the fact that each binary code is the corresponding 8421 code plus 0011(3).

Example: 1000 of 8421 = 1011 in Excess-3

Gray Code

The gray code belongs to a class of codes called minimum change codes, in which only one bit in the code changes when moving from one code to the next. The Gray code is non-weighted code, as the position of bit does not contain any weight.

The gray code is a reflective digital code which has the special property that any two subsequent numbers codes differ by only one bit. This is also called a unit-distance code. In digital Gray code has got a special place.

BINARY TO GRAY CONVERSION

- Gray Code MSB is binary code MSB.
- Gray Code MSB-1 is the XOR of binary code MSB and MSB-1.
- MSB-2 bit of gray code is XOR of MSB-1 and MSB-2 bit of binary code.
- MSB-N bit of gray code is XOR of MSB-N-1 and MSB-N bit of binary code.

2

Different Operating Conditions of a Transistor

INTRODUCTION

When a transistor is in the fully-off state (like an open switch), it is said to be *cutoff*. Conversely, when it is fully conductive between emitter and collector (passing as much current through the collector as the collector power supply and load will allow), it is said to be *saturated*. These are the two modes of operation explored thus far in using the transistor as a switch.

However, bipolar transistors don't have to be restricted to these two extreme modes of operation. As we learned in the previous section, base current "opens a gate" for a limited amount of current through the collector. If this limit for the controlled current is greater than zero but less than the maximum allowed by the power supply and load circuit, the transistor will "throttle" the collector current in a mode somewhere between cutoff and saturation. This mode of operation is called the *active* mode.

An automotive analogy for transistor operation is as follows: *cutoff* is the condition of no motive force generated by the mechanical parts of the car to make it move. In cutoff mode, the brake is engaged (zero base current), preventing motion (collector current). *Active mode* is the automobile cruising at a constant, controlled speed (constant, controlled collector current) as dictated by the driver.

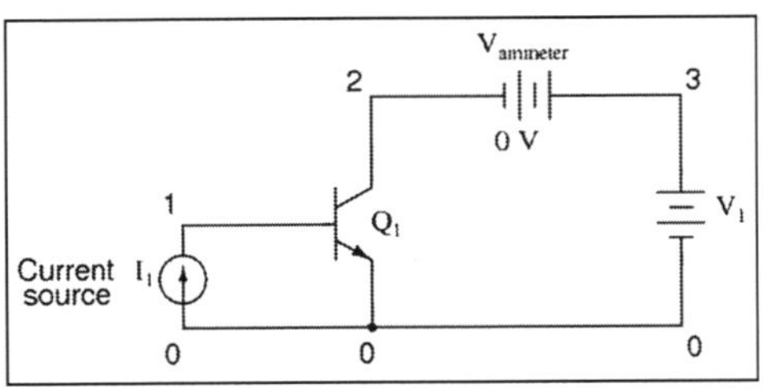

Saturation the automobile driving up a steep hill that prevents it from going as fast as the driver wishes. In other words, a "saturated" automobile is one with the accelerator pedal pushed all the way down (base current calling for more collector current than can be provided by the power supply/load circuit). Let's set up a circuit for SPICE simulation to demonstrate what happens when a transistor is in its active mode of operation.

```
bipolar transistor simulation
I1 0 1 dc 20u
Q1 2 1 0 mod1
vammeter 3 2 dc 0
V1 3 0 dc
.model mod1 npn
.dc V1 0 2 0.05
.plot dc i(vammeter)
.end
```

"Q" is the standard letter designation for a transistor in a schematic diagram, just as "R" is for resistor and "C" is for capacitor. In this circuit, we have an NPN transistor powered by a battery (V_1) and controlled by current through a *current source* (I_1). A current source is a device that outputs a specific amount of current, generating as much or as little voltage across its terminals to ensure that exact amount of current through it.

Current sources are notoriously difficult to find in nature (unlike voltage sources, which by contrast attempt to maintain a constant voltage, outputting as much or as little current in the fulfillment of that task), but can be simulated with a small collection of electronic components. As we are about to see, transistors themselves tend to mimic the constant-current behaviour of a current source in their ability to *regulate* current at a fixed value. In the SPICE simulation, we'll set the current source at a constant value of 20 μA, then vary the voltage source (V_1) over a range of 0 to 2 volts and monitor how much current goes through it. The "dummy" battery ($V_{ammeter}$) in Figure above with its output of 0 volts serves merely to provide SPICE with a circuit element for current measurement.

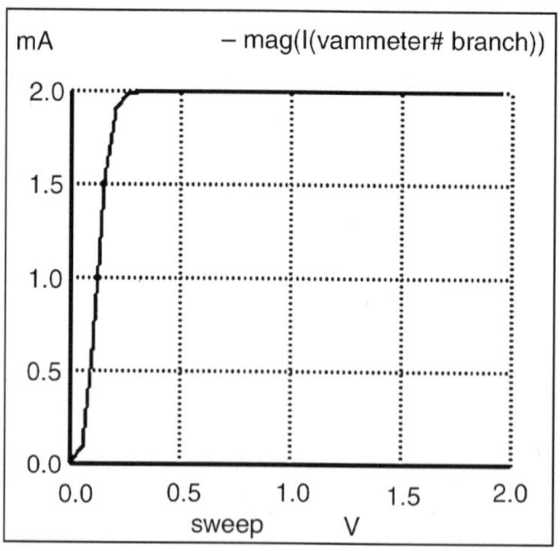

A Sweeping collector voltage 0 to 2 V with base current constant at 20 μA yields constant 2 mA collector current in the saturation region. The constant base current of 20 μA sets a collector current limit of 2 mA, exactly 100 times as much. Notice how flat the curve is in (Figure above for collector current over the range of battery voltage from 0 to 2 volts.

The only exception to this featureless plot is at the very beginning, where the battery increases from 0 volts to 0.25 volts. There, the collector current increases rapidly from 0 amps to its limit of 2 mA. Let's see what happens if we vary the battery voltage over a wider range, this time from 0 to 50 volts. We'll keep the base current steady at 20 μA.

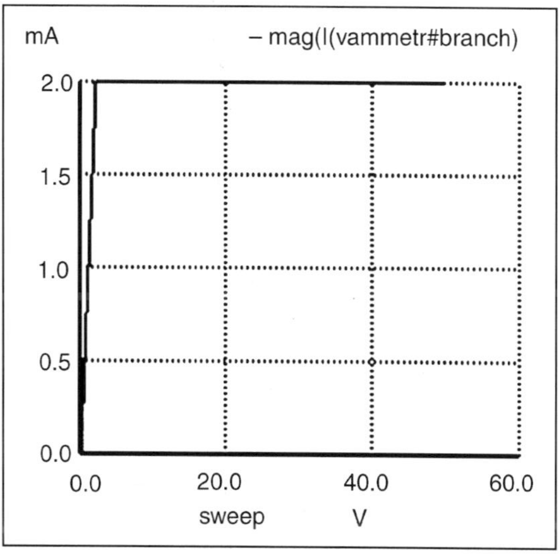


```
bipolar transistor simulation
i1 0 1 dc 20u
q1 2 1 0 mod1
vammeter 3 2 dc 0
v1 3 0 dc
.model mod1 npn
.dc v1 0 50 2
.plot dc i(vammeter)
.end
```

Sweeping collector voltage 0 to 50 V with base current constant at 20 μA yields constant 2 mA collector current. The collector current in Figure above holds absolutely steady at 2 mA, although the battery (v_1) voltage varies all the way from 0 to 50 volts. It would appear from our simulation that collector-to-emitter voltage has little effect over collector current, except at very low levels (just above 0 volts). The transistor is acting as a current regulator, allowing exactly 2 mA through the collector and no more. Now let's see what happens if we increase the controlling (I_1) current from 20 μA to 75 μA, once again sweeping the battery (V_1) voltage from 0 to 50 volts and graphing the collector current in Figure below.

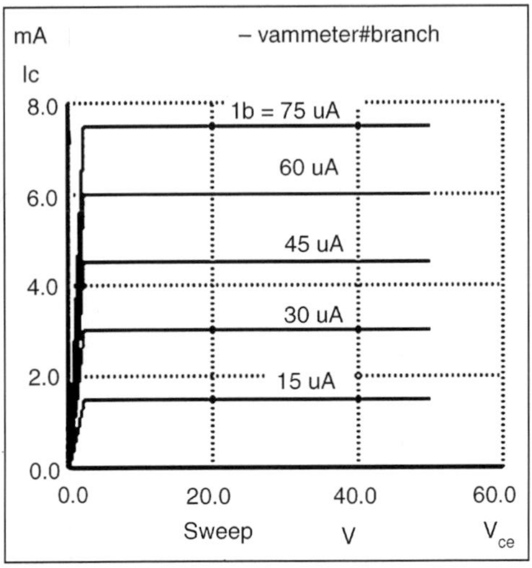


```
bipolar transistor simulation
i1 0 1 dc 75u
q1 2 1 0 mod1s
vammeter 3 2 dc 0
v1 3 0 dc
.model mod1 npn
.dc v1 0 50 2 i1 15u 75u 15u
.plot dc i(vammeter)
.end
```

Sweeping collector voltage 0 to 50 V (.dc v_1 0 50 2) with base current constant at 75 μA yields constant 7.5 mA collector current. Other curves are generated by current sweep (i1 15u 75u 15u) in DC analysis statement (.dc v_1 0 50 2 i_1 15u 75u 15u). Not surprisingly, SPICE gives us a similar plot: a flat line, holding steady this time at 7.5 mA—exactly 100 times the base current—over the range of battery voltages from just above 0 volts to 50 volts. It appears that the base current is the deciding factor for collector current, the V_1 battery voltage being irrelevant as long as it is above a certain minimum level.

This voltage/current relationship is entirely different from what we're used to seeing across a resistor. With a resistor, current increases linearly as the voltage across it increases. Here, with a transistor, current from emitter to collector stays limited at a fixed, maximum value no matter how high the voltage across emitter and collector increases. Often it is useful to superimpose several collector current/voltage graphs for different base currents on the same graph as in Figure below. A collection of curves like this—one curve plotted for each distinct level of base current—for a particular transistor is called the transistor's *characteristic curves*:

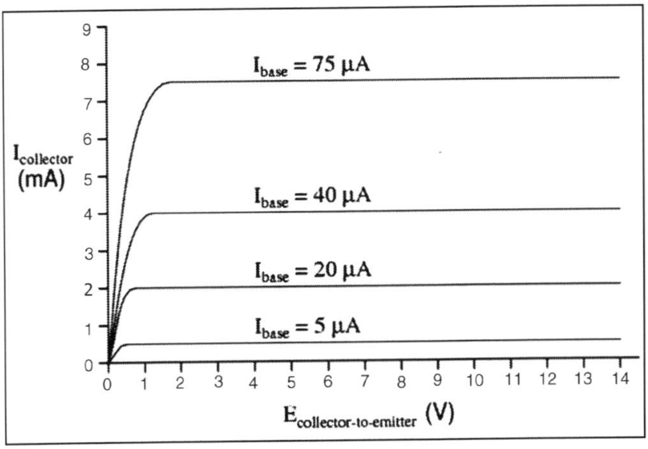

VOLTAGE COLLECTOR TO EMITTER VS COLLECTOR CURRENT FOR VARIOUS BASE CURRENTS

Each curve on the graph reflects the collector current of the transistor, plotted over a range of collector-to-emitter voltages, for a given amount of base current. Since a transistor tends to act as a current regulator, limiting collector current to a proportion set by the base current, it is useful to express this proportion as a standard transistor performance measure. Specifically, the ratio of collector current to base current is known as the *Beta* ratio (symbolized by the Greek letter β):

$$\beta = \frac{I_{Collector}}{I_{base}}.$$

β is also known as h_{fe}

Sometimes the β ratio is designated as "h_{fe}," a label used in a branch of mathematical semiconductor analysis known as "hybrid parameters" which strives to achieve precise predictions of transistor performance with detailed equations. Hybrid parameter variables are many, but each is labeled with the general letter "h" and a specific subscript. The variable "h_{fe}" is just another (standardized) way of expressing the ratio of collector current to base current, and is interchangeable with "β." The β ratio is unit less.

β for any transistor is determined by its design: it cannot be altered after manufacture. It is rare to have two transistors of the same design exactly match because of the physical variables affecting β. If a circuit design relies on equal β ratios between multiple transistors, "matched sets" of transistors may be purchased at extra cost. However, it is generally considered bad design practice to engineer circuits with such dependencies. The β of a transistor does not remain stable for all operating conditions. For an actual transistor, the β ratio may vary by a factor of over 3 within its operating current limits. For example, a transistor with advertised β of 50 may actually test with I_c/I_b ratios as low as 30 and as high as 100, depending on the amount of collector current, the transistor's temperature, and frequency of amplified signal, among other factors. For tutorial purposes it is adequate to assume a constant β for any given transistor; realise that real life is not that simple! Sometimes it is helpful for comprehension to "model" complex electronic components with a collection of simpler, better-understood components. The model in Figure below is used in many introductory electronics texts.

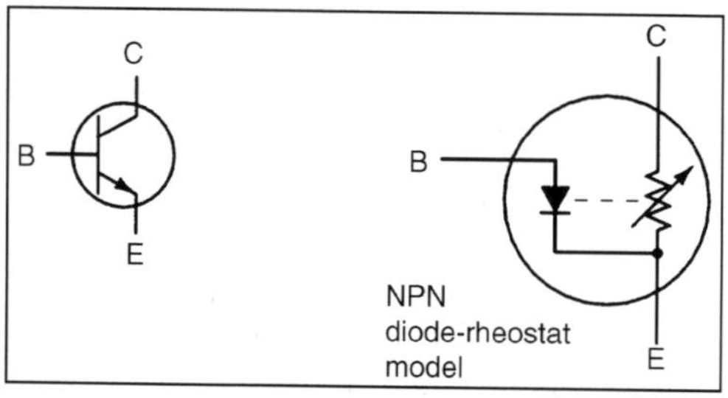

ELEMENTARY DIODE RESISTOR TRANSISTOR MODEL

This model casts the transistor as a combination of diode and rheostat (variable resistor). Current through the base-emitter diode controls the resistance of the collector-emitter rheostat, thus controlling collector current. An NPN transistor is modeled in the figure shown, but a PNP transistor would be only slightly different (only the base-emitter diode would be reversed). This model succeeds in illustrating the basic concept of transistor amplification: how the base current signal can exert control over the collector current. However, I don't like this model because it miscommunicates the notion of a set amount of collector-emitter resistance for a given amount of base current. If this were true, the transistor wouldn't *regulate* collector current at all like the characteristic curves show. Instead of the collector current curves flattening out after their brief rise as the collector-emitter voltage increases, the collector current would be directly proportional to collector-emitter voltage, rising steadily in a straight line on the graph. A better transistor model, often seen in more advanced textbooks, is shown in Figure below.

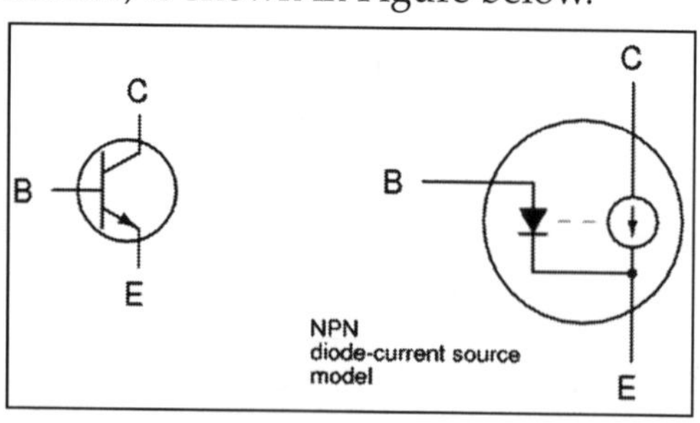

CURRENT SOURCE MODEL OF TRANSISTOR

It casts the transistor as a combination of diode and current source, the output of the current source being set at a multiple (β ratio) of the base current. This model is far more accurate in depicting the true input/output characteristics of a transistor: base current establishes a certain amount of collector *current*, rather than a certain amount of collector-emitter *resistance* as the first model implies.

Also, this model is favoured when performing network analysis on transistor circuits, the current source being a well-understood theoretical component. Unfortunately, using a current source to model the transistor's current-controlling behaviour can be misleading: in no way will the transistor ever act as a *source* of electrical energy. The current source does not model the fact that its source of energy is a external power supply, similar to an amplifier.

TRANSISTOR CONFIGURATIONS OR CONNECTIONS

You have to think in terms of circuit configurations and the voltage and current in each lead when discussing how transistors behave. There are 3 configurations—the emitter follower which is a current amplifier but has no voltage gain, the common emitter amplifier which has current and voltage gain, and the common base amplifier which has voltage gain but no current gain. In an emitter follower circuit with the collector connected to +V and a load connected between the emitter and ground, the voltage applied to the base minus the base emitter forward voltage drop (~0.6 V) will appear across the load (*i.e.*, 5 V base = 4.4 V emitter).

The only caveat is that the voltage source at the base must be able to supply about 5 per cent of the load current without appreciable voltage drop. This is a non-inverting voltage follower circuit. In a common emitter circuit with the emitter connected to ground and the load connected between the collector and +V, a voltage connected to the base which exceeds the base emitter forward voltage (0.6V) will rapidly turn on the transistor in proportion to the voltage rise as the base emitter current rapidly increases for a small increase in base voltage.

The base voltage source must be able to supply about 5 per cent of the load current into the base emitter diode (*i.e.*, short circuit) for the circuit to develop a large voltage across the load. This is an inverting voltage amplifier circuit. In a common base circuit with the base grounded (or at a reference voltage) and the load connected between the collector and +V, a control voltage connected to the emitter which is more negative than the base emitter forward voltage (~0.6V) causes the transistor to rapidly turn on.

The control voltage source must be able to supply about 105 per cent of the load current to develop the full voltage across the load. This is a non-inverting voltage amplifier circuit

COMMON-BASE (CB) CONFIGURATION

INTRODUCTION

As its name suggests, in the Common Base or grounded base configuration, the BASE connection is common to both the input signal AND the output signal with the input signal being applied between the base and the emitter terminals. The corresponding output signal is taken from between the base and the collector terminals as shown with the base terminal grounded or connected to a fixed reference voltage point.

The input current flowing into the emitter is quite large as its the sum of both the base current and collector current respectively therefore, the collector current output is less than the emitter current input resulting in a current gain for this type of circuit of "1" (unity) or less, in other words the common base configuration "attenuates" the input signal.

CIRCUIT

This type of amplifier configuration is a non-inverting voltage amplifier circuit, in that the signal voltagesV_{in} and Vout are in-phase. This type of transistor arrangement is not very common due to its unusually high voltage gain characteristics.

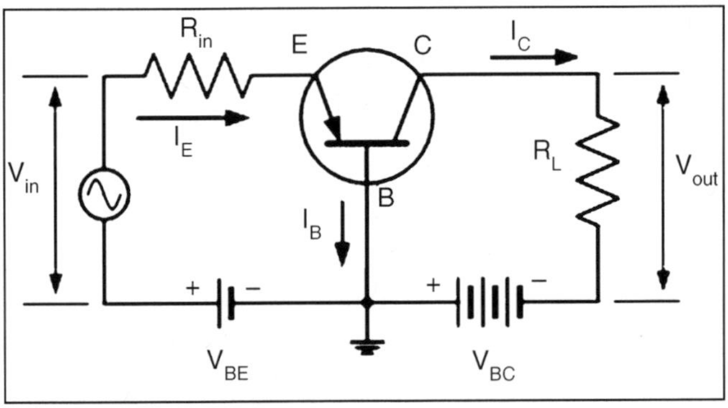

CHARCTERSTICS OF Cb CONFIGURATIONS

Its output characteristics represent that of a forward biased diode while the input characteristics represent that of an illuminated photo-diode. Also this type of bipolar transistor configuration has a high ratio of output to input resistance or more importantly "load" resistance (R_L) to "input" resistance (R_{in}) giving it a value of "Resistance Gain". Then the voltage gain (A_V) for a common base configuration is therefore given as:

VOLTAGE GAIN

$$A_V = \frac{Vout}{Vin} = \frac{I_C \times R_L}{I_E \times R_{IN}}$$

Where: I_c/I_e is the current gain, alpha (α) and R_L/R_{in} is the resistance gain.

The common base circuit is generally only used in single stage amplifier circuits such as microphone pre-amplifier or radio frequency (Rf) amplifiers due to its very good high frequency response.

COMMON-EMITTER (Ce) CONFIGURATION

INTRODUCTION

In the Common Emitter or grounded emitter configuration, the input signal is applied between the base, while the output is taken from between the collector and the emitter as shown. This type of configuration is the most commonly used circuit for transistor based amplifiers and which represents the "normal" method of bipolar transistor connection. The common emitter amplifier configuration produces the highest current and power gain of all the three bipolar transistor configurations.

This is mainly because the input impedance is LOW as it is connected to a forward-biased PN-junction, while the output impedance is HIGH as it is taken from a reverse-biased PN-junction.

CIRCUIT

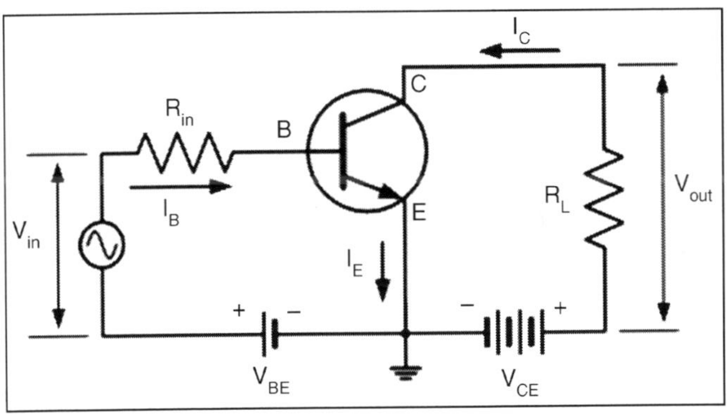

In this type of configuration, the current flowing out of the transistor must be equal to the currents flowing into the transistor as the emitter current is given as $I_e = I_c + I_b$. Also, as the load resistance (RL) is connected in series with the collector, the current gain of the common emitter transistor configuration is quite large as it is the ratio of Ic/Ib and is given the Greek symbol of Beta, (β). As the emitter current for a common emitter configuration is defined as $I_e = I_c + I_b$, the ratio of I_c/I_e is called Alpha, given the Greek symbol of á. Note: that the value of Alpha will always be less than unity.

Since the electrical relationship between these three currents, I_b, I_C and I_e is determined by the physical construction of the transistor itself, any small change in the base current (I_b), will result in a much larger change in the collector current (I_C). Then, small changes in current flowing in the base will thus control the current in the emitter-collector circuit. Typically, Beta has a value between 20 and 200 for most general purpose transistors. By combining the expressions for both Alpha, α and Beta, β the mathematical relationship between these parameters and therefore the current gain of the transistor can be given as:

$$\text{Alpha},(\alpha)=\frac{I_C}{I_E} \quad \text{and} \quad \text{Beta},(\beta)=\frac{I_C}{I_B}$$

$$\therefore \alpha=\frac{\beta}{\beta+1} \qquad \beta=\frac{\alpha}{1-\alpha}$$

$$I_E = I_C + I_B$$

Where: "I_C" is the current flowing into the collector terminal, "I_b" is the current flowing into the base terminal and "I_e" is the current flowing out of the emitter terminal. Then to summarise, this type of bipolar transistor configuration has a greater input impedance, current and power gain than that of the common base configuration but its voltage gain is much lower. The common emitter configuration is an inverting amplifier circuit resulting in the output signal being 180oout-of-phase with the input voltage signal.

COMMON COLLECTOR (Cc) CONFIGURATION

INTRODUCTION

In the Common Collector or grounded collector configuration, the collector is now common through the supply. The input signal is connected directly to the base, while the output is taken from the emitter load as shown. This type of configuration is commonly known as a Voltage Follower or Emitter Follower circuit. The emitter follower configuration is very useful for impedance matching applications because of the very high input impedance, in the region of hundreds of thousands of Ohms while having relatively low output impedance.

CIRCUIT

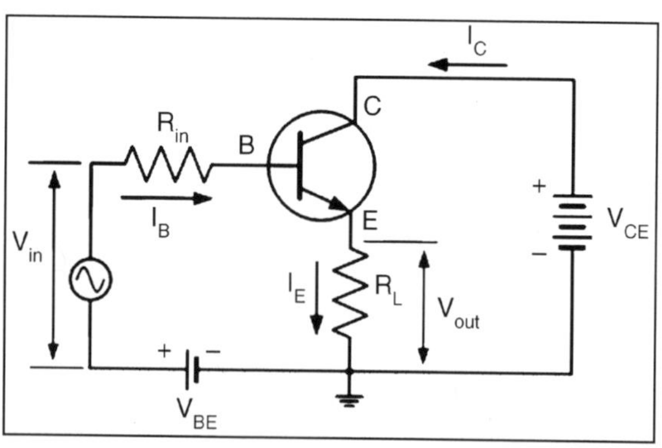

The common emitter configuration has a current gain approximately equal to the β value of the transistor itself. In the common collector configuration the load resistance is situated in series with the emitter so its current is equal to that of the emitter current. As the emitter current is the combination of the collector AND the base current combined, the load resistance in this type of transistor configuration also has both the collector current and the input current of the base flowing through it. Then the current gain of the circuit is given as:

GAIN

$$I_E = I_C + I_B$$

$$A_i = \frac{I_E}{I_B} = \frac{I_C + I_B}{I_B}$$

$$A_i = \frac{I_C}{I_B} + 1$$

$$A_i = \beta + 1.$$

This type of bipolar transistor configuration is a non-inverting circuit in that the signal voltages of Vin and Vout are in-phase. It has a voltage gain that is always less than "1" (unity). The load resistance of the common collector transistor receives both the base and collector currents giving a large current gain (as with the common emitter configuration) therefore, providing good current amplification with very little voltage gain.

COMPARISON OF THREE CONFIGURATIONS

INTRODUCTION

To summaries, the behaviour of the bipolar transistor in each one of the above circuit configurations is very different and produces different circuit characteristics with regards to input impedance, output impedance and gain whether this is voltage gain, current gain or power gain and this is summarised in the table below.

CHARACTERISTICS

The static characteristics for a Bipolar Transistor can be divided into the following three main groups.

Input Characteristics:-	Common Base -	ΔVEB / ΔIE
	Common Emitter -	ΔVBE / ΔIB
Output Characteristics:-	Common Base -	ΔVC / ΔIC
	Common Emitter -	ΔVC / ΔIC
Transfer Characteristics:-	Common Base -	ΔIC / ΔIE
	Common Emitter -	ΔIC / ΔIB

with the characteristics of the different transistor configurations given in the following table:

Characteristic	Common Base	Common Emitter	Common Collector
Input Impedance	Low	Medium	High
Output Impedance	Very High	High	Low
Phase Angle	0°	180°	0°
Voltage Gain	High	Medium	Low
Current Gain	Low	Medium	High
Power Gain	Low	Very High	Medium

In the next tutorial about Bipolar Transistors, we will look at the NPN Transistor in more detail when used in the common emitter configuration as an amplifier as this is the most widely used configuration due to its flexibility and high gain. We will also plot the output characteristics curves commonly associated with amplifier circuits as a function of the collector current to the base current.

OPERATING POINT (QUIESCENT, Q OR SILENT POINT)

The point Vo in the diagram above is where the output signal would be taken. For simplicity, the input signal and coupling capacitors have been omitted. For minimum distortion and clipping it is desirable to bias this point to half the supply voltage, 10 volts dc in this case.

This is also known as the quiescent point. The ac output signal would then be superimposed on the dc bias voltage. The Q-point is sometimes indicated on the output characteristics curves for a transistor amplifier. The quiescent point also refers to the dc conditions (bias conditions) of a circuit without an input signal.

Q-POINT VALUE

I have mentioned that setting the Q-point to half the supply voltage is a good idea. It gives a circuit the highest margin for overload. However, any amplifier will clip if the input amplitude exceeds the limit for which the circuit was designed.

However, there are certain cases when it is not necessary to bias a stage to half the supply voltage. Examples would be an RF amplifier design where the input signal is in microvolts or millivolts. If the stage had a gain of 200 then the output (assuming a 2mV peak input) would only need to swing up and down 400mV about the Q-point. Hence a stage with a supply voltage of 12 volts could have its Q-point set at 10 volts or even 2 volts without problems.

DIFFERENT POINT ON THE CHARACTERSTICS

The example would be a microphone stage where similar low level input signals are involved.

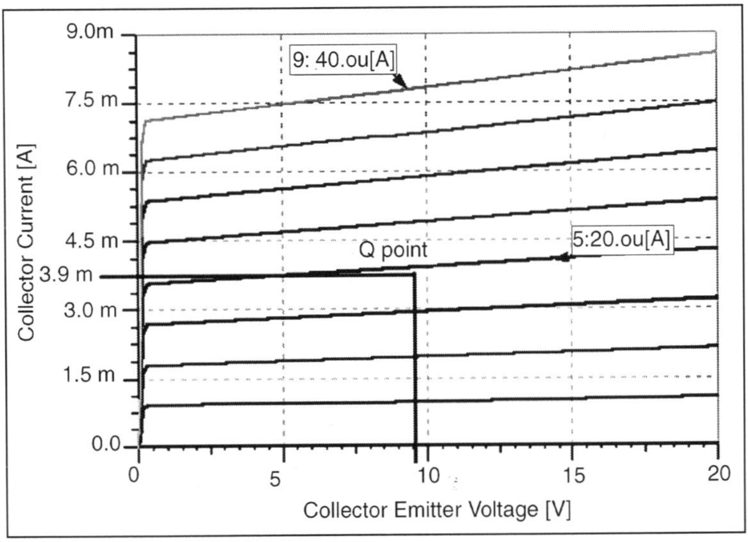

TYPES OF BJT'S

Transistors are three terminal active devices made from different semiconductor materials that can act as either an insulator or a conductor by the application of a small signal voltage. The transistor's ability to change between these two states enables it to have two basic functions: "switching" (digital electronics) or "amplification" (analogue electronics).

Then bipolar transistors have the ability to operate within three different regions:

1. *Active Region*: The transistor operates as an amplifier and Ic = β.Ib
2. *Saturation*: He transistor is "fully-ON" operating as a switch and Ic = I (saturation)
3. *Cut-off*: The transistor is "fully-OFF" operating as a switch and Ic = 0

Fig. Typical Bipolar Transistor

The word Transistor is an acronym, and is a combination of the words Transfer Varistor used to describe their mode of operation way back in their early days of development. There are two basic types of bipolar transistor construction, PNP and NPN, which basically describes the physical arrangement of the P-type and N-type semiconductor materials from which they are made. The Bipolar Transistor basic construction consists of two PN-junctions producing three connecting terminals with each terminal being given a name to identify it from the other two. These three terminals are known and labelled as the Emitter (E), the Base (B) and the Collector (C) respectively. Bipolar Transistors are current regulating devices that control the amount of current flowing through them in proportion to the amount of biasing voltage applied to their base terminal acting like a current-controlled switch. The principle of operation of the two transistor types PNP and NPN, is exactly the same the only difference being in their biasing and the polarity of the power supply for each type.

BIPOLAR TRANSISTOR CONSTRUCTION

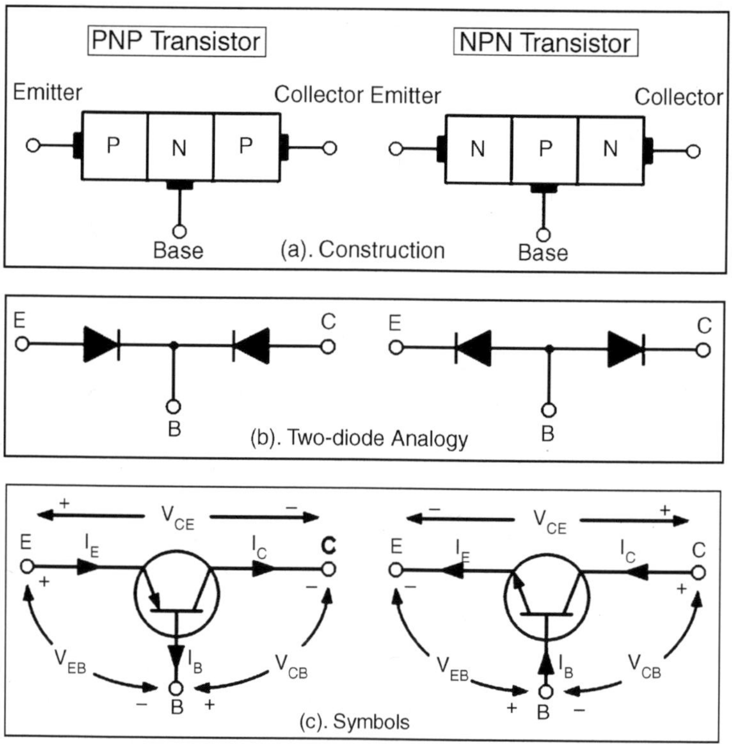

(a). Construction
(b). Two-diode Analogy
(c). Symbols

The construction and circuit symbols for both the PNP and NPN bipolar transistor are given above with the arrow in the circuit symbol always showing the direction of "conventional current flow" between the base terminal and its emitter terminal. The direction of the arrow always points from the positive P-type region to the negative N-type region for both transistor types, exactly the same as for the standard diode symbol.

A BJT consists of three differently doped semiconductor regions, the emitter region, the base region and the collector region. These regions are, respectively, p type, n type and p type in a PNP, and n type, p type and n type in a NPN transistor. Each semiconductor region is connected to a terminal, appropriately labeled: emitter (E), base (B) and collector (C). The base is physically located between the emitter and the collector and is made from lightly doped, high resistivity material. The collector surrounds the emitter region, making it almost impossible for the electrons injected into the base region to escape being collected, thus making the resulting value of α very close to unity, and so, giving the transistor a large β. A cross section view of a BJT indicates that the collector—base junction has a much larger area than the emitter—base junction.

The bipolar junction transistor, unlike other transistors, is usually not a symmetrical device. This means that interchanging the collector and the emitter makes the transistor leave the forward active mode and start to operate in reverse mode. Because the transistor's internal structure is usually optimized for forward-mode operation, interchanging the collector and the emitter makes the values of α and β in reverse operation much smaller than those in forward operation; often the α of the reverse mode is lower than 0.5.

The lack of symmetry is primarily due to the doping ratios of the emitter and the collector. The emitter is heavily doped, while the collector is lightly doped, allowing a large reverse bias voltage to be applied before the collector–base junction breaks down. The collector–base junction is reverse biased in normal operation. The reason the emitter is heavily doped is to increase the emitter injection efficiency: the ratio of carriers injected by the emitter to those injected by the base. For high current gain, most of the carriers injected into the emitter–base junction must come from the emitter.

TRANSISTOR TERMINALS

The essential usefulness of a transistor comes from its ability to use a small signal applied between one pair of its terminals to control a much larger signal at another pair of terminals. This property is called gain. A transistor can control its output in proportion to the input signal; that is, it can act as an amplifier. Alternatively, the transistor can be used to turn current on or off in a circuit as an electrically controlled switch, where the amount of current is determined by other circuit elements.

There are two types of transistors, which have slight differences in how they are used in a circuit. A *bipolar transistor* has terminals labeled base, collector, and emitter. A small current at the base terminal (that is, flowing from the base to the emitter) can control or switch a much larger current between the collector and emitter terminals. For a *field-effect transistor*, the terminals are labeledgate, source, and drain, and a voltage at the gate can control a current between source and drain. The image to the right represents a typical bipolar transistor in a circuit. Charge will flow between emitter and collector terminals depending on the current in the base.

Since internally the base and emitter connections behave like a semiconductor diode, a voltage drop develops between base and emitter while the base current exists. The amount of this voltage depends on the material the transistor is made from, and is referred to as V_{BE}.

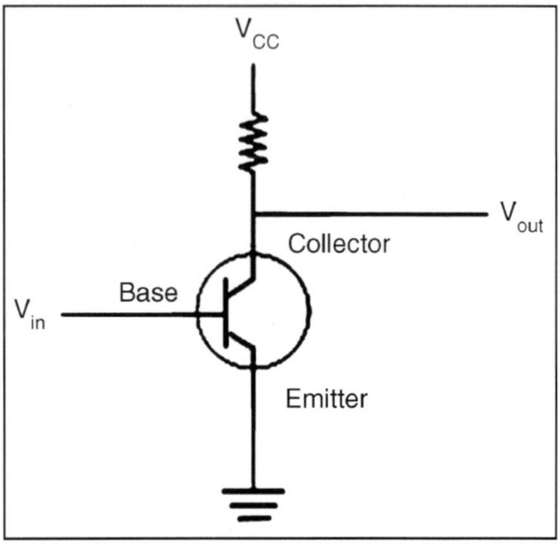

TRANSISTOR ACTION

Bipolar transistors are made from 3 sections of semiconductor material (alternating P-type and N-type), with 2 resulting P-N junctions. Schematically, a bipolartransistor can be thought of in this fashion:

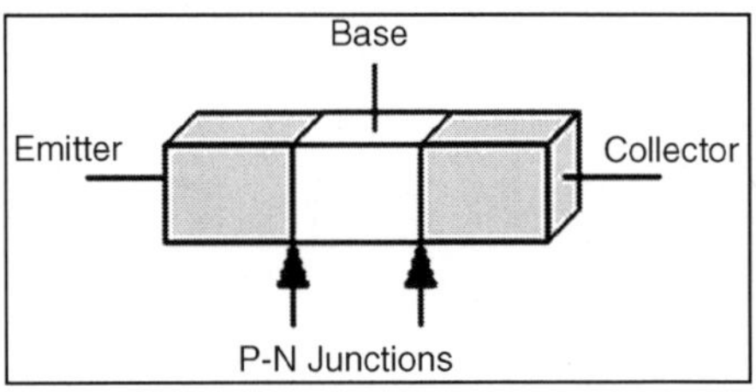

One P-N junction is between the emitter and the base; the other P-N junction is between the collector and the base. Note that the emitter and collector are usually doped somewhat differently, so they are rarely electrically interchangeable. While the terms "collector" and "emitter" go back to vacuum tube days, the base derives its name from the first point-contact transistors—here the center connection also formed the mechanical base for the structure. In modern practice, the base region is made as thin as possible to achieve reasonable levels of current gain; it is often only about one millionth of a meter thick. Bipolar transistors are classified as either NPN or PNP according to the arrangement of their N-type and P-type materials. Their basic construction and chemical treatment is implied by their names. So an NPN transistors is formed by introducing a thin region of P-type material between two regions of N-type material.

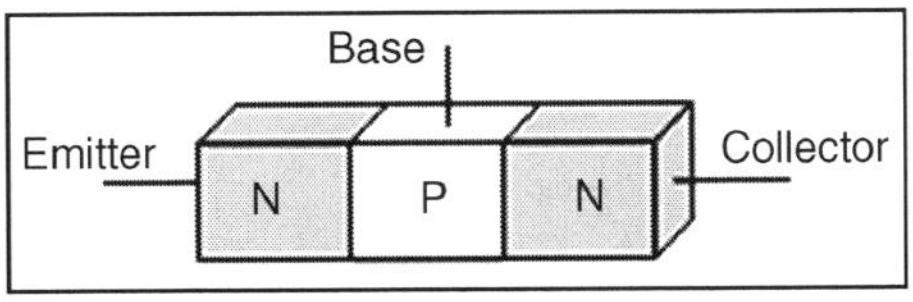

On the other hand, a PNP transistor is formed by introducing a thin region of N-type material between two regions of P-type material.

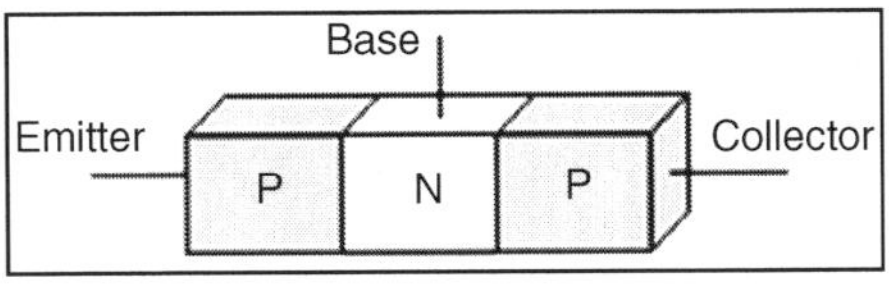

Since the majority and minority current carriers are different for N-type and P-type materials, it stands to reason that the internal operation of the NPN and PNPtransistors will also be different. These two basic types of transistors along with their circuit symbols are shown here:

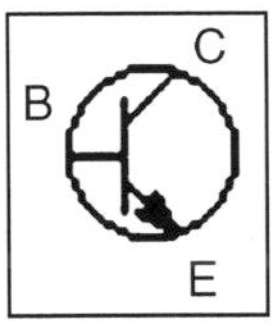

Fig. NPN

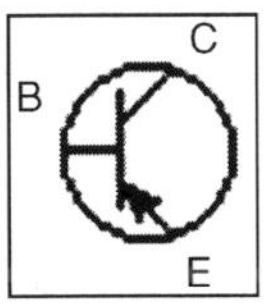

Fig. PNP

Note that the two symbols are subtly different. The vertical line represents the base (B), the angular line with the arrow on it represents the emitter (E), and the other angular line represents the collector (C). The direction of the arrow on the emitter distinguishes (graphically) the NPN from the PNP transistor. If the arrow points in, (Points iN) the transistor is a PNP. On the other hand if the arrow points out, the transistor is an NPN (Not Pointing iN). Bear in mind that the arrow always points in the direction of hole flow (current), or from the P-type to N-type sections, no matter whether the P-type section is theemitter or base.

On the other hand, electron flow is always "against" the arrow, just like in the junction diode. As a result, a PNP transistor is "triggered" when its base is pulled low; an NPN transistor is "triggered" when its base is brought high. Note that the bipolar transistor is a current-amplifying device, unlike the vacuum tube and the field-effect transistor (FET), both of which depend upon voltage changes to operate. It is the amount of current flowing in the base circuit that controls the amount of current flowing in the collector circuit.

TRANSISTOR BIASING

INTRODUCTION

The simplest bias circuit is shown below. It consists only of a fixed bias resistor and load resistor. The BJT is operating in common emitter mode. The dc current gain or beta, h_{FE} is the ratio of dc collector current divided by dc base current. The BJT is a BC107A. The values of Rb and Rc can be determined by either mathematical approach or by using the output characteristic curves for the BC107A.

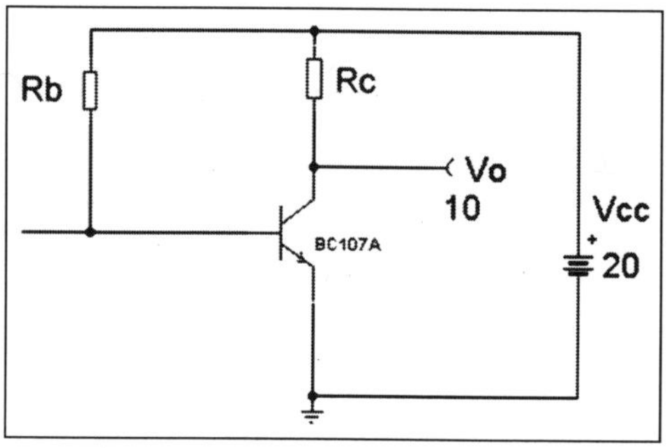

DESIGN

The collector voltage Vc for the simple bias design is 10 volt. The dc current gain, h_{FE} for the BC107A is obtained from the manufacturers data sheets and varies between devices. A typical beta is around 290. Taking a base current of 20uA and reading values direct from the output curves, the collector current, for a collector emitter voltage of 10 volts is around 3.9mA. As h_{FE}= Ic/Ib then a BC107A must have a beta of at least 3.9mA/20uA = 195 to work with this circuit. Also, the base emitter voltage, Vbe is typically 0.6v. Knowing the above data and using ohm's law, values for Rb and Rc can be determined:

Rb = Vcc–Vbe/Ib = (20–0.6)/20u = 970k use (1M)

Rc = Vc/Ic = 10/3.9m = 2.56K use (2.7K)

MATHEMATICAL APPROACH

Without using the output characteristic curve, values for Rb and Rc can still be calculated. A value for h_{FE} must be estimated first and a desired collector current. As h_{FE} varies in each transistor the value chosen should be the lowest value from the manufacturers data sheets. *The equations to use are*:

$$Rc = \frac{Vc}{Ic}$$

$$Ib = \frac{Ic}{h_{FE}}$$

Rb = Vcc–0.6/Ib.

Using the example above with Vcc=20 and h_{FE} =195 yields the same values.

NEED FOR BIASING A TRANSISTOR

A BJT (Bipolar Junction Transistor) require a voltage normally in the range of 0.7V for the internal junctions to become conductive. It is a fixed parameter of Silicon (Si) due to the amount of 1.1eV required to get electrons from the valence energy band into a conductive band. To be able jump the energy gap which is a forbidden band for electrons or to raise the Fermi energy level in the atom. The energy, whether it is electrically applied, thermally or optically, is required to be able change the state of a semiconductor from an insulator to an conductor. You can read more on "semiconductor theory" for better understanding.

Then with a non-linear relationship the conductivity will increase as one increase the forward bias current through the base to emitter junction. Biasing is used for classical transistor amplifier applications. Biasing is required to have the transistor half way saturated for Class-A amplification or barely switched on for Class-B power amplifiers. If a Class-B amplifier is not biased, then the lower 0.7V of the audio or sine wave will not be amplified causing crossover distortion. When you bias it correctly, the distortions will be gone, since the entire half wave will then fit into the on state of the transistor. If a Class-A amplifier is not correctly biased, premature clipping on the positive or negative part of the wave will occur.Biasing may be used for other applications as well, such as photo transistors, internal construction of IC's such as op-amps. This is not a problem for FM operation, where the drive level is constant, and always enough to 'turn on' the PA transistor. FM-only PAs usually have an RF choke to provide a DC return path directly from the base to ground.

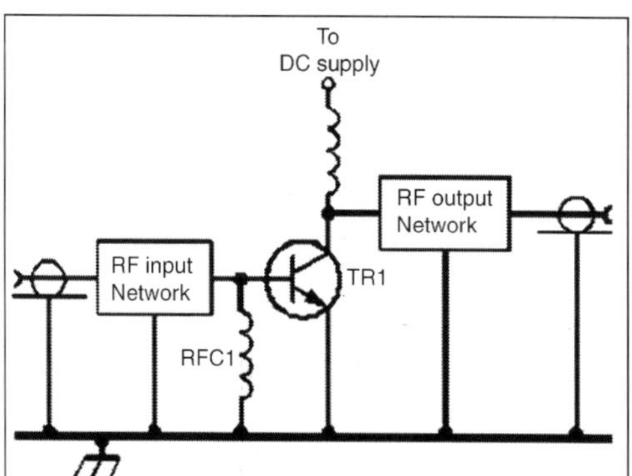

This circuit has no bias—only RFC1 from base to ground. This is sometimes called 'Class C' operation. But for SSB modulation, the delayed turn-on at low drive levels is disastrous: it means that all the low-level parts of the modulation are severely distorted and the amplifier only delivers RF power in bursts on speech peaks. This is why you must never use an FM-only power amplifier on SSB - the splatter is horrendous! For linear operation, it is *essential* to use a fixed DC bias to make sure that the transistor is already 'turned on' before any

RF drive arrives (so-called 'Class AB'). Typically, if the transistor is drawing about 100mA in 'standing current' with no RF drive, distortion will be quite low, provided that the bias supply can also cope with the higher demands of peak modulation. The standing collector current in the RF power transistor depends on the current flowing from the bias supply into the base, and on the beta of the transistor (ratio of collector current to base current). For a typical RF power transistor with a beta of 50, a standing collector current of 100mA needs a base current of 2mA. However, beta is not a very well-controlled value, so the next transistor might need only 2mA; or maybe 7mA. That's one reason why the bias supply must be adjustable. Another reason is that a very small change in base voltage can make a very big difference to the collector current.

WHAT HAPPENS IF A TRANSISTOR IS NOT BIASED

CONCEPT

It is very important that the bias supply maintains a fairly constant output voltage, even at maximum current demand; if it fails to do that, the RF drive will bias the transistor back towards Class C, causing heavy splatter on speech peaks. Another difficulty is that the base-emitter voltage of a transistor decreases as the transistor heats up. If the bias supply voltage remains constant, the transistor will draw more base current - and hence more collector current - when it's hot than when it's cool. More collector current means more power dissipation, which means more heat, which means more base current, which means more collector current... which can very quickly mean "goodbye transistor" due to thermal runaway. The solutions to this problem are a large, effective heatsink and a base bias supply whose output voltage *decreases* with temperature so that the PA collector current remains fairly constant.

BAD CIRCUITS

Here are two variants of a very common circuit - which generally works very badly.

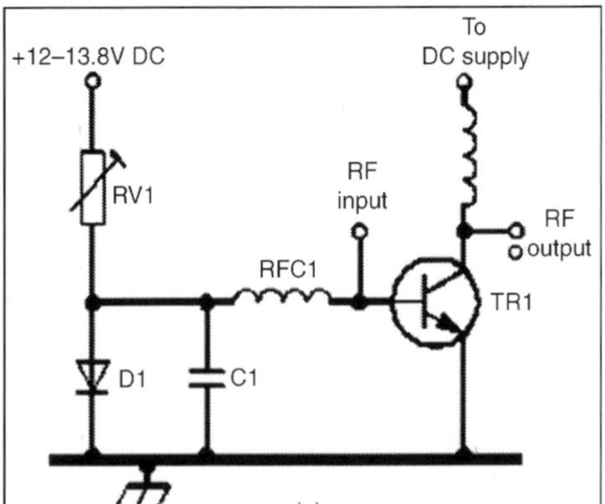

(a)

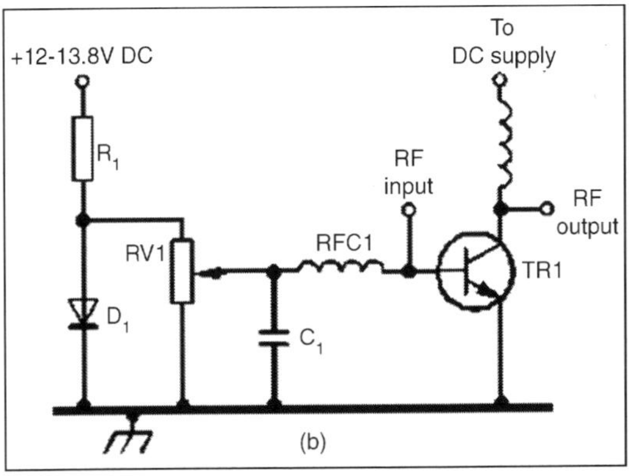

The voltage drop across the forward-biased diode D_1 is approximately the same as the voltage drop across the transistor's base-emitter junction, and by adjusting RV1 to send the correct current through D_1, the collector current in TR1 can be set to the desired value.

If D_1 is in thermal contact with TR1, the voltage across D_1 will drop as TR1 and D_1 heat up together, maintaining a constant and temperature-stabilized current through TR1. There are many problems with this simple circuit. The main one is that in order to maintain a constant voltage across D_1, the permanent standing current through D_1 must be several times higher than the maximum base current drawn by TR1 at the peak of RF drive. This requires an enormous standing current through RV1 and D_1 - one ampere or even more. Most designers fail to provide this. Some commercial circuits even use a low-current signal diode such as a IN914 for D_1! Bias regulation totally fails when peaks of RF drive create a heavy demand for base current, so this circuit is a real splatter-generator.

3

Digital Binary Numbers and Codes

DIGITAL BINARY NUMBERS

Binary representations of positive can be understood in the same way as their decimal counterparts.

For example,

$$86_{10} = 1*64 + 0*32 + 1*16 + 0*8 + 1*4 + 1*2 + 0*1$$

or

$$86_{10} = 1*2^6 + 0*2^5 + 1*2^4 + 0*2^3 + 1*2^2 + 1*2^1 + 0*2^0$$

or

$$86_{10} = 1010110_2$$

The subscript 2 denotes a binary number. Each digit in a binary number is called a bit. The number 1010110 is represented by 7 bits. Any number can be broken down this way, by finding all of the powers of 2 that add up to the number in question (in this case 2^6, 2^4, 2^2 and 2^1). You can see this is exactly analagous to the decimal deconstruction of the number 125 that was done earlier.

Likewise we can make a similar set of observations:

- To multiply a number by 2 you can simply shift it to the left by one digit, and fill in the rightmost digit with a 0. To divide a number by 2, simply shift the number to the right by one digit.
- To see how many digits a number needs, you can simply take the logarithm (base 2) of the number, and add 1 to it. The integer part of the result is the number of digits.

For instance,

$$\log_2(86) + 1 = 7.426.$$

The integer part of that is 7, so 7 digits are needed.

- With n digits, 2^n unique numbers (from 0 to 2^n-1) can be represented. If n=8, 256 (=2^8) numbers can be represented 0-255.

It is often convenient to handle groups of bits, rather than individually. The most common grouping is 8 bits, which forms a byte. A single byte can represent 256 (2^8) numbers. Memory capacity is usually referred to in bytes. Two bytes is usually called a word, or short word (though word-length depends on the application). A two-byte word is also the size that is usually used to represent integers in programming languages. A long word is usually twice as long as a word. A less common unit is the nibble which is 4 bits, or half of a byte.

It is cumbersome for humans to deal with writing, reading and remembering individual bits, because it takes many of them to represent even fairly small numbers. A number of different ways have been developed to make the handling of binary data easier for us. The most common is hexadecimal. In hexadecimal notation, 4 bits (a nibble) are represented by a single digit. There is obviously a problem with this since 4 bits gives 16 possible combinations, and there are only 10 unique decimal digits, 0 to 9. This is solved by using the first 6 letters (A..F) of the alphabet as numbers. The table shows the relationship between decimal, hexadecimal and binary.

Decimal	Hexadecimal	Binary
0	0	0000
1	1	0001
2	2	0010
3	3	0011
4	4	0100
5	5	0101
6	6	0110
7	7	0111
8	8	1000
9	9	1001
10	A	1010
11	B	1011
12	C	1100
13	D	1101
14	E	1110
15	F	1111

There are some significant advantages to using hexadecimal when dealing with electronic representations of numbers (if people had 16 fingers, we wouldn't be saddled with the awkward decimal system). Using hexadecimal makes it very easy to convert back and forth from binary because each hexadecimal digit corresponds to exactly 4 bits ($\log_2(16) = 4$) and each byte is two hexadecimal digit. In contrast, a decimal digit corresponds to $\log_2(10) = 3.322$ bits and a byte is 2.408 decimal digits. Clearly hexadecimal is better suited to the task of representing binary numbers than is decimal. As an example, the number $CA3_{16} = 1100\ 1010\ 0011_2$ ($1100_2 = C_{16}$, $1010_2 = A_{16}$, $0011_2 = 3_{16}$). It is convenient to write the binary number with spaces after every fourth bit to make it easier to read. Converting back and forth to decimal is more difficult, but can be done in the same way as before.

$$3235_{10} = C_{16}*256 + A_{16}*16 + 3_{16}*1 = C_{16}*16^2 + A_{16}*16^1 + 3_{16}*16^0$$

or

$$3235_{10} = 12*256 + 10*16 + 3*1 = 12*16^2 + 10*16^1 + 3*16^0$$

Octal notation is yet another compact method for writing binary numbers. There are 8 octal characters, 0...7. Obviously this can be represented by exactly 3 bits. Two octal digits can represent numbers up to 64, and three octal digits up to 512. A byte requires 2.667 octal digits. Octal used to be quiete common, it was the primary way of doing low level I/O on some old DEC computers. It is much less common today but is still used occasionally (*e.g.*, to set read, write and execute permissions on Unix systems)

DESCRIPTION OF BINARY NUMBERS

We will not be using a minus sign (–) to represent negative numbers. We would like to represent our binary numbers with only two symbols, 0 and 1. There are a few ways to represent negative binary numbers. The simplest of these methods is called ones complement, where the sign of a binary number is changed by simply toggling each bit (0's become 1's and vice-versa).

This has some difficulties, among them the fact that zero can be represented in two different ways (for an eight bit number these would be 0000 0000 and 1111 1111)., we will use a method called two's complement notation which avoids the pitfalls of one's complement, but which is a bit more complicated. To represent an n bit signed binary number the leftmost bit, has a special significance. The difference between a signed and an unsigned number is given in the table below for an 8 bit number.

Table. The Value of Bits in Signed and Unsigned Binary Numbers

	Bit 7	Bit 6	Bit 5	Bit 4	Bit 3	Bit 2	Bit 1	Bit 0
Unsigned	$2^7 = 128$	$2^6 = 64$	$2^5 = 32$	$2^4 = 16$	$2^3 = 8$	$2^2 = 4$	$2^1 = 2$	$2^0 = 1$
Signed	$-(2^7) = -128$	$2^6 = 64$	$2^5 = 32$	$2^4 = 16$	$2^3 = 8$	$2^2 = 4$	$2^1 = 2$	$2^0 = 1$

Let's look at how this changes the value of some binary numbers.

Binary	Unsigned	Signed
0010 0011	35	35
1010 0011	163	–93
1111 1111	255	–1
1000 0000	128	–128

If Bit 7 is not set (as in the first example) the representation of signed and unsigned numbers is the same. However, when Bit 7 is set, the number is always negative. For this reason Bit 7 is sometimes called the sign bit. Signed numbers are added in the same way as unsigned numbers, the only difference is in the way they are interpreted. This is important for designers of arithmetic circuitry because it means that numbers can be added by the same circuitry regardless of whether or not they are signed.

To form a two's complement number that is negative you simply take the corresponding positive number, invert all the bits, and add 1. The example below illustrated this by forming the number negative 35 as a two's complement integer:

$$35_{10} = 0010\ 0011_2$$
$$\text{invert} \rightarrow 1101\ 1100_2$$
$$\text{add } 1 \rightarrow 1101\ 1101_2$$

So 1101 1101 is our two's complement representation of -35. We can check this by adding up the contributions from the individual bits.

$$1101\ 1101_2 = -128 + 64 + 0 + 16 + 8 + 4 + 0 + 1 = -35.$$

The same procedure (invert and add 1) is used to convert the negative number to its positive equivalent. If we want to know what what number is represented by 1111 1101, we apply the procedure again.

$$? = 1111\ 1101_2$$
$$\text{invert} \rightarrow 0000\ 0010_2$$
$$\text{add } 1 \rightarrow 0000\ 0011_2$$

Since 0000 0011 represents the number 3, we know that 1111 1101 represents the number -3.

SIGNED BINARY NUMBERS

NUMBERS

So far we have considered how computers can represent integers as unsigned quantities. It is more realistic and practical to represent them as signed integers having both positive and negative values. Let's consider how this can be done. First, it should be observed that we will still be restricted to a uniform (finite) precision for representing signed integers. Thus, the same number of bits will now have to serve for for both negative and positive values. A reasonable approach would be to assign half of the binary values to negative decimal values and half to positive decimal values. For example, suppose that we had a precision of only four bits. Figure shows how these might be assigned in an orderly fashion.

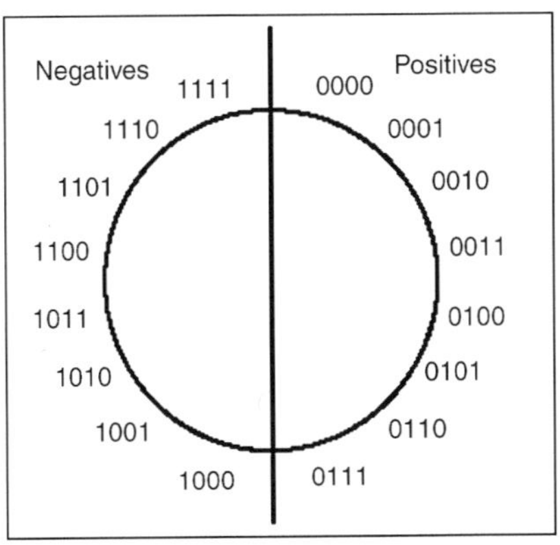

Fig. Dividing 4-bit Precision Binary into Positive and Negative Segments.

The binary values 0-7 could represent positive decimal values and the binary values 8-15 could signify negative decimal values. This divides the range into 8 values for positives and 8 values for negatives.

Notice that the binary values 0–7 representing positives have the most significant bit (MSB) of 0. The binary values 8–15 representing negatives have a MSB of 1. Thus, we could use the MSB to denote the sign and the remaining bits to signify the quantity or magnitude as shown in Figure. This scheme is appropriately called sign and magnitude.

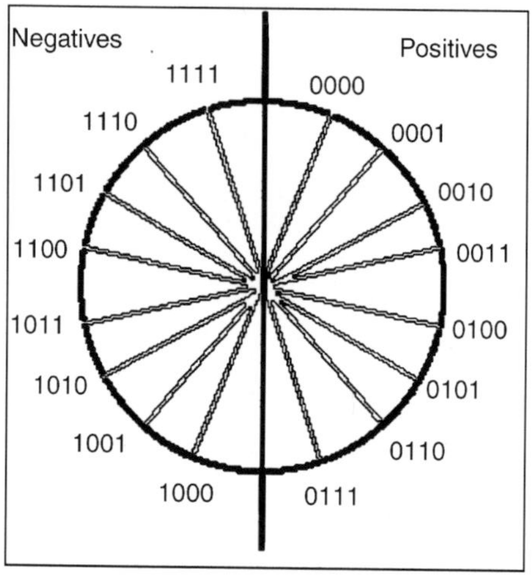

Fig. The Most Significant Bit Denotes the Sign and the Last Three Bits Signify the Magnitude.

As you can see in Figure, each positive has a corresponding negative value that differs only in the sign bit, *i.e.,* the MSB. With a 4-bit precision, our range is small, +7... –7. But, even if we extend the precision to 16 bits or 32 bits, there are other problems that remain. First, notice that there are codes for both +0 and –0; this is not convenient if, for example, we should have to decide whether a number is 0 or not. A more serious problem arises when doing arithmetic.

Recall that any binary integer can be represented by the sequence

+4 0100
+ -3 +1011
+1 1111
= –7

To do the arithmetic correctly, we have to consider the signs and the relative magnitudes of both numbers. It is much too complicated and therefore potentially expensive to implement as computer circuits.

There is another approach: using Ns-complement. Blaise Pascal, for example, employed this technique for his decimal calculating machine later known as the Pascaline. Suppose that we had a decimal precision of 4 digits. The range of values would be from 0000 to 9999. In 9s-complement (*i.e.,* N =

9), a negative value is determined by taking its additive inverse. This is the result of subtracting the magnitude from 9999. Here are some examples.

```
–11  9999
    –0011
=    9988
–53  9999
    –0053
=    9946
```

Simple addition operations can be used for both addition and subtraction. For example, adding a positive and negative number works provided that the carry-out value is added to adjust the sum.

```
+373     0373
+ –53  + 9946
+320   1 0319
(add carry) + 1
            0320
```

Subtraction can also be solved using addition provided that the term subtracted is complemented and then added to the other term. The example illustrates.

```
2430     2430
–11    + 9988
2419   1 2418
(add carry) + 1
            2419
```

Twos Complement

Most computer systems employ a variation of this method for representing signed integers called twos-complement. The procedures are similar.

Negative values are represented by:

1. Finding the complement (bit-value inverse) of the unsigned quantity.
2. The result is adjusted by adding +1.

Examples

Decimal Value	(Binary) Magnitude	(Binary) Inverse	Adjusted Result
-4	0100	1011	1100
		+1	
		1100	

Decimal Value	(Binary) Magnitude	(Binary) Inverse	Adjusted Result
-7	0111	1000	1001
		+1	
		1001	

One advantage of this scheme is that the MSB still serves to signify the sign of the number. In general, values for which the MSB = 1 are negative; values for which the MSB = 0 are positive. Addition and subtraction can also be handled by performing simple additions.

Examples

```
+7                        0111
+ –4                      +1100
+3                        1 0011
(ignore carry out)        = +3
+3                            011
- -4(convert to comp)     +0100
+7                            0111
                              = +7
```

But, in some instances, we can produce a value that it too large for our precision. This causes an overflow error condition. The results are incorrect. For instance,

```
+7                                  0111
– –4 (convert to comp) +0100
+11                                 1011
(too big)                           = –5
```

In short, adding two numbers with the same sign (MSB) results in overflow when the sign (MSB) changes.

INTEGER

Introduction

If we are given an *m*-bit computer word B with bits $b_{m-1}, b_{m-2}, \ldots, b_0$, we can interpret it as an unsigned number with value,

$$\text{unsigned}(B) = b_{m-1}*2^{m-1} + b_{m-2}*2^{m-2} + \ldots + b_0*2^0.$$

This gives us a representation for numbers from 0 to $2^m - 1$.

If we want to represent negative values as well, we can just change the sign of the high-order bit b_{m-1}, giving a signed number with value

$$\text{signed}(B) = -b_{m-1}*2^{m-1} + b_{m-2}*2^{m-2} + \ldots + b_0*2^0.$$

This is called the *m*-bit *2's complement* interpretation of B.

With $b_{m-1} = 0$, we get representations for numbers from 0 to $2^{m-1} - 1$. With $b_{m-1} = 1$, we get representations for numbers from -2^{m-1} to $-2^{m-1} + (2^{m-1} - 1) = -1$. Thus we have several important facts about the *m*-bit 2's complement representation.

- It represents numbers from -2^{m-1} to $2^{m-1} - 1$.
- If b_{m-1} is 1 then the value is negative; otherwise it is non-negative. Thus the high-order bit, b_{m-1} is called the *sign bit.*
- When the sign bit of B is 0, signed(B) = unsigned(B).

- When the sign bit of B is 1, signed(B) = unsigned(B) – 2^m.
- In either case, signed(B) — unsigned(B) is a multiple of 2^m.

The third fact tells you how to convert between a computer word with sign bit 0 and its 2's complement signed value, assuming you know how to convert between unsigned binary numbers and decimal. The fourth fact could be used to do the same when the sign bit is 1, but there is an alternative method described below that does not require that you remember powers of 2. The fifth fact can be used to determine when arithmetic with signed numbers fails.

Negation and the 2's Complement Operation

The one's complement operation is important bitwise operation for computer words. It converts each 0 bit in the word to 1 and each 1 bit in the word to 0. This operation is closely related to the negation operation for numbers. To see this, look at the follwing sum where B′ is the one's complement of B.

signed(B) + signed(B′) + 1 = $-b_{m-1}*2^{m-1} + b_{m-2}*2^{m-2} + ... + b_0*2^0 + -b'_{m-1}*2^{m-1} + b'_{m-2}*2^{m-2} + ... + b'_0*2^0 + 1 = -b_{m-1}*2^{m-1} + -b'_{mû1}*2^{m-1} + b_{m-2}*2^{m-2} + b'_{m-2}*2^{m-2} + ... + b_0*2^0 + b'_0*2^0 + 1 = -2^{m-1} + 2^{m-2} + ... + 2^0 + 1 = -2^{m-1} + 2^{m-1} - 1 + 1 = 0$

The terms in the third line are just the terms in the second line, rearranged to bring together like powers of 2. Then the b_is and the b'_is drop out because one of them is always 0 and the other is always 1. The equality between the fourth and fifth lines follows from the formula for summing a geometric series. The above formulas show that the negative of signed(B) is signed(B′) + 1. To make computer arithmetic reflect our arithmetic with numbers, addition on computer words is defined so that,

signed(B + C) = signed(B) + signed(C) Thus we can write

–signed(B) = signed(B′ + 1)

The operation on the right-hand side—doing a one's complement and adding one - is called the two's complement operation (not to be confused with the two's complement number representation). It is the computer equivalent of negating a number. There is one case where the two's complement operation fails to give us the same result as negation. This is to be expected when our computer operations use limited size words. Since the range of integers represented by an *m*-bit two's complement representation is from, -2^{m-1} to $2^{m-1} - 1$, there is number, -2^{m-1}, whose negative is not even representable. In this case, the add one step fails to work correctly.

CONVERTING SIGNED DECIMAL NUMBERS TO *M*-BIT 2'S COMPLEMENT

As noted above, the signed and unsigned *m*-bit representations are the same for representable non-negative integers. The equivalence of negation and the two's complement operation gives us a quick way of finding the *m*-bit two's complement representation of a negative integer: find the unsigned representation of its absolute value, then do a two's complement operation. Conversion in this direction fails whenever the decimal number is outside the range -2^{m-1} to $2^{m-1} - 1$.

Converting *m*-bit 2's Complement Numbers to Signed Decimal

To convert a *m*-bit two's complement number to decimal, you first look at the sign bit (the high order bit). If it is 0 the the number is non-negative and the determination of the decimal value is just an unsigned conversion from binary (or hexadecimal) to decimal. If the sign bit is 1, then do a two's complement operation, convert as an unsigned number, and affix a negative sign. Conversion in this direction never fails.

Signed Number Conversions in Hexadecimal

Since conversions are easier and more reliable in hexadecimal, it is useful to be able to to do the two's complement operation in hexadecimal.

To do this, you only need to be able to do the following:

- Recognize a negative number in hexadecimal
- Do a one's complement in hexadecimal
- Add one in hexadecimal

If the number of bits is a multiple of 4 then recognizing negative numbers in hexadecimal is easy: look at the high-order headecimal digit. If it is from 0 to 7 then the number is non-negative.

If it is from 8 to F then the number is negative. The following table shows how to do the one's complement step. The two hexadecimal digits in a row of the table are one's complements of each other. You can do a one's complement operation on a multi-digit hexadecimal number by converting each of the hexadecimal digit to its one's complement.

Hex	Binary	Decimal	Hex	Binary	Decimal
0	0000	0	F	1111	15
1	0001	1	E	1110	14
2	0010	2	D	1101	13
3	0011	3	C	1100	12
4	0100	4	B	1011	11
5	0101	5	A	1010	10
6	0110	6	9	1001	9
7	0111	7	8	1000	8

FIXED-LENGTH REPRESENTATIONS

Computers generally use fixed length representations for numbers. For example, in C and C^{++}, there are three types for signed integers: int (usually 32 bits), short (usually 16 bits), and char (8 bits). Recent compilers also support long long (64 bits). At times, it is necessary to coerce a signed integer from one type to another, resulting in a change in the number of bits used to represent the number. When a signed integer is coerced from a larger length to a smaller length, high order (leftmost) bits are discarded. If any of the duscarded bits are 1 then the coerced value is incorrect. Compilers will generally warn you of this possibility. When a signed integer is coerced from a smaller length to a larger length the original bits are padded on the left with copies of the sign bit of the original number. This is called sign extension.

REPRESENTATION OF UNSIGNED BINARY FRACTIONS

POSITIVE BINARY FRACTIONS

The representation of unsigned binary fractions proceeds in exactly the same way as decimal fractions.

For example,

$$0.625_{10} = 1*0.5 + 0*0.25 + 1*0.125 = 1*\ 2^{-1} + 0*\ 2^{-2} + 1*\ 2^{-3} = 0.101_2$$

Each place to the right of the decimal point represents a negative power of 2, just as for decimals they represent a negative power of 10. Likewise, if there are m bits to the right of a decimal, the precision of the number is 2^{-m} (versus 10^{-m} for decimal). Though it is possible to represent numbers greater than one by having digits to the left of the decimal place we will restrict ourselves to numbers less than one. These are commonly used by Digital Signal Processors. The largest number that can be represented by such a representation is $1–2^{-m}$, the smallest number is 2^{-m}. For a fraction with 15 bits of resolution this gives a range of approximately 0.99997 to 3.05E-5. Note that this representationis easily extended to represent all positive numbers by having the digits to the left of the decimal point represent the integer part, and the digits to the right representing the fractional part Thus, $6.625_{10} = 110.101_2$

SIGNED INTEGERS BINARY FRACTIONS

Signed binary fractions are formed much like signed integers. We will work with a single digit to the left of the decimal point, and this will represent the number –1 (= $-(2^0)$). The rest of the representation of the fraction remains unchanged. Therefore this leftmost bit represents a sign bit just as with two's complement integers. If this bit is set, the number is negative, otherwise the number is positive. The largest positive number that can be represented is still $1–2^{-m}$ but the largest negative number is –1. The resolution is still $1–2^{-m}$. There is a terminology for naming the resolution of signed fractions. If there are m bits to the right of the decimal point, the number is said to be in Q*m*format. For a 16 bit number (15 bits to the right of the decimal point) this results in Q15 notation.

DIGITAL BINARY CODES

DIGITAL COMPUTING

In 1832, Samuel F. B. Morse used the very same idea to propose that telegram *words* be coded into *binary addresses* or *binary codes* that could be transmitted over telegraph lines and decoded at the receiving end to unravel the telegram. Morse abandoned his scheme, illustrated in Figure, as too complicated and, in 1838, proposed his fabled Morse code for coding letters (instead of words) into objects (dots, dashes, spaces) capable of a threefold difference onely (sic).

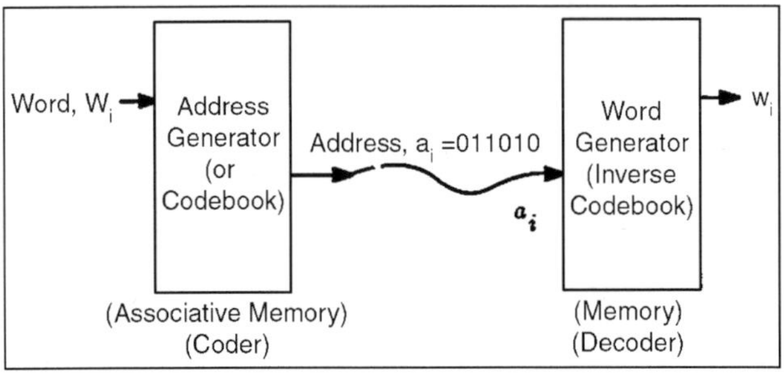

Fig. Generalized Coder-Decoder

The basic idea of Figure is used today in cryptographic systems, where the "address a_i" is an encyphered version of a messagew_i ; in vector quantizers, where the "address a_i" is the address of a close approximation to data w_i ; in coded satellite transmissions, where the "address a_i" is a data word w_i plus parity check bits for detecting and correcting errors; in digital audio systems, where the "address a_i" is a stretch of digitized and coded music; and in computer memories, where a_i is an address (a coded version of a word of memory) and w_i is a word in memory. In this chapter we study three fundamental questions in the construction of binary addresses or binary codes. First, what are plausible schemes for mapping symbols (such as words, letters, computer instructions, voltages, pressures, etc.) into binary codes? Second, what are plausible schemes for coding likely symbols with short binary words and unlikely symbols with long words in order to minimize the number of binary digits (bits) required to represent a message? Third, what are plausible schemes for "coding" binary words into longer binary words that contain "redundant bits" that may be used to detect and correct errors? These are not new questions. They have occupied the minds of many great thinkers. Sir Francis recognized that arbitrary messages had binary representations. Alan Turing, Alonzo Church, and Kurt Goedel studied binary codes for computations in their study of computable numbers and algorithms. Claude Shannon, R. C. Bose, Irving Reed, Richard Hamming, and many others have studied error control codes. Shan- non, David Huffman, and many others have studied the problem of efficiently coding information.

EXPLANATION

Did you know that everything a computer does is based on ones and zeroes? It's hard to imagine, because you hear people talking about the absolutely gargantuan (huge) numbers that computers "crunch". But all those huge numbers - they're just made up of ones and zeros. It's kind of like the computer is made up of a bunch of lightswitches, and each lightswitch controls just one lightbulb. On or Off. One or Zero. But if you took *all* of those lightbulbs together, and said "Let's make each sequence of On-and-Off represent a different number!" Well then, you could get some pretty large numbers.

Sequence

There are four different ways we could flip those switches:

- Both Off
- First Off, Second On
- First On, Second Off
- Both On

Binary Code takes each of those combinations and assigns a number to it, like this:

- Both Off = 0
- First Off, Second On = 1
- First On, Second Off = 2
- Both On = 3

Intermediate Explanation

Another way of thinking about it is this: let's give each lightbulb a point value. We'll say the first lightbulb is worth two points, and the second one is worth one point.

Now take a look at the combinations:

- Both Off = 0 + 0 = 0
- First Off, Second On = 0 + 1 = 1
- First On, Second Off = 2 + 0 = 2
- Both On = 2 + 1 = 3

If we added in another lightbulb, we would make it worth twice as many points as the 2 pointer. Then, if all the bulbs were on, the point value would be 4 + 2 + 1 = 7. And if we added in *another* bulb, we would make it worth 8 points (twice as much as four). Now if they are all turned on, that's worth 8 + 4 + 2 + 1 = 15. As you can see, it's going to take a lot of lightbulbs to make a really big number! Finally, even though we're giving point values to each of those lightbulbs, when we write them down we still only write them as ones and zeros. One means On, and Zero means Off.

So let's say we had 8 lightbulbs, and they were set up like this:

Off Off On On Off On Off Off.

The point values of those eight bulbs are:

0 + 0 + 32 + 16 + 0 + 4 + 0 + 0 (remember – we only give points if they're turned on!)

And that adds up to 52. So we would say the sequence of bulbs is worth 52. But how do we write it?

We write it like this: 00110100

So now we can say $00110100_{binary} = 52$.

8421 BCD CODE

In the 8421 Binary Coded Decimal (BCD) representation each decimal digit is converted to its 4-bit pure binary equivalent.

For example: $57_{dec} = 0101\ 0111_{bcd}$

Addition is analogous to decimal addition with normal binary addition taking place from right to left. For example,

6	0110	BCD for 6	42	0100 0010	BCD for 42
+3	0011	BCD for 3	+27	0010 0111	BCD for 27
	1001	BCD for 9		0110 1001	BCD for 69

Where the result of any addition exceeds 9(1001) then six (0110) must be added to the sum to account for the six invalid BCD codes that are available with a 4-bit number.

This is illustrated in the example below,

8	1001	BCD for 8
+7	0111	BCD for 7
	1111	exceeds 9 (1001) so
	0110	add six (0110)
	0001 0101	BCD for 15

Note that in the last example the 1 that carried forward from the first group of 4 bits has made a new 4-bit number and so represents the "1" in "15". In the examples above the BCD numbers are split at every 4-bit boundary to make reading them easier. This is not necessary when writing a BCD number down. This coding is an example of a binary coded (each decimal number maps to four bits) weighted (each bit represents a number, 1, 2, 4, etc.) code.

GRAY CODE

Gray coding is an important code and is used for its speed, it is also relatively free from errors. In pure binary coding or 8421 BCD then counting from 7 (0111) to 8 (1000) requires 4 bits to be changed simultaneously. If this does not happen then various numbers could be momentarily generated during the transition so creating spurious numbers which could be read. Gray coding avoids this since only one bit changes between subsequent numbers. To construct the code there are two simple rules. First start with all 0s and then proceed by changing the least significant bit (lsb) which will bring about a new state.

The first 16 Gray coded numbers are indicated below:

Decimal	Gray Code
0	0000
1	0001
2	0011
3	0010
4	0110
5	0111
6	0101
7	100
8	1100
9	1101
10	1111
11	1110
12	1010
13	1011
14	1001
15	1000

To convert a Gray-coded number to binary then follow this method:

- The binary number and the Gray-coded number will have the same number of bits.
- The binary MSB (left-hand bit) and Gray code MSB will always be the same.
- To get the binary next-to-MSB (*i.e.* next digit to the right) add the binary MSB and the gray code next-to-MSB. Re cord the sum, ignoring any carry.
- Continue in this manner right through to the end.

Gray coding is a non-BCD, non-weighted reflected binary code.

4221 BCD CODE

The 4221 BCD code is another binary coded decimal code where each bit is weighted by 4, 2, 2 and 1 respectively. Unlike BCD coding there are no invalid representations. The decimal numbers 0 to 9 have the following 4221 equivalents, the 1's complement of a 4221 representation is important in decimal arithmetic.

Decimal	4221	1's complement
0	0000	1111
1	0001	1110
2	0010	1101
3	0011	1100
4	1000	0111
5	0111	1000
6	1100	0011
7	1101	0010
8	1110	0001
9	1111	0000

In forming the code remember the following rules:

- Below decimal 5 use the right-most bit representing 2 first.
- Above decimal 5 use the left-most bit representing 2 first.
- Decimal 5 = 2+2+1 and not 4+1.

DECIMAL TO BINARY

Converting from decimal to binary notation is slightly more difficult conceptually, but can easily be done once you know how through the use of algorithms. Begin by thinking of a few examples. We can easily see that the number 3= 2+1. and that this is equivalent to $(1*2^1)+(1*2^0)$.

This translates into putting a "1" in the 2^1 column and a "1" in the 2^0 column, to get "11". Almost as intuitive is the number 5: it is obviously 4+1, which is the same as saying [(2*2) +1], or 2^2+1. This can also be written as $[(1*2^2)+(1*2^0)]$. Looking at this in columns,

2^2	2^2	2^0
1	0	1

or 101.

What we're doing here is finding the largest power of two within the number ($2^2=4$ is the largest power of 2 in 5), subtracting that from the number (5–4=1), and finding the largest power of 2 in the remainder ($2^0=1$ is the largest power of 2 in 1). Then we just put this into columns. This process continues until we have a remainder of 0. Let's take a look at how it works. We know that:

- $2^0 = 1$
- $2^1 = 2$
- $2^2 = 4$
- $2^3 = 8$
- $2^4 = 16$
- $2^5 = 32$
- $2^6 = 64$
- $2^7 = 128$

and so on. To convert the decimal number 75 to binary, we would find the largest power of 2 less than 75, which is 64. Thus, we would put a 1 in the 2^6 column, and subtract 64 from 75, giving us 11. The largest power of 2 in 11 is 8, or 2^3. Put 1 in the 2^3 column, and 0 in 2^4 and 2^5. Subtract 8 from 11 to get 3. Put 1 in the 2^1 column, 0 in 2^2, and subtract 2 from 3. We're left with 1, which goes in 2^0, and we subtract one to get zero. Thus, our number is 1001011.

Making this algorithm a bit more formal gives us:

- Let D=number we wish to convert from decimal to binary
- Repeat until D = 0

  - Find the largest power of two in D. Let this equal P.
  - Put a 1 in binary column P.
  - Subtract P from D.
- Put zeros in all columns which don't have ones.

This algorithm is a bit awkward. Particularly step 3, "filling in the zeros." Therefore, we should rewrite it such that we ascertain the value of each column individually, putting in 0's and 1's as we go:

- Let D= the number we wish to convert from decimal to binary
- Find P, such that 2^P is the largest power of two smaller than D.
- Repeat until P<0
  - If 2^P<=D then
    a. put 1 into column P
    b. subtract 2^P from D
- Else
  a. put 0 into column P
- End if
- Subtract 1 from P

Now that we have an algorithm, we can use it to convert numbers from decimal to binary relatively painlessly. Let's try the number D=55.

- Our first step is to find P. We know that 2^4=16, 2^5=32, and 2^6=64. Therefore, P=5.
- $2^5 \leqslant$=55, so we put a 1 in the 2^5 column: 1———.
- Subtracting 55-32 leaves us with 23. Subtracting 1 from P gives us 4.
- Following step 3 again, $2^4 \leqslant$=23, so we put a 1 in the 2^4 column: 11——.
- Next, subtract 16 from 23, to get 7. Subtract 1 from P gives us 3.
- 2^3>7, so we put a 0 in the 2^3 column: 110—-
- Next, subtract 1 from P, which gives us 2.
- $2^2 \leqslant$=7, so we put a 1 in the 2^2 column: 1101—
- Subtract 4 from 7 to get 3. Subtract 1 from P to get 1.
- $2^1 \leqslant$=3, so we put a 1 in the 2^1 column: 11011-
- Subtract 2 from 3 to get 1. Subtract 1 from P to get 0.
- $2^0 \leqslant$=1, so we put a 1 in the 2^0 column: 110111
- Subtract 1 from 1 to get 0. Subtract 1 from P to get -1.
- P is now less than zero, so we stop.

Another algorithm for converting decimal to binary

However, this is not the only approach possible. We can start at the right, rather than the left.

All binary numbers are in the form

$$a[n]*2^n + a[n-1]*2^{(n-1)}+...+a[1]*2^1 + a[0]*2^0$$

where each a[i] is either a 1 or a 0 (the only possible digits for the binary system). The only way a number can be odd is if it has a 1 in the 2^0 column, because all powers of two greater than 0 are even numbers (2, 4, 8, 16...). This gives us the rightmost digit as a starting point. Now we need to do the remaining digits. One idea is to "shift" them. It is also easy to see that multiplying and dividing by 2 shifts everything by one column: two in binary is 10, or $(1*2^1)$. Dividing $(1*2^1)$ by 2 gives us $(1*2^0)$, or just a 1 in binary. Similarly, multiplying by 2 shifts in the other direction: $(1*2^1)*2=(1*2^2)$ or 10 in binary. Therefore

$$\{a[n]*2^n + a[n-1]*2^{(n-1)} +... + a[1]*2^1 + a[0]*2^0\}/2$$

is equal to,

$$a[n]*2^{(n-1)} + a[n-1]*2^{(n-2)} +... + a[1]2^0$$

Let's look at how this can help us convert from decimal to binary. Take the number 163. We know that since it is odd, there must be a 1 in the 2^0 column (a[0]=1). We also know that it equals 162+1. If we put the 1 in the 2^0 column, we have 162 left, and have to decide how to translate the remaining digits. Two's column: Dividing 162 by 2 gives 81. The number 81 in binary would also have a 1 in the 2^0 column. Since we divided the number by two, we "took out" one power of two. Similarly, the statement $a[n-1]*2^{(n-1)} + a[n-2]*2^{(n-2)} +... + a[1]*2^0$ has a power of two removed. Our "new" 2^0 column now contains a1. We learned earlier that there is a 1 in the 2^0 column if the number is odd. Since 81 is odd, a[1]=1. Practically, we can simply keep a "running total", which now stands at 11 (a[1]=1 and a[0]=1). Also note that a1 is essentially "remultiplied" by two just by putting it in front of a[0], so it is automatically fit into the correct column.

Four's column: Now we can subtract 1 from 81 to see what remainder we still must place (80). Dividing 80 by 2 gives 40. Therefore, there must be a 0 in the 4's column, (because what we are actually placing is a 2^0 column, and the number is not odd). *Eight's column*: We can divide by two again to get 20. This is even, so we put a 0 in the 8's column. Our running total now stands at a[3]=0, a[2]=0, a[1]=1, and a[0]=1.

We can continue in this manner until there is no remainder to place.

Let's formalize this algorithm:

- Let D= the number we wish to convert from decimal to binary.
- Repeat until D=0:
  - If D is odd, put "1" in the leftmost open column, and subtract 1 from D.
  - If D is even, put "0" in the leftmost open column.
  - Divide D by 2.

  End Repeat

For the number 163, this works as follows:

- Let D=163

- D is odd, put a 1 in the 2^0 column.
  Subtract 1 from D to get 162.
- Divide D=162 by 2.
  Temporary Result: 01 New D=81
  D does not equal 0, so we repeat step 2.
- D is odd, put a 1 in the 2^1 column.
  Subtract 1 from D to get 80.
- Divide D=80 by 2.
  Temporary Result: 11 New D=40
  D does not equal 0, so we repeat step 2.
- D is even, put a 0 in the 2^2 column.
- Divide D by 2.
  Temporary Result: 011 New D=20
- D is even, put a 0 in the 2^3 column.
- Divide D by 2.
  Temporary Result: 0011 New D=10
- D is even, put a 0 in the 2^4 column.
- Divide D by 2.
  Temporary Result: 00011 New D=5
- D is odd, put a 1 in the 2^5 column.
  Subtract 1 from D to get 4.
- Divide D by 2.
  Temporary Result: 100011 New D=2
- D is even, put a 0 in the 2^6 column.
- Divide D by 2.
  Temporary Result: 0100011 New D=1
- D is odd, put a 1 in the 27 column.
  Subtract 1 from D to get D=0.
- Divide D by 2.
  Temporary Result: 10100011 New D=0

D=0, so we are done, and the decimal number 163 is equivalent to the binary number 10100011. Since we already knew how to convert from binary to decimal, we can easily verify our result. 10100011 = $(1*2^0) + (1*2^1)+(1*2^5)+(1*2^7)=1+2+32+128 = 163$.

INFORMATION OF HAMMING CODES

Several Teletext packets contain information protected by hamming. This is a method for encoding data such that errors in reception can be detected, and if the error is sufficiently small, corrected. Teletext uses two hamming codes. The simpler and more robust version encodes 4 bits of data in one 8-bit byte. This code is used extensively to protect the fields that have meaning to the Teletext system itself. The more efficient code encodes 18 bits of data in three 8-bit bytes. It is used for to protect some of the data fields inside Teletext packets. Both codes are designed such that any one-bit error can be corrected, and any 2-bit error can be detected.

8/4 HAMMING

The 8/4 code is quite simple; if the input nibble is the 4-bit value:

```
b3, b2, b1, b0
```

with b3 being the most significant bit, then the output hammed byte is the 8-bit value:

```
b3, b3^b2^b1, b2, !b2^b1^b0, b1, !b3^b1^b0,b0, !b3^b2^b0
```

where ^ represents bitwise exclusive-or and ! is bitwise not.

This code has the property that every value is four bits different from all other such values. A one-bit error is therefore unambiguously correctable, being only one bit away from a valid code. A two-bit error is detectable but not correctable, being equidistant between two valid codes.

Here is the table of all 16 encoded nibbles:

```
Data nibble     Hammed byte
0 = 0 0 0 0     15 = 0 0 0 1 0 1 0 1
1 = 0 0 0 1     02 = 0 0 0 0 0 0 1 0
2 = 0 0 1 0     49 = 0 1 0 0 1 0 0 1
3 = 0 0 1 1     5E = 0 1 0 1 1 1 1 0
4 = 0 1 0 0     64 = 0 1 1 0 0 1 0 0
5 = 0 1 0 1     73 = 0 1 1 1 0 0 1 1
6 = 0 1 1 0     38 = 0 0 1 1 1 0 0 0
7 = 0 1 1 1     2F = 0 0 1 0 1 1 1 1
8 = 1 0 0 0     D0 = 1 1 0 1 0 0 0 0
9 = 1 0 0 1     C7 = 1 1 0 0 0 1 1 1
A = 1 0 1 0     8C = 1 0 0 0 1 1 0 0
B = 1 0 1 1     9B = 1 0 0 1 1 0 1 1
C = 1 1 0 0     A1 = 1 0 1 0 0 0 0 1
D = 1 1 0 1     B6 = 1 0 1 1 0 1 1 0
E = 1 1 1 0     FD = 1 1 1 1 1 1 0 1
F = 1 1 1 1     EA = 1 1 1 0 1 0 1 0
      | |       | |  |  | |  | |  | |
  b3 b2 b1 b0        b3 |b2 |b1 |b0 |
                       |  |    |  |
                     321 !210 !310 !320
```

Decoding a hammed byte back in to a 4-bit nibble can be done using the table below, or by a bit-twiddling algorithm.

The algorithmic approach shows what is going on more clearly. Assuming the hammed byte is,

```
h7, h6, h5, h4, h3, h2, h1, h0
```

with h7 being the most significant bit, we compute

```
p  = h7 ^ h6 ^ h5 ^ h4 ^ h3 ^ h2 ^ h1 ^ h0
c0 = h7 ^ h5 ^ h1 ^ h0
c1 = h7 ^ h3 ^ h2 ^ h1
c2 = h5 ^ h4 ^ h3 ^ h1
```

If the parity, p, is correct (equal to 1) then either 0 or 2 errors occurred. If all the check bits, c0, c1, c2 are correct (equal to 1) then the byte was received intact, (no errors) otherwise it was damaged beyond repair (two errors). *If p is 0, then there was a single bit error which can be recovered*:

c_0	c_1	c_2	meaning
1	1	1	error in bit h6
1	1	0	error in bit h4
1	0	1	error in bit h2
0	1	1	error in bit h0
0	0	1	error in bit h7
0	1	0	error in bit h5
1	0	0	error in bit h3
0	0	0	error in bit h1

The erroneous bit should be flipped. Note that there is actually no need to fix errors in bits h6, h4, h2 and h0 since they are not used in the decoded byte.

After flipping bits if necessary, the decoded byte is then:

```
h7, h5, h3, h1
```

24/18 HAMMING

The more efficient 24/18 code is based on the same principle of interleaved check bits and an overall parity bit as the simpler 8/4 code.

Assuming the input bits are:

```
b17, b16, b15, b14, b13, b12, b11, b10, b9, b8,
b7, b6, b5, b4, b3, b2, b1, b0
```

with b17 being the most significant bit, the six hamming check bits are:

```
c0 = ! b17 ^ b15 ^ b13 ^ b11 ^ b10 ^ b8 ^ b6
^ b4 ^ b3 ^ b1 ^ b0
c1 = ! b17 ^ b16 ^ b13 ^ b12 ^ b10 ^ b9 ^ b6
^ b5 ^ b3 ^ b2 ^ b0
c2 = ! b17 ^ b16 ^ b15 ^ b14 ^ b10 ^ b9 ^ b8
^ b7 ^ b3 ^ b2 ^ b1
c3 = ! b10 ^ b9 ^ b8 ^ b7 ^ b6 ^ b5 ^ b4
c4 = ! b17 ^ b16 ^ b15 ^ b14 ^ b13 ^ b12 ^ b11
c5 = b17 ^ b14 ^ b12 ^ b11 ^ b10 ^ b7 ^ b5 ^
b4 ^ b2 ^ b1 ^ b0
```

where ^ represents bitwise exclusive-or and ! is bitwise not.C5 can alternatively and equivalently be computed as the odd parity of all the other data and check bits.

The output bytes are then:

```
c3, b3, b2, b1, c2, b0, c1, c0
c4, b10, b9, b8, b7, b6, b5, b4
c5, b17, b16, b15, b14, b13, b12, b11
```

in byte transmission order, with the most significant bit of each byte on the left.

To decode a hammed byte triplet:

```
h7, h6, h5, h4, h3, h2, h1, h0
h15, h14, h13, h12, h11, h10, h9, h8
h23, h22, h21, h20, h19, h18, h17, h16
```

with h0 being the least significant bit of the first byte and h23 being the most significant bit of the third byte, we compute,

```
p = h23 ^ h22 ^ h21 ^ h20 ^... ^ h1 ^ h0
c0 = h0 ^ h2 ^ h4 ^ h6 ^ h8 ^ h10 ^ h12 ^ h14
^ h16 ^ h18 ^ h20 ^ h22
c1 = h1 ^ h2 ^ h5 ^ h6 ^ h9 ^ h10 ^ h13 ^ h14
^ h17 ^ h18 ^ h21 ^ h22
c2 = h3 ^ h4 ^ h5 ^ h6 ^ h11 ^ h12 ^ h13 ^ h14
^ h19 ^ h20 ^ h21 ^ h22
c3 = h7 ^ h8 ^ h9 ^ h10 ^ h11 ^ h12 ^ h13 ^ h14
c4 = h15 ^ h16 ^ h17 ^ h18 ^ h19 ^ h20 ^ h21 ^
h22
```

If the parity, p, is correct (equal to 1) then either 0 or 2 errors occurred. If all the check bits, c0, c1, c2, c3, c4, c5 are correct (equal to 1), then the byte was received intact, (no errors) otherwise it was damaged beyond repair (two errors).

If p is 0, then there was a single bit error which can be recovered. For the check bits which are incorrect (equal to 0), add the following powers of two together:

```
if c0 = 0 add 1
if c1 = 0 add 2
if c2 = 0 add 4
if c3 = 0 add 8
if c4 = 0 add 16
```

The sum gives the bit position 1--24 corresponding to h0--h23 which is in error. The erroneous bit should be flipped. Note that there is actually no need to fix errors in bits h23, h15, h7, h3, h1 and h0 since they are not used in the decoded byte.

The output data bits, d17--d0 are:

```
h22, h21, h20, h19, h18, h17, h16, h14, h13, h12, h11,
h10, h9, h8, h6, h5, h4, h2
```

ERROR DETECTING

R. W. Hamming wrote the paper that both opened and closed this field in 1950. His interest was in providing a means of self-checking in computers, which were just being developed at the time he wrote this. the paper appeared in the Bell System Technical Journal, April, 1950. Definitely worth tracking down in the library and reading.

Bit Strings

The best starting point for understanding ECC codes is to consider bit strings as addresses in a binary hypercube. A hypercube is a generalization of a cube to various dimensions; we're probably most familiar with the notion of a four-dimensional hypercube.

Here's a picture of binary hypercubes for several different dimensionalities:

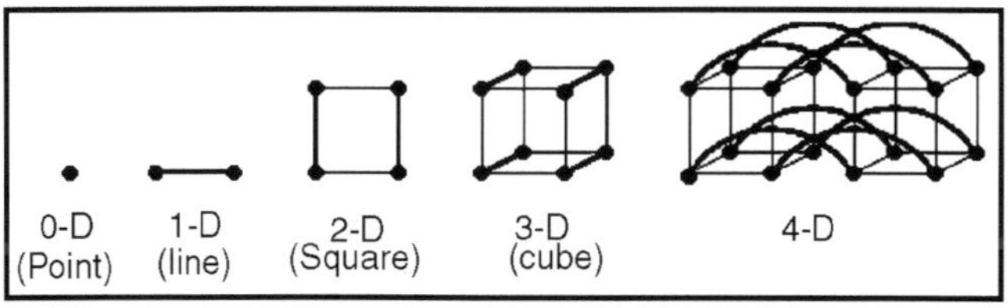

Each of them was created by copying the one to the left twice, and connecting corresponding vertices.

We can assign each vertex in a hypercube a location in a coordinate space determined by the dimensionality of the hypercube.

- A zero-dimensional hypercube requires no coordinates to know where you are
- A one-dimensional hypercube can use one bit to tell whether you're at the bottom or the top of the line segment.
- A two-dimensional hypercube can use two bits: first bit is left vs. right, second is inherited from the line.
- A three-dimensional hypercube can use a bit to tell front square from back, and inherit two bits from the square.
- A four-dimensional hypercube can use a bit to tell left cube from right, and inherits three bits from cube.

The Hamming distance between two bit strings is the number of bits you have to change to convert one to the other: this is the same as the number of edges you have to traverse in a binary hypercube to get from one of the vertices to the other. The basic idea of an error correcting code is to use extra bits to increase the dimensionality of the hypercube, and make sure the Hamming distance between any two valid points is greater than one.

- If the Hamming distance between valid strings is only one, a single-bit error results in another valid string. This means we can't detect an error.

- If it's two, then changing one bit results in an invalid string, and can be detected as an error. Unfortunately, changing just one more bit can result in another valid string, which means we can't know which bit was wrong: so we can detect an error but not correct it.
- If the Hamming distance between valid strings is three, then changing one bit leaves us only one bit away from the original error, but two bits away from any other valid string. This means if we have a one-bit error, we can figure out which bit is the error; but if we have a two-bit error, it looks like one bit from the other direction. So we can have single bit correction, but that's all.
- Finally, if the Hamming distance is four, then we can correct a single-bit error and detect a double-bit error. This is frequently referred to as a SECDED.

Parity

The simplest case is by adding a parity bit. Suppose we have a three-bit word (so the bit strings define points in a cube). If we add a fourth bit, we can decree that any time we want to switch a bit in the original three-bit string, we also have to switch the parity bit.

If we start with 000 in the left cube, so the full string is 0000, changing any one of the original three bits requires us to change to the other cube: 1001, 1010, and 1100. Now if we change a second bit, we have to move back to the left cube: 0011, 0101, 0110. And if we change the third bit, we move back to the right cube: 0111.

So, there is a Hamming distance of two between any two valid strings. If we get a one-bit error, we know it is an error because it's on one of the invalid vertices. This can be computed by counting the number of 1's, and making sure it's always even (so this is called even parity). We could have selected exactly the opposite set of vertices as the valid ones, which would have given us odd parity.

THEORY OF ERROR-CORRECTING CODES

The theory of error detecting and correcting codes is that branch of engineering and mathematics which deals with the reliable transmission and storage of data. Information media are not 100 per cent reliable in practice, in the sense that noise (any form of interference) frequently causes data to be distorted.

To deal with this undesirable but inevitable situation, some form of redundancy is incorporated in the original data. With this redundancy, even if errors are introduced (up to some tolerance level), the original information can be recovered, or at least the presence of errors can be detected. We saw in class how adding to the original message the parity bit or the arithmetic sum allows the detection of a (certain type of) error. However, that kind of redundancy doesn't allow for the correction of the error. Error-correcting codes do exactly this: they add redundancy to the original message in such a way that it is possible for the receiver to detect the error and correct it, recovering the original message. This is crucial for certain applications where the re-sending of the message is not possible (for example, for interplanetary communications and storage of data). The crucial problem to be resolved then is how to add this redundancy in order to detect and correct as many errors as possible in the most efficient way.

This document starts with an overview of the applications of the error-correcting codes, followed by a session describing the fundamental concepts. It then addresses some of the issues involved in the design of the codes. The last session is a brief introduction of the very last discovery in the theory of error-correcting codes: the turbo codes.

APPLICATIONS OF ERROR CORRECTING CODES

The increasing reliance on digital communication and the emergence of the digital computer as an essential tool in a technological society have placed error-correcting codes in a most prominent position. We cite here a few specific applications, in an attempt to indicate their practicality and importance. Many computers now have error-correcting capabilities built into their random access memories; it is less expensive to compensate for errors through the use of error-correcting codes than to build integrated circuits that are 100 per cent reliable. The single error-correcting Hamming codes, and linear codes in general, are of use here.

Disk storage is another area of computing where error-coding is employed. Storage capacity has been greatly increased through the use of disks of higher and higher density. With this increase in density, error probability also increases, and therefore information is now stored on many disks using error-correcting codes.

In 1972, the *Mariner* space probe flew past Mars and transmitted pictures back to earth. The channel for such transmissions is space and the earth's atmosphere. Solar activity and atmospheric conditions can introduce errors into weak signals coming from the spacecraft. In order that most of the pictures sent could be correctly recovered here on earth, the following coding scheme was used. The source alphabet consisted of 64 shades of gray. The source encoder encoded each of these into binary 6-tuples and the channel encoder produced binary 32-tuples. The source decoder could correct up to 7 errors in any 32-tuple. This was done with the Reed-Muller codes.

In 1979, the *Voyager* probes began transmitting color pictures of Jupiter. For color pictures the source alphabet needed to be much larger and was chosen to have 4096 color shades. The source encoder produced binary 12-tuples for each color shade and the channel encoder produced 24-tuples (*i.e.*

24 dimensional vectors). This code would correct up to 3 errors in any 24-tuple, and is the Golay code. The increasing popularity of digital audio is due in part to the powerful error-correcting codes that the digitization process facilitates. Information is typically stored on a small aluminized disk as a series of microscopic pits and smooth areas, the pattern representing a sequence of 0's and 1's.

A laser beam is used as the playback mechanism to retrieve stored data. Because the data is digital, error correction schemes can be easily incorporated into such a system. Given an error-coded digital recording, a digital audio system can on playback, correct errors introduced by fingerprints, scratches, or even imperfections originally present in the storage medium. The compact disc system pioneered by Philips Corporation of the Netherlands in cooperation with Sony Corporation of Japan, allowing playback of pre-recorded digital audio disks, is an excellent example of the application of error-correcting codes to digital communication; *cross interleaved Reed-Solomon* codes are used for error correction in this system. Digital audio tape (DAT) systems have also been developed, allowing digital recording as well as playback. Error-correcting codes are particularly suited when the transmission channel is noisy. This is the case of wireless communication. Nowadays, all digital wireless communi-cations use error-correcting codes.

Fundamental Concepts

We begin with a few definitions, in order to develop a working vocabulary. Let A be an alphabet of q symbols. For example, A = {a,b,c...,z) is the standard lower case alphabet for the English language, and A = (0,1) is the binary alphabet.

Definition: A block code of length n containing M codewords over the alphabet A is a set of M n-tuples where each n-tuple takes its components from A. We refer to such a block code as an [n,M]-code over A.

In practice, we most frequently take A to be the binary alphabet. Given a code C of block length n over an alphabet A, those specific n-tuples over A which are in C are referred to as codeword's. Note that while the channel encoder transmits codeword's, the n-tuples received by the channel decoder may or may not be codeword's, due to the possible occurrence of errors during transmission.

Example: Suppose the information we are to transmit comes from the set of symbols {A, B, C, D}. For practical considerations we associate sequences of 0's and l's with each of these symbols.

$A \rightarrow 00$

$B \rightarrow 01$

$C \rightarrow 10$

$D \rightarrow 11$

This is the source encoding. Now we want to add some redundancy (channel encoding).

A → 00 → 00000
B → 01 → 10110
C → 10 → 01011
D → 11 → 11101

We have just constructed a [5,4]-code over a binary alphabet. That is, we constructed a code with 4 codeword's, each being a 5-tuple (block length 5), with each component of the 5-tuple being O or 1. The code is the set of n-tuples produced by the channel encoder (as opposed to the source encoder). The source encoder transforms messages into k-tuples (k=2 in the example above) over the code alphabet A, and the channel encoder assigns to each of these information k-tuples a codeword of length n (n=5 in the example).

Since the channel encoder is adding redundancy, we have n > k and hence we have message expansion. While the added redundancy is desirable from the point of view of error control, it decreases the efficiency of the communication channel by reducing its effective capacity. The ratio k to n is a measure of the fraction of information in the channel which is non-redundant.

Definition: The rate of an [n,M]-code which encodes information k-tuples is, R = K/n The rate of the simple code given in example 1 is 2/5. The quantity r = n-k is sometimes called the redundancy of the code.

A fundamental parametre associated with an [n,M]-code C is the Hamming distance for C. Before we can define the Hamming distance for a code, we must define the Hamming distance between two codeword's.

Definition: The Hamming distance d(x,y) between two codewords x and y is the number of coordinate positions in which they differ.

Example: Over the alphabet A = (0,1}, the codewords x and y x=(10110) y=(11O11) have Hamming distance d(x,y) =3.

Example. The codeword's u and v over the alphabet A = (0,1,2), given by u = (21002) v=(12001) have Hamming distance d(u,v) =3.

Definition: Let C be an [n,M]-code.

The Hamming distance d of the code C is d= min {d(x,y): x,y belong to C, x != y}.

In other words, the Hamming distance of a code is the minimum distance between two distinct codeword's, over all pairs of codeword's.

Example: Consider C = (c_0,c_1,c_2,c_3} where c_0=(00000) c_1 =(10110) c_2= (01011) c_3= (11101) This code has distance d = 3. It is the [5,4] code constructed earlier.

Suppose we have an [n,M]-code C with distance d. We need to adopt a strategy for the channel decoder (or just decoder). When the decoder receives an n-tuple r it must make some decision.

This decision may be one of:

- No errors have occurred; accept r as a codeword.
- Errors have occurred; correct r to a codeword c.
- Errors have occurred; no correction is possible.

In general, the decoder will not always make the correct decision; for example, consider the possibility of an error pattern occurring which changes a transmitted codeword into another codeword.

The goal is that the decoder takes the course of action which has the greatest probability of being correct. One usually makes the assumption that errors are introduced by the channel at random, and that the probability of an error in one coordinate is independent of errors in adjacent coordinates. The decoding strategy we shall adopt, called nearest neighbour decoding, can then be specified as follows.

Nearest Neighbour Decoding If an n-tuple r is received, and there is a unique codeword c that belongs to C such that d(r,c) is a minimun, then correct r to the c. If no such c exists, report that errors have been detected, but no correction is possible. By nearest neighbour decoding, a received vector is decoded to the codewords"closest" to it, with respect to Hamming distance. The figure below illustrates the concept. The red dots are the codeword's, the green ones are the received words that can be corrected to the closest codeword's and the blue dot is a received word that is equidistant from 2 codeword's and therefore cannot be corrected.

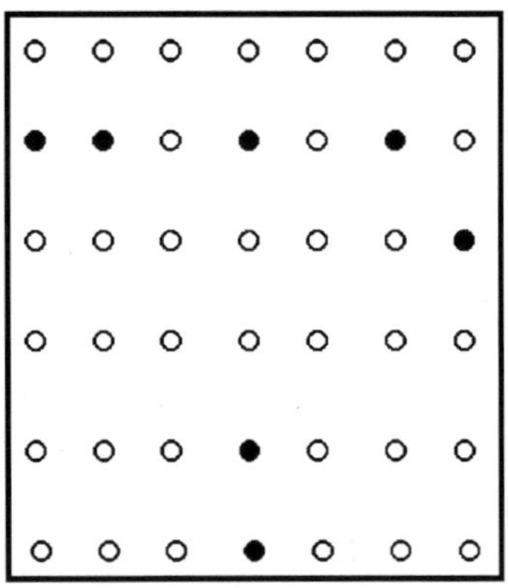

A code is said to correct e errors if a decoder using the above scheme is capable of correcting any pattern of e or fewer errors introduced by the channel. In this case, the decoder can correct any transmitted codeword which has been altered in e or fewer coordinate positions.

Theorem: Let C be an [n,M]-code having distance d = 2e+1. Then C can correct e errors. If used for error detection only, C can detect 2e errors.

Let c be one codeword of C and S be the set of all n-tuples over the alphabet of C and define:

S(c) = {x belongs to S: d(x,c) $\Leftarrow$ e).

S(c) is called the sphere of radius e about the codeword c. It consists of all n-tuples within distance e of the codeword c, which we think of as being at the centre of the sphere. In the figure below, the"spheres" arount the codewords of the previous figure.

The radius is in this case is 1:

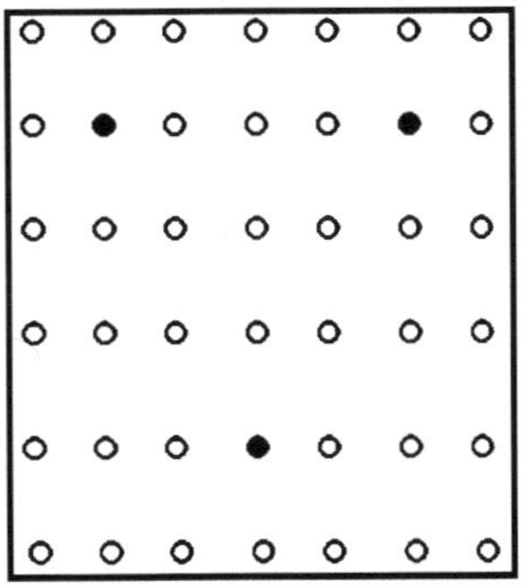

Given 2 codewords, their spheres don't intersect, hence if codeword c is transmitted and t⇐ e errors are introduced, the received word r is an n-tuple in the sphere S(c) and thus c is the unique codeword closest to r. The decoder can always correct any error pattern of this type.

If we use the code only for error detection, then at least 2e+1 errors must occur in a codeword to carry it into another codeword. If at least 1 and at most 2e errors are introduced, the received word will never be a codeword and error detection is always possible. The spheres have to be disjoint in order to be able to correct errors. But if a received word happens to be in the space between the spheres, correction is not possible: that space doesn't belong to any sphere, *i.e.* to any codeword: the error is detected but not corrected. Therefore, we want to find codes such that the the spheres around the codewords are disjoint (to correctly correct the errors) but as close as possible to each other, to correct ALL the errors. If all the space is taken by the sphere, all the words received will fall into the sphere of a codeword and therefore can be corrected to that codeword. These are the perfect codes. Lets give the formal definition of perfect codes.

Definition: A perfect code is an e-error-correcting [n, M]-code over an alphabet A such that every n-tuple over A is in the sphere of radius e about some codework. In a perfect code of block length n, the sphere of radius e about code works are not only disjoint (since the code is e-error-correcting) but exhaust the entire space of n-tuples.

Issues

Designing a good code is a very hard problem. Also, lots of factors need to be taken in account. For instance, in practice the code should be designed appropriately depending on the expected rate of errors for the particular channel being employed. If it is known that the probability that the channel will introduce 2 errors into any transmitted codeword is extremely small, then it is likely not necessary to construct a code that will correct all 2-bit error patterns. A single error correcting code will likely suffice. Conversely, if double errors are frequent and a single error correcting code is being used, then decoding errors will be frequent. From this brief introduction, a number of questions arise.

- Given n, M and d, can we determine if an [n Al] code with distance d exists?
- Assuming such a code does exist, how would one be constructed in practice?
- How should information k-tuples be associated with codeword n-tuples to facilitate efficient channel encoding?
- How should channel decoding be performed?

Lets examine the issue of channel decoding in greater detail. When a word is received and it's not a codeword, finding the closest codeword involves computing the distance from the received word to each codeword, requiring M comparisons. While this might be acceptable for small M, in practice we usually find M quite large. Suppose a code C is used with M = 2^50 codewords, which is not unrealistic. If we could carry out 1 million distance computations per second, it would take around 20 years to make a single correction. Clearly, this is not tolerable and more efficient techniques are required. Wishing to retain the nearest neighbour decoding strategy, we seek more efficient techniques for its implementation. The theory of error-correcting code is concerned with constructing codes for various values of n, M and d, and the consideration of appropriate encoding and decoding techniques. Most of the best known codes are algebraic in nature like the linear codes. Linear codes are an important and general class of error-correcting codes. For example, theBCH codes used for CDs are linear codes. They are heavily mathematical and an appropriate description here is not possible. The next session describes instead the last"discovery" in the theory of error correcting codes, the Turbo codes.

Turbo Codes

In session 3, when we introduced the Nearest Neighbour Decoding, we didn't mention the fact that what the decoding actually does is maximizing the probability P(r | c) that r is received, given that c is sent. *i.e.* choosing the nearest codeword is equivalent to choosing the most likely input message c given the received tuple r. This decoding strategy is known as maximum likelihood decoding. We can then state the decoding problem in the following manner. Let U be the original message, X the encoded message and Y the message received after the noisy channel. This is schematized in the following figure.

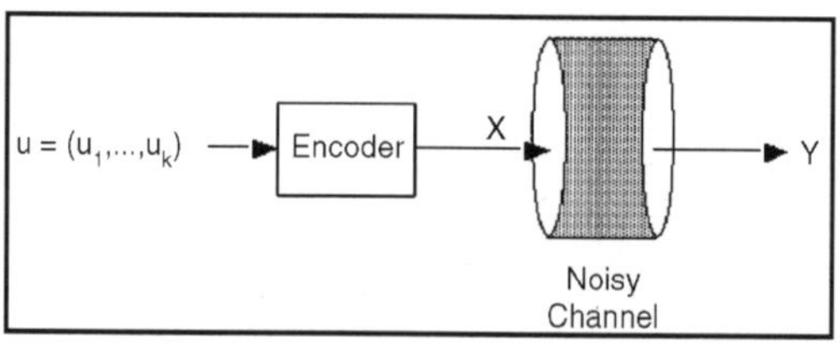

The receiver knows Y and the model of the encoder, *i.e.* is has a knowledge of how the original message was originally encoded. The problem now is finding the U that maximizes the probability that U was sent given that Y was received, *i.e.* the probability P(U | Y). Having stated the decoding problem in probabilistic terms, we can take advantage of various methods that deal with probability estimations. A class of such methods is the class of graphical models.

The simplest graphical model:

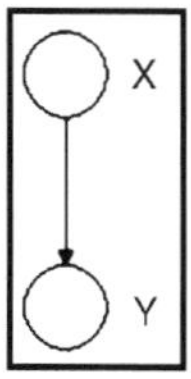

A classical problem of probability estimation is finding the probability distribution P(X | Y) where X and Y are 2 random variables. The graphical model framework allows for such probability estimations to be calculated in an efficient way.

Note that the calculation of P(X | Y) from P(Y | X) and P(X) is just Bayes rule – P(X | Y) = P(Y | X)P(X)/P(Y) – and that graphical model inference algorithms can be viewed as generalizations of Bayes rule to arbitrary graphs. Lets now see how we can view error correcting codes as graphical models. In the figure below, a convolution code as a graphical model.Let U be the original message, X the encoded message and Y the message received after the noisy channel.

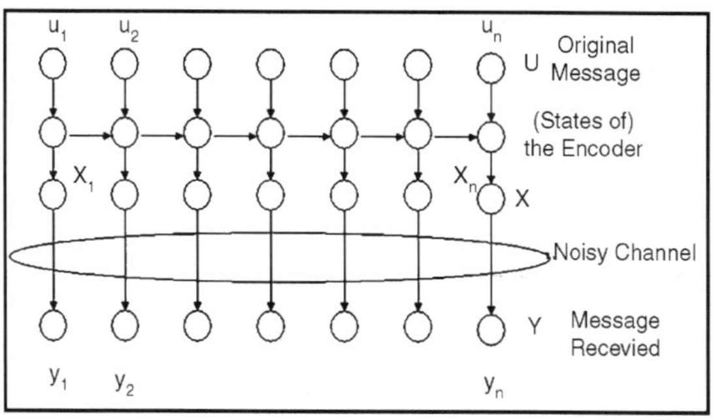

Now, the decoding problem of finding U that maximizes p(U | Y) can be tackled within the framework of graphical models. We have introduced the convolutional codes mainly because the Turbo codes are two convolutional codes put together. The following figure illustrate the graphical representation of a turbo code. It should be mentioned that general inference in graphical models is NP-hard, and, in particular, exact inference, calculating P(U | Y), for turbo codes is infeasible and therefore an approximate inference algorithm is used.

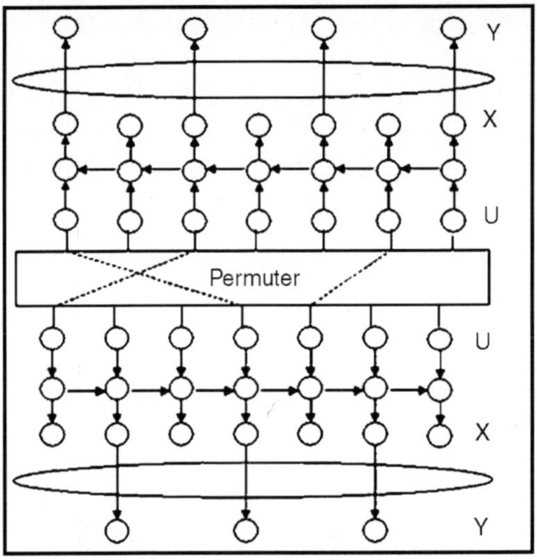

Turbo codes were discovered very recently. There is much excitement about them. They outperform all other kinds of error-correcting codes in the case of long block lengths, although the reason why they do so is not yet clear.

4

Digital Electronic Circuits

INTRODUCTION

Digital circuits are circuits dealing with signals restricted to the extreme limits of zero and some full amount. This stands in contrast to *analog* circuits, in which signals are free to vary continuously between the limits imposed by power supply voltage and circuit resistances. These circuits find use in "true/false" logical operations and digital computation. The circuits in this chapter make use of *IC*, or *integrated circuit*, components. Such components are actually networks of interconnected components manufactured on a single wafer of semiconducting material.

Integrated circuits providing a multitude of pre-engineered functions are available at very low cost, benefitting students, hobbyists and professional circuit designers alike. Most integrated circuits provide the same functionality as "discrete" semiconductor circuits at higher levels of reliability and at a fraction of the cost. Circuits in this chapter will primarily use *CMOS* technology, as this form of IC design allows for a broad range of power supply voltage while maintaining generally low power consumption levels. Though CMOS circuitry is susceptible to damage from static electricity (high voltages will puncture the insulating barriers in the MOSFET transistors), modern CMOS ICs are far more tolerant of electrostatic discharge than the CMOS ICs of the past, reducing the risk of chip failure by mishandling.

Proper handling of CMOS involves the use of anti-static foam for storage and transport of IC's, and measures to prevent static charge from building up on your body (use of a grounding wrist strap, or frequently touching a grounded object). Circuits using *TTL* technology require a regulated power supply voltage of 5 volts, and will not tolerate any substantial deviation from this voltage level. Any TTL circuits in this chapter will be adequately labeled as such, and it will be expected that you realise its unique power supply requirements.

When building digital circuits using integrated circuit "chips," it is highly recommended that you use a breadboard with power supply "rail" connections along the length. These are sets of holes in the breadboard that are electrically common along the entire length of the board. Connect one to the positive terminal of a battery, and the other to the negative terminal, and DC power will be available to any area of the breadboard via connection through short jumper wires:

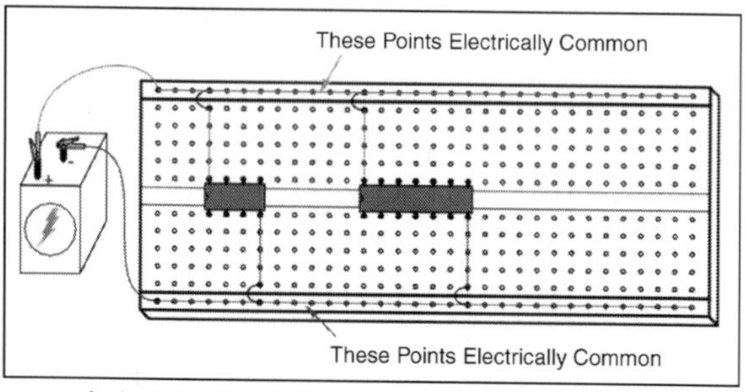

With so many of these integrated circuits having "reset," "enable," and "disable" terminals needing to be maintained in a "high" or "low" state, not to mention the V_{DD} (or V_{CC}) and ground power terminals which require connection to the power supply, having both terminals of the power supply readily available for connection at any point along the board's length is very useful.

Most breadboards that I have seen have these power supply "rail" holes, but some do not. Up until this point, I've been illustrating circuits using a breadboard lacking this feature, just to show how it isn't absolutely necessary. However, digital circuits seem to require more connections to the power supply than other types of breadboard circuits, making this feature more than just a convenience.

DIGITAL INTEGRATED CIRCUITS

Digital integrated circuits, sometimes called an IC, chip or microchip, are the building blocks for nearly every type of modern electronics and electrical devices, whether for home or office, work or pleasure.

Origin

Digital integrated circuit development was necessary to resolve the fundamental issues of vacuum tubes, the leading technology of the first half of the 20th century. Vacuum tubes are bulky, fragile, power hungry, hot and failed frequently.

History

On Sept. 12, 1958, Jack Kilby successfully demonstrated the first IC with a single transistor and all its components on a single piece of germanium semiconductor material. In the first 50 years, ICs have advanced from single transistors to complex microprocessors with multiple CPU cores. On Dec. 3, 2009, the Helsinki University of Technology announced that a team of researchers had succeeded in building the first single atom transistor, the theoretical minimum component size. Technological alternatives such as quantum computing evolved as semiconductor technology approached theoretical limits.

Features

Digital integrated circuits operate based on binary mathematics using electrical signals to represent "ones" and "zeros." Digital integrated circuits can perform any number of operations, from a simple switch to a complex microprocessor.

HISTORY OF INTEGRATED CIRCUITS

The experiments performed on semi conductors revealed that they can perform the variety of vacuum tube functions. The incorporation of bulk of puny transistors on a small chip was a major leap in manually assembling electronic components on a really small circuit. Mass production and efficiency of Integrated Circuits greatly replaced the discrete transistors from many devices.

The two main features of integrated circuits like low cost and high performance gave it edge over the discrete transistors. The low cost is associated to the bulk production and printing using photolithography. The material used in constructing an IC is less than that used in discrete circuits. The high performance can be contributed to the quick switching and low power consumption.

The idea of IC was developed by the scientists working for Royal Radar. The idea propagated further when Jack Kilby and Robert Noyce working separately brought a remarkable invention. The chips made by both of them were meant to perform same functions whereas the material used was not the same. Noyce made a silicone chip and the Kilby manufactured a germanium chip. The development in this field was not new it was in 1949 when the first idea related to integrated chip came to view. From then onwards the development and growth is continued.

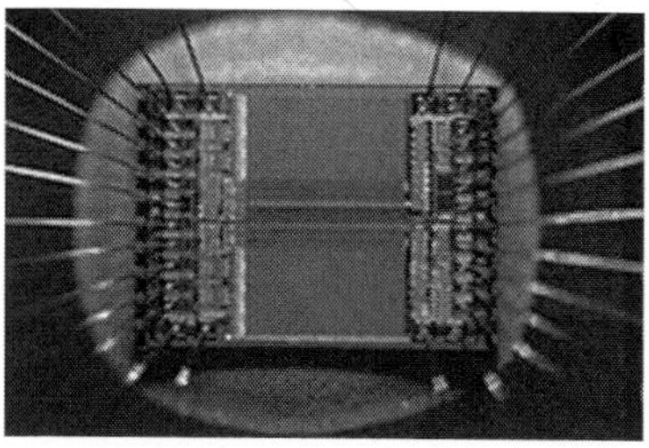

Applications of Integrated Circuts

Integrated circuits today have become ubiquitous. It seems that it was this invention which has led to the growth in technology. This remarkable invention has helped companies and manufacturers of electronic devices to design and introduce new and advance products. It can be said that it was due to the micro chips that we can use portable digital devices today. The integrated chip is an important component of laptops, palm tops, MP3s, playstaions, mobile phones, net books and an unlimited array of electronic devices.

The existence of all modern communication and electronic devices is based today on the use of integrated circuits. This chip is small but really efficient and swift when it comes to the performance. It is due to this desirable feature that it is part of almost all cell phones and we carry them anywhere in the world without being worrying about performance decline.

Taxonomy of Integrated Circuits

The integrated circuits can be divided into three broad categories like digital ICs, analog ICs and mixed signal ICs. Digital integrated circuits contain many flip flops, multiplexers and logic gates in a single chip comprising only few millimeters. This small size has provided its edge over all other technologies. Therefore, the manufactures of digital devices now prefer it over discrete transistors. These small chips consume less power and they are efficient. The manufacturing of these circuits help in reducing manufacturing cost due to the wide scale integration.

The working of the digital microchips is guided by the binary mathematical process in the form of 1 and 0 signals. On the contrary the analog micro circuits work by continuous flow of signals. The various examples of analog circuits include power management circuits, sensors and operational amplifiers.

These integrated circuits are used for performing functions like active filtering, demodulation, amplification and mixing. The expertly designed analog circuits remove the need for manufacturing an entirely new circuit from abrasion. This provides the facility to the mobile phone manufactures to buy and install the IC instead of preparing one. The digital and analog circuits can be combined in on one chip to enhance the performance.

DIGITAL ELECTRONICS

HALF ADDER CIRCUIT

To understand what is a half adder you need to know what is an adder first. Adder circuit is a combinational digital circuit that is used for adding two numbers. A typical adder circuit produces a sum bit (denoted by *S*) and a carry bit (denoted by *C*) as the output.

Typically adders are realised for adding binary numbers but they can be also realised for adding other formats like BCD (binary coded decimal, XS-3, etc. Besides addition, adder circuits can be used for a lot of other applications in digital electronics like address decoding, table index calculation, etc. Adder circuits are of two types: Half adder ad Full adder. Full adder s have been already explained in a previous article and in this topic I am giving stress to half adders.

Half adder is a combinational arithmetic circuit that adds two numbers and produces a sum bit (*S*) and carry bit (*C*) as the output. If *A* and *B* are the input bits, then sum bit (*S*) is the X-OR of *A* and *B* and the carry bit (*C*) will be the AND of A and B. From this it is clear that a half adder circuit can be easily constructed using one X-OR gate and one AND gate.

Half adder is the simplest of all adder circuit, but it has a major disadvantage. The half adder can add only two input bits (*A* and *B*) and has nothing to do with the carry if there is any in the input. So if the input to a half adder have a carry, then it will be neglected it and adds only the *A* and B bits. That means the binary addition process is not complete and that's why it is called a half adder. The truth table, schematic representation and XOR// AND realisation of a half adder are shown in the figure below.

Inputs		Outputs	
A	B	S	C
0	0	0	0
1	0	1	0
0	1	1	0
1	1	0	1

Truth Table

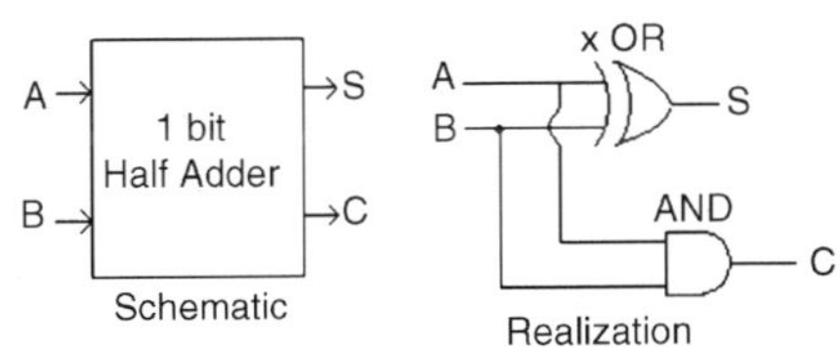

Fig. Truth Table, Schematic and Realisation of Half Adder

NAND gates or NOR gates can be used for realising the half adder in universal logic and the relevant circuit diagrams are shown in the figure below.

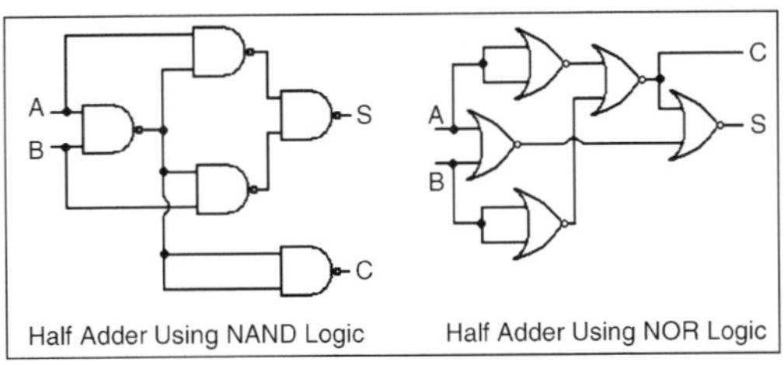

Fig. Half Adder Using NAND and NOR Logic

RIPPLE CARRY ADDER CIRCUIT

Multiple full adder circuits can be cascaded in parallel to add an *N*-bit number. For an *N*- bit parallel adder, there must be *N* number of full adder circuits.

A ripple carry adder is a logic circuit in which the carry-out of each full adder is the carry in of the succeeding next most significant full adder. It is called a ripple carry adder because each carry bit gets rippled into the next stage. In a ripple carry adder the sum and carry out bits of any half adder stage is not valid until the carry in of that stage occurs.Propagation delays inside the logic circuitry is the reason behind this. Propagation delay is time elapsed between the application of an input and occurance of the corresponding output.

Consider a NOT gate, When the input is "03 the output will be "13 and vice versa. The time taken for the NOT gate's output to become "03 after the application of logic "13 to the NOT gate's input is the propagation delay here. Similarly the carry propagation delay is the time elapsed between the application of the carry in signal and the occurance of the carry out (Cout) signal. Circuit diagram of a 4-bit ripple carry adder is shown below.

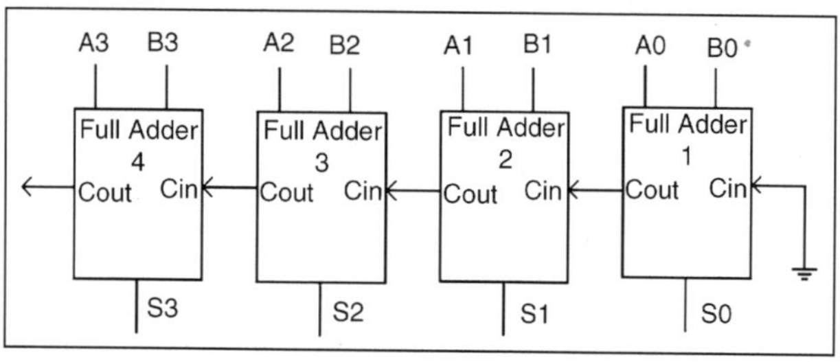

Fig. Ripple Carry Adder

Sum out S0 and carry out Cout of the Full Adder 1 is valid only after the propagation delay of Full Adder 1. In the same way, Sum out S3 of the Full Adder 4 is valid only after the joint propagation delays of Full Adder 1 to Full Adder 4. In simple words, the final result of the ripple carry adder is valid only after the joint propogation delays of all full adder circuits inside it.

Full Adder

To understand the working of a ripple carry adder completely, you need to have a look at the full adder too. Full adder is a logic circuit that adds two input operand bits plus a Carry in bit and outputs a Carry out bit and a sum bit..

The Sum out (Sout) of a full adder is the XOR of input operand bits *A*, *B* and the Carry in (Cin) bit. Truth table and schematic of a 1 bit Full adder is shown below There is a simple trick to find results of a full adder. Consider the second last row of the truth table, here the operands are 1, 1, 0 ie (*A*, *B*, Cin). Add them together ie 1+1+0 = 10.

In binary system, the number order is 0, 1, 10, 11……. and so the result of 1+1+0 is 10 just like we get 1+1+0 =2 in decimal system. 2 in the decimal system corresponds to 10 in the binary system. Swapping the result "103 will give S=0 and Cout = 1 and the second last row is justified. This can be applied to any row in the table.

Inputs			Outputs	
A	B	Cin	Cout	S
0	0	0	0	0
1	0	0	0	1
0	1	0	0	1
1	1	0	1	0
0	0	1	0	1
1	0	1	1	0
0	1	1	1	0
1	1	1	1	1

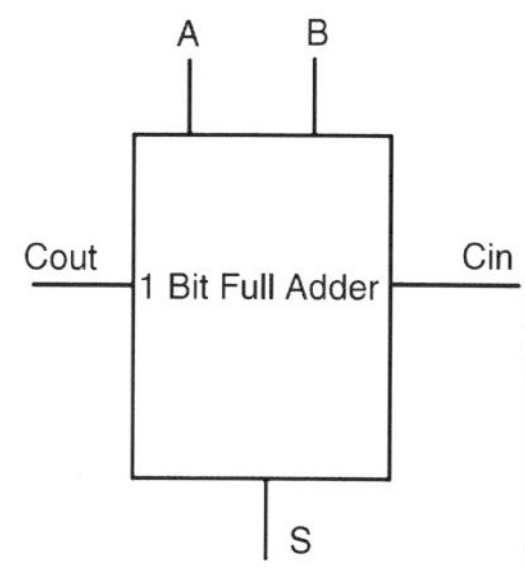

Fig. Bit Full Adder Schematic and Truth Table

A Full adder can be made by combining two half adder circuits together *(a half adder is a circuit that adds two input bits and outputs a sum bit and a carry bit).*

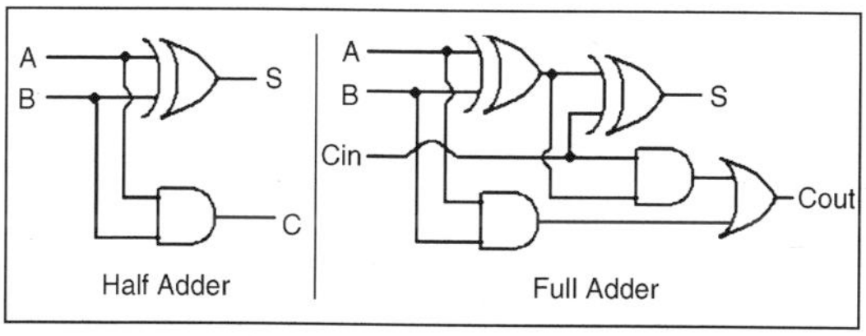

Fig. Full Adder and Half Adder Circuit

Full Adder Using NAND or NOR Logic

Alternatively the full adder can be made using NAND or NOR logic. These schemes are universally accepted and their circuit diagrams are shown below.

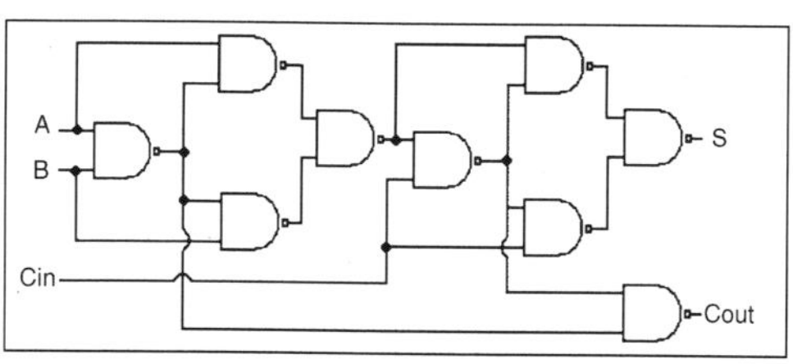

Fig. Full Adder Using NAND Logic

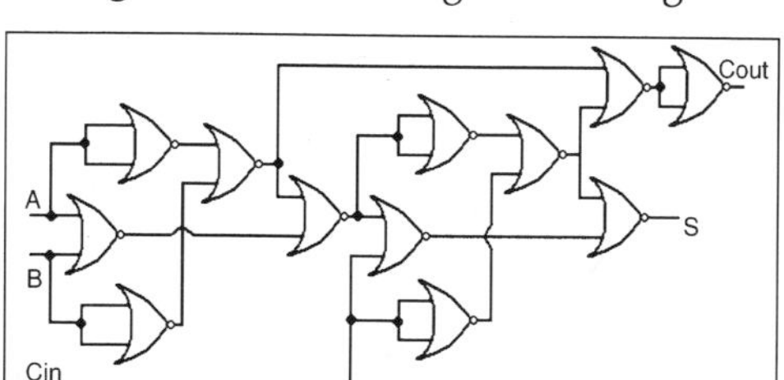

Fig. Full Adder Using NOR Logic

FLIP FLOP – TRIGGERING METHODS

After going through my post on flip flop, you must have understood the importance of triggering a flip flop. The output of a flip flop can be changed by bring a small change in the input signal. This small change can be brought with the help of a clock pulse or commonly known as a trigger pulse. When such a trigger pulse is applied to the input, the output changes and thus the flip flop is said to be triggered. Flip flops are applicable in designing counters or registers which stores data in the form of multi-bit numbers.But such registers need a group of flip flops connected to each other as sequential circuits. And these sequential circuits require trigger pulses.

The number of trigger pulses that is applied to the input of the circuit determines the number in a counter. A single pulse makes the bit move one position, when it is applied onto a register that stores multi-bit data. In the case of SR Flip Flops, the change in signal level decides the type of trigger that is to be given to the input. But the original level must be regained before giving a second pulse to the circuit.

If a clock pulse is given to the input of the flip flop at the same time when the output of the flip flop is changing, it may cause instability to the circuit. The reason for this instability is the feedback that is given from the output combinational circuit to the memory elements. This problem can be solved to a certain level by making the flip flop more sensitive to the pulse transition rather than the pulse duration. There are mainly four types of pulse-triggering methods. They differ in the manner in which the electronic circuits respond to the pulse. They are

High Level Triggering

When a flip flop is required to respond at its HIGH state, a HIGH level triggering method is used. It is mainly identified from the straight lead from the clock input. Take a look at the symbolic representation shown below.

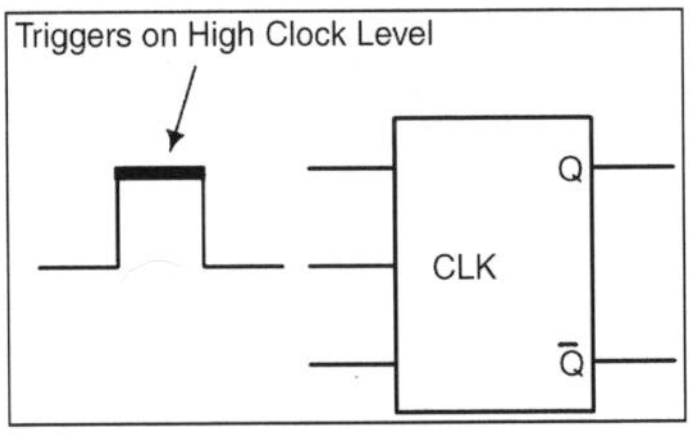

Fig. High Level Triggering

Low Level Triggering

When a flip flop is required to respond at its LOW state, a LOW level triggering method is used.. It is mainly identified from the clock input lead along with a low state indicator bubble. Take a look at the symbolic representation shown below.

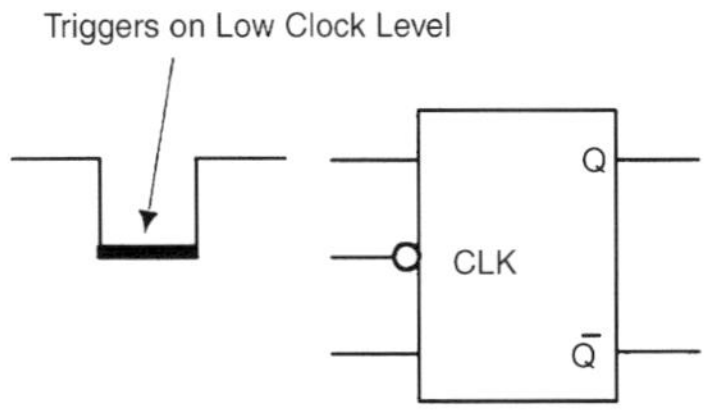

Fig. Low Level Triggering

Positive Edge Triggering

When a flip flop is required to respond at a LOW to HIGH transition state, POSITIVE edge triggering method is used. It is mainly identified from the clock input lead along with a triangle. Take a look at the symbolic representation shown below.

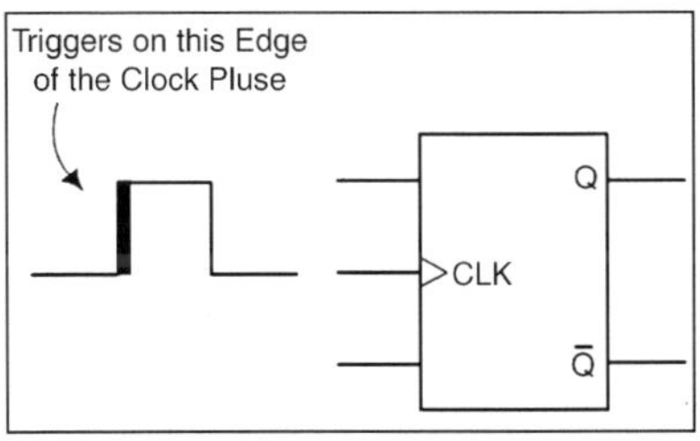

Fig. Positive Edge Triggering

Negative Edge Triggering

When a flip flop is required to respond during the HIGH to LOW transition state, a NEGATIVE edge triggering method is used.. It is mainly identified from the clock input lead along with a low-state indicator and a triangle. Take a look at the symbolic representation shown below.

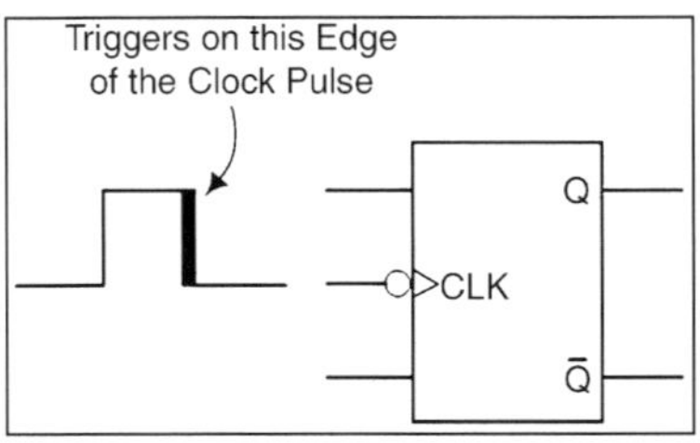

Fig. Negative Edge Triggering

CLOCK PULSE TRANSITION

The movement of a trigger pulse is always from a 0 to 1 and then 1 to 0 of a signal. Thus it takes two transitions in a single signal. When it moves from 0 to 1 it is called a positive transition and when it moves from 1 to 0 it is called a negative transition. To understand more take a look at the images below.

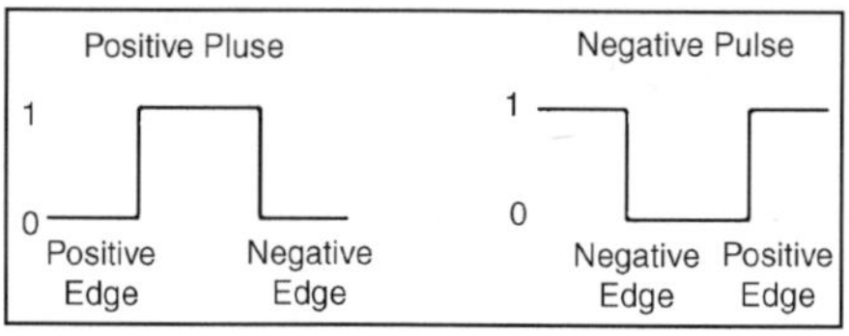

Fig. Clock Pulse Transition

The clocked flip-flops already introduced are triggered during the 0 to 1 transition of the pulse, and the state transition starts as soon as the pulse reaches the HIGH level. If the other inputs change while the clock is still 1, a new output state may occur. If the flip-flop is made to then the multiple-transition problem can be eliminated. The multi-transition problem can be stopped is the flip flop is made to respond to the positive or negative edge transition only, other than responding to the entire pulse duration.

CLEANING AND ETCHING OF WAFERS

Surface of semiconductor wafer gets contaminated during device processing. The source of contaminants are ambient air, storage ambient, process gases, chemicals, materials, water etc which are used in the fabrication processes. Processing tools as well as personnel operating in the clean- rooms are also sources of contamination. The most prevalent contaminants are particles and they may cause a catastrophic failure during device manufacturing process.

The measure of the air quality of a clean room is described in Federal Standard 209. Clean rooms are rated as Class 10K, where there exist no more than 10,000 particles larger than 0.5 microns in any given cubic foot of air; Class 1K, where there exists no more than 1000 particles; and Class 100, where there exist no more than 100 particles. These small particles are controlled in a clean-room by using High Efficiency Particulate Air (HEPA) filters. Another type of contaminants which degrade the devices are metallic contaminants originate primarily from liquid chemicals, water and process tools. The most common metallic contaminants are iron (*Fe*), aluminum (*Al*), copper (*Cu*), nickel (Ni) as well as ionic metals such as sodium (*Na*) and calcium (*Ca*). Organic contaminants are present in ambient air, storage containers and can arise from photoresists.

Organic compounds readily adsorb surfaces adversely affect device properties. Native oxides as well as moisture from the ambient air or wet processes adversely affect the devices and can be considered as a contaminant and its removal is a part of cleaning process. As total elimination of contaminants is not possible, methods of semiconductor surface cleaning are employed throughout the device manufacturing sequence. The cleaning can be achieved by a chemical reaction with a reactant and contaminant on the surface, by the physical interaction between cleaning ambient and the surface, the momentum transfer between high kinetic energy particles directed towards the contaminant, etc.

In Wet Cleaning, contaminant is removed via selective chemical reaction in the liquid-phase by its dissolution in the solvent, or its conversion into, the soluble compound. Typically, process is enhanced ultrasonic agitation. In Dry Cleaning, contaminant is removed via chemical reaction in the gas phase converting it into a volatile compound. Wet cleaning is the dominant cleaning technology in semiconductor device manufacturing. Wet cleans use combinations of acids and solvents, oxidise, etch, and scrub contaminants from the wafer surface. An integral part of every wet cleaning scheme is rinses in ultra-pure deionised (DI) water which stops chemical reaction on the wafer surface and washes off reactants and reaction products. Wet cleaning is always completed with a wafer drying process.

RCA clean Wet cleaning recipes were first proposed over 30 years ago presents a complete cleaning process to remove from the surface heavy organics, particles, and metallic contaminants as well as native/chemical oxide. Typically the first step is to remove organic contamination remaining on the surface. The H_2SO_4:H_2O_2 solution at 100°C-130°C, also known as SPM (Sulfuric Peroxide Mixture), or "piranha" clean. NH_4OH: H_2O_2: H_2O mixture 1:1:50, at temperature ~ 70°C with ultrasonic agitation is used to remove particles.

This Ammonium hydroxide-hydrogen Peroxide Mixture (APM) is also known as Standard Clean 1 (*SC*1 or *RCA* 1). To remove metallic contamination, *HCl*: H_2O_2: H_2O mixture is used. This Hydrochloric acid - hydrogen Peroxide-water Mixture (*HPM*) is also known as Standard Clean 2 (*SC*2 or *RCA* 2). Dilution and bath temperature are similar to APM. Native/chemical oxide etch is carried out in diluted HF:H_2O solution at the ratio of 1:100 or weaker. Thin films are very fragile and material loss also can result by such very resourceful and time consuming cleaning processes. In practice it is simplified by less aggressive cleans. In many applications a sequence involving just one cleaning step followed with D.I. water rinse and dry is enough.

In a dry cleaning technology, removal of contaminant fro m the surface takes place via chemical reaction in the gas- phase converting it into a volatile compound. Gas sources like O_2, H_2, CO_2, Ozone, $SiCl_4$, HCl, are used for dry cleaning. Methods like Laser, Sputtering etc are based momentum transfer between specie impinging on the surface. Gas-phase cleaning methods lack a shear chemical and physical strength of liquid cleaning ambient. However gas-phase surface processing methods are fully capable of controlling organic contamination.

Etching

Etch is a process that removes unwanted materials from the surface of a substrate by various dry and wet techniques. These techniques are used to remove silicon dioxide, silicon nitride, polysilicon, aluminum, tungsten, contamination particles, and other layer materials. This process step creates the layer definition that is based on the outcome of a previous photolithography process step. These etch processes transform a single layer of semiconductor material into the patterns, features, lines, and interconnects.

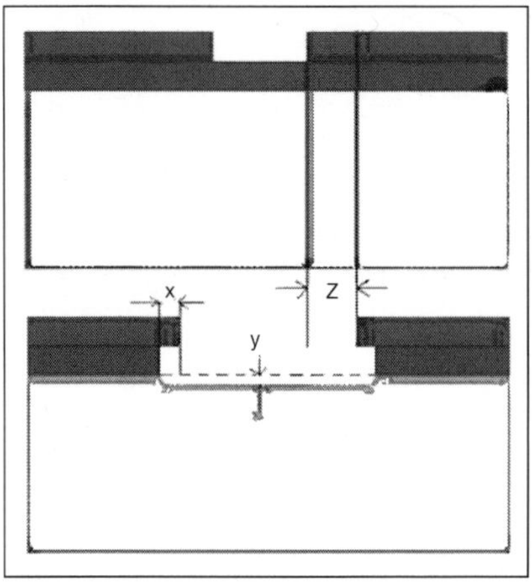

Fig. Etching Profiles Before and After the Pro

A typical etching profile is given in Figure above. In this case the red region is the mask (protective layer) used, blue layer is to be removed selectively from regions not protected by mask and grey layer is the substrate which should not be etched. The profile after the etching indicates that there is a horizontal etching as well etching of underlying substrate. Selectivity is the characteristic of etch whereby the desired layer is etched without damaging the underlying or masking layers. The etching system's ability to do this depends on the ratio of etch rates in the two materials. The selectivity can be quantified as:

$$S_{A-B} = \frac{\text{desired layer eatch rate}(A)}{\text{undersired layer etch rate}(B)}$$

Anisotropy is the characteristic of etch whereby the desired layer is etched in one direction only. The degree of anisotropy can be quantified as:

$$A = 1 - \frac{\text{lateral eatch rate}(A)}{\text{vertical etch rate}(B)}$$

In the above figure dimension 'x' shows the degree of anisotropy, 'y' shows the lack of selectivity with respect to the underlying layer and 'z' shows the lack of selectivity with respect to the masking layer:

- A poorly selective etch removes the desired layer, but also attacks the underlying material.

- A highly selective etch leaves the underlying material unharmed.
- A perfectly isotropic etch produces round sidewalls.
- A perfectly anisotropic etch produces vertical sidewalls

The wet etching processes used liquid-phase ("wet") etchants. The wafer is immersed in a bath of etchant, which must be agitated to achieve good process control. For instance, buffered hydrofluoric acid (*HF*) was used commonly to etch silicon dioxide over a silicon substrate. Wet etchants are usually isotropic, which leads to undercuts when etching thick films. They also require the disposal of large amounts of toxic waste. For these reasons, they are seldom used in state-of-the-art processes.

Modern VLSI processes avoid wet etching, and use plasma etching instead. The plasma produces energetic radicals, neutrally charged, that react at the surface of the wafer. Since neutral particles attack the wafer from all angles, this process is isotropic. The source gas for the plasma usually contains small molecules rich in chlorine or fluorine. For instance, carbon tetrachloride (CCl_4) etches silicon and aluminium, and trifluoromethane etches silicon dioxide and silicon nitride. A plasma containing oxygen is used to oxidise ("ash") photoresist and facilitate its removal.

In Ion milling, or sputter etching, lower pressures, energetic ions of noble gases, often Ar+, bombards the wafer with which knock atoms from the substrate by transferring momentum. Because the etching is performed by ions, which approach the wafer approximately from one direction, this process is highly anisotropic. On the other hand, it tends to display poor selectivity. Reactive-ion etching (RIE) operates under conditions intermediate between sputter and plasma. Deep reactive-ion etching (DRIE) modifies the RIE technique to produce deep, narrow features.

The fabrication of an integrated circuit involves a sequence of processes that may be repeated many times before a circuit is complete. In this section, we have discussed about the first step involved in semiconductor device fabrication, *i.e.*, the cleaning of wafers. Briefly we also have studied about the etching of thin films. Generally, the next step involved is oxidation of the wafer surface.

5

Design of Biasing Circuits

A bipolar junction transistor, (BJT) is very versatile. It can be used in many ways, as an amplifier, a switch or an oscillator and many other uses too. Before an input signal is applied its operating conditions need to be set. This is achieved with a suitable bias circuit, some of which I will describe. A bias circuit allows the operating conditions of a transistor to be defined, so that it will operate over a pre-determined range. This is normally achieved by applying a small fixed dc voltage to the input terminals of a transistor. Bias design can take a mathematical approach or can be simplified using transistor characteristic curves. The characteristic curves predict the performance of a BJT. There are three curves, an input characteristic curve, a transfer characteristic curve and an output characteristic curve. Of these curves, the most useful for amplifier design is the output characteristics curve. The output characteristic curves for a BJT are a graph displaying the output voltages and currents for different input currents. The linear (straight) part of the curve needs is utilized for an amplifier or oscillator. For use as a switch,a transistor is biased at the extremities of the graph, these conditions are known as "cut-off" and "saturation".

CURVES

For each transistor configuration, common emitter, common base and emitter follower the output curves are slightly different.

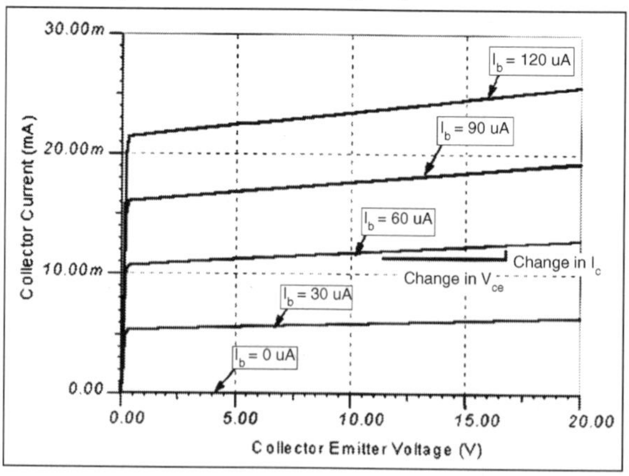

A typical output characteristic for a BJT in common emitter mode are shown above diagram. After the initial bend, the curves approximate a straight line. The slope or gradient of each line represents the output impedance, for a particular input base current. So what has all this got to do with biasing ? Take, for example the middle curve. The collector emitter voltage is displayed up to 20 volts. Let's assume that we have a single stage amplifier, working in common emitter mode, and the supply voltage is 10 volts. The output terminal is the collector, the input is the base, where do you set the bias conditions? The answer is anywhere on the flat part of the graph. However, imagine the bias is set so that the collector voltage is 2 volts. What happens if the output signal is 4 volts peak to peak ? Depending on whether the transistor used is a PNP or NPN, then one half cycle will be amplified cleanly, the other cycle will approach the limits of the power supply and will "clip". This is shown below:

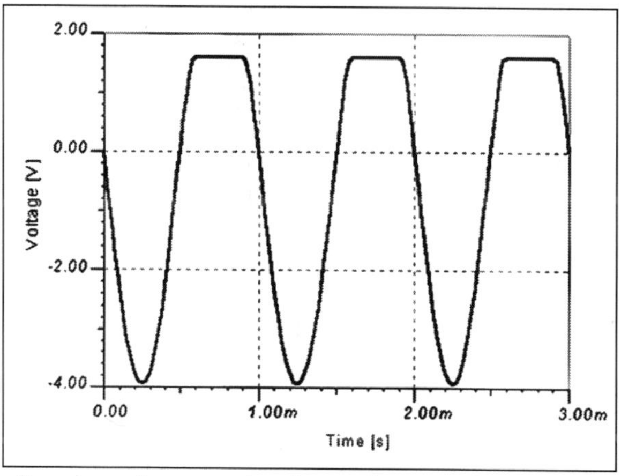

The above diagram shows a 4 volt peak to peak waveform with clipping on the positive half cycle. This is caused by setting the bias at a value other than half the supply voltage.

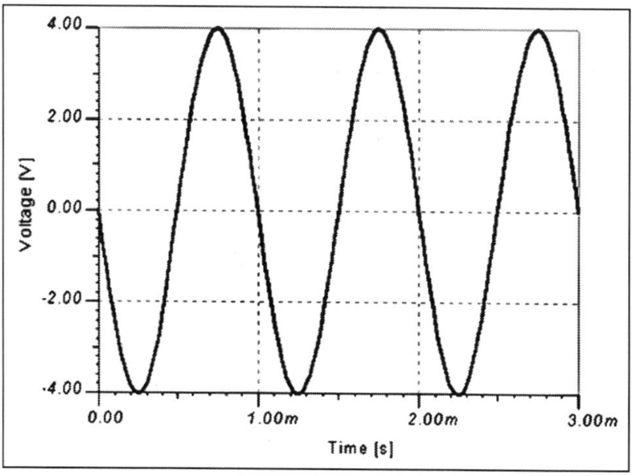

The lower diagram shows the same amplifier, but here the bias is set so that collector voltage is half the value of the supply voltage. Hence, it is a good idea to set the bias for a single stage amplifier to half the supply voltage, as this allows maximum output voltage swing in both directions of an output waveform.

CHARACTERISTIC

Before describing the bias circuits, it is worthwhile looking at a typical input characteristic curve for a small signal BJT. The following is the input characteristic for a transistor in common emitter mode, it is a plot of input base emitter voltage verses base current. It is shown with both x and y axis slightly zoomed.

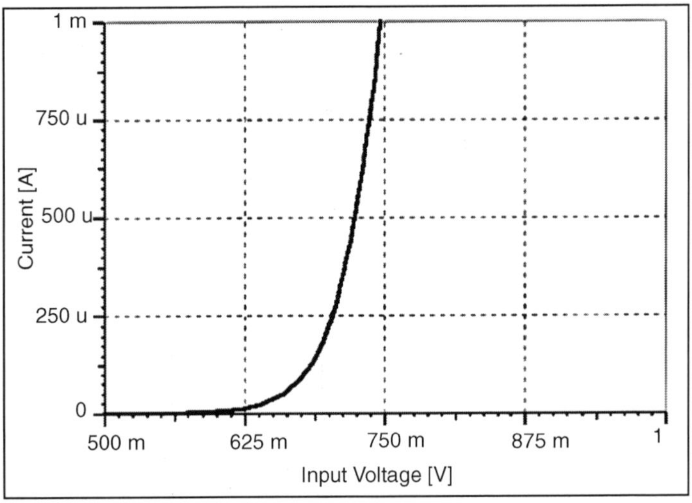

The base emitter voltage, Vbe is quoted in most text books as either 0.6 V or 0.7 V Both values are an approximation, and as can be seen from the above graph the value of Vbe varies between this range. For small signal work with base currents of 50uA or below a value for Vbe of 0.6 volts is a reasonable quote. For higher base currents, a Vbe of 0.7 V is a better approximation. In fact, in a large power transistor, the Vbe value can be even higher. The value of Vbe also varies widely with temperature change.

CIRCUIT

The simplest bias circuit is shown below. It consists only of a fixed bias resistor and load resistor. The BJT is operating in common emitter mode. The dc current gain or beta, h_{FE} is the ratio of dc collector current divided by dc base current. The BJT is a BC107A. The values of Rb and Rc can be determined by either mathematical approach or by using the output characteristic curves for the BC107A.

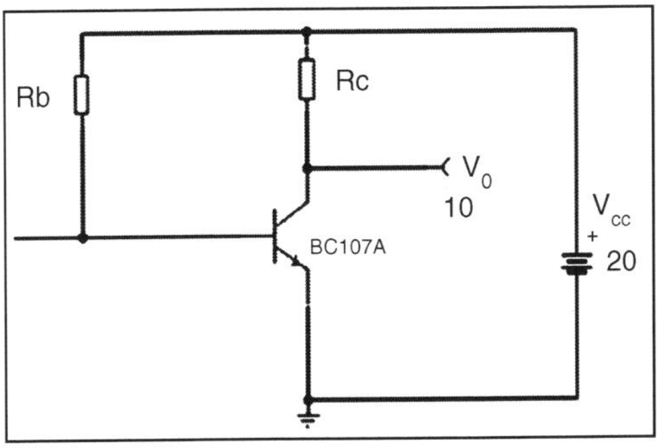

VOLTAGE OR POTENTIAL DIVIDER BIASING

This is the most widely used biasing scheme in general electronics. For a single stage amplifier this circuit offers the best resilience against changes in temperature and device characteristics. The disadvantage is that a couple of extra resistors are required, but this is outweighed by the advantage of excellent stability. The circuits below:

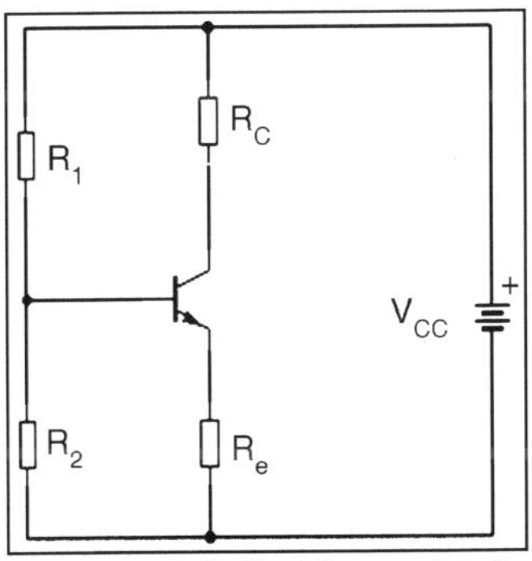

Here R_1 and R_2 form a potential divider, which will fix the base potential of the transistor. The current through this bias chain is usually set at 10 times greater than the base current required by the transistor. The base emitter voltage drop of the transistor is approximated as 0.6 volt. There will also be a voltage drop across the emitter resistor, Re, this is generally set to about 10 per cent of the supply voltage. The inclusion of this resistor also helps to stabilize the bias: If the temperature increases, then extra collector current will flow. If Ic increases, then so will Ie as Ie= Ib + Ic. The extra current flow through Re increases the voltage drop across this resistor reducing the effective base emitter voltage and therefore stabilizing the collector current. The equations follow:

$R_c = V_c/I_c$

Ie = Ib + Ic as Ic >> Ib then Ie ~ Ic

Ve = 10% * Vcc

$Re = V_e/I_e$

$V_b = V_e + 0.6$

$R_2 = V_b/10 * I_b$

$R_1 = V_{cc} - V_b/10 * I_b$

AN EXAMPLE

Using the values of the previous examples a direct comparison of stability can be demonstrated. The values are;

V_{cc}=20V, V_c=10V, I_c = 1mA, transistor is BC107A with h_{FE}=195

R_c= Vc/I_c = 10/1m = 10k

V_e = 10% * 20 = 2V

R_e = V_e/I_e= 2/1= 2k

V_b = 2+ 0.6 = 2.6V

I_b = I_c/h_{FE} = 1/195 =0.005128mA

R_2 = V_b/10* Ib = 2.6/0.05128 = 50.7k (use 47K)

R_1 = V_{cc}–V_b/10 * I_b = (20–2.6)/0.05128 = 339.3k (use 330K)

Using these values and plotting the change in quiescent conditions for V_c and I_c over a temperature range of–50 to +50 celcius is displayed below:

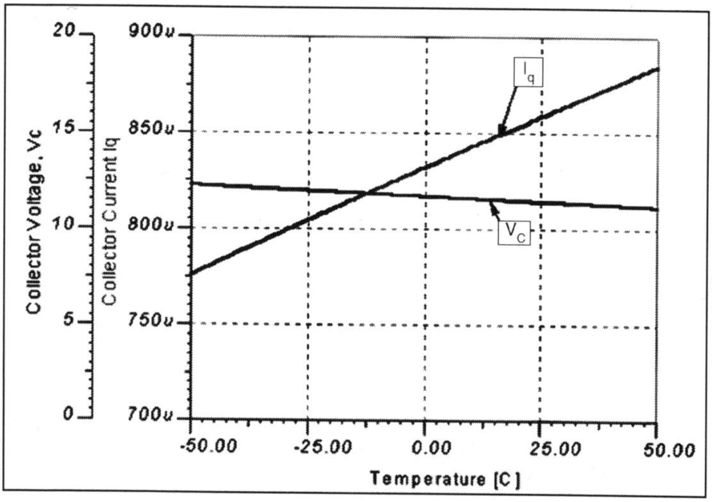

As shown above, this bias circuit gives the best stability against variations in V_C and I_C over a very wide temperature range. As the resistor values were approximated the quiescent voltage point is slightly different from the intended value. Using a load line gives a slightly more accurate design.

TWO BATTERY BIAS STABILISATION

INTRODUCTION

Transistors are inevitable parts of Electronic circuits. The success of a circuit design lies in the selection of proper transistor type and calculation of voltage and current flowing through it. A small variation in the voltage or current level in the transistor will affects the working of the whole circuit. Here explains how a transistor works.

The Fig. explains how voltage and current are flowing through a bipolar transistor. Input voltage to the circuit is 12 volt DC. The base of T_1 is connected to a potential divider R_1–R_2. If they have equal values, half supply voltage will be available at the base of T_1. Here the value of R_1 is 3.2 Ohms.

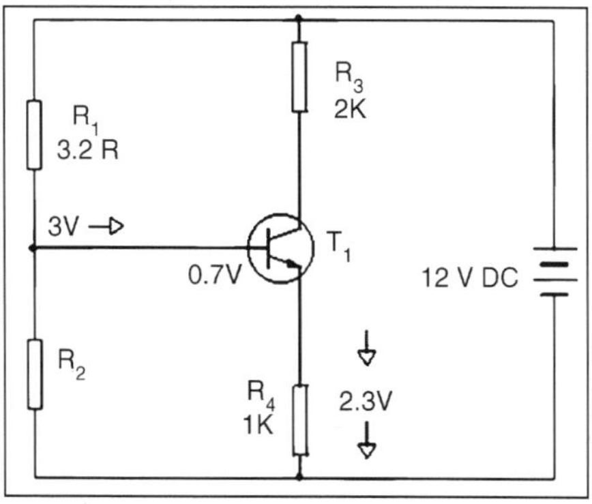

If the value of R_1 is three times greater than R_2, then three quarter of 12V drops by R_1 and allow one quarter to pass through R_2. Therefore the base voltage of T_1 will be 12/4 = 3 V. Thus the voltage provided by R1 to the base of T_1 is 3 volts. The emitter voltage of T_1 will be 0.7 volts less than 3 volts since T1 drops 0.7 volts for its biasing. Thus the emitter voltage appears as 3–0.7 = 2.3 volts. If the value of the emitter resistor R_4 is 1K, then if 2.3 volt passes through it, emitter current will be 2.3V/1 = 2.3 mA. Collector current also remains same. If the value of the load resistor R_3 is 2K, two times higher than that of R_4, then the voltage drop across it will be 2 × 2.3V = 4.6 volts. There fore the collector voltage of T1 remains as 12–4.6 = 7.4 volts.

LOAD CURRENT

In the circuit shown in Fig volt DC supply is provided. T1 is a general purpose NPN transtior like BC 548. A potential divider comprising R_1 and R_2 bias the base of T1. Minimum base voltage necessary for biasing T1 is 0.7 volts. The potential divider R_1-R_2 drops 6-0.7 = 6.3 volts. If the load takes 4 volts,then the collector voltage will be 2 volts. 6-4=2 volts.

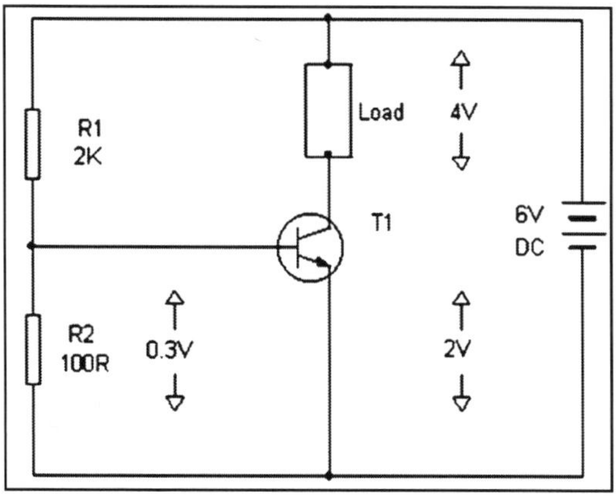

Value of the collector current depends on the base voltage. When the base voltage increases, collector current also increases. This results in more volts in the load. In short, 0.1 volt increase in base voltage causes 1 Volt increases in the load.

CURRENT IN THE TRANSISTOR AMPLIFIER

Normally when a High volt is present at the collector and Low volt in the base, Base-Emitter junction of T1 will be reverse biased.If the collector remains open, collector voltage will be 0 and hence the base current will be 100 mA. If collector of T1 is connected to the Vcc, 98 mA current flows through the collector and 2mA to the base.That is

Emitter current = Base current + Collector current = 2mA + 98mA = 100mA
Collector current = Emitter current–Base current = 100mA–2 mA =98 mA
Base current = Emitter current–Collector current = 100mA–98mA = 2 mA

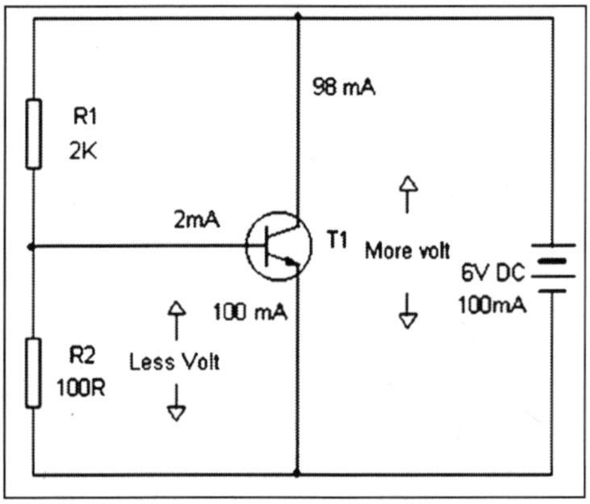

The condition is just reversed in the case of a PNP transistor as shown in Fig. The base-emitter junction of T1 forward biased and the base-collector junction is reverse biased. In this state,T1 remains non conducting. If we makes the base more negative, T1 conducts and collector current appears.

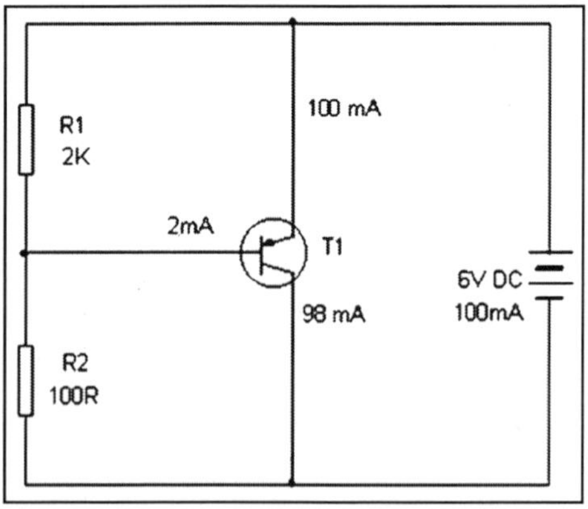

THERMAL RESISTANCE

There is an electrical analogy with conduction heat transfer that can be exploited in problem solving. The analog of $\dot{Q}$ is current, and the analog of the temperature difference, $T_1 - T_2$, is voltage difference. From this perspective the slab is a pure resistance to heat transfer and we can define,

$$\dot{Q} = \frac{T_1 - T_2}{R}$$

where $R = L / kA$, the thermal resistance. The thermal resistance R increases as L increases, as A decreases, and as k decreases.

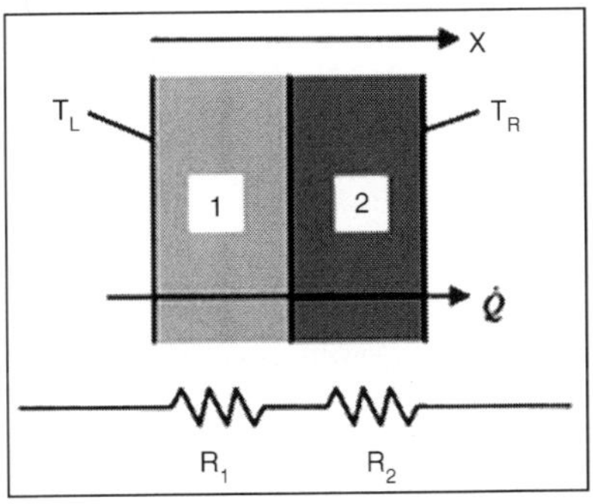

Fig. Heat Transfer Across a Composite Slab (Series Thermal Resistance)

The concept of a thermal resistance circuit allows ready analysis of problems such as a composite slab (composite planar heat transfer surface). In the composite slab shown in Figure, the heat flux is constant with x. The resistances are in series and sum to $R = R_1 + R_2$. If T_L is the temperature at the left, and T_R is the temperature at the right, the heat transfer rate is given by,

$$\dot{Q} = \frac{T_L - T_R}{R} = \frac{T_L - T_R}{R_1 + R_2}.$$

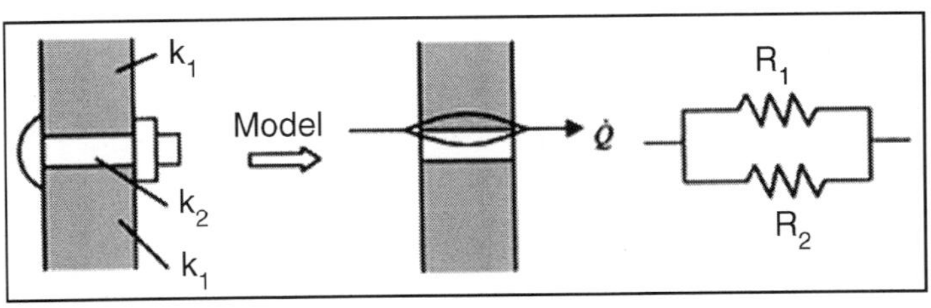

Fig. Heat Transfer for a Wall with Dissimilar Materials (Parallel Thermal Resistance)

Another example is a wall with a dissimilar material such as a bolt in an insulating layer. In this case, the heat transfer resistances are in parallel. Figure shows the physical configuration, the heat transfer paths and the thermal resistance circuit.

DETERMINE OF OPERATING POINT IN PRESENCE OF SELF HEATING

For this situation, the total heat flow $\dot{Q}$ is made up of the heat flow in the two parallel paths, $\dot{Q} = \dot{Q}_1 + \dot{Q}_2$,, with the total resistance given by,

$$\frac{1}{R} = \frac{1}{R_1} + \frac{1}{R_2}.$$

More complex configurations can also be examined; for example, a brick wall with insulation on both sides.

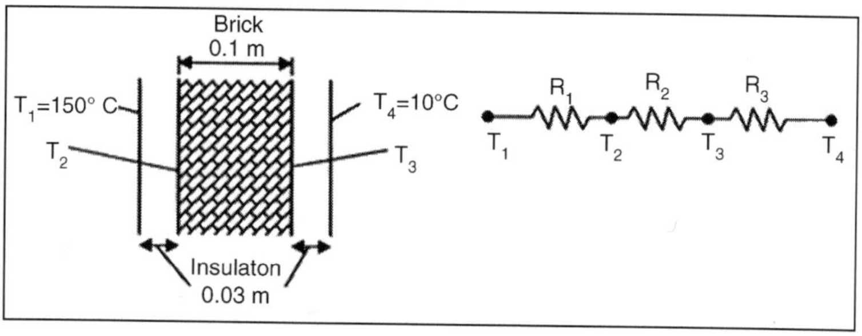

Fig. Heat Transfer Through an Insulated Wall

The overall thermal resistance is given by

$$R = R_1 + R_2 + R_3 = \frac{L_1}{k_1 A_1} + \frac{L_2}{k_2 A_2} + \frac{L_3}{k_3 A_3}.$$

Some representative values for the brick and insulation thermal conductivity are:

$$k_{brik} = k_2 \qquad = 0.7 W/m-K$$

$$k_{insulation} = k_1 = k_3 \qquad = 0.07 W/m-K$$

Using these values, and noting that $A_1 = A_2 = A_3 = A$, we obtain,

$$Ar_1 = Ar_3 = \frac{L_1}{k_1} = \frac{0.03}{0.07 W/m-k} = 0.42 m^2 k/W$$

$$Ar_2 = \frac{L_2}{k_2} = \frac{0.1m}{0.7 W/m-k} = 0.14 m^2 k/W.$$

This is a series circuit so,

$$\dot{q} = \frac{\dot{Q}}{A} = \text{Constant throughout} = \frac{T_1 - T_4}{RA} = \frac{140}{0.98 m^2 K/W} = 142 W/m^2.$$

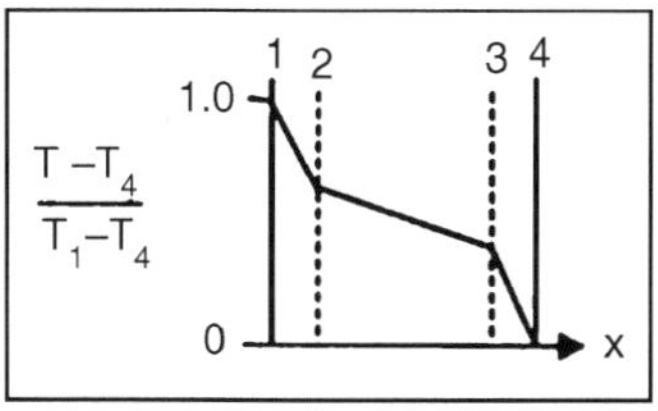

Fig. Temperature Distribution Through an Insulated Wall

The temperature is continuous in the wall and the intermediate temperatures can be found from applying the resistance equation across each slab, since $\dot{Q}$ is constant across the slab. For example, to find T_2:

$$\dot{q} = \frac{T_1 - T_2}{R_1 A} = 142 W/m^2.$$

This yields $T_1 - T_2 = 60k$ or $T_2 = 90°$.

The same procedure gives $T_3 = 90°$. As sketched in Figure, the larger drop is across the insulating layer even though the brick layer is much thicker.

BIAS COMPENSATION

The Minimum Statistics noise power spectral density (psd) estimation approach is based on tracking minima of a short term power spectral density (psd) estimate in frequency subbands. Since the short term minimum power is always smaller than (or in trivial cases equal to) the mean power, the minimum noise power estimate is a biased estimate of the mean power. For an accurate noise power estimate this bias must be compensated.In this paper we review bias compensation methods for moving average and first-order recursive smoothed psd estimates.

While for some cases exact expressions for the bias are available, approximations are required in general. We present approximations which allow an efficient computation and compensation of the bias. We discuss factors that influence the bias and show that the method is to some extent robust to variations of the signal statistics. Besides different smoothing methods, we discuss the effect of overlapping spectral analysis windows and of signal correlation.

BASE RESISTOR/FIXED BIAS CIRCUIT

The first biasing method, called *Base Current Bias* or sometimes FIXED BIAS, was used in the picture below. As you recall, it consisted basically of a resistor (RB) connected between the collector supply voltage and the base. Unfortunately, this simple arrangement is quite thermally unstable. If the temperature of the transistor rises for any reason (due to a rise in ambient temperature or due to current flow through it), collector current will increase. This increase in current also causes the dc operating point, sometimes called the quiescent or static point, to move away from its desired position (level). This reaction to temperature is undesirable because it affects amplifier gain (the number of times of amplification) and could result in distortion, as you will see later in this discussion.

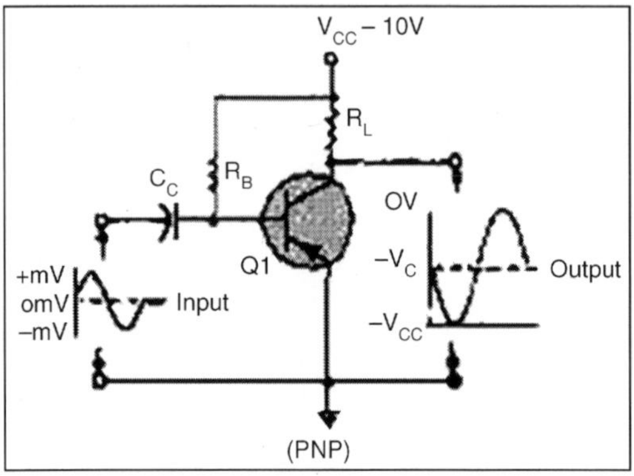

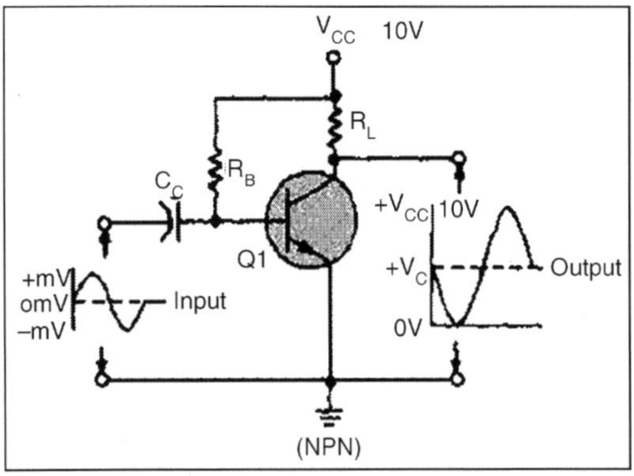

BIASING WITH A FEEDBACK RESISTOR

INTRODUCTION

If some percentage of an amplifier's output signal is connected to the input, so that the amplifier amplifies part of its own output signal, we have what is known as *feedback*. Feedback comes in two varieties:*positive* (also called *regenerative*), and *negative* (also called *degenerative*). Positive feedback reinforces the direction of an amplifier's output voltage change, while negative feedback does just the opposite.

A familiar example of feedback happens in public-address ("PA") systems where someone holds the microphone too close to a speaker: a high-pitched "whine" or "howl" ensues, because the audio amplifier system is detecting and amplifying its own noise. Specifically, this is an example of *positive* or *regenerative*feedback, as any sound detected by the microphone is amplified and turned into a louder sound by the speaker, which is then detected by the microphone again, and so on... the result being a noise of steadily increasing volume until the system becomes "saturated" and cannot produce any more volume.

One might wonder what possible benefit feedback is to an amplifier circuit, given such an annoying example as PA system "howl." If we introduce positive, or regenerative, feedback into an amplifier circuit, it has the tendency of creating and sustaining oscillations, the frequency of which determined by the values of components handling the feedback signal from output to input. This is one way to make an *oscillator* circuit to produce AC from a DC power supply. Oscillators are very useful circuits, and so feedback has a definite, practical application for us. "Phase shift oscillator", for a practical application of positive feedback.

Negative feedback, on the other hand, has a "dampening" effect on an amplifier: if the output signal happens to increase in magnitude, the feedback signal introduces a decreasing influence into the input of the amplifier, thus opposing the change in output signal. While positive feedback drives an amplifier circuit toward a point of instability (oscillations), negative feedback drives it the opposite direction: toward a point of stability.

An amplifier circuit equipped with some amount of negative feedback is not only more stable, but it distorts the input waveform less and is generally capable of amplifying a wider range of frequencies. The tradeoff for these advantages (there just *has* to be a disadvantage to negative feedback, right?) is decreased gain. If a portion of an amplifier's output signal is "fed back" to the input to oppose any changes in the output, it will require a greater input signal amplitude to drive the amplifier's output to the same amplitude as before. This constitutes a decreased gain. However, the advantages of stability, lower distortion, and greater bandwidth are worth the tradeoff in reduced gain for many applications.

Let's examine a simple amplifier circuit and see how we might introduce negative feedback into it, starting with Figure below.

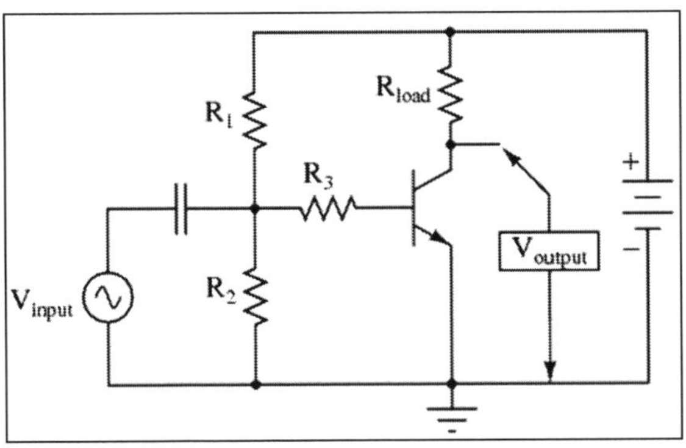

COMMON-EMITTER AMPLIFIER WITHOUT FEEDBACK.

The amplifier configuration shown here is a common-emitter, with a resistor bias network formed by R_1 and R_2. The capacitor couples V_{input} to the amplifier so that the signal source doesn't have a DC voltage imposed on it by the R_1/R_2 divider network. Resistor R_3 serves the purpose of controlling voltage gain. We could omit it for maximum voltage gain, but since base resistors like this are common in common-emitter amplifier circuits, we'll keep it in this schematic. Like all common-emitter amplifiers, this one *inverts* the input signal as it is amplified. In other words, a positive-going input voltage causes the output voltage to decrease, or move toward negative, and vice versa. The oscilloscope waveforms are shown in Figure below.

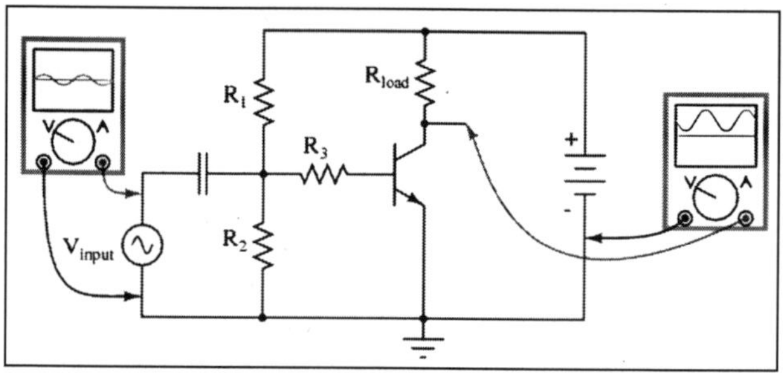

COMMON-EMITTER AMPLIFIER, NO FEEDBACK, WITH REFERENCE WAVEFORMS FOR COMPARISON

Because the output is an inverted, or mirror-image, reproduction of the input signal, any connection between the output (collector) wire and the input (base) wire of the transistor in Figure below will result in *negative* feedback.

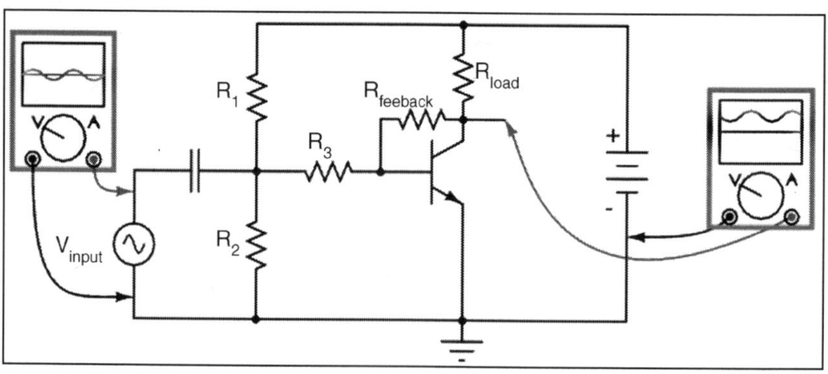

NEGATIVE FEEDBACK, COLLECTOR FEEDBACK, DECREASES THE OUTPUT SIGNAL

The resistances of R_1, R_2, R_3, and $R_{feedback}$ function together as a signal-mixing network so that the voltage seen at the base of the transistor (with respect to ground) is a weighted average of the input voltage and the feedback voltage, resulting in signal of reduced amplitude going into the transistor. So, the amplifier circuit in Figure above will have reduced voltage gain, but improved linearity (reduced distortion) and increased bandwidth.

EMITTER RESISTANCE BIASING (OR SELF BIAS)

A better method of biasing is obtained by inserting the bias resistor directly between the base and collector, as shown in the next illustration below. By tying the collector to the base in this manner, feedback voltage can be fed from the collector to the base to develop forward bias. This arrangement is called SELF-BIAS.

Now, if an increase of temperature causes an increase in collector current, the collector voltage (VC) will fall because of the increase of voltage produced across the load resistor (R_L). This drop in VC will be fed back to the base and will result in a decrease in the base current. The decrease in base current will oppose the original increase in collector current and tend to stabilize it. The exact opposite effect is produced when the collector current decreases.

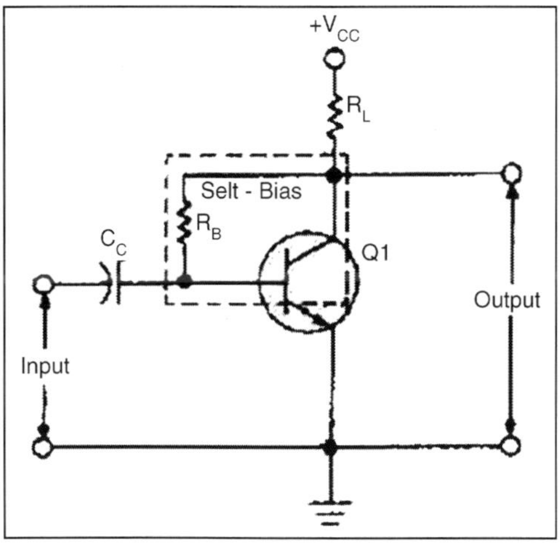

Self-bias has two small drawbacks:

1. It is only partially effective and, therefore, is only used where moderate changes in ambient temperature are expected;
2. It reduces amplification since the signal on the collector also affects the base voltage.

This is because the collector and base signals for this particular amplifier configuration are 180 degrees out of phase (opposite in polarity) and the part of the collector signal that is fed back to the base cancels some of the input signal. This process of returning a part of the output back to its input is known as *Degeneration* or *Negative Feedback*. Sometimes degeneration is desired to prevent amplitude distortion (an output signal that fails to follow the input exactly) and self-bias may be used for this purpose.

6

Equivalent Circuits of Transistor Amplifier

A *port* is a pair of terminals of a network (circuit). Across the port is a voltage, *v*, and through it flows a current, *i*, as shown below.

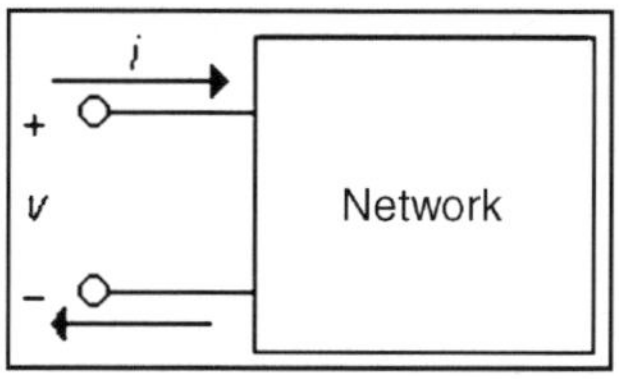

Amplifiers have two ports, input and output. An electrical *waveform* is a voltage or current as a function of time. A waveform to be amplified is applied to the input port and another waveform appears at the output port that is larger than the input waveform. Input and output quantities can be either voltages or currents, resulting in four basic kinds of amplifiers:

Amplifier Type	Input Quantity	Output Quantity
Voltage, A_v	voltage, v_i	voltage, v_o
Current, A_i	current, i_i	current, i_o
Transresistance, R_m	current, i_i	voltage, v_o
Transconductance, G_m	voltage, v_i	current, i_o

In the table under amplifier type is the expression for amplification or *gain* (or *transfer function*), which is the output quantity divided by the input quantity. In general, $A = x_o/x_i$, where *x*is either a voltage or current. An ideal input port is not affected by input source resistance nor is an ideal output port affected by output load resistance. The general amplifier is shown below:

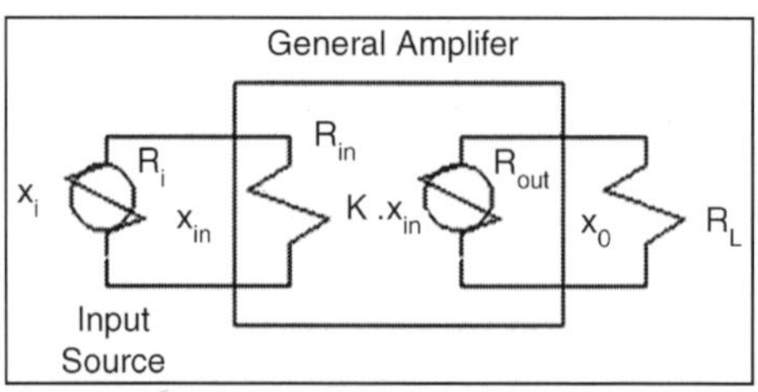

The combination source/resistance symbol is a generalized source: either a Thevenin or Norton equivalent circuit. The amplifier has an input resistance R_{in} and output resistance, R_{out}.

The input source, x_i (where x_i is v_i or i_i), has resistance R_i. It forms a divider (voltage or current) with R_{in} so that $x_i \neq x_{in}$. Similarly, output resistance R_{out} forms a divider with output port load resistance R_L so that the output $x_{out} = K \times x_{in} \neq x_0$.

The amplification of x_{in} by K results in x_{out} that is K times larger. K is the gain, and it scales x_{in}. (Gain less than 1 is called *attenuation*.) If source or load resistance is unknown or varies with K, then error in the overall amount of gain results. An accurate (or at least unchanging) gain is required for calibrated sensor circuits, so that the transducer output is multiplied by a known (and constant) amount.

An example of a voltage amplifier is shown below:

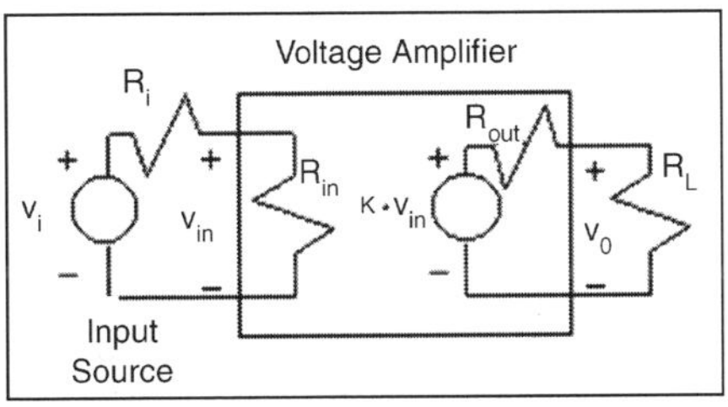

The overall voltage *gain* is:

$$A_v = \frac{v_0}{v_i} = \left(\frac{v_{in}}{v_i}\right)\left(\frac{v_{out}}{v_{in}}\right)\left(\frac{v_0}{v_{out}}\right)$$

$$= \left(\frac{R_{in}}{R_i + R_{in}}\right)(k)\left(\frac{R_L}{R_0 + R_L}\right)$$

The first factor is the input voltage divider attenuation, the second is the amplifier voltage gain and the third is the output voltage divider attenuation. For the ideal voltage amplifier, $A_v = K$. This is achieved when R_{in} approaches infinity (open-circuit input) and $R_0 = 0$.

The ideal port resistances are given in the following table:

Port Type	**Ideal Resistance**
Voltage input	infinite (open)
Current input	zero
Voltage output	zero
Current output	infinite (open)

In practice, good amplifier design approaches the ideal so that input and output loading does not affect the overall amplifier gain accuracy.

TRANSISTOR CONFIGURATIONS

Transistors have three terminals connected to input and output circuit loops. One-transistor amplifiers are two-port networks; one of the three transistor terminals must be shared by both input and output ports as the common terminal. This results in three possibilities. The first is the *common emitter* (CE) amplifier. The emitter is common to both input and output, as shown below.

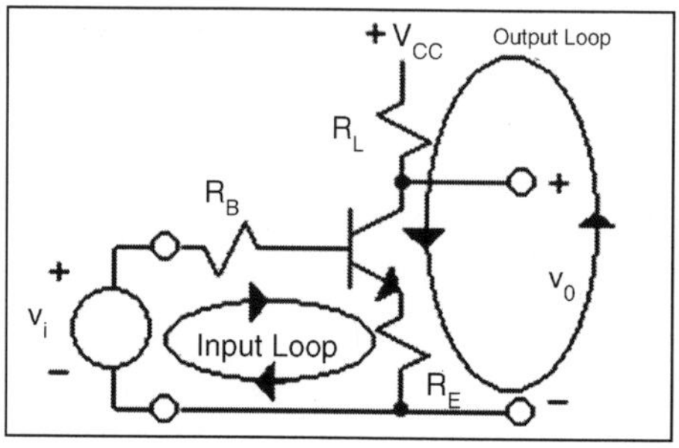

The emitter is part of both input and output loops. It is the common terminal of the transistor that is connected to both an input and output port terminal. With a series emitter resistor R_E the emitter terminal is still common to both loops.

The output loop current is shown flowing from the power supply ($+V_{CC}$), through R_L and the BJT, through R_E to ground, which is connected to the negative terminal of the supply. The closure of the output loop from ground to $+V_{CC}$ implies flow through the voltage-source, $+V_{CC}$.

The common-base (CB) configuration is shown below:

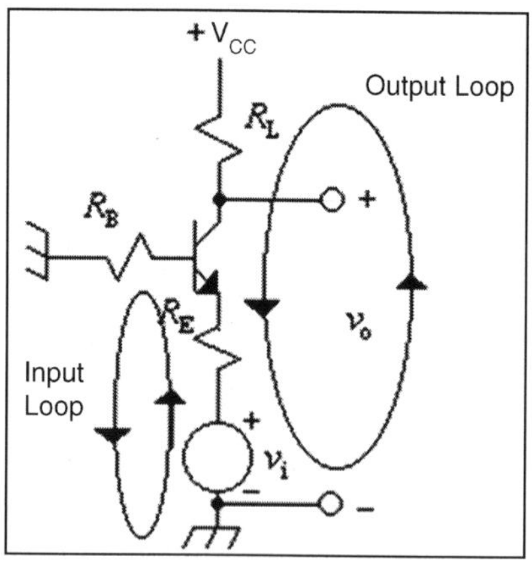

The common-collector (CE) configuration, also known as the *emitter-follower*, is shown below.

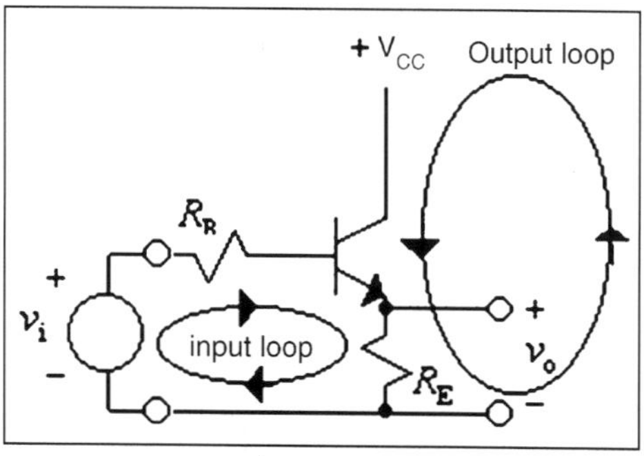

VOLTAGE AND POWER GAINS

Then the gain of an amplifier can be said to be the relationship that exists between the signal measured at the output with the signal measured at the input. There are three different kinds of Amplifier Gain, Voltage Gain, (Av), Current Gain (Ai) and Power Gain (Ap) and examples of these are given below.

AMPLIFIER GAIN OF THE INPUT SIGNAL

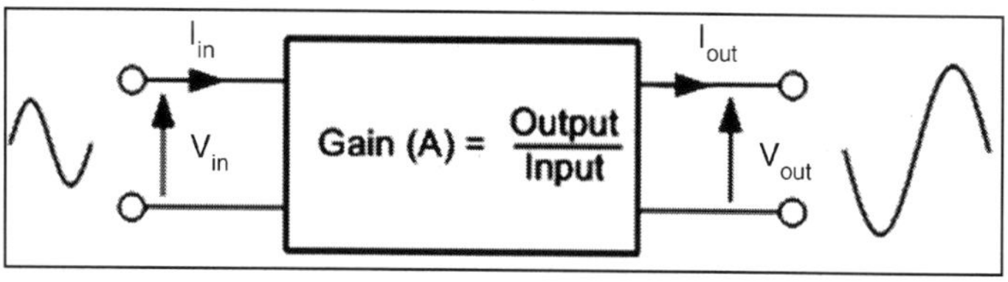

Fig. Amplification Stage

VOLTAGE AMPLIFIER GAIN

$$Voltage\,Gain(A_v) = \frac{Output\,Voltage}{Input\,Voltage} = \frac{V_{out}}{V_{in}}$$

CURRENT AMPLIFIER GAIN

$$Current\,Gain(A_i) = \frac{Output\,Current}{Input\,Current} = \frac{I_{out}}{I_{in}}.$$

POWER AMPLIFIER GAIN

$$Power\,Gain(A_p) = A_v \times A_i.$$

Note that for the Power Gain you can also divide the power obtained at the output with the power obtained at the input. Also when calculating the gain of an amplifier, the subscripts v, i and p are used to denote the type of signal gain being used. The power Gain or power level of the amplifier can also be expressed in Decibels, (dB). The Bel is a logarithmic unit (base 10) of measurement that has no units. Since the Bel is too large a unit of measure, it is prefixed with *deci* making it Decibels instead with one decibel being one tenth (1/10th) of a Bel. To calculate the gain of the amplifier in Decibels or dB, we can use the following expressions.

- Voltage Gain in dB: $a_v = 20 \log Av$
- Current Gain in dB: $a_i = 20 \log Ai$
- Power Gain in dB: $a_p = 10 \log Ap$

Note that the DC power gain of an amplifier is equal to ten times the common log of the output to input ratio, where as voltage and current gains are 20 times the common log of the ratio. Note however, that 20dB is not twice as much power as 10dB because of the log scale. Also, a positive value of dB represents a Gain and a negative value of dB represents a Loss within the amplifier.

For example, an amplifier gain of +3dB indicates that the amplifiers output signal has "doubled", (x2) while an amplifier gain of -3dB indicates that the signal has "halved", (x0.5) or in other words a loss. The -3dB point of an amplifier is called the half-power point which is -3dB down from maximum, taking 0dB as the maximum output value.

ALTERNATIVE AC EQUIVALENT CIRCUITS FOR THE AMPLIFIER

An *operational amplifier* ("op-amp") is a DC-coupled high-gain electronic voltage amplifier with a differential input and, usually, a single-ended output. An op-amp produces an output voltage that is typically hundreds of thousands times larger than the voltage *difference* between its input terminals.

Operational amplifiers are important building blocks for a wide range of electronic circuits. They had their origins in analog computers where they were used in many linear, non-linear and frequency-dependent circuits. Their popularity in circuit design largely stems from the fact that characteristics of the final op-amp circuits with negative feedback (such as their gain) are set by external components with little dependence on temperature changes and manufacturing variations in the op-amp itself.

Op-amps are among the most widely used electronic devices today, being used in a vast array of consumer, industrial, and scientific devices. Many standard IC op-amps cost only a few cents in moderate production volume; however some integrated or hybrid operational amplifiers with special performance specifications may cost over $100 US in small quantities.Op-amps may be packaged as components, or used as elements of more complex integrated circuits. The op-amp is one type of differential amplifier. Other types of differential amplifier include the fully differential amplifier (similar to the op-amp, but with two outputs), the instrumentation amplifier (usually built from three op-amps), the isolation amplifier (similar to the instrumentation amplifier, but with tolerance to common-mode voltages that would destroy an ordinary op-amp), and negative feedback amplifier (usually built from one or more op-amps and a resistive feedback network).

RELATIONSHIP BETWEEN INPUT AND OUTPUT OF A TRANSISTOR AMPLIFIER

The current flowing between emitter and collector of a transistor is much greater than that flowing between base and emitter. So a small base current is controlling the much larger emitter collector current. The ratio of the two currents, I_{CE}/I_{BE} is constant, provided that the collector emitter voltage V_{CE} is constant.

Therefore, if the base current rises, so does collector current. This ratio is the CURRENT GAIN of the transistor and is given the symbol h_{fe}. A fairly low gain transistor might have a current gain of 20 to 50, while a high gain type may have a gain of 300 to 800 or more. The spread of values of h_{fe} for any given transistor is quite large, even in transistors of the same type and batch.

CHARACTERISTIC

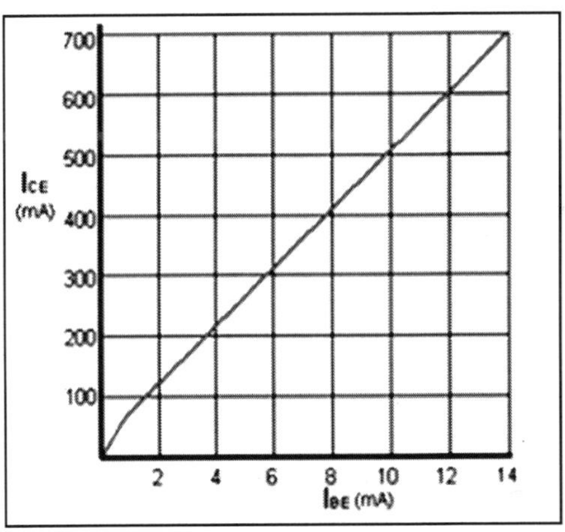

Fig. Transfer Characteristic

The graph of I_{CE}/I_{BE} shown (right) is called the *Transfer Characterstic* and the slope of the graph shows the h_{fe} for that transistor.

Characteristic curves (graphs) can be drawn to show other parameters of a transistor, and are used both to detail the performance of a particular device and as an aid to the design of amplifiers.

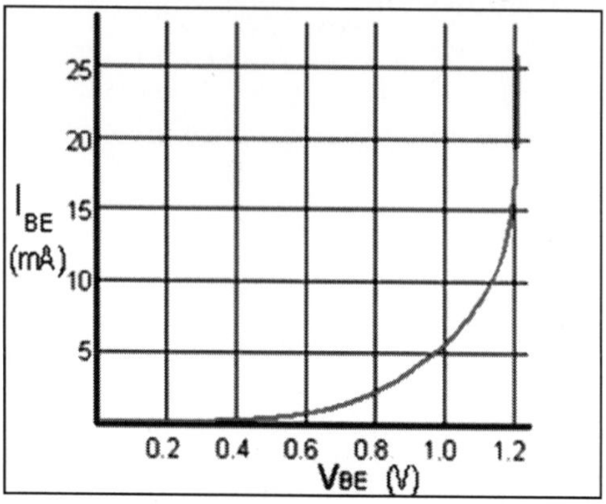

Fig. Input Characteristic

The *Input Characterstic* is a graph of base emitter current I_{BE} against base emitter voltage V_{BE} (I_{BE}/V_{BE}) shows the input *Conductance* of the transistor. As conductance I/V is the reciprocal of RESISTANCE (V/I) this curve can be used to determine the input resistance of the transistor.

The steepness of this particular curve when the V_{BE} is above 1 volt shows that the input conductance is very high, and there is a large increase in current (in practice, usually enough to destroy the transistor!) for a very small increase in V_{BE}. Therefore the input RESISTANCE must be low. Around 0.6 to 0.7 volts the graph curves shows that the input resistance of a transistor varies, according to the amount of base current flowing, and below about 0.5 volts base current ceases.

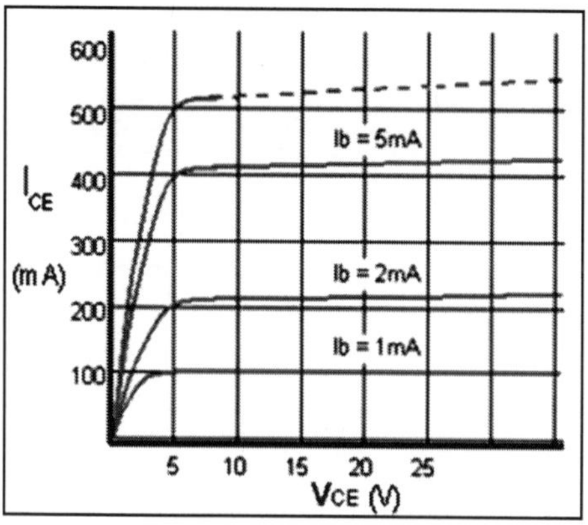

Fig. Output Characteristic

Figure shows the *Output Characterstic* whose slope gives the value of output conductance (and by implication output resistance). The near horizontal parts of the graph lines show that a change in collector emitter voltage V_{CE} has almost no effect on collector current in this region, just the effect to be expected if the transistor output had a large value resistor in series with it. Therefore the graph shows that the output resistance of the transistor is high.

The above characteristic graphs show that, for a silicon transistor with an input applied between base and emitter, and output taken between collector and emitter (a method of connection called common emitter mode) one would expect;

- Low input resistance (from the input characteristic).
- Fairly high gain (from the transfer characteristic).
- High output resistance (from the output characteristic).

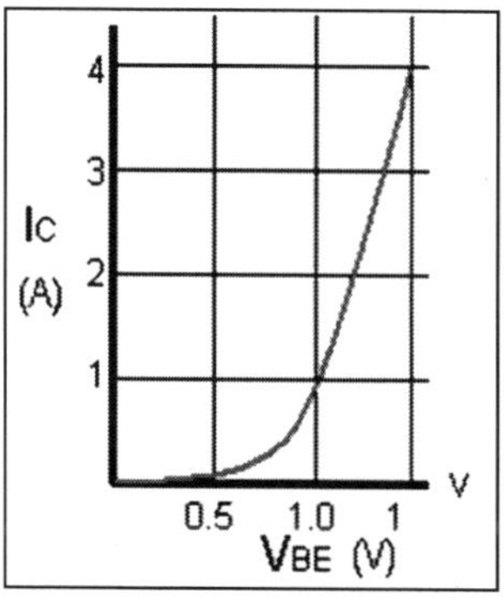

Fig. Mutual Characteristic

Figure shows, the *Mutual Characteristic* shows a graph of *Mutual Conductance* I_C/V_{BE} and illustrates the change in collector current which takes place for a given change in base emitter voltage, (*i.e.* input signal voltage). This graph is for a typical silicon power transistor. Notice the large collector currents possible, and the nearly linear relationship between the input voltage and output current. The characteristics described on this page are those relating to a typical power transistor connected in the "common emitter" mode.

Note: In many transistors the currents will be much smaller than shown here. For small signal amplifiers, base currents will be a few micro"amps rather than milli"amps.

ANALYSIS OF TRANSISTOR AMPLIFIER

In the Bipolar Transistor tutorial, we saw that the most common circuit configuration for an NPN transistor is that of the Common Emitter Amplifier and that a family of curves known commonly as theOutput Characteristics Curves, relates the Collector current (Ic), to the output or Collector voltage (Vce), for different values of Base current (Ib).

All types of transistor amplifiers operate using AC signal inputs which alternate between a positive value and a negative value so some way of "presetting" the amplifier circuit to operate between these two maximum or peak values is required. This is achieved using a process known as Biasing.

Biasing is very important in amplifier design as it establishes the correct operating point of the transistor amplifier ready to receive signals, thereby reducing any distortion to the output signal. We also saw that a static or DC load line can be drawn onto these output characteristics curves to show all the possible operating points of the transistor from fully "ON" to fully "OFF", and to which the quiescent operating point or Q-point of the amplifier can be found. The aim of any small signal amplifier is to amplify all of the input signal with the minimum amount of distortion possible to the output signal, in other words, the output signal must be an exact reproduction of the input signal but only bigger (amplified).

To obtain low distortion when used as an amplifier the operating quiescent point needs to be correctly selected. This is in fact the DC operating point of the amplifier and its position may be established at any point along the load line by a suitable biasing arrangement. The best possible position for this Q-point is as close to the centre position of the load line as reasonably possible, thereby producing a Class A type amplifier operation, *i.e.* Vce = 1/2Vcc. Consider the Common Emitter Amplifier circuit shown below.

The Common Emitter Amplifier Circuit

The single stage common emitter amplifier circuit shown above uses what is commonly called "Voltage Divider Biasing".

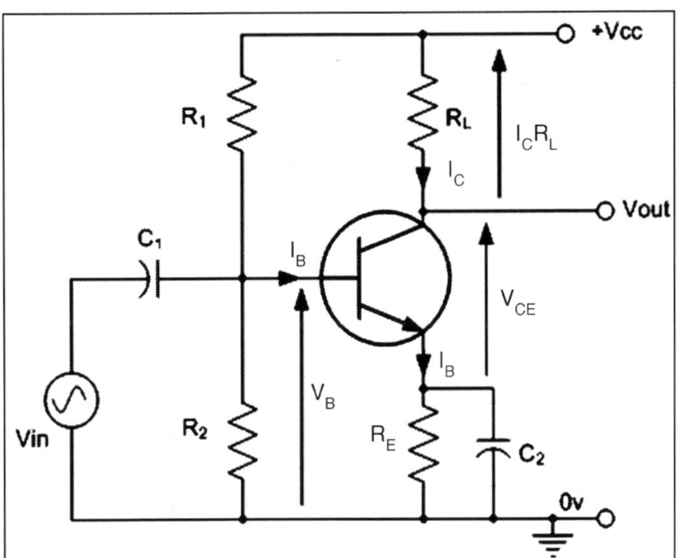

This type of biasing arrangement uses two resistors as a potential divider network and is commonly used in the design of bipolar transistor amplifier circuits.

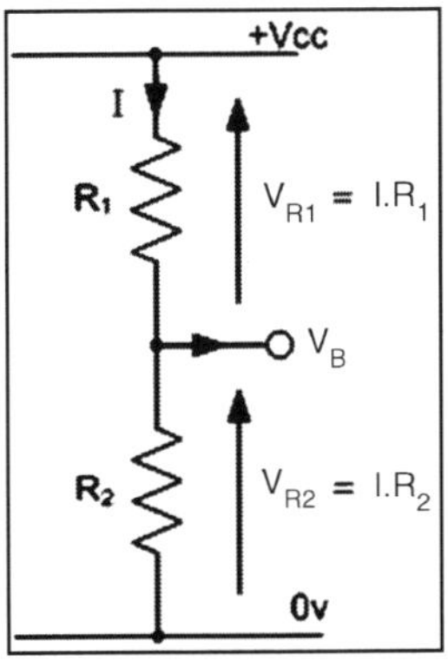

This method of biasing the transistor greatly reduces the effects of varying Beta, (β) by holding the Base bias at a constant steady voltage level allowing for best stability. The quiescent Base voltage (V_b) is determined by the potential divider network formed by the two resistors, R_1, R_2 and the power supply voltage V_{cc} as shown with the current flowing through both resistors. Then the total resistance RT will be equal to $R_1 + R_2$ giving the current as $i = V_{cc}/RT$. The voltage level generated at the junction of resistors R_1 and R_2 holds the Base voltage (V_b) constant at a value below the supply voltage. Then the potential divider network used in the common emitter amplifier circuit divides the input signal in proportion to the resistance.

This bias reference voltage can be easily calculated using the simple voltage divider formula below:

$$V_B = \frac{V_{CC} R_2}{R_1 + R_2}.$$

The same supply voltage, (V_{CC}) also determines the maximum Collector current, Ic when the transistor is switched fully "ON" (saturation), Vce = 0. The Base current Ib for the transistor is found from the Collector current, Ic and the DC current gain Beta, β of the transistor.

$$\beta = \frac{\Delta I_C}{\Delta I_B}.$$

Beta is sometimes referred to as h_{FE} which is the transistors forward current gain in the common emitter configuration. Beta has no units as it is a fixed ratio of the two currents, I_C and I_b so a small change in the Base current will cause a large change in the Collector current. One final point about Beta. Transistors of the same type and part number will have large variations in their Beta value for example, the BC107 NPN Bipolar transistor has a DC current gain Beta value of between 110 and 450 (data sheet value) this is because Beta is a characteristic of their construction and not their operation.

As the Base/Emitter junction is forward-biased, the Emitter voltage, Ve will be one junction voltage drop different to the Base voltage. If the voltage across the Emitter resistor is known then the Emitter current,Ie can be easily calculated using *Ohm's Law*. The Collector current, Ic can be approximated, since it is almost the same value as the Emitter current.

CIRCUIT OF COMMON EMITTER AMPLIFIER

Then to summarize. The Common Emitter Amplifier circuit has a resistor in its Collector circuit. The current flowing through this resistor produces the voltage output of the amplifier. The value of this resistor is chosen so that at the amplifiers quiescent operating point, Q–point this output voltage lies half way along the transistors load line.

The Base of the transistor used in a common emitter amplifier is biased using two resistors as a potential divider network. This type of biasing arrangement is commonly used in the design of bipolar transistor amplifier circuits and greatly reduces the effects of varying Beta, (b) by holding the Base bias at a constant steady voltage.

This type of biasing produces the greatest stability. A resistor can be included in the emitter leg in which case the voltage gain becomes$-R_L/R_E$. If there is no external Emitter resistance, the voltage gain of the amplifier is not infinite as there is a very small internal resistance, R_e in the Emitter leg. The value of this internal resistance is equal to $25mV/I_E$

In the next tutorial about Amplifiers we will look at the Junction Field Effect Amplifier commonly called theJFET Amplifier. Like the transistor, the JFET is used in a single stage amplifier circuit making it easier to understand. There are several different kinds of field effect transistor that we could use but the easiest to understand is the junction field effect transistor, or JFET which has a very high input impedance making it ideal for amplifier circuits.

CIRCUIT

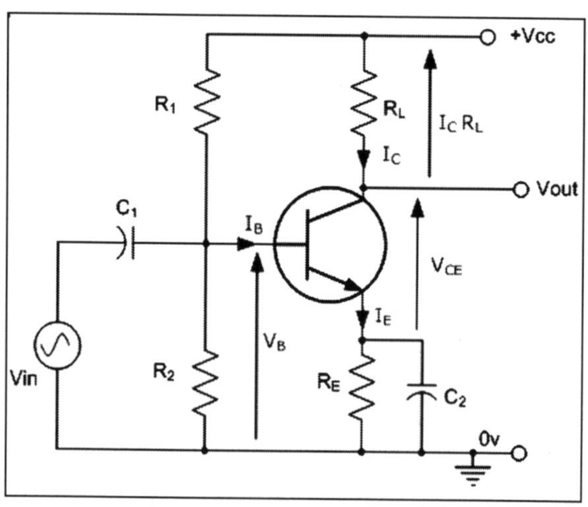

The single stage common emitter amplifier circuit shown above uses what is commonly called "Voltage Divider Biasing". This type of biasing arrangement uses two resistors as a potential divider network and is commonly used in the design of bipolar transistor amplifier circuits. This method of biasing the transistor greatly reduces the effects of varying Beta, (β) by holding the Base bias at a constant steady voltage level allowing for best stability.

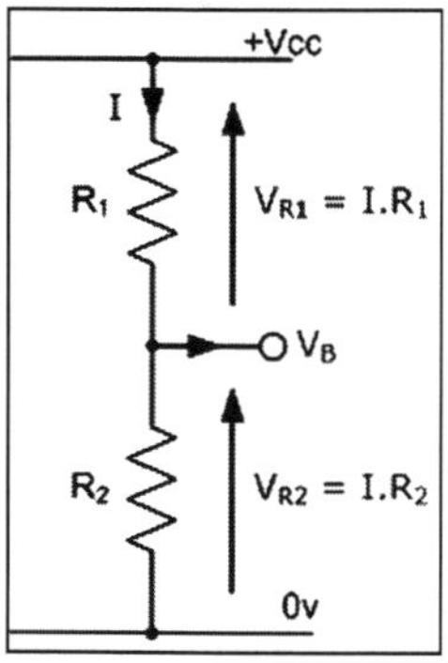

The quiescent Base voltage (Vb) is determined by the potential divider network formed by the two resistors, R_1, R_2 and the power supply voltage Vcc as shown with the current flowing through both resistors. Then the total resistance RT will be equal to $R_1 + R_2$ giving the current as $i = V_{CC}/RT$. The voltage level generated at the junction of resistors R_1 and R_2 holds the Base voltage (V_b) constant at a value below the supply voltage. Then the potential divider network used in the common emitter amplifier circuit divides the input signal in proportion to the resistance. This bias reference voltage can be easily calculated using the simple voltage divider formula below:

$$V_B = \frac{V_{CC} R_2}{R_1 + R_2}$$

The same supply voltage, (V_{CC}) also determines the maximum Collector current, I_c when the transistor is switched fully "ON" (saturation), $V_{ce} = 0$. The Base current Ib for the transistor is found from the Collector current, Ic and the DC current gain Beta, β of the transistor.

$$\beta = \frac{\Delta I_C}{\Delta I_B}.$$

Beta is sometimes referred to as hFE which is the transistors forward current gain in the common emitter configuration. Beta has no units as it is a fixed ratio of the two currents, I_c and I_b so a small change in the Base current will cause a large change in the Collector current. One final point about Beta. Transistors of the same type and part number will have large variations in their Beta value for example, the BC107 NPN Bipolar transistor has a DC current gain Beta value of between 110 and 450 (data sheet value) this is because Beta is a characteristic of their construction and not their operation.

As the Base/Emitter junction is forward-biased, the Emitter voltage, Ve will be one junction voltage drop different to the Base voltage. If the voltage across the Emitter resistor is known then the Emitter current,Ie can be easily calculated using Ohm's Law. The Collector current, I_c can be approximated, since it is almost the same value as the Emitter current.

COUPLING CAPACITORS

In Common Emitter Amplifier circuits, capacitors C_1 and C_2 are used as Coupling Capacitors to separate the AC signals from the DC biasing voltage. This ensures that the bias condition set up for the circuit to operate correctly is not effected by any additional amplifier stages, as the capacitors will only pass AC signals and block any DC component. The output AC signal is then superimposed on the biasing of the following stages. Also a bypass capacitor, CE is included in the Emitter leg circuit.

This capacitor is an open circuit component for DC bias meaning that the biasing currents and voltages are not affected by the addition of the capacitor maintaining a good Q-point stability. However, this bypass capacitor short circuits the Emitter resistor at high frequency signals and only RL plus a very small internal resistance acts as the transistors load increasing the voltage gain to its maximum. Generally, the value of the bypass capacitor, CE is chosen to provide a reactance of at most, 1/10th the value of REat the lowest operating signal frequency.

OUTPUT CHARACTERISTICS CURVES

Ok, so far so good. We can now construct a series of curves that show the Collector current, I_c against the Collector/Emitter voltage, Vce with different values of Base current, Ib for our simple common emitter amplifier circuit. These curves are known as the "Output Characteristic Curves" and are used to show how the transistor will operate over its dynamic range. A static or DC load line is drawn onto the curves for the load resistor RL of 1.2kΩ to show all the transistors possible operating points.

When the transistor is switched "OFF", Vce equals the supply voltage Vcc and this is point B on the line. Likewise when the transistor is fully "ON" and saturated the Collector current is determined by the load resistor, RL and this is point A on the line. We calculated before from the DC gain of the transistor that the Base current required for the mean position of the transistor was 45.8μA and this is marked as point Q on the load line which represents the Quiescent point or Q-point of the amplifier.

We could quite easily make life easy for ourselves and round off this value to 50μA exactly, without any effect to the operating point. Point Q on the load line gives us the Base current Q-point of Ib = 45.8μA or 46μA. We need to find the maximum and minimum peak swings of Base current that will result in a proportional change to the Collector current, Ic without any distortion to the output signal. As the load line cuts through the different Base current values on the DC characteristics curves we can find the peak swings of Base current that are equally spaced along the load line.

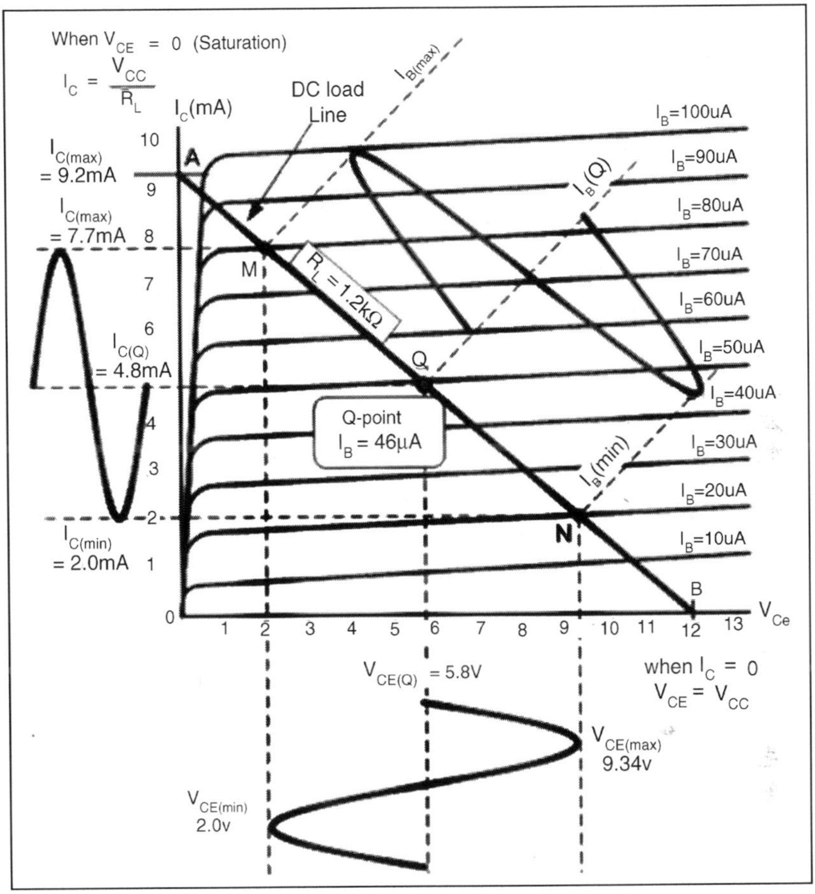

Fig. Output Characteristics Curves

These values are marked as points N and M on the line, giving a minimum and a maximum Base current of 20μA and 80μA respectively. These points, N and M can be anywhere along the load line that we choose as long as they are equally spaced from Q. This then gives us a theoretical maximum input signal to the Base terminal of 60μA peak-to-peak, (30ìμA peak) without producing any distortion to the output signal. Any input signal giving a Base current greater than this value will drive the transistor to go beyond point N and into its Cut-off region or beyond point M and into its Saturation region thereby resulting in distortion to the output signal in the form of "clipping".

Using points N and M as an example, the instantaneous values of Collector current and corresponding values of Collector-emitter voltage can be projected from the load line. It can be seen that the Collector-emitter voltage is in anti-phase (–180°) with the collector current.

As the Base current Ib changes in a positive direction from 50μA to 80μA, the Collector-emitter voltage, which is also the output voltage decreases from its steady state value of 5.8v to 2.0v. Then a single stage Common Emitter Amplifier is also an "Inverting Amplifier" as an increase in Base voltage causes a decrease in Vout and a decrease in Base voltage produces an increase in Vout.

VOLTAGE GAIN

The Voltage Gain of the common emitter amplifier is equal to the ratio of the change in the input voltage to the change in the amplifiers output voltage. Then ΔVL is Vout and ΔVB is Vin. But voltage gain is also equal to the ratio of the signal resistance in the Collector to the signal resistance in the Emitter and is given as:

$$Voltage\,Gain = \frac{V_{out}}{V_{in}} = \frac{\Delta V_L}{\Delta V_B}$$

$$= -\frac{R_L}{R_E}$$

We mentioned earlier that as the signal frequency increases the bypass capacitor, CE starts to short out the Emitter resistor. Then at high frequencies RE = 0, making the gain infinite.

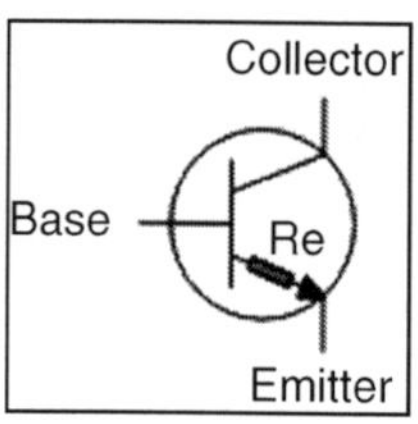

However, bipolar transistors have a small internal resistance built into their Emitter region called Re. The transistors semiconductor material offers an internal resistance to the flow of current through it and is generally represented by a small resistor symbol shown inside the main transistor symbol. Transistor data sheets tell us that for a small signal bipolar transistors this internal resistance is the product of 25mV ÷ Ie (25mV being the internal volt drop across the Base/Emitter junction depletion layer), then for our common Emitter amplifier circuit above this resistance value will be equal to:

$$R_e = \frac{25mV}{I_E}$$
$$= \frac{25mV}{4.58mA}$$
$$= 5.5\Omega.$$

This internal Emitter leg resistance will be in series with the external Emitter resistor, RE, then the equation for the transistors actual gain will be modified to include this internal resistance and is given as:

$$Voltage\,Gain = -\frac{R_L}{(R_E + R_e)}$$

At low frequency signals the total resistance in the Emitter leg is equal to $R_E + R_e$. At high frequency, the bypass capacitor shorts out the Emitter resistor leaving only the internal resistance R_e in the Emitter leg resulting in a high gain. Then for our common emitter amplifier circuit above, the gain of the circuit at both low and high signal frequencies is given as:

At Low Frequencies,

$$Gain = -\frac{R_L}{(R_E + R_e)}$$
$$= -\frac{1200}{220 + 5.5}$$
$$= -5.32$$

At High Frequencies

$$Gain = -\frac{R_L}{R_e}$$
$$= -\frac{1200}{5.5}$$
$$= -2.18$$

One final point, the voltage gain is dependent only on the values of the Collector resistor, R_L and the Emitter resistance, $(R_E + R_e)$ it is not affected by the current gain Beta, β (hFE) of the transistor.

So, for our simple example above we can now summarise all the values we have calculated for our common emitter amplifier circuit and these are:

	Minimum	**Mean**	**Maximum**
Base Current	20μA	50μA	80μA
Collector Current	2.0mA	4.8mA	7.7mA
Output Voltage Swing	2.0V	5.8V	9.3V
Amplifier Gain	-5.32		-218

SUMMARY

The Common Emitter Amplifier circuit has a resistor in its Collector circuit. The current flowing through this resistor produces the voltage output of the amplifier. The value of this resistor is chosen so that at the amplifiers quiescent operating point, Q-point this output voltage lies half way along the transistors load line.

The Base of the transistor used in a common emitter amplifier is biased using two resistors as a potential divider network. This type of biasing arrangement is commonly used in the design of bipolar transistor amplifier circuits and greatly reduces the effects of varying Beta, (β) by holding the Base bias at a constant steady voltage.

This type of biasing produces the greatest stability. A resistor can be included in the emitter leg in which case the voltage gain becomes -RL/RE. If there is no external Emitter resistance, the voltage gain of the amplifier is not infinite as there is a very small internal resistance, Re in the Emitter leg. The value of this internal resistance is equal to 25mV/IE.

EFFECT ON AN EMITTER BYPASS CAPACITOR

Amplitude distortion occurs when the peak values of the frequency waveform are attenuated causing distortion due to a shift in the Q–point and amplification may not take place over the whole signal cycle. This non–linearity of the output waveform is shown below.

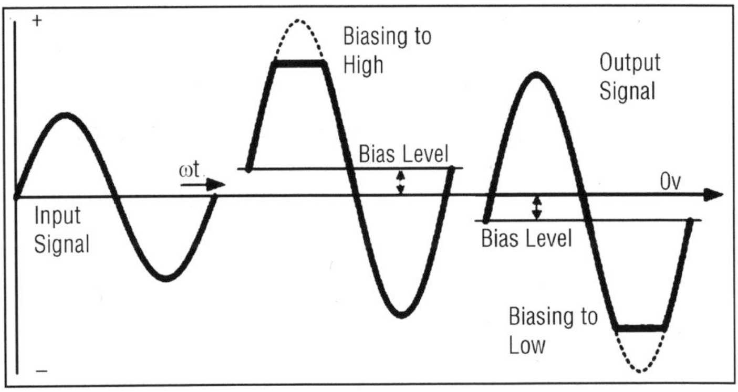

Fig. Amplitude Distortion due to Incorrect Biasing

If the bias is correct the output waveform should look like that of the input waveform only bigger, (amplified). If there is insufficient bias the output waveform will look like the one on the right with the negative part of the output waveform "cut–off".

If there is too much bias the output waveform will look like the one on the left with the positive part "cut–off". When the bias voltage is too small, during the negative part of the cycle the transistor does not conduct fully so the output is set by the supply voltage. When the bias is too great the positive part of the cycle saturates the transistor and the output drops almost to zero. Even with the correct biasing voltage level set, it is still possible for the output waveform to become distorted due to a large input signal being amplified by the circuits gain.

The output voltage signal becomes clipped in both the positive and negative parts of the waveform an no longer resembles a sine wave, even when the bias is correct. This type of amplitude distortion is called Clipping and is the result of "Over–driving" the input of the amplifier. When the input amplitude becomes too large, the clipping becomes substantial and forces the output waveform signal to exceed the power supply voltage rails with the peak (+ve half) and the trough (–ve half) parts of the waveform signal becoming flattened or "Clipped–off". To avoid this the maximum value of the input signal must be limited to a level that will prevent this clipping effect as shown above.

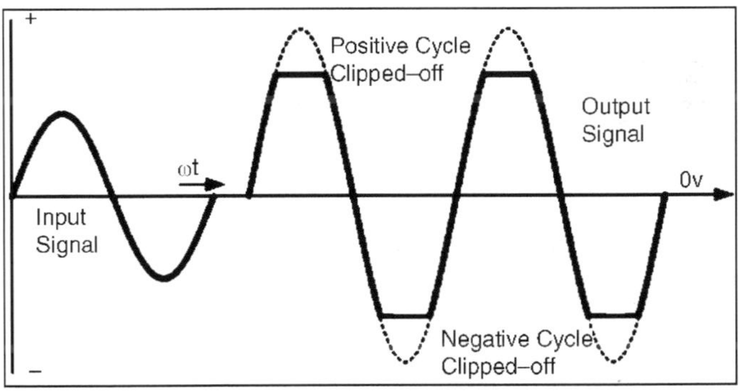

Fig. Amplitude Distortion due to Clipping

Amplitude Distortion greatly reduces the efficiency of an amplifier circuit. These "flat tops" of the distorted output waveform either due to incorrect biasing or over driving the input do not contribute anything to the strength of the output signal at the desired frequency.

Having said all that, some well known guitarist and rock bands actually prefer that their distinctive sound is highly distorted or "overdriven" by heavily clipping the output waveform to both the +ve and–ve power supply rails. Also, excessive amounts of clipping can also produce an output which resembles a "square wave" shape which can then be used in electronic or digital circuits.

We have seen that with a DC signal the level of gain of the amplifier can vary with signal amplitude, but as well as Amplitude Distortion, other types of distortion can occur with AC signals in amplifier circuits, such as Frequency Distortion and Phase Distortion.

FREQUENCY RESPONSE

Frequency Distortion occurs in a transistor amplifier when the level of amplification varies with frequency. Many of the input signals that a practical amplifier will amplify consist of the required signal waveform called the "Fundamental Frequency" plus a number of different frequencies called "Harmonics" superimposed onto it. Normally, the amplitude of these harmonics are a fraction of the fundamental amplitude and therefore have very little or no effect on the output waveform. However, the output waveform can become distorted if these harmonic frequencies increase in amplitude with regards to the fundamental frequency. For example, consider the waveform below:

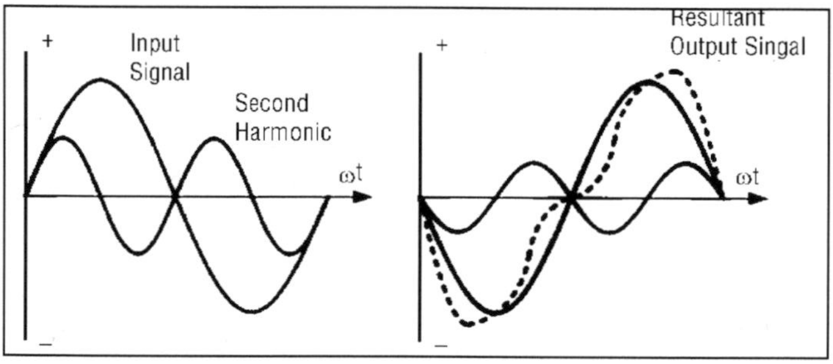

Fig. Frequency Distortion due to Harmonics

In the example above, the input waveform consists a the fundamental frequency plus a second harmonic signal. The resultant output waveform is shown on the right hand side. The frequency distortion occurs when the fundamental frequency combines with the second harmonic to distort the output signal.

Harmonics are therefore multiples of the fundamental frequency and in our simple example a second harmonic was used. Therefore, the frequency of the harmonic is 2 times the fundamental, 2 × f or 2f. Then a third harmonic would be 3f, a fourth, 4f, and so on. Frequency distortion due to harmonics is always a possibility in amplifier circuits containing reactive elements such as capacitance or inductance.

PHASE DISTORTION

Phase Distortion or Delay Distortion occurs in a non–linear transistor amplifier when there is a time delay between the input signal and its appearance at the output. If we call the phase change between the input and the output zero at the fundamental frequency, the resultant phase angle delay will be the difference between the harmonic and the fundamental. This time delay will depend on the construction of the amplifier and will increase progressively with frequency within the bandwidth of the amplifier. For example, consider the waveform below:

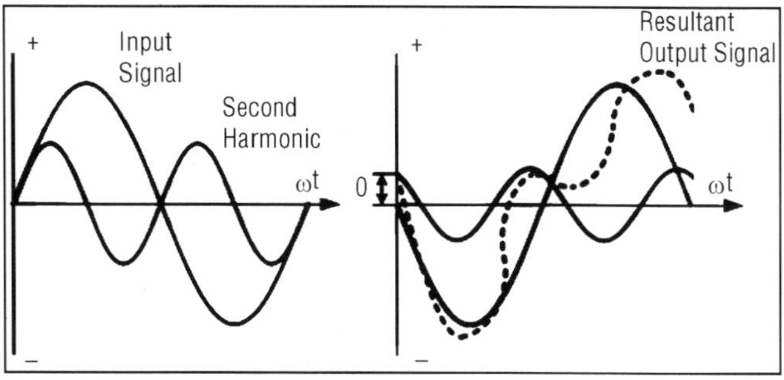

Fig. Phase Distortion due to Delay

Any practical amplifier will have a combination of both "Frequency" and "Phase" distortion together with amplitude distortion but in most applications such as in audio amplifiers or power amplifiers, unless the distortion is excessive or severe it will not generally affect the operation of the system. In the next tutorial about Amplifiers we will look at the Class A Amplifier. Class A amplifiers are the most common type of amplifier output stage making them ideal for use in audio power amplifiers.

Common emitter amplifiers are the most commonly used type of amplifier as they have a large voltage gain. They are designed to produce a large output voltage swing from a relatively small input signal voltage of only a few millivolt's and are used mainly as "small signal amplifiers" as we saw in the previous tutorials. However, sometimes an amplifier is required to drive large resistive loads such as a loudspeaker or to drive a motor in a robot and for these types of applications where high switching currents are needed Power Amplifiers are required. The main function of the power amplifier, which are also known as a "large signal amplifier" is to deliver power, which is the product of voltage and current to the load. Basically a power amplifier is also a voltage amplifier the difference being that the load resistance connected to the output is relatively low, for example a loudspeaker of 4 or 8Ws resulting in high currents flowing through the collector of the transistor. Because of these high load currents the output transistor(s) used for power amplifier output stages such as the 2N3055 need to have higher voltage and power ratings than the general ones used for small signal amplifiers such as the BC107. Since we are interested in delivering maximum AC power to the load, while consuming the minimum DC power possible from the supply we are mostly concerned with the "conversion efficiency" of the amplifier.

However, one of the main disadvantage of power amplifiers and especially the Class A amplifier is that their overall conversion efficiency is very low as large currents mean that a considerable amount of power is lost in the form of heat. Percentage efficiency in amplifiers is defined as the r.m.s. output power dissipated in the load divided by the total DC power taken from the supply source as shown below.

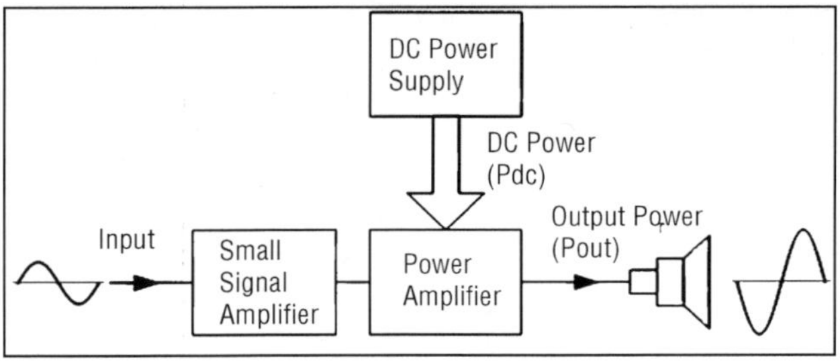

Fig. Power Amplifier Efficiency

$$\eta\% = \frac{P_{OUT}}{P_{DC}} \times 100.$$

Where:

- $\eta\%$: Is the efficiency of the amplifier.
- *Pout:* Is the amplifiers output power delivered to the load.
- *Pdc*: Is the DC power taken from the supply.

For a power amplifier it is very important that the amplifiers power supply is well designed to provide the maximum available continuous power to the output signal.

COMMON SOURCE AMPLIFIER AT HIGH FREQUENCIES

In electronics, a common-source amplifier is one of three basic single-stage field-effect transistor (FET) amplifier topologies, typically used as a voltage or transconductance amplifier. The easiest way to tell if a FET is common source, common drain, or common gate is to examine where the signal enters and leaves.

The remaining terminal is what is known as "common". In this example, the signal enters the gate, and exits the drain. The only terminal remaining is the source. This is a common-source FET circuit. The analogous bipolar junction transistor circuit is the common-emitter amplifier.

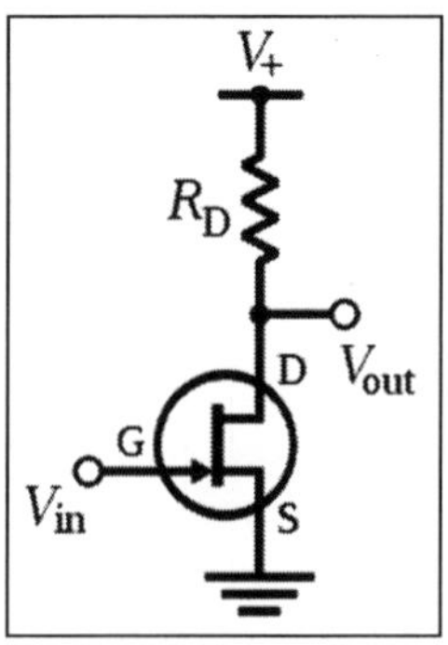

The common-source (CS) amplifier may be viewed as a transconductance amplifier or as a voltage amplifier. As a transconductance amplifier, the input voltage is seen as modulating the current going to the load. As a voltage amplifier, input voltage modulates the amount of current flowing through the FET, changing the voltage across the output resistance according to Ohm's law. However, the FET device's output resistance typically is not high enough for a reasonable transconductance amplifier (ideally infinite), nor low enough for a decent voltage amplifier (ideally zero).

Another major drawback is the amplifier's limited high-frequency response. Therefore, in practice the output often is routed through either a voltage follower (common-drain or CD stage), or a current follower (common-gate or CG stage), to obtain more favorable output and frequency characteristics. The CS–CG combination is called a cascade amplifier. The bandwidth of the common-source amplifier tends to be low, due to high capacitance resulting from the Miller effect.

The gate-drain capacitance is effectively multiplied by the factor $1+|A_V|$, thus increasing the total input capacitance and lowering the overall bandwidth. Figure shows a MOSFET common-source amplifier with an active load. Figure shows the corresponding small-signal circuit when a load resistor R_L is added at the output node and a Thévenin driver of applied voltage V_A and series resistance R_A is added at the input node.

The limitation on bandwidth in this circuit stems from the coupling of parasitic transistor capacitance C_{gd} between gate and drain and the series resistance of the source R_A. (There are other parasitic capacitances, but they are neglected here as they have only a secondary effect on bandwidth.) Using Miller's theorem, the circuit of Figure is transformed to that of Figure, which shows the *Miller capacitance* C_M on the input side of the circuit. The size of C_M is decided by equating the current in the input circuit of Figure through the Miller capacitance, say i_M, which is:

$$i_M - j\omega C_{MGS} = j\omega C_M v_G,$$

to the current drawn from the input by capacitor C_{gd} in Figure, namely $j\omega C_{gd}$ v_{GD}. These two currents are the same, making the two circuits have the same input behaviour, provided the Miller capacitance is given by:

$$C_M = C_{gd}\frac{v_{GD}}{v_{GS}} = C_{gd}\left(1-\frac{v_D}{v_G}\right).$$

Usually the frequency dependence of the gain v_D/v_G is unimportant for frequencies even somewhat above the corner frequency of the amplifier, which means a low-frequency hybrid-pi model is accurate for determining v_D/v_G. This evaluation is *Miller's approximation* and provides the estimate.

$$\frac{v_D}{v_G} \approx -g_m\left(r_0 / R_L\right),$$

So the Miller capacitance is,

$$C_M = C_{gd}\left(1 + g_m\left(r_0 // R_L\right)\right)$$

The gain $g_m\ (r_O//R_L)$ is large for large R_L, so even a small parasitic capacitance C_{gd} can become a large influence in the frequency response of the amplifier, and many circuit tricks are used to counteract this effect.

One trick is to add a common-gate(current-follower) stage to make a cascode circuit. The current-follower stage presents a load to the common-source stage that is very small, namely the input resistance of the current follower (R_L H≈ $1/g_m$ H≈ $V_{ov}/(2I_D)$. Small R_L reduces C_M. The article on the common-emitter amplifier discusses other solutions to this problem.

BIASING IN MOS AMPLIFIER CIRCUITS

Biasing is the static voltage and current settings for a given device for certain functions of operation. Depending on the needs of the circuit, there may be as many as six different biasing schemes.

But for the most part there are four basic biasing schemes. They are Class A, Class B, Class C and Class AB.

- *Class A*: This is where the device is biased at a point where it will conduct and amplify for the entire signal.
- *Class B*: This is where the device is biased such that it will conduct for only half of the signal.
- *Class C*: This is where the device will only conduct for a small portion of the peak of the signal. It can also be described as any biasing point where the device conducts for less than half of the signal. This biasing scheme is never used in audio and can be found in R.F. applications.
- *Class AB*: This is where the device conducts for more than half of the signal but less than the full signal.

This is as far as I will go here regarding biasing classes. Here we will discuss practical implementation of the different biasing schemes. With tube amplifiers, biasing has been the subject of many many articles and discussions on news group threads. It also seems to be one of the least understood subjects with regard tube sound.

BIAS SETTING SOUND “BETTER” THAN ANOTHER

First, let us examine a simple single stage triode circuit with a standard bias and bypass capacitor:

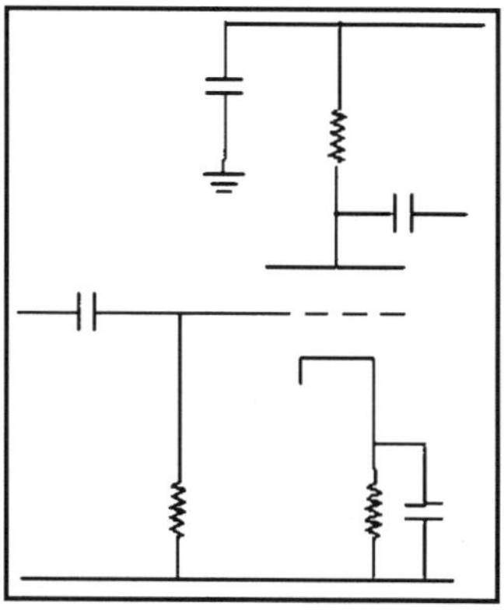

The above circuit is biased at the half points of the tube's maximum parameters. It has a nice sound to it and is loud but has some noise (hiss). However, at strong loud bassy passages, it tends to seem limited but warmer. Sometimes it even seems to drop out. Why is this? Some would claim insufficient transient response from the power supply. It sounds slow, as many would say. But let's take a closer look at this circuit. Let us rotate the circuit 90 degrees to the left. Now let's remove the grid circuit for a minute.

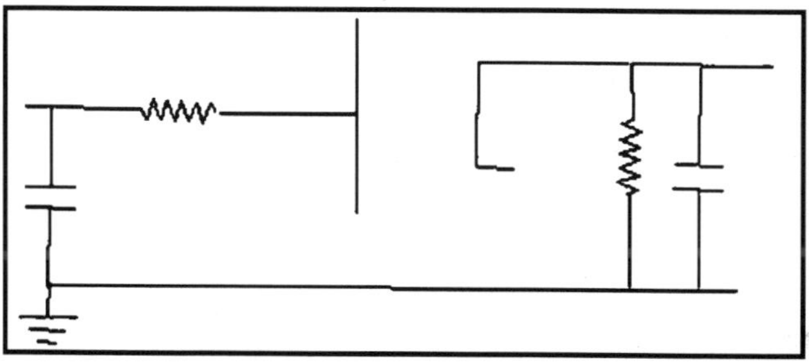

What does it look like now? That's right, a power supply rectifier! A half wave rectifier to be exact. So now what do the cathode resistor and bypass cap look like? A load and *filter*. The bypass cap sees a constant DC signal accompanied by an AC component. To a filter cap, or any capacitor for that matter, this appears as a fluctuating DC, or power supply ripple! To get a bit deeper into the physics of the thing, if one were to calculate the time constant of the RC circuit at the cathode, one will find that for the above circuit the time constant is t=RC, or for the sake of argument, we will use the values I used for the actual circuit, 2200 X.000022 (22 microfarads). The answer is.0484 seconds. What that means is that the capacitor resistor circuit requires about.0484 seconds to charge 63 percent of its full capacity. For the first.0484 seconds, if the capacitor were a 25 volt capacitor, and the bias were set to 2 volts, it would only take the first time constant to reach 2 volts. 0484 seconds factors out to a frequency of 20 hertz (1/t). If I took a 20 hertz signal of.7 volt RMS and inserted it, the positive peak will be 1 volt above the bias of 2 volts. Since the time constant is as small as it is, it wouldn't take much to increase the voltage of the capacitor. This also simultaneously changes the bias of the circuit by about.4 volts (0.404 X Vpeak. The average of the positive portion of a sine wave). Looking at the curve chart below for a triode, this will change the characteristics of the tube which is then amplified through the tube. A larger capacitor will do this more and make things worse.

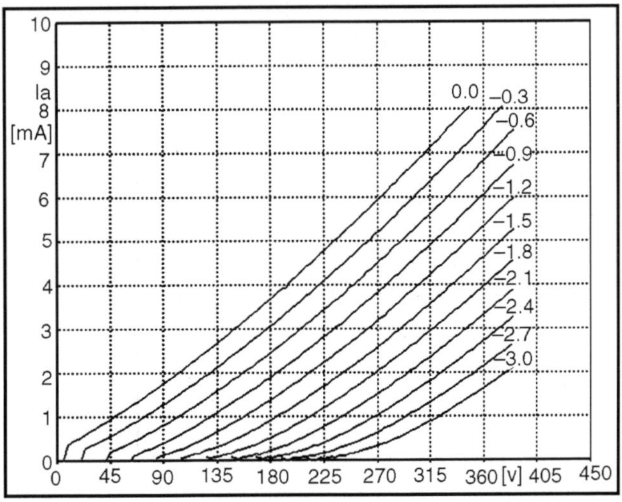

Looking at this chart, go to the 225 on the bottom line. This is the B+. Then go up to the 2.5 line from the left (the Y axis). This is the quiescent, or no input signal, current. For these conditions, it is showing a -1.4 volt grid bias. If the bias were anything different, then one would have to follow the line in the following chart to see the amount of voltage swing the input would accept before clipping. A method for biasing a tube is to draw a line from the B+ voltage to the desired current and choose a bias setting accordingly.

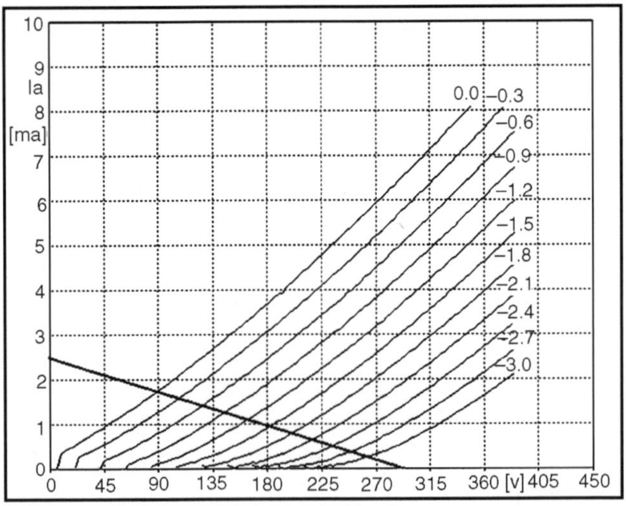

This line is drawn for the modified version of the above circuit I currently listen to. The B+ is 290 volts and the current is about 2 milliamps. If you were to place a pointer at the bias point you designed the amp for, and follow the line, you will see the varying current and the voltage it will produce. Say I had biased the tube for 1.5 volts ("I had a biased point for 1.5 volts"). No I didn't mean for *you* to say it! I start at 1.5 volts on the line, go to zero and I will see that the plate voltage has gone down to 50 volts, while the current went up to 1.8 mA or so.

Then I take the voltage down to -3 volts. This would be a full peak to peak input swing. We can see that the voltage went to about 260 volts, where the current went down to about.3 mA. So the conclusion is that we use the above graph to set static voltages and predict to a relatively good degree the gain. So the output voltage swings about 210 volts peak to peak. This makes it about 74 volts RMS. So the gain can be calculated as Vout/Vin, or 74/1.06= about 70. Theoretically, that is.

For the sound quality we want, we need to use a transfer chart in conjunction with this one. It is a chart which shows the relationship between grid voltage and plate current. If we bias the tube along the most linear part of this line, and follow it with a nominal voltage swing across to the above chart, then one can find where clean signals end and clipping begins. Unfortunately I do not have a true chart, but the below will illustrate what I mean.

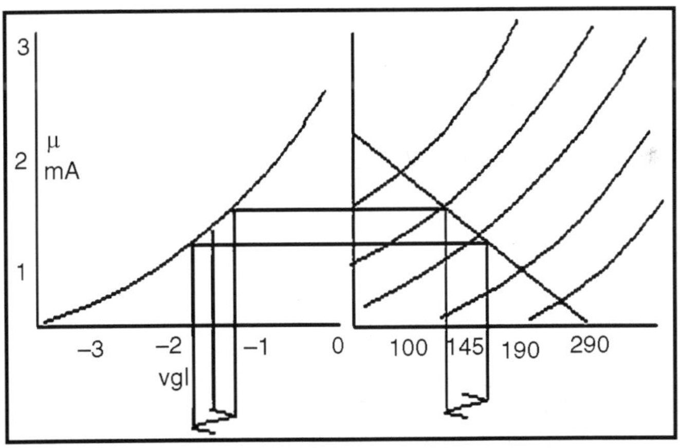

The diagram assumes accuracy, but it is not. The transfer curve is usually straighter in the area above the near cut-off region (depending on the tube type). However, if the circuit parameters are B+ 290 volts, Vp 145 volts, Vg -1.5 volts and Ip 1.5 milliamps, then a grid signal of about.75 volts peak to peak will output a plate voltage of about 45 volts peak to peak. That gives a voltage gain of about 60 according to the above chart. Actual gain is not like this, but circuit parameters might cause a higher or lower gain, depending on the design of the tube and the resistors chosen for biasing. A fixed bias circuit could allow for the resistors to set gain by the simple gain equation G=Rp/Rk. If the plate resistance is 65 kilo ohms and the effective cathode resistor is 680 Ohms, the gain could be 100, and the grid bias can be exactly 1.5 volts. Certain tubes have a top gain (12AX7 and 6EU7 for example) of 100. This is known as the tube's amplification factor or mu. The curve on the left, which is the transfer curve, is actually more curved as one approaches the more negative voltage level. Biasing down there will not yield a very linear response. So fixed biasing has its advantages, one being the possibility of not using a bypass resistor. Another is accurate biasing that doesn't change much with time or heat, providing better linearity.

In audio, with one instrument or even the fundamental being at a high amplitude, the instant that the peak reaches this area, another signal of a higher frequency may suffer the effects of distortion. This is a form of modulation distortion. Capacitors cause current to lag the voltage, so the bias will not follow the signal, hence altering the incoming signal's nature, and the overall sound quality. What this means is that a signal whose current component and voltage component are in phase will come out of a capacitor with current being 60 degrees behind the voltage signal. This may not necessarily be a problem if there is no grid resistor (some circuits do this), but if there is a grid resistor, then the resistor will react to the varying current and add to the original voltage signal the resultant voltage signal across the resistor and cause a slight phase distortion.

This is because, not only do the biasing schemes mentioned at the outset of this discussion alter dramatically the sound quality, but also variations within the most popular, the class A, also alter the sound quality. You will find that the schemes that use the lower voltages and currents are more popular because they are the least linear. This may seem like a contradiction to what an audiophile would want from a sound system, especially one that uses tube and expensive irons. It is being a purist who is also a tube lover, I find this to be perplexing.

In my opinion, wherever the tubes are biased, it is still far superior to many solid state high end designs. It takes many transistors in a circuit to come close to the amplification ability and linearity *before distortion reducing schemes* that it takes only one twin triode to do. In an amplifier configuration using a 6NS7 tube (a twin triode) where one half of the tube amplifies and the other half acts as a follower, a biasing scheme where the output is taken from the cathode and it doesn't amplify voltage but current, but the first half does the amplifying of voltage. This particular circuit had an open loop (no NFB) distortion rating of less than 0.2 per cent! Astonishingly low.

PUSH PULL AMPLIFIER

One of the controversies about push pull biasing is that there exists a cross over distortion. What this means is that when the signal input to either tube causes the tube to cut off there is a less than linear transition for the other tube to "take up" when it begins to conduct for the other half of the wave (I hope you aren't confused *yet*). In a pure class B biased circuit, this means that there is a gap between when one tube stops conducting and the other starts to conduct. This makes for a wave form that kind of looks like this:

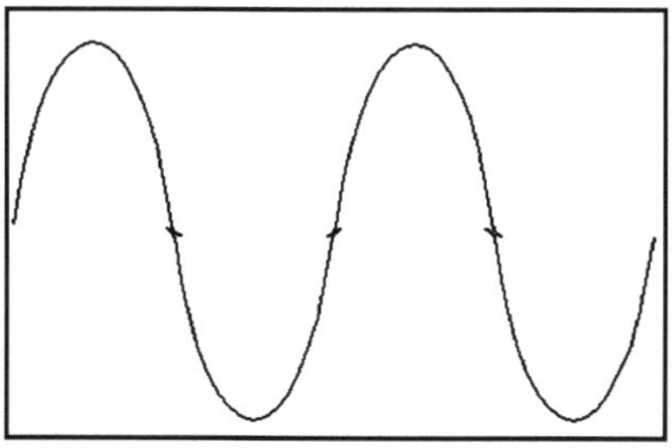

Notice the bends where the wave crosses the zero line. Class AB makes up for this by causing the tubes to conduct a little bit more of the cycle so as to overlap the cut off to turn on times. In other words, those bends are now in the signal past the zero crossing.

The result is a "purer" sine wave. The resulting spikes can then be filtered out with a small value capacitor that will not affect the audible high frequencies. Inverted feedback will also reduce this "crossover distortion". Also eliminated is the low volume level distorted sound of the crossover problem in pure class B operation. In essence, the tubes conduct as class A for low level signals, and as class B on loud level signals.

The real audible difference in a push-pull configuration, even in class A push-pull, is the fact of reduced even order harmonics. Or, increased odd order harmonics. Whichever textbook you wish to refer to, the fact is that odd order harmonics dominate in the push-pull stage. This is where the *real* sonic differences between push-pull and single ended amplifiers occur. This is not to imply that the crossover distortion is not real, just that the distortion is virtually eliminated by biasing and filtering. Transformers, too, naturally filter out the spikes.

Solid state amps don't have transformers to do this, so many persons complain about the buzz, grainy or raspy sound they hear. It is actually the crossover spikes they are listening to. It could also be a higher amplitude high end which causes the high end to sound (subjectively speaking) like an icing on cake, and not the cake itself, which is what we want to hear. Better amps usually use a small choke in line with the output to the speaker to reduce the spikes that NFB doesn't. OTL (output transformer less) tube amps usually work in class A anyway so there is no problem with cross-over distortion there either.

In many high end tube amplifiers there are two potentiometers per channel that are user accessible. They are labeled "bias". These potentiometers are there to set the bias for the output tubes so that they match each other. This allows both tubes to amplify their respective half of the signal *equally*. This also causes the tubes to cancel the even order harmonics (or *whatever*). Many audiophiles mis-align the biasing.

They claim that the amp sounds better. What is really happening is that now even order harmonics are showing up because of not being as canceled out by the push pull configuration.

7

Semiconductor Diode

INTRODUCTION

If we join a section of N-type semiconductor material with a similar section of P-type semiconductor material, we obtain a device known as a PN JUNCTION. (The area where the N and P regions meet is appropriately called the junction.) The usual characteristics of this device make it extremely useful in electronics as a diode rectifier. The diode rectifier or PN junction diode performs the same function as its counterpart in electron tubes but in a different way. The diode is nothing more than a two-element semiconductor device that makes use of the rectifying properties of a PN junction to convert alternating current into direct current by permitting current flow in only one direction. The schematic symbol of a PN junction diode is shown in figure below. The vertical bar represents thecathode (N-type material) since it is the source of electrons and the arrow represents the anode. (P-type material) since it is the destination of the electrons. The label "CR1" is an alphanumerical code used to identify the diode. In this figure, we have only one diode so it is labeled CR1 (crystal rectifier number one). If there were four diodes shown in the diagram, the last diode would be labeled CR4. The heavy dark line shows electron flow. Notice it is against the arrow. For further clarification, a pictorial diagram of a PN junction and an actual semiconductor (one of many types) are also illustrated.

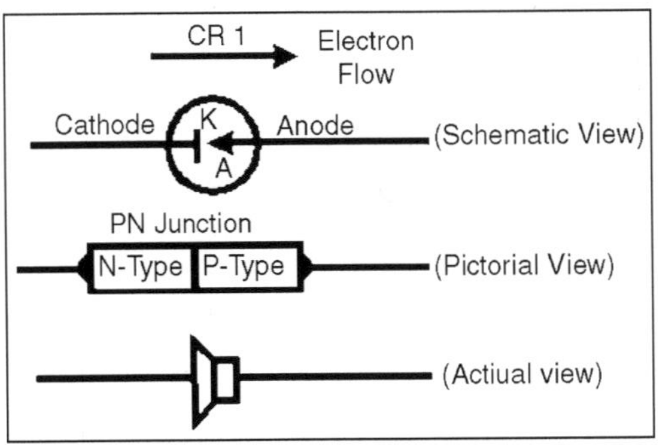

CONSTRUCTION

Merely pressing together a section of P material and a section of N material, however, is not sufficient to produce a rectifying junction. The semiconductor should be in one piece to form a proper PN junction, but divided into a P-type impurity region and an N-type impurity region. This can be done in various ways. One way is to mix P-type and N-type impurities into a single crystal during the manufacturing process. By so doing, a P-region is grown over part of a semiconductor's length and N-region is grown over the other part. This is called a GROWN junction and is illustrated in view A of figure below.

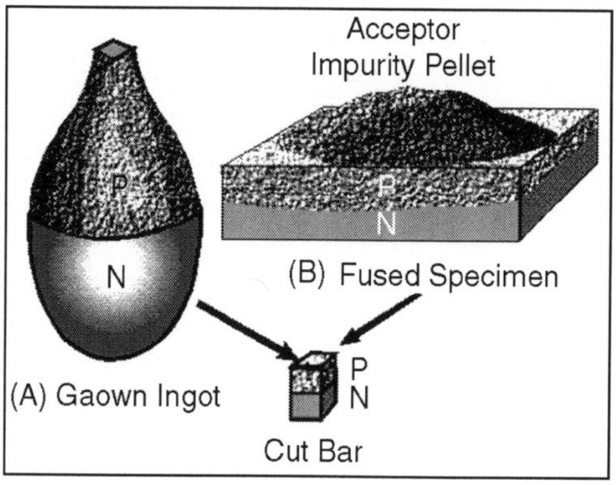

Another way to produce a PN junction is to melt one type of impurity into a semiconductor of the opposite type impurity. For example, a pellet of acceptor impurity is placed on a wafer of N-type germanium and heated. Under controlled temperature conditions, the acceptor impurity fuses into the wafer to form a P-region within it, as shown in view B of figure above. This type of junction is known as an ALLOY or FUSED-ALLOY junction, and is one of the most commonly used junctions. In figure shown below, a POINT-CONTACT type of construction is shown.

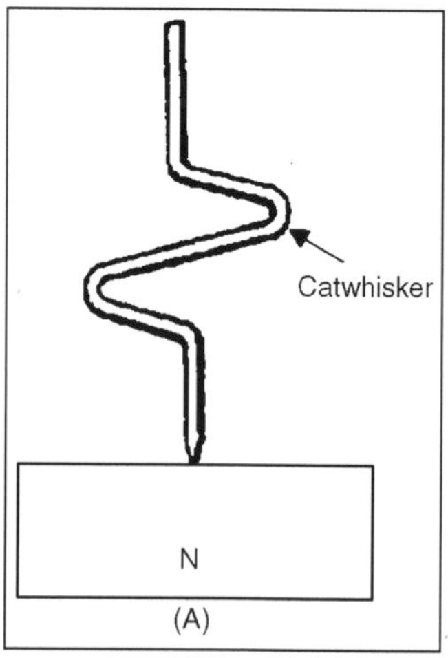

It consists of a fine metal wire, called a cat whisker, that makes contact with a small area on the surface of an N-type semiconductor as shown in view A of the figure. The PN union is formed in this process by momentarily applying a high-surge current to the wire and the N-type semiconductor. The heat generated by this current converts the material nearest the point of contact to a P-type material (view B).

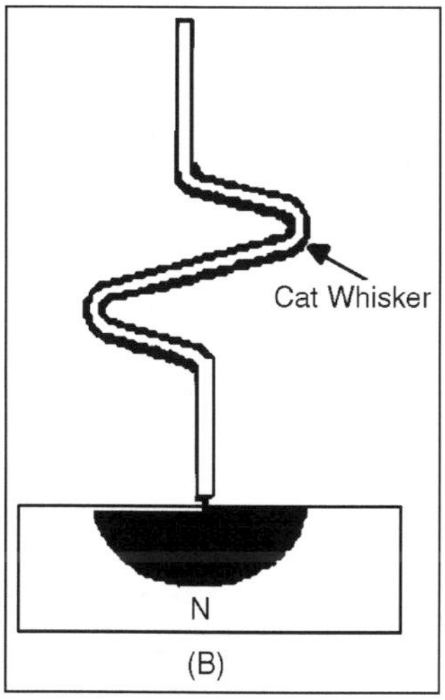

RECTIFIERS

The first diode in figure below is a semiconductor diode which could be a small signal diode of the 1N914 type commonly used in switching applications, a rectifying diode of the 1N4004 (400V 1A) type or even one of the high power, high current stud mounting types. You will notice the straight bar end has the letter "k", this denotes the "cathode" while the "a" denotes anode. Current can only flow from anode to cathode and not in the reverse direction, hence the "arrow" appearance. This is one very important property of diodes.

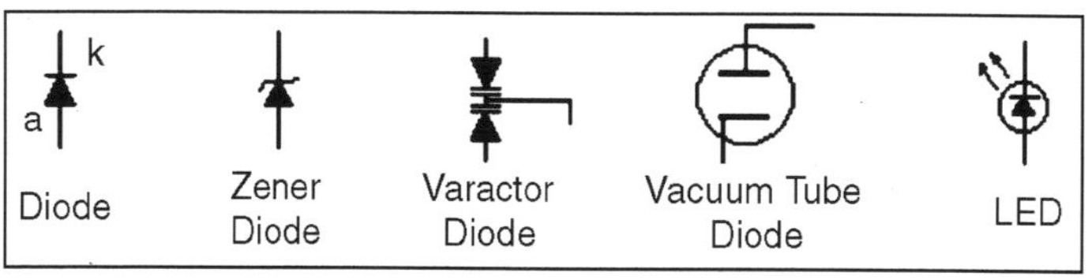

The second of the diodes is a zener diode which are fairly popular for the voltage regulation of low current power supplies. Whilst it is possible to obtain high current zener diodes, most regulation today is done electronically with the use of dedicated integrated circuits and pass transistors.

The next of the diodes in the schematic is a varactor or tuning diode. Depicted here is actually two varactor diodes mounted back to back with the DC control voltage applied at the common junction of the cathodes. These cathodes have the double bar appearance of capacitors to indicate a varactor diode. When a DC control voltage is applied to the common junction of the cathodes, the capacitance exhibited by the diodes (all diodes and transistors exhibit some degree of capacitance) will vary in accordance with the applied voltage.

A typical example of a varactor diode would be the Philips BB204G tuning diodes of which there are two enscapsulated in a TO-92 transistor package. At a reverse voltage Vr (cathode to anode) of 20V each diode has a capacitance of about 16 pF and at Vr of 3V this capacitance has altered to about 36 pF. Being low cost diodes, tuning diodes have virtually replaced air variable capacitors in radio applications today.

The next diode is the simplest form of vacuum tube or valve. It simply has the old cathode and anode. These terms were passed on to modern solid state devices. Vacuum tube diodes are mainly only of interest to restorers and tube enthusiasts.

The last diode depicted is of course a light emitting diode or LED. A led actually doesn't emit as much light as it first appears, a single LED has a plastic lens installed over it and this concentrates the amount of light. Seven LED's can be arranged in a bar fashion called a seven segment LED display and when decoded properly can display the numbers 0–9 as well as the letters A to F.

RECTIFYING DIODES

The principal early application of diodes was in rectifying 50/60 Hz AC mains to raw DC which was later smoothed by choke transformers and/ or capacitors. This procedure is still carried out today and a number of rectifying schemes for diodes have evolved, half wave, full wave and bridge rectifiers.

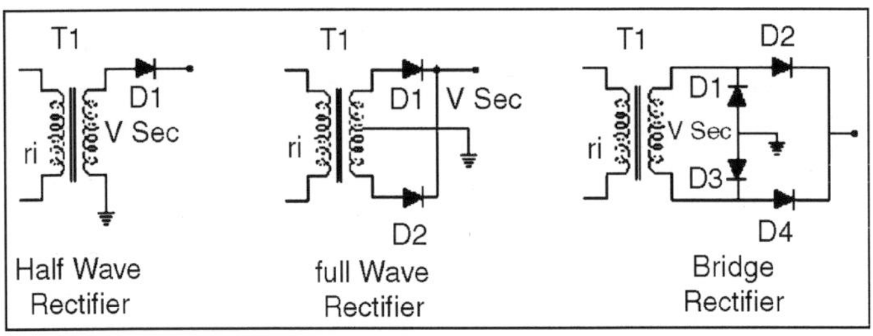

Fig. Rectifying Diodes

As examples in these applications the half wave rectifier passes only the positive half of successive cycles to the output filter through D1. During the negative part of the cycle D1 does not conduct and no current flows to the load.

In the full wave application it essentially is two half wave rectifiers combined and because the transformer secondary is centre tapped, D1 conducts on the positive half of the cycle while D2 conducts on the negative part of the cycle. Both add together. This is more efficient. The full wave bridge rectifier operates essentially the same as the full wave rectifier but does not require a cetre tapped transformer. Further discussion may be seen on the topic power supplies. A further application of rectifying diodes is in the conversion or detection of rf modulated signals to audio frequencies. Typical examples are am modulated signals being detected and early detection schemes for fm also used diodes for detecting modulation.

CHARACTERISTICS OF DIODE

Diodes have the following characteristics:

- Diodes are two terminal devices like resistors and capacitors. They don't have many terminals like transistors or integrated circuits.
- In diodes current is directly related to voltage, like in a resistor. They're not like capacitors where current is related to the time derivative of voltage or inductors where the derivative of current is related to voltage.
- In diodes the current is not linearly related to voltage, like in a resistor.
- Diodes only consume power. They don't produce power like a battery. They are said to be passive devices.
- Diodes are nonlinear, two terminal, passive electrical devices.

Semiconductor diodes have properties that enable them to perform many different electronic functions. To do their jobs, engineers and technicians must be supplied with data on these different types of diodes. The information presented for this purpose is called *Diode Characteristics.*

These characteristics are supplied by manufacturers either in their manuals or on specification sheets (data sheets). Because of the scores of manufacturers and numerous diode types, it is not practical to put before you a specification sheet and call it typical. Aside from the difference between manufacturers, a single manufacturer may even supply specification sheets that differ both in format and content. Despite these differences, certain performance and design information is normally required. We will discuss this information in the next few paragraphs.

A standard specification sheet usually has a brief description of the diode. Included in this description is the type of diode, the major area of application, and any special features. Of particular interest is the specific application for which the diode is suited. The manufacturer also provides a drawing of the diode which gives dimension, weight, and, if appropriate, any identification marks.

In addition to the above data, the following information is also provided: a static operating table (giving spot values of parameters under fixed conditions), sometimes a characteristic curve similar to the one in figure (showing how parameters vary over the full operating range), and diode ratings (which are the limiting values of operating conditions outside which could cause diode damage). In general, diodes tend to permit current flow in one direction, but tend to inhibit current flow in the opposite direction. The graph below shows how current can depend upon voltage for a diode.

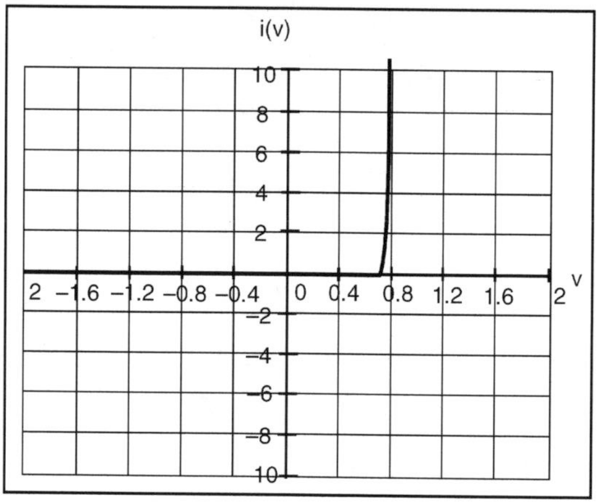

Note the following:

- When the voltage across the diode is positive, a lot of current can flow once the voltage becomes large enough.
- When the voltage across the diode is negative, virtually no current flows.

The circuit symbol for a diode is designed to remind you that current flows easily through a diode in one direction. The circuit symbol for a diode is shown below together with common conventions for current through the diode and voltage across the diode.

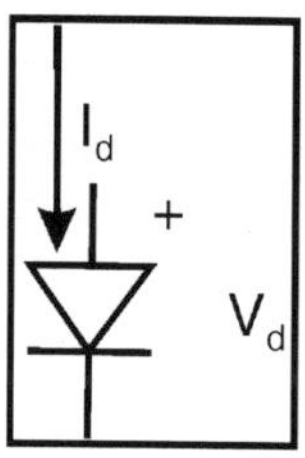

HALF WAVE RECTIFIER

Now we come to the most popular application of the diode: rectification. Simply defined, rectification is the conversion of alternating current (AC) to direct current (DC). This involves a device that only allows one-way flow of electrons. As we have seen, this is exactly what a semiconductor diode does. The simplest kind of rectifier circuit is the *half-wave* rectifier. It only allows one half of an AC waveform to pass through to the load. (Figure below)

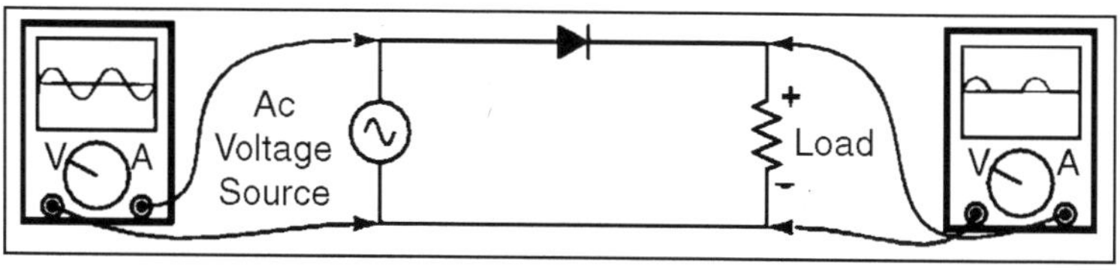

Fig. Half-wave Rectifier Circuit.

For most power applications, half-wave rectification is insufficient for the task. The harmonic content of the rectifier's output waveform is very large and consequently difficult to filter. Furthermore, the AC power source only supplies power to the load one half every full cycle, meaning that half of its capacity is unused. Half-wave rectification is, however, a very simple way to reduce power to a resistive load. Some two-position lamp dimmer switches apply full AC power to the lamp filament for "full" brightness and then half-wave rectify it for a lesser light output. (Figure below)

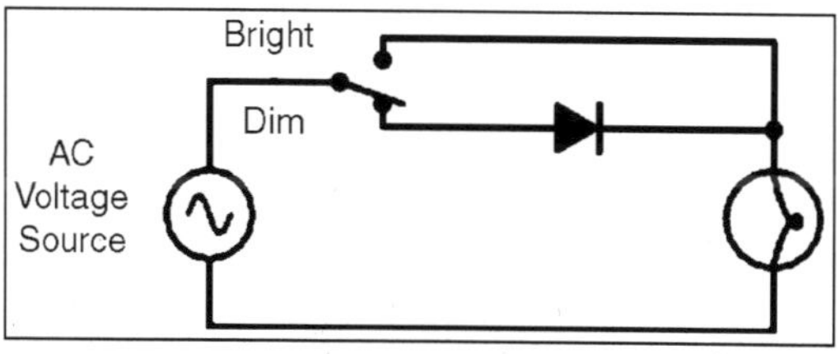

Fig. Half-wave Rectifier Application: Two Level Lamp Dimmer.

In the "Dim" switch position, the incandescent lamp receives approximately one-half the power it would normally receive operating on full-wave AC. Because the half-wave rectified power pulses far more rapidly than the filament has time to heat up and cool down, the lamp does not blink. Instead, its filament merely operates at a lesser temperature than normal, providing less light output. This principle of "pulsing" power rapidly to a slow-responding load device to control the electrical power sent to it is common in the world of industrial electronics. Since the controlling device (the diode, in this case) is either fully conducting or fully nonconducting at any given time, it dissipates little heat energy while controlling load power, making this method of power control very energy-efficient. This circuit is perhaps the crudest possible method of pulsing power to a load, but it suffices as a proof-of-concept application.

VOLTAGE REGULATOR

A Zener Diode is an electronic component which can be used to make a very simple voltage regulator circuit. This circuit enables a fixed stable voltage to be taken from an unstable voltage source such as thebattery bank of a renewable energy system which will fluctuate depending on the state of charge of the bank.

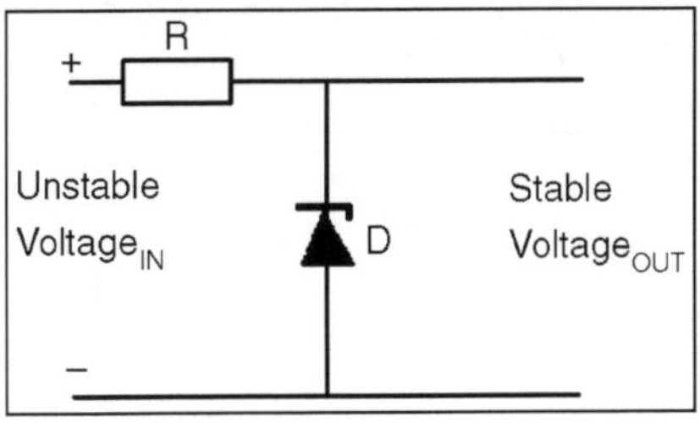

Fig. Zener Diode Voltage Regulator Circuit

Pictured above is a very simple voltage regulator circuit requiring just one zener diode (available from the REUK Shop) and one resistor. As long as the input voltage is a few volts more than the desired output voltage, the voltage across the zener diode will be stable. As the input voltage increases the current through the Zener diode increases but the voltage drop remains constant - a feature of zener diodes. Therefore since the current in the circuit has increased the voltage drop across the resistor increases by an amount equal to the difference between the input voltage and the zener voltage of the diode.

SEMI CONDUCTOR MEMORIES

RAM ARCHITECTURE

Memory inside a computer is organised in a matrix of rows and collums. Each word of memory (or location as it is often caleld) is uniquely identified by the combined row and column values - known as the address. This arrangement resembles a set of pigeon holes used to sort post. Each item of post has an assigned address, which indicates the pigeon hole into which it is to be placed:

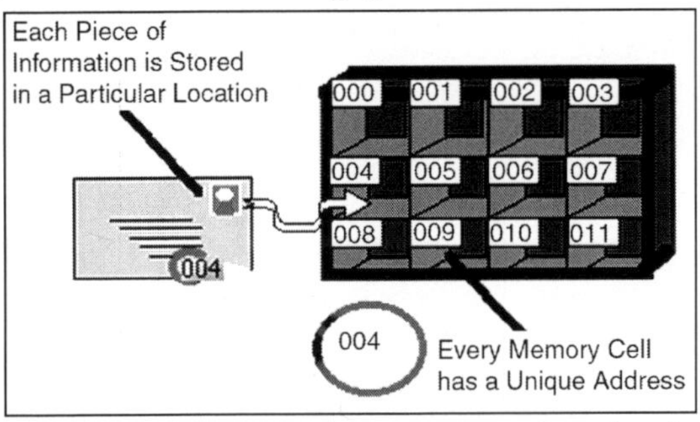

For instance to read the value stored at a memory location 4, the following steps of actions are performed:

- Set the memory address value to 4 to indicate that we are going to deal with the 4th memory location
- Set the memory control logic to READ (enables the memory)
- The data register returns the value at the location specified by the memory address (*e.g.* 23 in this example)
- Disable the memory control logic

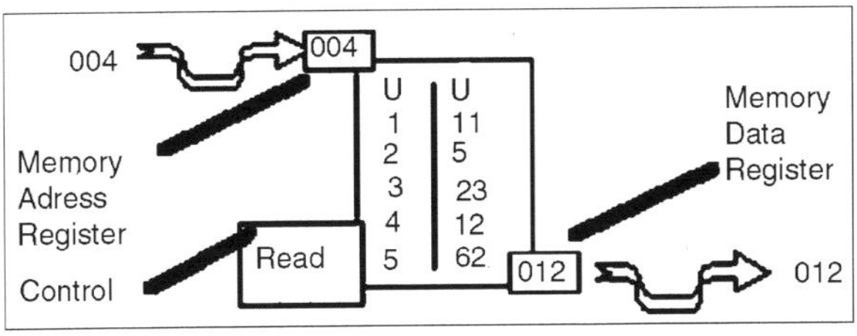

MEMORY HIERARCHY

As often is the case, we utilize a number of logical models of our memory system, depending on the point we want to make. The simplest view of memory is that of a monolithic linear memory; specifically a memory fabricated as a single unit (monolithic) that is organized as a singly dimensioned array (linear). This is satisfactory as a logical model, but it ignores very many issues of considerable importance. Consider a memory in which an M-bit word is the smallest addressable unit. For simplicity, we assume that the memory contains N = 2K words and that the address space is also N = 2K. The memory can be viewed as a one-dimensional array, declared something like *Memory*: Array [0.. (N–1)] of M-bit word. The monolithic view of the memory is shown in the following figure.

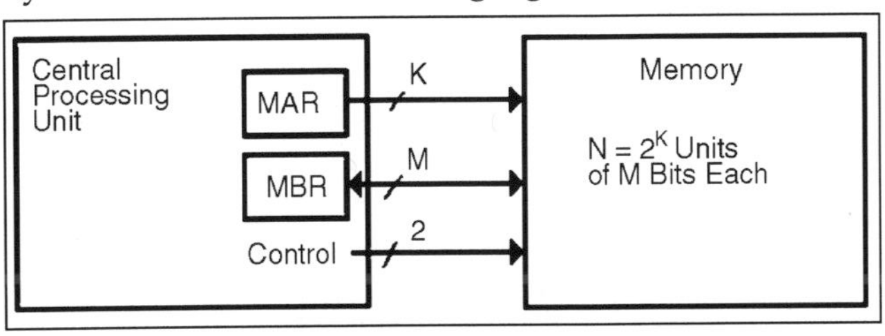

Fig. Monolithic View of Computer Memory

In this monolithic view, the CPU provides K address bits to access N = 2K memory entries, each of which has M bits, and at least two control signals to manage memory. The linear view of memory is a way to think logically about the organization of the memory. This view has the advantage of being rather simple, but has the disadvantage of describing accurately only technologies that have long been obsolete. However, it is a consistent model that is worth mention. The following diagram illustrates the linear model.

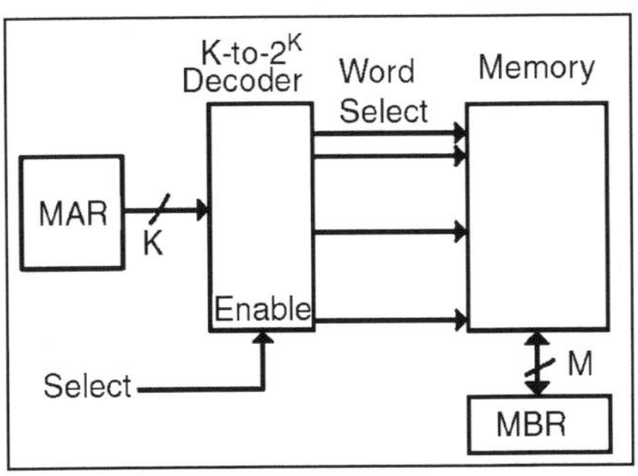

There are two problems with the above model, a minor nuisance and a"show-stopper". The minor problem is the speed of the memory; its access time will be exactly that of plain variety DRAM (dynamic random access memory), which is about 50 nanoseconds. We must have better performance than that, so we go to other memory organizations. The"show-stopper" problem is the design of the memory decoder. Consider two examples for common memory sizes: 1MB (220 bytes) and 4GB (232 bytes) in a byte-oriented memory. A 1MB memory would use a 20-to-1,048,576 decoder, as 220 = 1,048,576. A 4GB memory would use a 32-to-4,294,967,296 decoder, as 232 = 4,294,967,296. Neither of these decoders can be manufactured at acceptable cost using current technology. One should note that since other designs offer additional benefits, there is no motivation to undertake such a design task. We now examine two design choices that produce easy-to-manufacture solutions that offer acceptable performance at reasonable price. The first is the memory hierarchy, using various levels of cache memory, offering faster access to main memory. Before discussing the ideas behind cache memory, we must first speak of two technologies for fabricating memory.

STATIC RAM (SRAM)

Static RAM is a type of RAM that holds its data without external refresh, for as long as power is supplied to the circuit. This is contrasted to dynamic RAM (DRAM), which must be refreshed many times per second in order to hold its data contents. SRAMs are used for specific applications within the PC, where their strengths outweigh their weaknesses compared to DRAM:

- *Simplicity*: SRAMs don't require external refresh circuitry or other work in order for them to keep their data intact.
- *Speed*: SRAM is faster than DRAM.

In contrast, SRAMs have the following weaknesses, compared to DRAMs:

- *Cost*: SRAM is, byte for byte, several times more expensive than DRAM.
- *Size*: SRAMs take up much more space than DRAMs (which is part of why the cost is higher).

These advantages and disadvantages taken together obviously show that performance-wise, SRAM is superior to DRAM, and we would use it exclusively if only we could do so economically. Unfortunately, 32 MB of SRAM would be prohibitively large and costly, which is why DRAM is used for system memory. SRAMs are used instead for level 1 cache and level 2 cache memory, for which it is perfectly suited; cache memory needs to be very fast, and not very large. SRAM is manufactured in a way rather similar to how processors are: highly-integrated transistor patterns photo-etched into silicon. Each SRAM bit is comprised of between four and six transistors, which is why SRAM takes up much more space compared to DRAM, which uses only one (plus a capacitor). Because an SRAM chip is comprised of thousands or millions of identical cells, it is much easier to make than a CPU, which is a large die with a non-repetitive structure. This is one reason why RAM chips cost much less than processors do. See this discussion of how processors are manufactured; this process is similar (but simplified somewhat) for making memory circuits.

DYNAMIC RAM (DRAM)

Dynamic RAM is a type of RAM that only holds its data if it is continuously accessed by special logic called a refresh circuit. Many hundreds of times each second, this circuitry reads the contents of each memory cell, whether the memory cell is being used at that time by the computer or not. Due to the way in which the cells are constructed, the reading action itself refreshes the contents of the memory. If this is not done regularly, then the DRAM will lose its contents, even if it continues to have power supplied to it. This refreshing action is why the memory is called dynamic. All PCs use DRAM for their main system memory, instead of SRAM, even though DRAMs are slower than SRAMs and require the overhead of the refresh circuitry. It may seem weird to want to make the computer's memory out of something that can only hold a value for a fraction of a second. In fact, DRAMs are both more complicated and slower than SRAMs.

The reason that DRAMs are used is simple: they are much cheaper and take up much less space, typically 1/4 the silicon area of SRAMs or less. To build a 64 MB core memory from SRAMs would be very expensive. The overhead of the refresh circuit is tolerated in order to allow the use of large amounts of inexpensive, compact memory. The refresh circuitry itself is almost never a problem; many years of using DRAM has caused the design of these circuits to be all but perfected.

DRAMs are smaller and less expensive than SRAMs because SRAMs are made from four to six transistors (or more) per bit, DRAMs use only one, plus a capacitor. The capacitor, when energized, holds an electrical charge if the bit contains a "1" or no charge if it contains a "0". The transistor is used to read the contents of the capacitor. The problem with capacitors is that they only hold a charge for a short period of time, and then it fades away. These capacitors are tiny, so their charges fade particularly quickly. This is why the refresh circuitry is needed: to read the contents of every cell and refresh them with a fresh "charge" before the contents fade away and are lost. Refreshing is done by reading every "row" in the memory chip one row at a time; the process of reading the contents of each capacitor re-establishes the charge. For an explanation of how these "rows" are read, and thus how refresh is accomplished, refer to this section describing memory access. DRAM is manufactured using a similar process to how processors are: a silicon substrate is etched with the patterns that make the transistors and capacitors (and support structures) that comprise each bit. DRAM costs much less than a processor because it is a series of simple, repeated structures, so there isn't the complexity of making a single chip with several million individually-located transistors. See here for details on how processors are manufactured; the principles for DRAM manufacture are similar.

DECODERS

Decoders can detect a code and activate a single output to signal the presence of that code. Decoders have many applications, from producing system alerts in alarm systems to performing the task of driving multiple devices in microprocessor systems (*e.g.* memory).

BASIC BINARY DECODER

The function of the binary decoder is to determine if a given input combination has occurred. For example, if we wish to detect that 1011 occurs on the inputs of a digital circuit we must design a decoder which only outputs '1' for this instance. Accordingly, a 4-input AND gate and an Inverter may be employed as illustrated in.

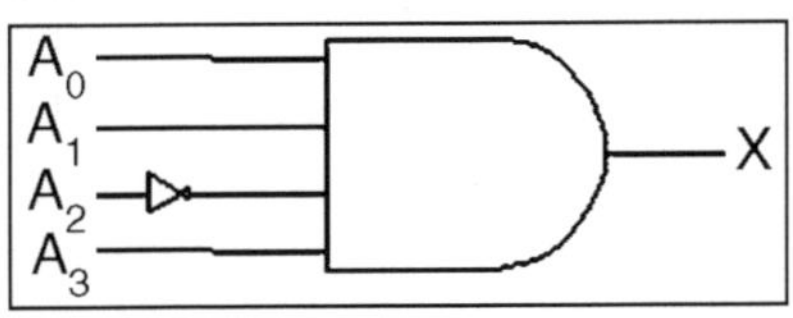

Fig. Decoding circuit for X=1011

THE THREE BIT BINARY DECODER

In order to decode all possible combinations of three bits, eight (2^3=8) decoding logic gates are required. This type of decoder is called the *3-line-to-8-line* decoder because they are 3 inputs and 8 outputs.

Let us consider the design of such a decoder and assume that we require ACTIVE HIGH outputs. That is, for a given input combination the decoder outputs '1'. To illustrate lets consider Table which list the decoding functions and truth tables for the 3-line-to-8-line decoder.

Table. Decoding Functions and Truth Tables for the 3-line-to-8-line Decoder

Decimal Digit	Binary Inputs			Logic Function	Outputs							
					D_0	D_1	D_2	D_3	D_4	D_5	D_6	D_7
0	0	0	0	$\bar{A}_2\bar{A}_1\bar{A}_0$	1	0	0	0	0	0	0	0
1	0	0	1	$\bar{A}_2\bar{A}_1A_0$	0	1	0	0	0	0	0	0
2	0	1	0	$\bar{A}_2A_1\bar{A}_0$	0	0	1	0	0	0	0	0
3	0	1	1	$\bar{A}_2A_1A_0$	0	0	0	1	0	0	0	0
4	1	0	0	$A_2\bar{A}_1\bar{A}_0$	0	0	0	0	1	0	0	0
5	1	0	1	$A_2\bar{A}_1A_0$	0	0	0	0	0	1	0	0
6	1	1	0	$A_2A_1\bar{A}_0$	0	0	0	0	0	0	1	0
7	1	1	1	$A_2A_1A_0$	0	0	0	0	0	0	0	1

Now, we can develop a decoder based on each logic function and implement the SOP logic circuit. This is illustrated below in Figure.

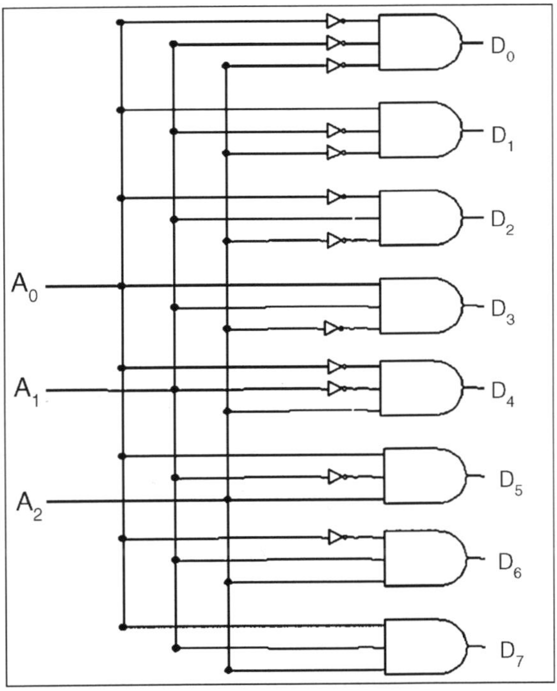

Fig. Internal Circuitry for 3-line-to-8-line decoder

It is far more convenient to use the logic symbol for the3-line-to-8-line decoder as illustrated in Figure rather than repeating the complex internal circuitry each time.

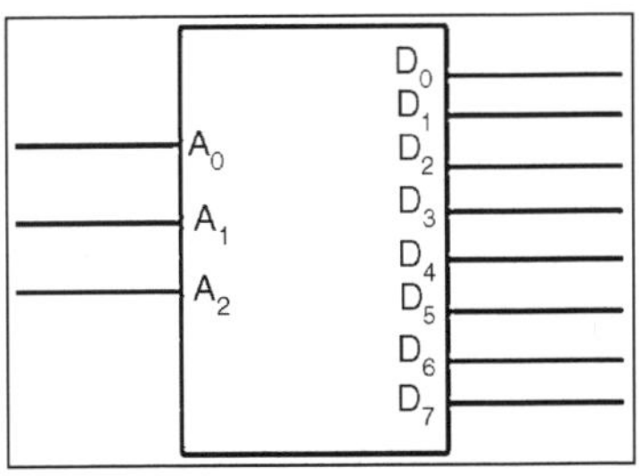

Fig. Logic Symbol for 3-line-to-8-line decoder

Note the 3-line-to-8-line is sometimes referred to as the 3 × 8 decoder

THE BCD-TO-DECIMAL DECODER

The BCD-to-decimal decoder converts each BCD code to its decimal equivalent. The technique employed is very similar to the one used in developing the 3-line-to-8-line decoder. Again assuming active high outputs are required, Table lists the decoding functions for BCD-to-decimal decoder

Table. Decoding Functions for the BCD-to-Decimal Decoder

Decimal Digit	Binary Inputs				Logic Function
0	0	0	0	0	$\bar{A}_3\bar{A}2\bar{A}_1\bar{A}_0$
1	0	0	0	1	$\bar{A}_3\bar{A}_2\bar{A}_1A_0$
2	0	0	1	0	$\bar{A}_3\bar{A}_2A_1\bar{A}_0$
3	0	0	1	1	$\bar{A}_3\bar{A}_2A_1A_0$
4	0	1	0	0	$\bar{A}_3A_2\bar{A}_1\bar{A}_0$
5	0	1	0	1	$\bar{A}_3A_2\bar{A}_1A_0$
6	0	1	1	0	$\bar{A}_3A_2A_1\bar{A}_0$
7	0	1	1	1	$\bar{A}_3A_2A_1A_0$
8	1	0	0	0	$A_3\bar{A}_2\bar{A}_1\bar{A}_0$
6	1	0	0	1	$A_3\bar{A}_2\bar{A}_1A_0$

Now, we can develop a decoder based on each logic function and implement the SOP logic circuit. This is illustrated.

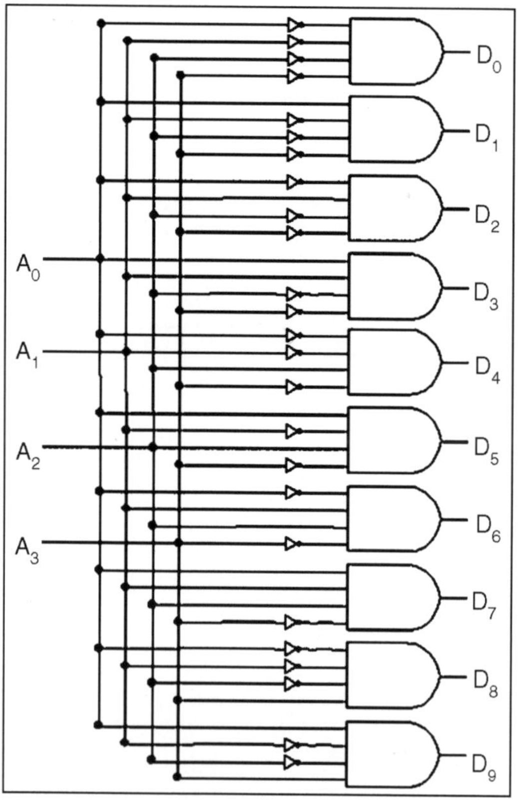

Fig. Logic Circuit for BCD Decoder

PRINCIPLE OF VARACTOR OR TUNING DIODES

These types of diodes work on the principle that all diodes exhibit some capacitance. Indeed the zener diode BZX79C12 quoted above has, according to the data book, a capacitance of 65–85 pF at 0V and measured at 1 Mhz. For AM Radio band applications a specific diode has been devised. The Philips BB212 in a TO-92 case is one such type. Each of the diodes has a capacitance of 500 - 620 pF at a reverse bias of 0.5V and <22 pF at 8V. This diode's capacitance ratio is quoted at 22.5:1 which could not be achieved easily if at all with an air variable capacitor. This type of diode is depicted in figure above.

Several obvious advantages come immediately to mind, a small transistor type package, very low cost, ease of construction on a circuit board, can be mounted away from heat generating devices, frequency determining circuitry entirely dependent upon resistor values and ratios, DC voltage control can be either from frequency synthesiser circuits or perhaps a multi-turn potentiometer. Such a potentiometer aids band spreading and fine tuning if two potentiometers are used. The only real limitation is your imagination and the calculations involved.

DIODES AS FREQUENCY MULTIPLIERS

Just one more example of the versatility of diodes is the frquency doubling circuit depicted in Figure. Now if that looks a lot like the full wave rectifier from figure above you would be correct. That is why the ripple frequency for 50/60 Hz always comes out at 100/120 Hz.

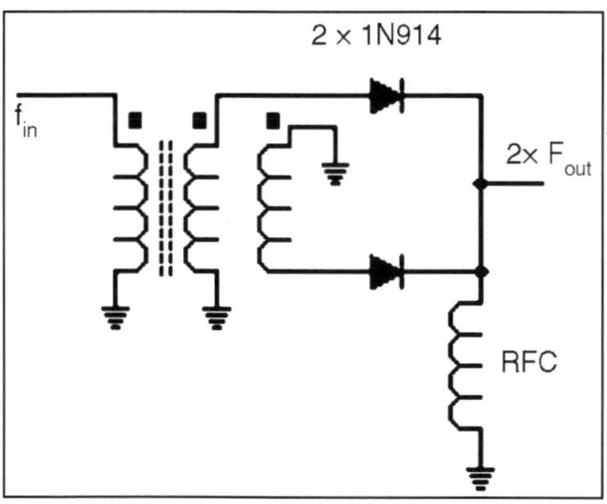

Fig. Diodes as Frequency Multipliers

Here the input is a wide band transformer and the signal passes to a full wave rectifier comprising two 1N914 diodes. The DC component caused by the rectification passes to ground through RFC which of course presents a high impedance to the rf porion of the signal but essentially a short circuit for DC. The original signal should be down about 40 dB and with this type of circuit there would be a loss of somewhere around 7.5 dB so the 2 X signal would require further amplification to restore that loss.

DIODES AS MIXERS

With some subtle re-arrangement to figure we can get the circuit to function as a two diode frequency mixer. Note that there are other diode arrangements as well in this application.

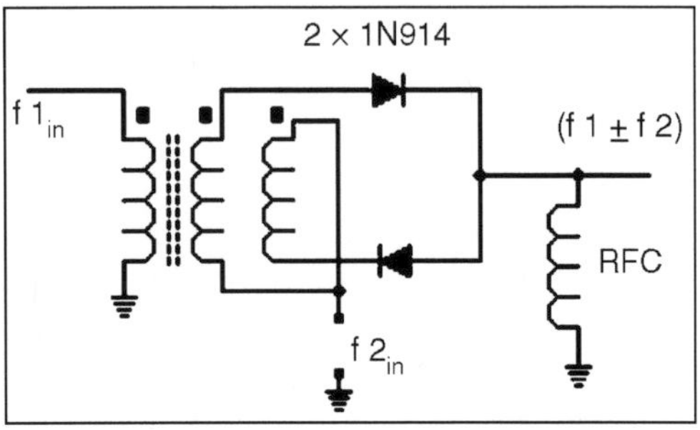

Fig. Diodes as Frequency Mixers

The diodes here act as switches and it can be mathematically shown that only the sum and difference signals will result. For example, if F1 was 5 Mhz and F2 was 3 Mhz then the sum and difference signals from the diodes would be 8 Mhz and 2 Mhz. None of the original signals appear at the output and this is a most important property of using diodes as mixers. It should be noted that although 1N914 diodes are depicted you would normally use hot carrier diodes in any serious application and the diodes need to be well matched.

APPLICATIONS OF SWITCHING DIODES

Similar types of diodes have been developed specifically for band switching purposes. Although a typical 1N914 type switching diode can be used for such purposes it is preferable to use diodes which have been optimised for such purposes because the Rd on is much lower. This means the diode resistance Rd can have a serious affect on rf circuits in particular the "Q" of a tuned circuit. One example of a low Rd device is the Philips BA482 diode used for band switching in television tuners. It has a typical Rd of 0.4 ohms at a forward current of 10 mA.

In figureabove we have one application where switching diodes operate. All diodes serve to switch in or out capacitors in the diagram which is presented here just to illustrate one single application of switching diodes, many, many more applications exist. Again the limit is your imagination. The switching diodes in figure switch in or out successively higher values of capacitors as each control select line is "grounded". The voltage from the +5V feed line proceeds through the diode at DC thus opening the diode and making it appear "transparent" for rf purposes. The capacitor with the value attached is then "switched" into circuit. Other components marked RFC and Cbp are chokes and bypass capacitors for "clean" switching. The bypass capacitors and choke values would be determined by the frequency of operation.

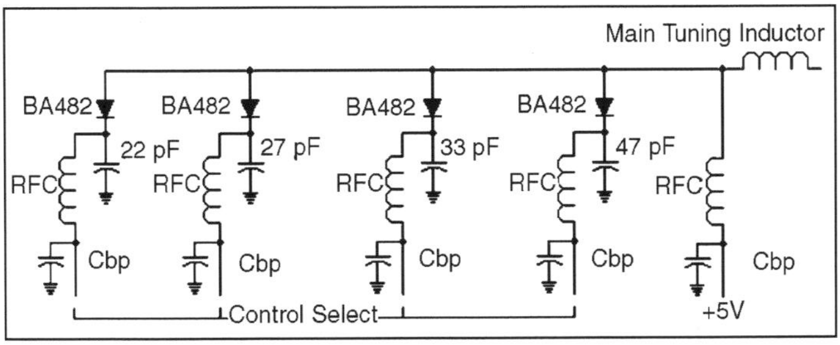

Fig. Applications of Switching Diodes

We could just have easily have switched inductors instead of capacitors. Note why Rd is quite important on overall circuit performance. If we were using inductors the diode resistance Rd would have a significant affect on inductor "Q" which in turn would affect filter performance, if it was in fact an LC filter application.

SWITCHING DIODES IN LOGIC CIRCUITS

If you you completed the tutorial on digital basics you should be aware of binary numbers. There are a whole range of digital building blocks available and just by way of one illustration of using diodes we have presented the 74HC4040 twelve stage binary ripple counter (there are others with varying number of stages). In the schematic of figure we have this counter which divides by successive division of two for twelve stages.

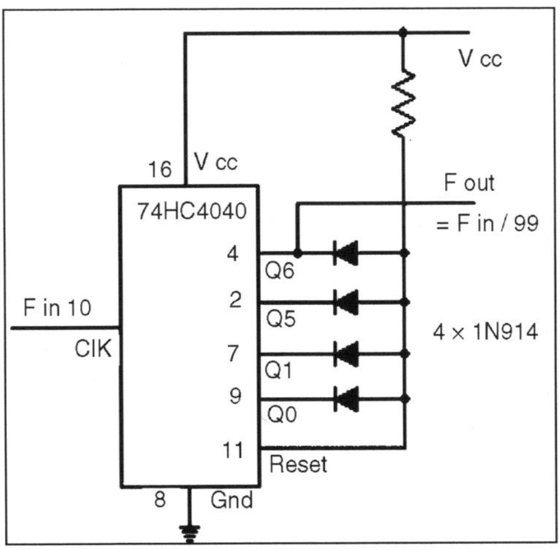

Fig. Applications of Switching Diodes in Digital Logic Circuits

Initially because there is no voltage drop across the resistor a high appears on all anodes as well as on pin 4 the master reset causing the counter to reset forcing all outputs low and in turn a voltage drop across each diode and across the resistor and a low on reset. Progressively each of the outputs change from low to high for a certain period of time and without unduly complicating matters when all outputs as selected by our diode combination (in this particular case 1 + 2 + 32 + 64 = 99) are simultaneously high the voltage drop across the resistor will cease and cause pin 11 (reset which was formerly low) to go high and reset all the internal ripple counters. At the same time pin 4 changes state also with reset. It can been shown this happens once every 99 periods. Simply by placing diodes on the right outputs we can select to divide by any number up to 4095 using this particular counter.

8

Combinational Circuits Design

Combinational logic is probably the easiest circuitry to design. The outputs from a combinational logic circuit depend only on the current inputs. The circuit has no remembrance of what it did at any time in the past. Much of logic design involves connecting simple, easily understood circuits to construct a larger circuit that performs a much more complicated function. Several simple, often-used combinational logic circuits are the following:

LOGIC CIRCUITS AND DESIGN PROCEDURE

Logic circuits for digital systems may be combinational or sequential. A combinational circuit consists of logic gates whose outputs at any time are determined by combining the values of the applied inputs using logic operations. A combinational circuit performs an operation that can be specified logically by a set of Boolean expression. In addition to using logic gates, sequential circuits employ elements that store bit values. Sequential circuit outputs are a function of inputs and the bit value in storage elements. These values, in turn, are a function of previously applied inputs and stored values. As a consequence, the outputs of a sequential circuit depend not only on the presently applied values of the inputs, but also on pas inputs, and the behaviour of the circuit must be specified by a sequence in time of inputs and internal stored bit values. A combinational circuit consists of input variables, output variables, logic gates and interconnections.

The interconnected logic gates accept signals from the inputs and generate signals at the output. The n input variables come from the environment of the circuit, and the m output variables are available for use by the environment. Each input and output variable exists physically as a binary signal that represents logic 1 or logic 0. For n input variables, there are 2^n possible binary input combinations. For each binary combination of the input variables, there is one possible binary value on each output. Thus, a combinational circuit can be specified by a truth table that lists the output values for each combination of the input variables. A combinational circuit can also be described by m Boolean function, one for each output variable. Each such function is expressed as function of the n input variables.

COMBINATIONAL CIRCUIT DESIGN

The design of combinational circuit starts from a specification of the problem and culminates in a logic diagram or set of Boolean equations from which the logic diagram can be obtained.

The procedure involves the following steps:

- From the specifications of the circuit, determine the required number of inputs and outputs, and assign a letter symbol to each.
- Derive the truth table that defines the required relation ship between inputs and outputs.
- Obtain the simplified Boolean functions of each outputs as function of the input variables.
- Draw the logic diagram.
- Verify the correctness of the design.

COMBINATIONAL ANALYSIS PROCEDURE

The bulk of the Combinational Analysis module is accessed through a single window of that name allowing you to view truth tables and Boolean expressions. This window can be opened in two ways.

WINDOW MENU

Select Combinational Analysis, and the current Combinational Analysis window will appear. If you haven't viewed the window before, the opened window will represent no circuit at all. Only one Combinational Analysis window exists within Logisim, no matter how many projects are open. There is no way to have two different analysis windows open at once.

PROJECT MENU

From a window for editing circuits, you can also request that Logisim analyse the current circuit by selecting the Analyse Circuit option from the Project menu. Before Logisim opens the window, it will compute Boolean expressions and a truth table corresponding to the circuit and place them there for you to view. For the analysis to be successful, each input must be attached to an input pin, and each output must be attached to an output pin. Logisim will only analyse circuits with at most eight of each type, and all should be single-bit pins. Otherwise, you will see an error message and the window will not open.

In constructing Boolean expressions corresponding to a circuit, Logisim will first attempt to construct a Boolean expressions corresponding exactly to the gates in the circuit. But if the circuit uses some non-gate components (such as a multiplexer), or if the circuit is more than 100 levels deep (unlikely), then it will pop up a dialog box telling you that deriving Boolean expressions was impossible, and Logical will instead derive the expressions based on the truth table, which will be derived by quietly trying each combination of inputs and reading the resulting outputs. After analyzing a circuit, there is no continuing relationship between the circuit and the Combinational Analysis window. That is, changes to the circuit will not be reflected in the window, nor will changes to the Boolean expressions and/or truth table in the window be reflected in the circuit. Of course, you are always free to analyse a circuit again; and, as we will see later, you can replace the circuit with a circuit corresponding to what appears in the Combinational Analysis window.

LIMITATIONS

Logical will not attempt to detect sequential circuits: If you tell it to analyse a sequential circuit, it will still create a truth table and corresponding Boolean expressions, although these will not accurately summarize the circuit behaviour. (In fact, detecting sequential circuits is provably impossible, as it would amount to solving the Halting Problem. Of course, you might hope that Logical would make at least some attempt - perhaps look for flip-flops or cycles in the wires - but it does not.) As a result, the Combinational Analysis system should not be used indiscriminately: Only use it when you are indeed sure that the circuit you are analyzing is indeed combinational! Logical will make a change to the original circuit that is perhaps unexpected: The Combinational Analysis system requires that each input and output have a unique name that conforming to the rules for Java identifiers. (Roughly, each character must either a letter or a digit, and the first character must be a letter. No spaces allowed!) It attempts to use the pins' existing labels, and to use a list of defaults if no label exists. If an existing label doesn't follow the Java-identifier rule, then Logical will attempt to extract a valid name from the label if at all possible. Incidentally, the ordering of the inputs in the truth table will match their top-down ordering in the original circuit, with ties being broken in left-right order.

ARITHMETIC CIRCUIT

Suppose we wanted to build a device that could add two binary bits together. Such a device is known as a half-adder, and its gate circuit looks like this:

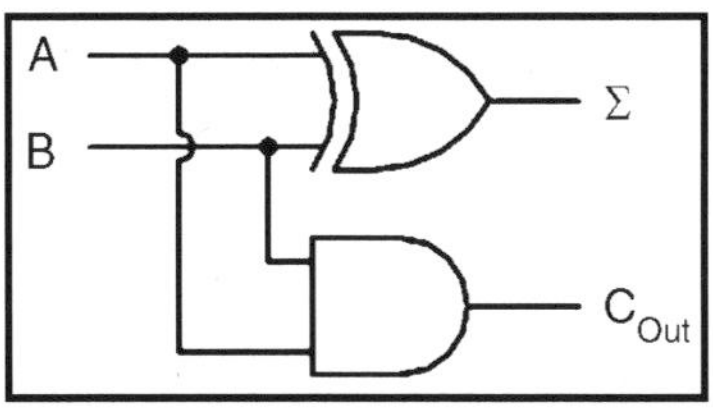

The Σ symbol represents the "sum" output of the half-adder, the sum's least significant bit (LSB). C_{out} represents the "carry" output of the half-adder, the sum's most significant bit (MSB). If we were to implement this same function in ladder (relay) logic, it would look like this:

Either circuit is capable of adding two binary digits together. The mathematical "rules" of how to add bits together are intrinsic to the hard-wired logic of the circuits. If we wanted to perform a different arithmetic operation with binary bits, such as multiplication, we would have to construct another circuit. The above circuit designs will only perform one function: add two binary bits together. To make them do something else would take re-wiring, and perhaps different compo entry.

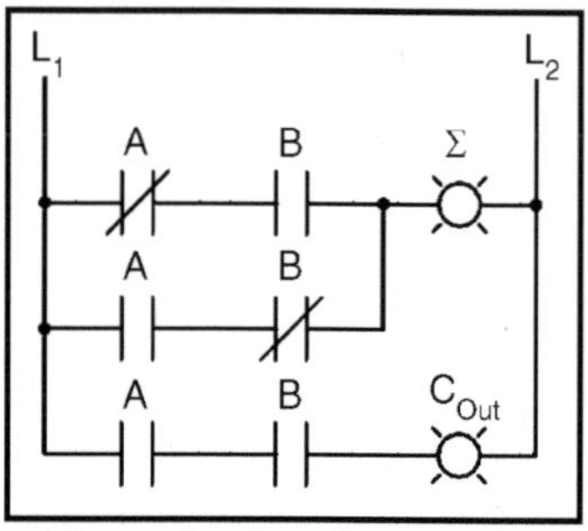

In this sense, digital arithmetic circuits aren't much different from analog arithmetic (operational amplifier) circuits: they do exactly what they're wired to do, no more and no less. We are not, however, restricted to designing digital computer circuits in this manner. It is possible to embed the mathematical "rules" for any arithmetic operation in the form of digital data rather than in hard-wired connections between gates. The result is unparalleled flexibility in operation, giving rise to a whole new kind of digital device: the programmable computer.

LOOK-UP TABLES

Having learned about digital memory devices in the last chapter, we know that it is possible to store binary data within solid-state devices. Those storage "cells" within solid-state memory devices are easily addressed by driving the "address" lines of the device with the proper binary value(s). Suppose we had a ROM memory circuit written, or programmed, with certain data, such that the address lines of the ROM served as inputs and the data lines of the ROM served as outputs, generating the characteristic response of a particular logic function. Theoretically, we could programme this ROM chip to emulate whatever logic function we wanted without having to alter any wire connections or gates. Consider the following example of a 4 × 2 bit ROM memory (a very small memory!) programmed with the functionality of a half adder:

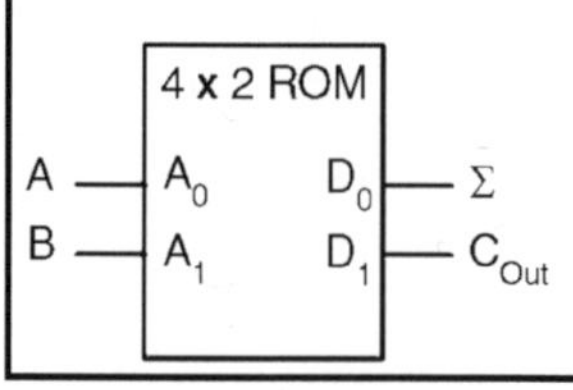

Address		Data	
A	B	C_{Out}	Σ
0	0	0	0
0	1	0	1
1	0	0	1
1	1	1	0

If this ROM has been written with the above data (representing a half-adder's truth table), driving the A and B address inputs will cause the respective memory cells in the ROM chip to be enabled, thus outputting the corresponding data as the Ó (Sum) and C_{out} bits.

Unlike the half-adder circuit built of gates or relays, this device can be set up to perform any logic function at all with two inputs and two outputs, not just the half-adder function. To change the logic function, all we would need to do is write a different table of data to another ROM chip. We could even use an EPROM chip which could be re-written at will, giving the ultimate flexibility in function.

It is vitally important to recognize the significance of this principle as applied to digital circuitry. Whereas the half-adder built from gates or relays processes the input bits to arrive at a specific output, the ROM simply remembers what the outputs should be for any given combination of inputs. This is not much different from the "times tables" memorized in grade school: rather than having to calculate the product of 5 times 6 (5 + 5 + 5 + 5 + 5 + 5 = 30), school-children are taught to remember that 5 × 6 = 30, and then expected to recall this product from memory as needed.

Likewise, rather than the logic function depending on the functional arrangement of hard-wired gates or relays (hardware), it depends solely on the data written into the memory (software). Such a simple application, with definite outputs for every input, is called a look-up table, because the memory device simply "looks up" what the output(s) should to be for any given combination of inputs states.

This application of a memory device to perform logical functions is significant for several reasons:

- Software is much easier to change than hardware.
- Software can be archived on various kinds of memory media (disk, tape), thus providing an easy way to document and manipulate the function in a "virtual" form; hardware can only be "archived" abstractly in the form of some kind of graphical drawing.
- Software can be copied from one memory device (such as the EPROM chip) to another, allowing the ability for one device to "learn" its function from another device.
- Software such as the logic function example can be designed to perform functions that would be extremely difficult to emulate with discrete logic gates (or relays!).

The usefulness of a look-up table becomes more and more evident with increasing complexity of function. Suppose we wanted to build a 4-bit adder circuit using a ROM. We'd require a ROM with 8 address lines (two 4-bit numbers to be added together), plus 4 data lines (for the signed output):

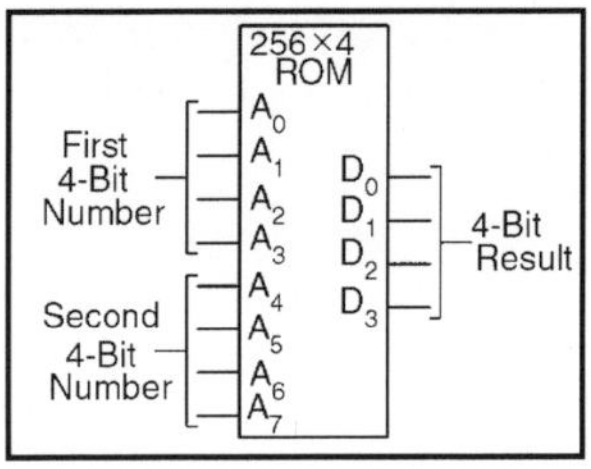

With 256 addressable memory locations in this ROM chip, we would have a fair amount of programming to do, telling it what binary output to generate for each and every combination of binary inputs. We would also run the risk of making a mistake in our programming and have it output an incorrect sum, if we weren't careful. However, the flexibility of being able to configure this function (or any function) through software alone generally outweighs that costs. Consider some of the advanced functions we could implement with the above "adder." We know that when we add two sets of numbers in 2's complement signed notation, we risk having the answer overflow. For instance, if we try to add 0111 (decimal 7) to 0110 (decimal 6) with only a 4-bit number field, the answer we'll get is 1001 (decimal -7) instead of the correct value, 13 (7 + 6), which cannot be expressed using 4 signed bits. If we wanted to, we could avoid the strange answers given in overflow conditions by programming this look-up table circuit to output something else in conditions where we know overflow will occur (that is, in any case where the real sum would exceed +7 or -8). One alternative might be to programme the ROM to output the quantity 0111 (the maximum positive value that can be represented with 4 signed bits), or any other value that we determined to be more appropriate for the application than the typical overflowed "error" value that a regular adder circuit would output. It's all up to the programmer to decide what he or she wants this circuit to do, because we are no longer limited by the constraints of logic gate functions. The possibilities don't stop at customised logic functions, either. By adding more address lines to the 256 × 4 ROM chip, we can expand the look-up table to include multiple functions:

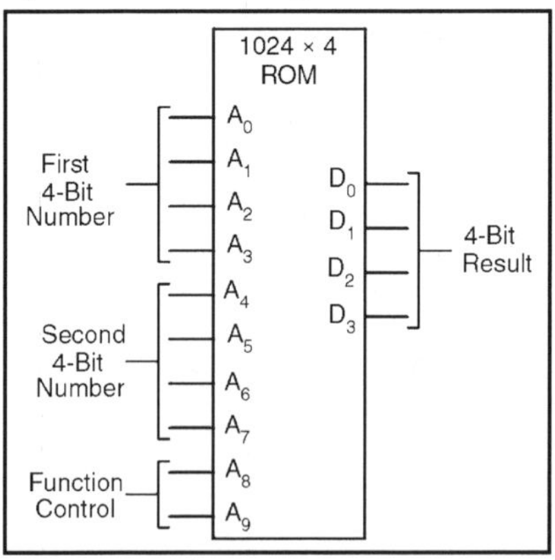

With two more address lines, the ROM chip will have 4 times as many addresses as before (1024 instead of 256). This ROM could be programmed so that when A8 and A9 were both low, the output data represented the sum of the two 4-bit binary numbers input on address lines A0 through A7, just as we had with the previous 256 × 4 ROM circuit. For the addresses A8=1 and A9=0, it could be programmed to output the difference (subtraction) between the first 4-bit binary number (A0 through A3) and the second binary number (A4 through A7).

For the addresses A8=0 and A9=1, we could programme the ROM to output the difference (subtraction) of the two numbers in reverse order (second - first rather than first - second), and finally, for the addresses A8=1 and A9=1, the ROM could be programmed to compare the two inputs and output an indication of equality or inequality. What we will have then is a device that can perform four different arithmetical operations on 4-bit binary numbers, all by "looking up" the answers programmed into it. If we had used a ROM chip with more than two additional address lines, we could programme it with a wider variety of functions to perform on the two 4-bit inputs. There are a number of operations peculiar to binary data (such as parity check or Exclusive-ORing of bits) that we might find useful to have programmed in such a look-up table.

Devices such as this, which can perform a variety of arithmetical tasks as dictated by a binary input code, are known as Arithmetic Logic Units (ALUs), and they comprise one of the essential components of computer technology. Although modern ALUs are more often constructed from very complex combinational logic (gate) circuits for reasons of speed, it should be comforting to know that the exact same functionality may be duplicated with a "dumb" ROM chip programmed with the appropriate look-up table(s). In fact, this exact approach was used by IBM engineers in 1959 with the development of the IBM 1401 and 1620 computers, which used look-up tables to perform addition, rather than binary adder circuitry. The machine was fondly known as the "CADET," which stood for "Can't Add, Doesn't Even Try."

A very common application for look-up table ROMs is in control systems where a custom mathematical function needs to be represented. Such an application is found in computer-controlled fuel injection systems for automobile engines, where the proper air/fuel mixture ratio for efficient and clean operation changes with several environmental and operational variables. Tests performed on engines in research laboratories determine what these ideal ratios are for varying conditions of engine load, ambient air temperature, and barometric air pressure. The variables are measured with sensor transducers, their analog outputs converted to digital signals with A/D circuitry, and those parallel digital signals used as address inputs to a high-capacity ROM chip programmed to output the optimum digital value for air/fuel ratio for any of these given conditions. Sometimes, ROMs are used to provide one-dimensional look-up table functions, for "correcting" digitized signal values so that they more accurately represent their real-world significance. An example of such a device is a thermocouple transmitter, which measures the millivoltage signal generated by a junction of dissimilar metals and outputs a signal which is supposed to directly correspond to that junction temperature. Unfortunately, thermocouple junctions do not have perfectly linear temperature/voltage responses, and so the raw voltage signal is not perfectly proportional to temperature.

By digitizing the voltage signal (A/D conversion) and sending that digital value to the address of a ROM programmed with the necessary correction values, the ROM's programming could eliminate some of the nonlinearity of the thermocouple's temperature-to-millivoltage relationship, so that the final output of the device would be more accurate. The popular instrumentation term for such a look-up table is a digital characterizer.

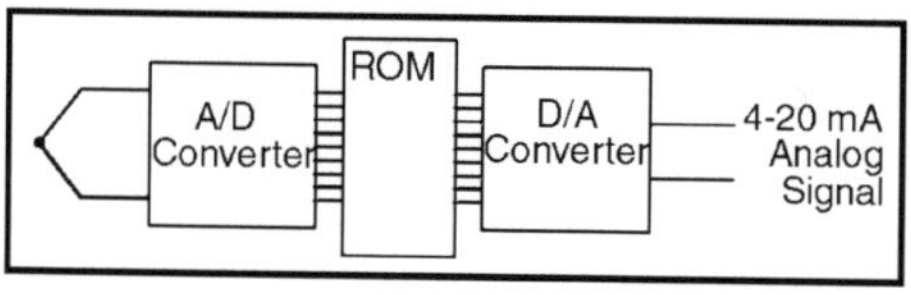

Another application for look-up tables is in special code translation. A 128 x 8 ROM, for instance, could be used to translate 7-bit ASCII code to 8-bit EBCDIC code:

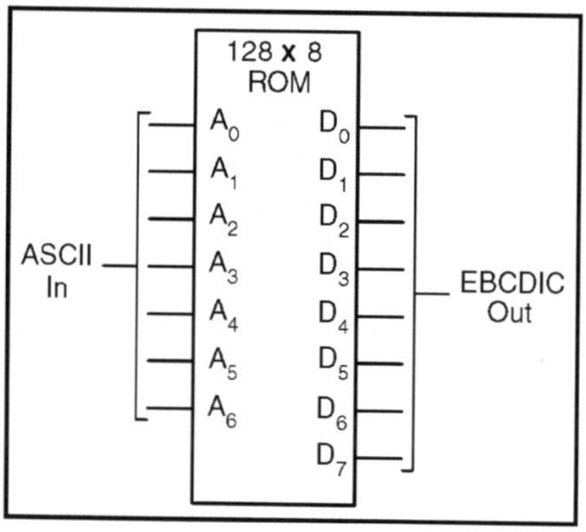

Again, all that is required is for the ROM chip to be properly programmed with the necessary data so that each valid ASCII input will produce a corresponding EBCDIC output code.

ARITHMETIC LOGIC UNI

Devices which can perform a variety of arithmetical tasks as dictated by a binary input code, are known as*Arithmetic Logic Units* (ALUs), and they comprise one of the essential components of computer technology. Although modern ALUs are more often constructed from very complex combinational logic (gate) circuits for reasons of speed, it should be comforting to know that the exact same functionality may be duplicated with a "dumb" ROM chip programmed with the appropriate look-up table(s). In fact, this exact approach was used by IBM engineers in 1959 with the development of the IBM 1401 and 1620 computers, which used look-up tables to perform addition, rather than binary adder circuitry.

The machine was fondly known as the "CADET," which stood for "Can't Add, Doesn't Even Try." A very common application for look-up table ROMs is in control systems where a custom mathematical function needs to be represented. Such an application is found in computer-controlled fuel injection systems for automobile engines, where the proper air/fuel mixture ratio for efficient and clean operation changes with several environmental and operational variables.

Tests performed on engines in research laboratories determine what these ideal ratios are for varying conditions of engine load, ambient air temperature, and barometric air pressure. The variables are measured with sensor transducers, their analog outputs converted to digital signals with A/D circuitry, and those parallel digital signals used as address inputs to a high-capacity ROM chip programmed to output the optimum digital value for air/fuel ratio for any of these given conditions. Sometimes, ROMs are used to provide one-dimensional look-up table functions, for "correcting" digitized signal values so that they more accurately represent their real-world significance. An example of such a device is a *thermocouple transmitter*, which measures the millivoltage signal generated by a junction of dissimilar metals and outputs a signal which is supposed to *directly* correspond to that junction temperature.

Unfortunately, thermocouple junctions do not have perfectly linear temperature/voltage responses, and so the raw voltage signal is not perfectly proportional to temperature. By digitizing the voltage signal (A/D conversion) and sending that digital value to the address of a ROM programmed with the necessary correction values, the ROM's programming could eliminate some of the nonlinearity of the thermocouple's temperature-to-millivoltage relationship, so that the final output of the device would be more accurate. The popular instrumentation term for such a look-up table is a digital *characterizer*.

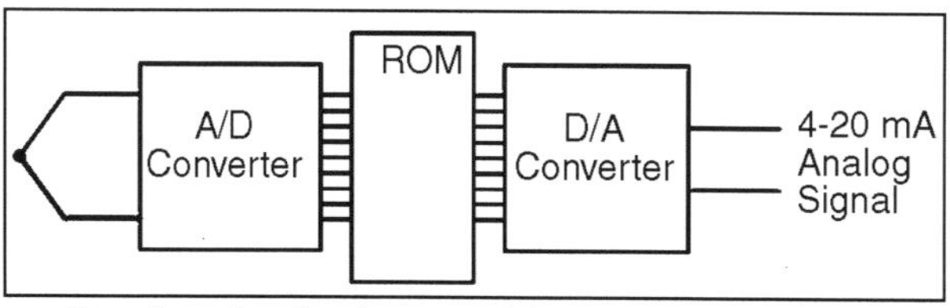

Another application for look-up tables is in special code translation. A 128 × 8 ROM, for instance, could be used to translate 7-bit ASCII code to 8-bit EBCDIC code:

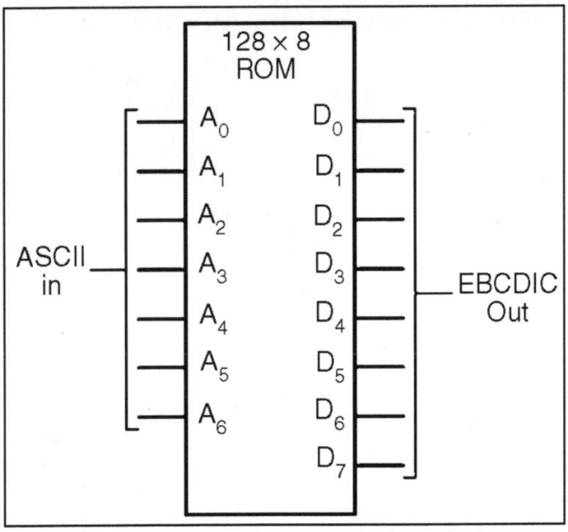

Again, all that is required is for the ROM chip to be properly programmed with the necessary data so that each valid ASCII input will produce a corresponding EBCDIC output code.

MULTIPLEXES CIRCUIT

A multiplexer is a combinatorial circuit that is given a certain number (usually a power of two) data inputs, let us say 2n, and n address inputs used as a binary number to select one of the data inputs. The multiplexer has a single output, which has the same value as the selected data input.

In other words, the multiplexer works like the input selector of a home music system. Only one input is selected at a time, and the selected input is transmitted to the single output. While on the music system, the selection of the input is made manually, the multiplexer chooses its input based on a binary number, the address input.

The truth table for a multiplexer is huge for all but the smallest values of n. We therefore use an abbreviated version of the truth table in which some inputs are replaced by `-' to indicate that the input value does not matter.

Here is such an abbreviated truth table for n = 3. The full truth table would have 2(3 + 23) = 2048rows.

a_2	a_1	a_0	d_7	d_6	d_5	d_4	d_3	d_2	d_1	d_0	|	x
-	-	-	-	-	-	-	-	-	-	-	---	-
0	0	0	-	-	-	-	-	-	-	0	|	0
0	0	0	-	-	-	-	-	-	-	1	|	1
0	0	1	-	-	-	-	-	-	0	-	|	0
0	0	1	-	-	-	-	-	-	1	-	|	1
0	1	0	-	-	-	-	-	0	-	-	|	0
0	1	0	-	-	-	-	-	1	-	-	|	1
0	1	1	-	-	-	-	0	-	-	-	|	0
0	1	1	-	-	-	-	1	-	-	-	|	1

1	0	0	-	-	-	0	-	-	-	-	|	0
1	0	0	-	-	-	1	-	-	-	-	|	1
1	0	1	-	-	0	-	-	-	-	-	|	0
1	0	1	-	-	1	-	-	-	-	-	|	1
1	1	0	-	0	-	-	-	-	-	-	|	0
1	1	0	-	1	-	-	-	-	-	-	|	1
1	1	1	0	-	-	-	-	-	-	-	|	0
1	1	1	1	-	-	-	-	-	-	-	|	1

We can abbreviate this table even more by using a letter to indicate the value of the selected input, like this:

a_2	a_1	a_0	d_7	d_6	d_5	d_4	d_3	d_2	d_1	d_0	|	x
-	-	-	-	-	-	-	-	-	-	-	---	-
0	0	0	-	-	-	-	-	-	-	c	|	c
0	0	1	-	-	-	-	-	-	c	-	|	c
0	1	0	-	-	-	-	-	c	-	-	|	c
0	1	1	-	-	-	-	c	-	-	-	|	c
1	0	0	-	-	-	c	-	-	-	-	|	c
1	0	1	-	-	c	-	-	-	-	-	|	c
1	1	0	-	c	-	-	-	-	-	-	|	c
1	1	1	c	-	-	-	-	-	-	-	|	c

The same way we can simplify the truth table for the multiplexer, we can also simplify the corresponding circuit. Indeed, our simple design method would yield a very large circuit.

The simplified circuit looks like this:

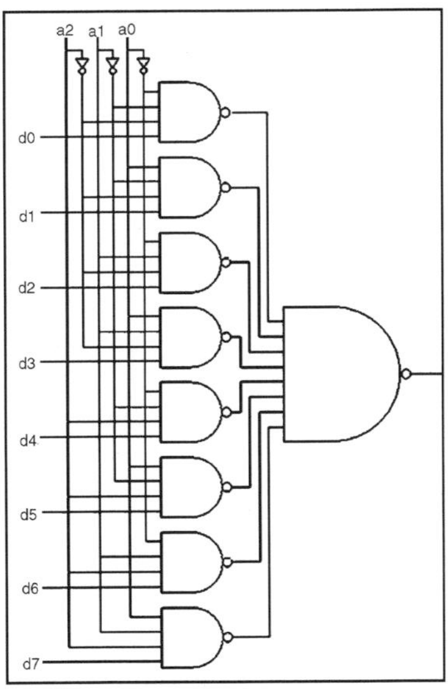

A multiplexer performs the function of selecting the input on any one of'n' input lines and feeding this input to one output line. Multiplexers are used as one method of reducing the number of integrated circuit packages required by a particular circuit design. This in turn reduces the cost of the system. Assume that we have four lines, C0, C1, C2 and C3, which are to be multiplexed on a single line, Output (f). The four input lines are also known as the Data Inputs. Since there are four inputs, we will need two additional inputs to the multiplexer, known as the Select Inputs, to select which of the C inputs is to appear at the output. Call these select lines A and B.

The gate implementation of a 4-line to 1-line multiplexer is shown below:

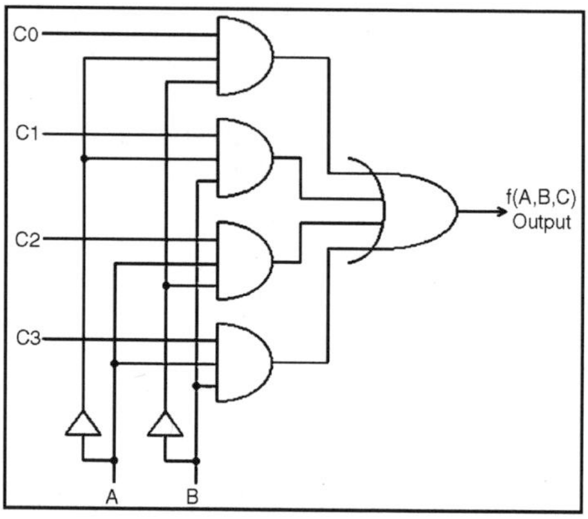

The circuit symbol for the above multiplexer is:

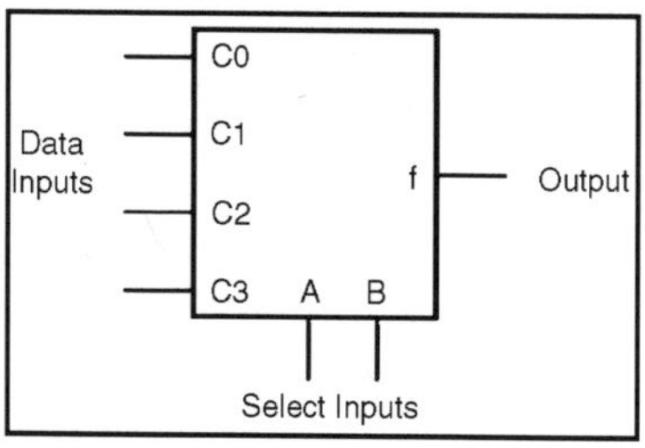

4 INPUT MULTIPLEXER

The multiplexer concept is not limited to two data inputs. If we add a second addressing input, B, we can control as many as four data inputs, as shown to the left. A third and fourth addressing input will allow the multiplexer to control eight or sixteen inputs, respectively. Inputs A and B are the addressing inputs to this multiplexer.

They select which of the four data inputs will be transmitted to the final output, X. If the data inputs are to be multiplexed for transmission to a distant location, the inputs must cycle through all four possible addresses more than twice for each single cycle of each of the data inputs. Otherwise the input data cannot be reconstructed accurately at the receiving end.

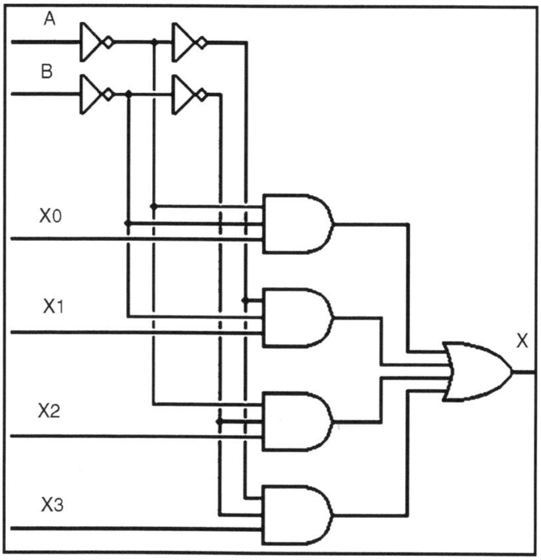

CIRCUITS DECODERS

In both the multiplexer and the demultiplexer, part of the circuits decode the address inputs, *i.e.* it translates a binary number of n digits to 2n outputs, one of which (the one that corresponds to the value of the binary number) is 1 and the others of which are 0. It is sometimes advantageous to separate this function from the rest of the circuit, since it is useful in many other applications. Thus, we obtain a new combinatorial circuit that we call the decoder.

It has the following truth table (for n = 3):

```
a2 a1 a0 | d7 d6 d5 d4 d3 d2 d1 d0
----------------------------------
0  0  0  | 0  0  0  0  0  0  0  1
0  0  1  | 0  0  0  0  0  0  1  0
0  1  0  | 0  0  0  0  0  1  0  0
0  1  1  | 0  0  0  0  1  0  0  0
1  0  0  | 0  0  0  1  0  0  0  0
1  0  1  | 0  0  1  0  0  0  0  0
1  1  0  | 0  1  0  0  0  0  0  0
1  1  1  | 1  0  0  0  0  0  0  0
```

DECODER GENERATION

X86's decoder is generated using an ISA description like all the other ISAs, although how it does that is a bit different. Most of the instructions for most of the other ISAs are defined by passing chunks of code that perform the instruction into an instruction format. The format is basically a template which puts wraps that bit of code in the structure needed to support it and you have your instruction object. Because almost all of the instructions in x86 are microcoded and many can be encoded in multiple ways and hence appear in the decoder more than once, and because the same non-trivial decoding rules apply to many different instructions, X86 uses the decoder as a layer of indirection and defines the majority of its instructions elsewhere.

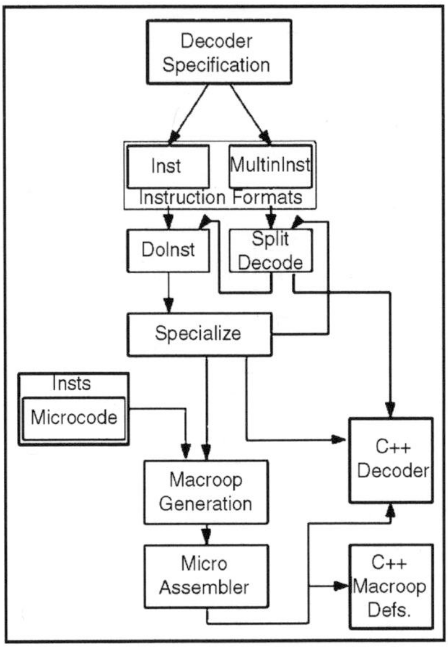

X86 almost exclusively uses only two different instruction formats, Inst and MultiInst. MultiInst is just a compact way of describing multiple related Insts. An Inst essentially selects an instruction like XOR and provides a specification for its operands.

Inside the instruction format, the instruction name and operand specification are passed to a python function called"specializeInst" which figures out what to do with it. If the operand specification describes more than one version of the instruction, for instance one that uses memory and one that uses registers, the instruction's information is passed into another funciton,"doSplitDecode", which separates out those versions and passes each individually back through the same system.

This goes on until the instructions have been fully split out and code has been generated to figure out what version to use. As a nice bonus, the MultiInst format doesn't add much complexity to this model since it can simply jump right into do SplitDecode and continue as normal.

There is one additional format for string instructions that works similar to MultiInst, except instead of specializing the instruction based on its operands, it specializes it based on its prefixes. There are also a few instructions that don't use this system, but because there are so few and because they work like the instructions in other ISAs I won't describe them here. At this point, the code for selecting the right version of an instruction is put into the C++ decoder function. Almost all of this function is built this way, with the minor exception of small bits of logic that glue everything together and make large scale distinctions the number of opcode bytes.

3 TO 8 DECODER

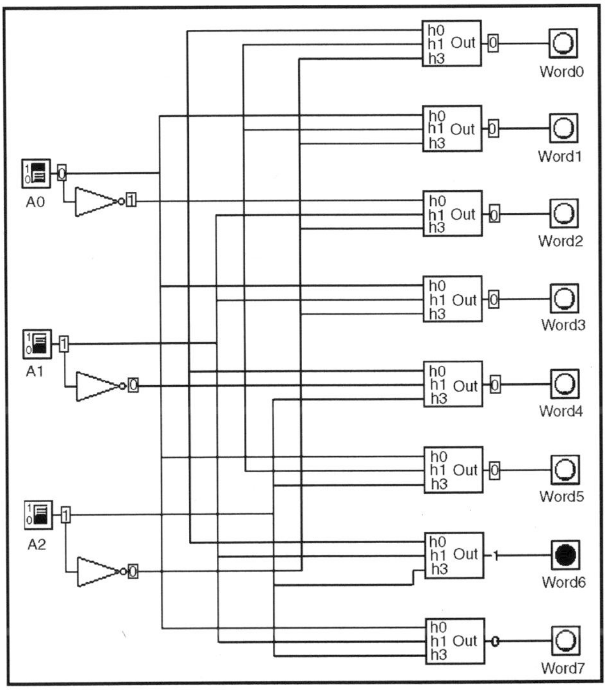

The 3 to 8 decoder unit takes 3 address lines as input and outputs 8 address enable lines. Which of the 8 output is enabled is dependant upon the configuration of the 3 address line. If A0, A1, and A2 are all 0, then address 0 is enabled. If A0=0, A1=1, A2=0, then address 3 is enables. With 3 address lines, the number of words that can be addressed is 8 (2^3=8).

ENCODERS

An encoder is a circuit that changes a set of signals into a code. Lets begin making a 2-to-1 line encoder truth table by reversing the 1-to-2 decoder truth table.

D_1	D_0	A
0	1	0
1	0	1

This truth table is a little short. A complete truth table would be,

D_1	D_0	A
0	0	
0	1	0
1	0	1
1	1	

One question we need to answer is what to do with those other inputs? Do we have them generate an additional error output? In many circuits this problem is solved by adding sequential logic in order to know not just what input is active but also which order the inputs became active.

A more useful application of combinational encoder design is a binary to 7-segment encoder. The seven segments are given according,

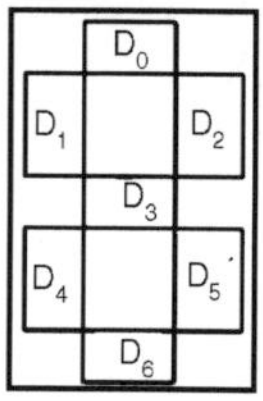

Our truth table is:

I_3	I_2	I_1	I_0	D_6	D_5	D_4	D_3	D_2	D_1	D_0
0	0	0	0	1	1	1	0	1	1	1
0	0	0	1	0	0	1	0	0	1	0
0	0	1	0	1	0	1	1	1	0	1
0	0	1	1	1	0	1	1	0	1	1
0	1	0	0	0	1	1	1	0	1	0
0	1	0	1	1	1	0	1	0	1	1
0	1	1	0	1	1	0	1	1	1	1
0	1	1	1	1	0	1	0	0	1	0
1	0	0	0	1	1	1	1	1	1	1
1	0	0	1	1	1	1	1	0	1	1

Deciding what to do with the remaining six entries of the truth table is easier with this circuit. This circuit should not be expected to encode an undefined combination of inputs, so we can leave them as"don't care" when we design the circuit. The boolean equations are,

$$D_0 = I_3 + I_1 + \bar{I}_3\bar{I}_2\bar{I}_1 I_3$$

$$D_1 = I_3 + \bar{I}_2\bar{I}_1 + \bar{I}_2\bar{I}_1 + I_2\bar{I}_0$$

$$D_2 = I_2 + \bar{I}_3\bar{I}_2\bar{I}_1\bar{I}_0 + \bar{I}_3 I_2 I_1 I_0$$

$$D_3 = I_3 + I_1\bar{I}_0 + I_2\bar{I}_1$$

$$D_4 = I_1\bar{I}_0 + \bar{I}_2\bar{I}_1\bar{I}_0$$

$$D_5 = I_3 + I_2 + I_0$$

$$D_6 = I_3 + I_1\bar{I}_0 + \bar{I}_3\bar{I}_2\bar{I}_1 + \bar{I}_3 I_2\bar{I}_1 I_0$$

and the circuit is,

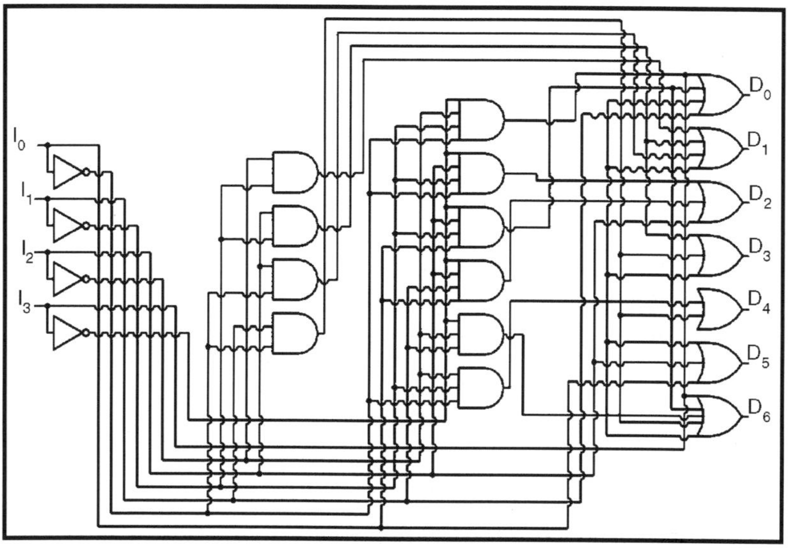

FUNCTION OF MAGNITUDE COMPARATOR

74L85 4-BIT MAGNITUDE COMPARATOR

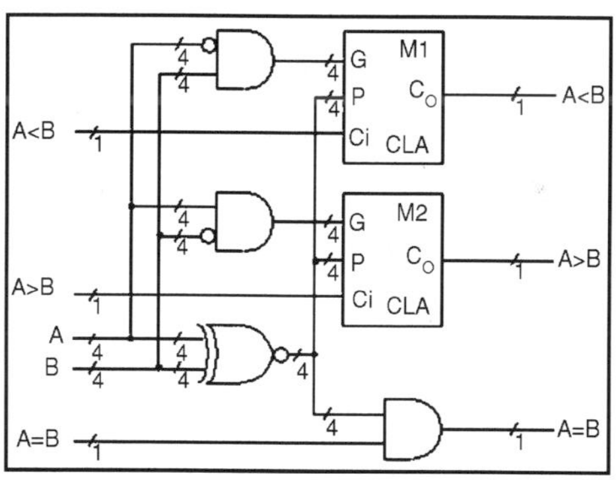

STATISTICS

11 inputs; 3 outputs; 33 gates;

FUNCTION

The 74L85 magnitude comparator can be functionally modeled as above. This is a simplification of implementing a magnitude comparator by a carry function with an inverted input bus as shown.

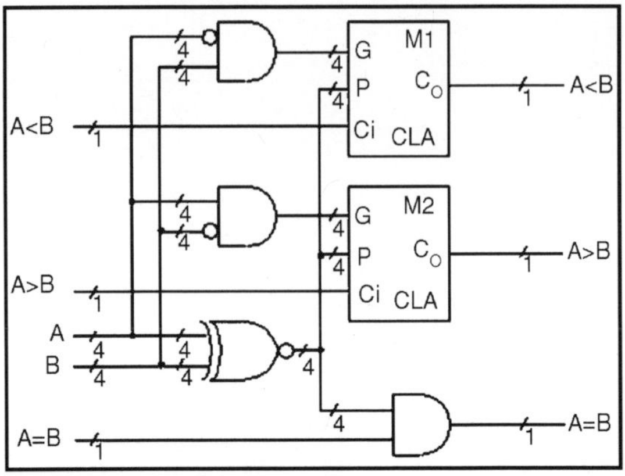

Using this concept, common elements of the three comparator functions A < B, A > B, and A = B are combined to construct the model shown above, which maps directly onto the gate-level realization of the 74L85.

TECHNIQUE OF BINARY MULTIPLIER

Binary multiplication uses the same technique as decimal multiplication. In fact, binary multiplication is much easier because each digit we multiply by is either zero or one. Consider the simple problem of multiplying 1102 by 102. We can use this problem to review some terminology and illustrate the rules for binary multiplication.

- First, we note that 1102 is our multiplicand and 102 is our multiplier.

```
 110
× 10
```

- We begin by multiplying 1102 by the rightmost digit of our multiplier which is 0. Any number times zero is zero, so we just write zeros below.

```
 110
× 10
 ---
 000
```

- Now we multiply the multiplicand by the next digit of our multiplier which is 1. To perform this multiplication, we just need to copy the multiplicand and shift it one column to the left as we do in decimal multiplication.

```
  110
 × 10
  ---
  000
 110
```

- Now we add our results together. The product of our multiplication is 1100_2.

$$\begin{array}{r} 110 \\ \times\ 10 \\ \hline 000 \\ 110 \\ \hline 1100 \end{array}$$

When performing binary multiplication, remember the following rules:

- Copy the multiplicand when the multiplier digit is 1. Otherwise, write a row of zeros.
- Shift your results one column to the left as you move to a new multiplier digit.
- Add the results together using binary addition to find the product.

SUBTRACTOR OF BINARY ADDER

HALF ADDER/SUBTRACTOR

This figure shows the configuration for a Half Adder/Subtractor. The first logic gate which is a XOR allows the circuit to do the complement of the binary bit when we want to do a subtraction. In the case that is needed to implement a addition the XOR keep the number the same.

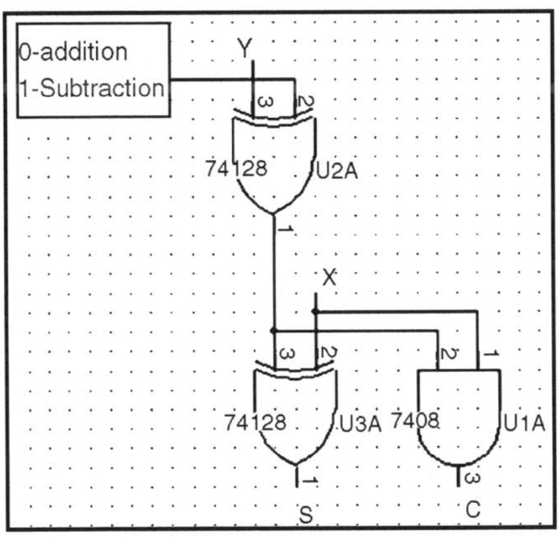

Truth Table

A	B	C	S
0	0	0	0
0	1	0	1
1	0	0	1
1	1	1	0

FULL ADDER/SUBTRACTOR

Full Adder Circuit

This circuit adds two binary one bit numbers. Also, it manages a carry that could come from another circuit.

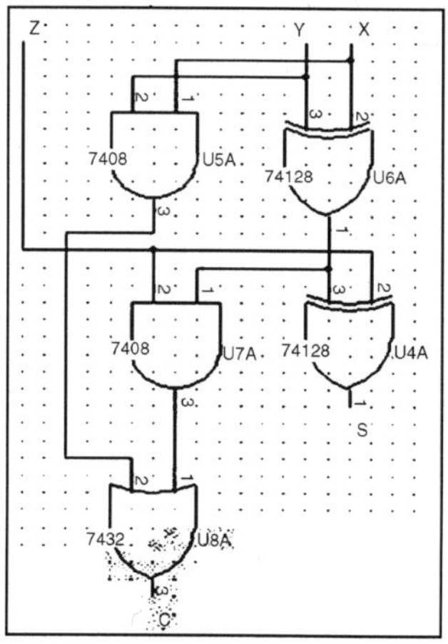

$[(AA)'*(BB)']' = A+B$

X	Y	Z	C	S
0	0	0	0	0
0	0	1	0	1
0	1	0	0	1
0	1	1	1	0
1	0	0	0	1
1	0	1	1	0
1	1	0	1	0
1	1	1	1	1

This figure shows the configuration for a Full Adder/Subtractor. The box with the name of"Full Adder" has all the logic to do the addition and subtraction depending of the inputs that it receives. The XOR gate that is outside the box allows the circuit to do the complement of the binary bit when we want to do a subtraction. In the case that is needed to implement an addition the XOR keep the number the same. In the previous graph the internal logic for the box"Full Adder" is shown.

3-BIT ADDER/SUBTRACTOR

The 3-bit adder/Subtractor was implemented with three Full adder circuits and three XOR gates outside which implemented the operation (addition/ subtraction) selected by the user. In this circuit, we have three inputs for the first three bits binary number and three inputs for the second three bits binary number. When the addition is selected the XOR gates keep the binary numbers the same and add them together. On the other hand, when a subtraction is selected the XOR gates complement the second number which is represented with a"Y" and after that, the Full Adder circuit adds both numbers together.

The 3-bit Adder/Subtractor circuit has four outputs. The first three outputs represent the three bits that were the result of the subtraction or addition. The last bit represents a carry.

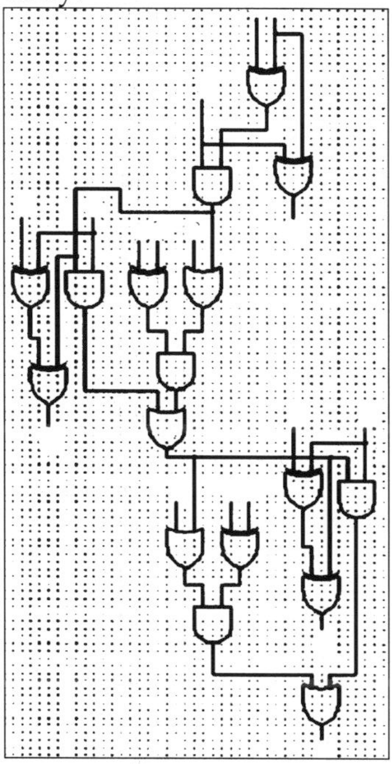

9

Analysis of Sequential Circuits

CIRCUIT ANALYSIS

Circuit analysis begins with a circuit diagram or a black box and ends with an identification of the sequential circuit implemented by the device - normally a truth table.

The steps are:

- Identify the inputs and the outputs.
- Express each output as a Boolean function of the inputs and the present state Q(T).
- Identify the circuit if possible.

CIRCUIT FOR ANALYSIS

We first study the analysis of digital circuits, then we study their design. There are a number of steps in the analysis of a circuit. Where to begin depends on what one has.

When given a circuit diagram, the following steps are used to begin the analysis:

- Determine the inputs and outputs of the circuit. Assign variables to represent these.
- Determine the inputs and outputs of the flip-flops.
- Construct the Next State and Output Tables.
- Construct the State Diagram.
- If possible, identify the circuit. There are no good rules for this step.

Consider the following circuit. We want to discover what it does.

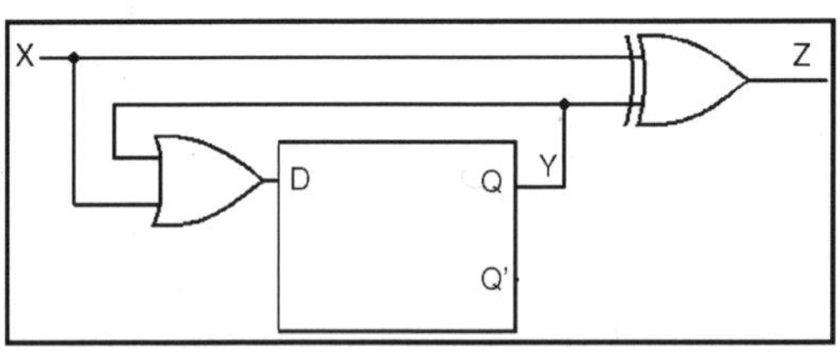

Fig. Circuit to Be Analysed

Step 1: Identify and Label the Inputs, Outputs, and Internal States

We use the following variables in the analysis of this circuit with a single flip-flop. X denotes the input, Y denotes the output of the flip-flop (Y' also), and Z the output of the circuit. If we had more than one flip-flop, we would label the flip-flop with a number beginning at 0 and use that as a subscript, so flip-flop 0 would have output Y0, etc.

Step 2: Determine the Inputs and Outputs of the Flip-flops

The next step is to determine the equations for Z, the output, and D, the input to the flip-flop. By inspection, we determine the following for the equations:

$Z = X \oplus Y$

$D = X + Y$

Step 3: Construct the Next State and Output Tables.

We begin this state by recalling the characteristic table of each flip-flop that is used in the design. Here we have only one flip-flip, a D with a very simple characteristic table that is better represented as an equation: Q(t+1) = D - the next state is what you put in now.

Noting that Q(t) = Y (the state of a flip-flop is also its output) we construct the following Next-State diagram for the flip-flop, based on the characteristic table of a D flip-flop and the equation we derived for the D input: D = X + Y. One simple caution here is that the input to a flip-flop is a function of the present state only, having nothing to do with the next state (as we have no crystsal balls). Thus Y = Q(t). Here is the present state (PS)/next state (NS) diagram for the circuit.

X	Q(t) = Y	D = X + Y	Q(t+1)
0	0	0	0
0	1	1	1
1	0	1	1
1	1	1	1

The output table is similarly constructed, using the equation $Z = X \oplus Y = Z = X \oplus Q(t)$. Again, note that the output is not a function of the next state.

X	Q(t)	Z
0	0	0
0	1	1
1	0	1
1	1	0

These two tables are combined to form the transition/output table.

X	Q(t) = Y	D = X + Y	Q(t+1)/Z
0	0	0	0/0
0	1	1	1/1
1	0	1	1/1
1	1	1	1/0

At this point, we should produce a state table in the standard format. This involves assigning labels to each of the two states, currently identified only as Q(t) = 0 and Q(t) = 1. For lack of anything more imaginative, we label the states 0 and 1.

Table. State Table for Circuit to be Analysed

Present State	Next State/Output	
	X = 0	X = 1
0	0/0	1/1
1	1/1	1/0

Step 4: Construct the State Diagram

The final step in the process may be the creation of the state diagram.

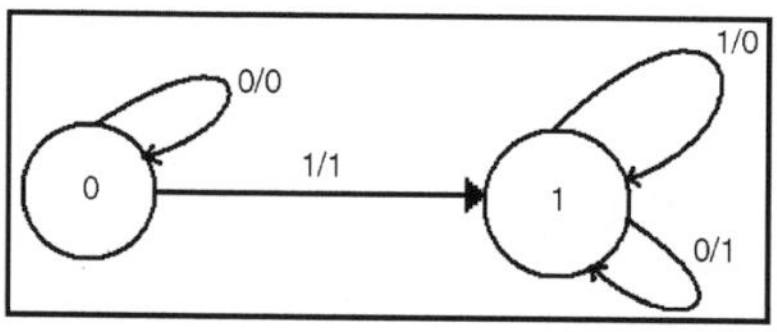

At this point, we have a complete description of the circuit. It may be possible to proceed from this diagram to obtain an understanding of what the circuit does.

Step 5: If Possible, Identify the Circuit.

This circuit is a 2-state device, with memory represented by one bit. The circuit stays in state 0 from the start until a 1 is input at which time it transitions to state 1 and remains there. Note the relation of the output to the input, depending on the state of the machine.

Input	Q(t)	Output	
0	0	0	For Q(t) = 0, the output is X
1	0	1	
0	1	1	For Q(t) = 1, the output is X'.
1	1	0	

A verbal description of the circuit is then that it copies its input to the output until the first 1 is encountered in the input stream. After that event, all input is output as complemented.

What this circuit does is take the two's-complement of a binary integer, presented to the circuit least-significant bit first. It is easy to prove that such a strategy produces the two's complement of a number. First, consider a number ending in 1, say $X_nX_{n-1}.... X_2X_{11}$.

The one's complement of this number is $X_n'X_{n-1}'$ .... $X_2'X_{1'0}$. Adding 1 to this produces the number $X_n'X_{n-1}'$ .... $X_2'X_{1'1}$, in which the least significant 1 is copied and the remaining bits are complemented. The proof is completed by supposing that the number terminates in a one or more zeroes; *i.e.*, its least significant bits are 10 .... 0, where the count of zeroes is not important.

The one's-complement of this number will end with 01 .... 1, where each zero in the original has turned to a 1. But 01 .... 1 + 1 = 10 .... 0, and up to the least significant 1 the two's-complement is a copy of the bits in the integer itself. Note that there is no carry out of the addition that produced the right-most 1, so the remainder of the integer is formed by the one's-complement. Thus we have a complete description of the circuit.

SEQUENTIAL CIRCUITS

Digital electronics is classified into combinational logic and sequential logic. Combinational logic output depends on the inputs levels, whereas sequential logic output depends on stored levels and also the input levels.

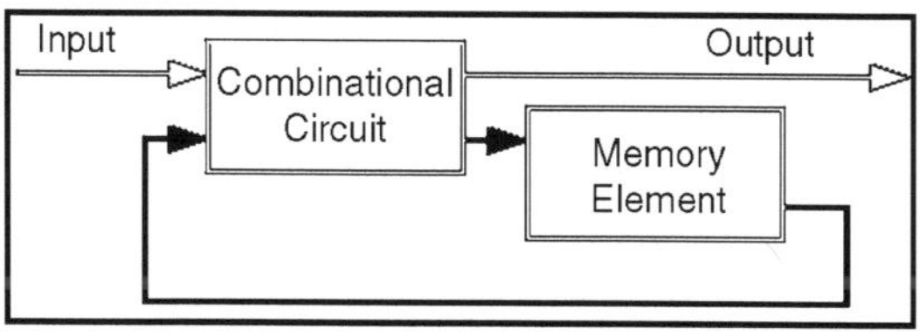

The following figure shows a way to consider sequential circuits.

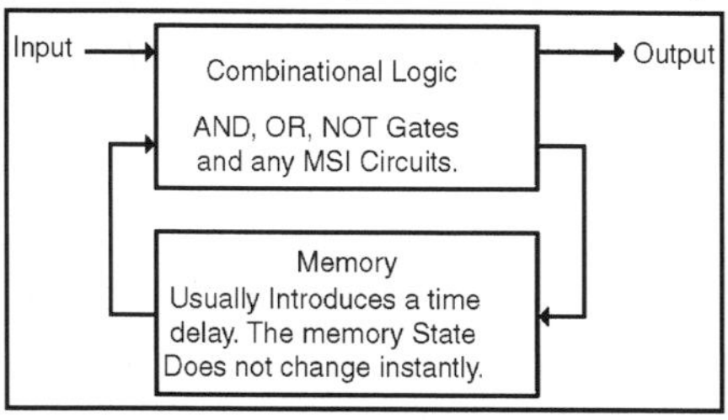

Fig. Sequential Logic Includes Combinational Logic and Memory

Sequential circuits can be characterized into two broad classes - synchronous and asynchronous. As a general rule, asynchronous circuits are faster, but much harder to design. We shall focus totally on synchronous circuits.

By Q(T) we denote the state of a sequential circuit at time T - this is basically its memory. We watch the state of the circuit change from Q(T) to Q(T + 1) as the clock ticks.

The constraint on synchronous circuits is that the state of the circuit changes after the input, thus we have a typical sequence as follows:

- At time T, we have input (denoted by X) and state Q(T).
- As a result of the input X and state Q(T), a new state is computed,

This becomes available to the input only at time (T + 1) and so is called Q(T + 1). The fact that the new state, computed as a result of X and Q(T), is not available to the input of the sequential circuit until the next time step greatly facilitates the design and analysis of the specific circuit.

DESIGN OF SEQUENTIAL CIRCUITS

Having seen how to analyse digital circuits, we now investigate how to design digital circuits. We assume that we are given a complete and unambiguous description of the circuit to be designed as a starting point. At this level, most design problems focus on one of two topics: modulo-N counters and sequence detectors.

Here is an overview of the design procedure for a sequential circuit:

- Derive the state diagram and state table for the circuit.
- Count the number of states in the state diagram (call it N) and calculate the umber of flip-flops needed (call it P) by solving the equation 2P-1 < N 2P. This is best solved by guessing the value of P.
- Assign a unique P-bit binary number (state vector) to each state. Often, the first state = 0, the next state = 1, etc.
- Derive the state transition table and the output table.
- Separate the state transition table into P tables, one for each flip-flop.

  WARNING: Things can get messy here; neatness counts.
- Decide on the types of flip-flops to use. When in doubt, use all JK's.
- Derive the input table for each flip-flop using the excitation tables for the type.
- Derive the input equations for each flip-flop based as functions of the input and current state of all flip-flops.
- Summarize the equations by writing them in one place.
- *Draw the circuit diagram*: Most homework assignments will not go this far, as the circuit diagrams are hard to draw neatly.

ANALYSIS OF CLOCKED SEQUENTIAL CIRCUITS

Analysis consists of obtaining a state-table or a state-diagram from a given sequential circuit implementation. In other words analysis closes the loop by forming state-table from a given circuit-implementation. We will show the analysis procedure by deriving the state table of the example circuit we considered in synthesis.

The circuit is shown in Figure.

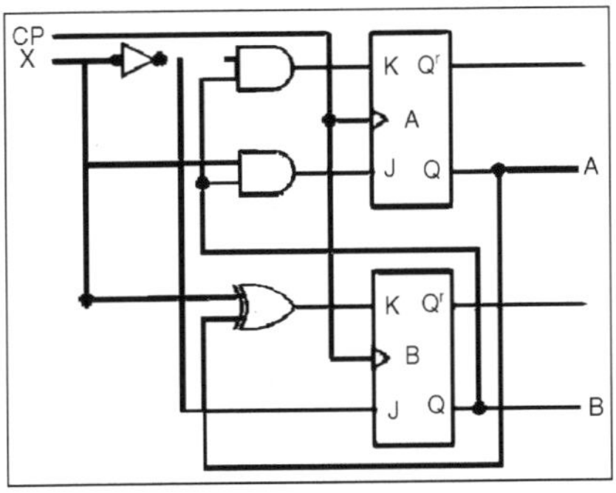

Fig. A Clocked Sequential Circuit

The circuit has:

- Clock input, CP.
- One input x
- One output y
- One clocked JK flip-flop
- One clocked D flip-flop (the machine can be in maximum of 4 states)

A State table is representation of sequence of inputs, outputs, and flip-flop states in a tabular form. Two forms of state tables are shown.

Present State		**Next State**		**Output**	
		x = 0	**x = 1**	**x = 0**	**x = 1**
A	B	A	B	y	y
0	0				
0	1				
1	0				
1	1				

Analysis is the generation of state table from the given sequential circuit. The number of rows in the state table is equal to 2 (number of flip-flops+ number of inputs). For the circuit under consideration, number of rows = 2(2+1) = 2(3) = 8

Table: State Table - Form 2

Present State		**Input**	**NextState**	**Output**
A(t)	B(t)	x	A(t+1) B(t+1)	y
0	0	0		
0	0	1		
0	1	0		
0	1	1		
1	0	0		
1	0	1		
1	1	0		
1	1	1		

In the present case there are two flip-flops and one input, thus a total of 8 rows as shown in the table.

Present State		Input	NextState		Output
A(t)	B(t)	x	A(t+1)	B(t+1)	y
0	0	0	0	0	0
0	0	1	0	1	0
0	1	0	1	0	0
0	1	1	0	1	0
1	0	0	0	0	0
1	0	1	0	0	0
1	1	1	1	1	0
1	1	1	0	1	1

The analysis can start from any arbitrary state. Let us start deriving the state table from the initial state 00.

As a first step, the input equations to the flip-flops and to the combinational circuit must be obtained from the given logic diagram.

These equations are:

$J_A = BX'$

$K_A = BX + B'X'$

$D_B = X$

$y = ABX$

The first row of the state-table is obtained as follows:

When input X = 0; and present states A = 0 and B = 0 (as in the first row); then, using the above equations we get:

$$y = 0,\ J_A = 0,\ K_A = 1, \text{ and } D_B = 0.$$

The resulting state table is exactly same from which we started our design example. Thus analysis is opposite to design and combined they act as a closed loop.

STATE REDUCTION

Ring the input-output relationships. In other words, to reduce the number of states, redundant states should be eliminated. A redundant state Si is a state which is equivalent to another state Sj. Two states are said to be equivalent if, for each member of the set of inputs, they give exactly the same output and send the circuit either to the same state or to an equivalent state.

Since'm' flip-flops can describe a state machine of up to 2m states, reducing the number of states may (or may not) result in a reduction in the number of flip-flops. For example, if the number of states are reduced from 8 to 5, we still need 3 flip-flops. However, state reduction will result in more don't care states. The increased number of don't care states can help obtain a simplified circuit for the state machine.

Consider the shown state diagram.

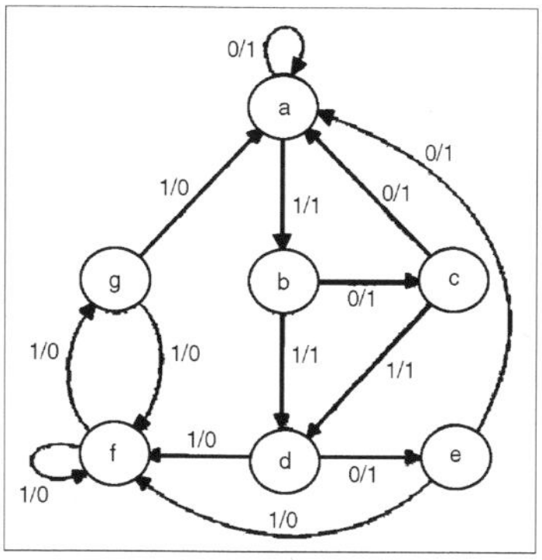

Fig. State Diagram

The state reduction proceeds by first tabulating the information of the state diagram into its equivalent state-table form (as shown in the table) The problem of state reduction requires identifying equivalent states. Each N states is replaced by 1 state.

Consider the following state table.

Table. State Table After Reduction

Present State	Next State		Output	
	x = 0	x = 1	x = 0	x = 1
a	a	b	1	1
b	c	d	1	1
c	a	d	1	1
d	e	~~f~~ d	1	0
e	a	~~f~~ d	1	0
~~f~~	~~g~~ e	f	1	0
~~g~~	a	f	1	0

States'g' and'e' produce the same outputs, *i.e.*'1' and'0', and take the state machine to same next-states,'a' and'f', on inputs'0' and'1' respectively. Thus, states'g' and'e' are equivalent states.

We can now remove state'g' and replace it with'e' as shown. We next note that the above change has caused the states'd' and'f' to be equivalent. Thus in the next step, we remove state'f' and replace it with'd'. There are no more equivalent states remaining. The reduced state table results in the following reduced state diagram.

STATES ASSIGNMENT

When constructing a state diagram, variable names are used for states as the final number of states is not known a priori. Once the state diagram is constructed, prior to implementation (using gates and flip-flops), we need to perform the step of'state reduction'. The step that follows state reduction is state assignment. In state assignment, binary patterns are assigned to state variables.

Table: Possible State Assignments

State	Assignment 1	Assignment 2	Assignment 3
a	001	000	000
b	010	010	100
c	011	011	010
d	100	101	101
e	101	111	011

For a given machine, there are several state assignments possible. Different state assignments may result in different combinational circuits of varying complexities. State assignment procedures try to assign binary values to states such that the cost (complexity) of the combinational circuit is reduced. There are several heuristics that attempt to choose good state assignments (also known as state encoding) that try to reduce the required combinational logic complexity, and hence cost. As mentioned earlier, for the reduced state machine obtained in the previous example, there can be a number of possible assignments. As an example, three different state assignments are shown in the table for the same machine.

SINGLE BINARY BIT OF FLIP FLOPS

A flip-flop is a"bit box"; it stores a single binary bit. By Q(t), we denote the state of the flip-flop at the present time, or present tick of the clock; either Q(t) = 0 or Q(t) = 1. The student will note that throughout this textbook we make the assumption that all circuit elements function correctly, so that any binary device is assumed to have only two states. A flip-flop must have an output; this is called either Q or Q(t). This output indicates the current state of the flip-flop, and as such is either a binary 0 or a binary 1. We shall see that, as a result of the way in which they are constructed, all flip-flops also output $\overline{Q(t)}$, the complement of the current state. Each flip-flop also has, as input, signals that specify how the next state, Q(t + 1), is to relate to the present state, Q(t). Every flip-flop also has an input derived from the system clock, which allows it to function as a synchronous circuit. It also has connections to power and ground. Here are the symbols for SR and D flip-flops, which we have not yet defined. Note the small triangles on the clock input; this says"edge triggered".

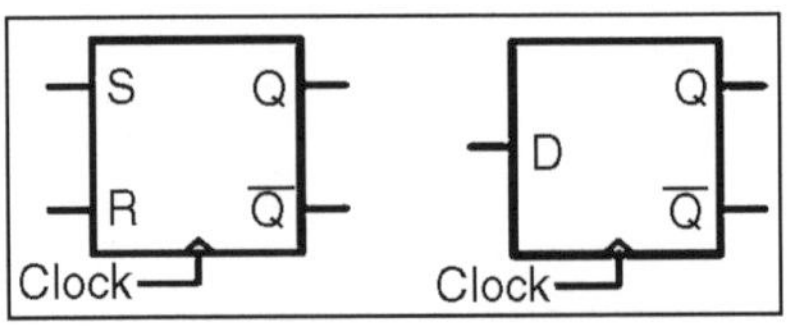

One should note that the more common symbols for flip-flops show the clock input coming in"from the side" as shown in the next figure.

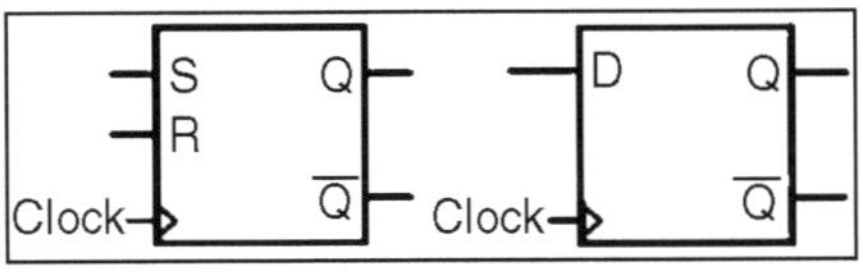

THE CLOCK

The most fundamental characteristic of synchronous sequential circuits is a system clock. This is an electronic circuit that produces a repetitive train of logic 1 and logic 0 at a regular rate, called the clock frequency. Most computer systems have a number of clocks, usually operating at related frequencies; for example – 2 GHz, 1GHz, 500MHz, and 125MHz.

The inverse of the clock frequency is the clock cycle time. As an example, we consider a clock with a frequency of 2 GHz (2•109 Hertz). The cycle time is $1.0/(2 \bullet 10^9)$ seconds, or 0.5•10-9 seconds = 0.500 nanoseconds = 500 picoseconds. Synchronous sequential circuits are sequential circuits that use a clock input to order events. Asynchronous sequential circuits do not use a common clock and, as hinted at above, are much harder to design and test. As we shall focus only on synchronous circuits, we immediately launch a discussion of the clock. The following figure illustrates some of the terms commonly used for a clock.

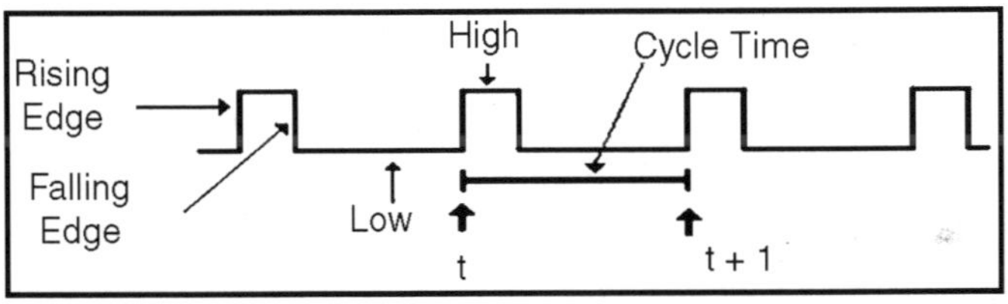

The clock input is very important to the concept of a sequential circuit. At each"tick" of the clock the output of a sequential circuit is determined by its input and by its state. We now provide a common definition of a"clock tick" - it occurs at the rising edge of each pulse. We use t to represent the time at a clock tick and (t + 1) to denote the time at the next clock tick - the difference between the two is the clock cycle time. Suppose a 2 GHz clock, which corresponds to a clock cycle time of 0.5 nanosecond. Strictly speaking, we should label our timings in nanoseconds: 1.0, 1.5. 2.0. 2.5, etc. The convention is just to count the ticks, referring to the present clock pulse as occurring at time t and the next one at time (t + 1).

DESCRIPTION

By definition, a flip-flop is an edge-triggered latch. We must now show how achieve edge triggering. In essence, what we shall do is take a level triggered latch and give it a clock pulse with a very short positive (logical 1) phase. The key component of an edge-triggered flip-flop is a pulse generator that we studied in a previous chapter. This could be based on the gate delay of a NOT gate. More modern devices likely use a different circuit so as to generate a shorter pulse.

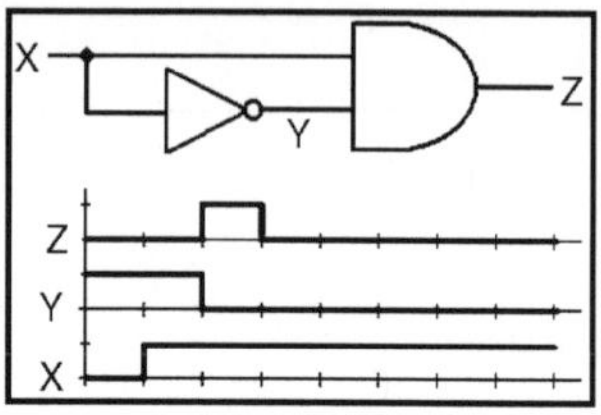

Now that we have a method to generate a short pulse, we can build an edge-triggered device. The following is a diagram of the components of two typical edge-triggered flip-flops. The top one is a SR flip-flop and the bottom one is a D flip-flop.

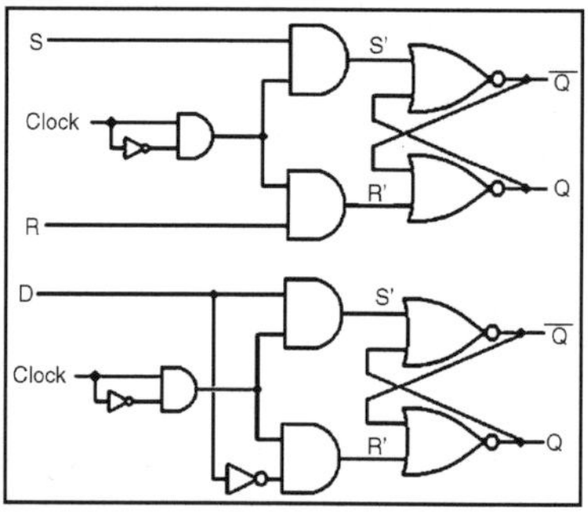

TYPES OF FLIP-FLOPS

In order to avoid the simple example, we shall examine the general case. Here is the circuit for consideration. We postulate a total of gate delays (including that of the D flip-flop) to be the time interval signified by. Thus at time after the D latch is first sensitive to its input, the circuitry has output a new value to become D. But the flip-flop is activated by a short pulse, of time length.

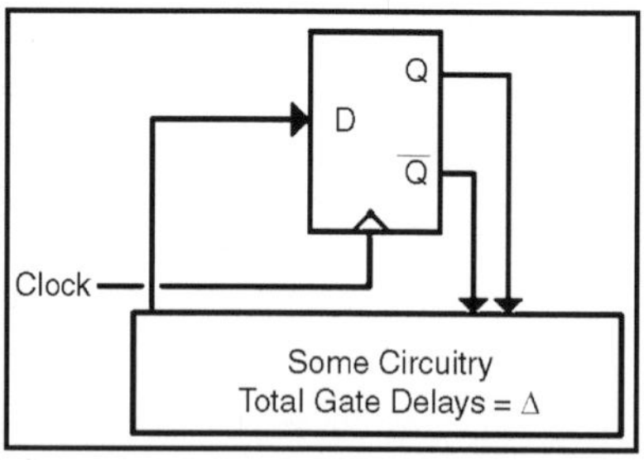

The timing diagram below shows the interruption of the uncontrolled feedback loop. By the time that the output of the circuitry has changed, the D flip-flop is no longer sensitive to input. The input will not become effective until the beginning of the next clock cycle.

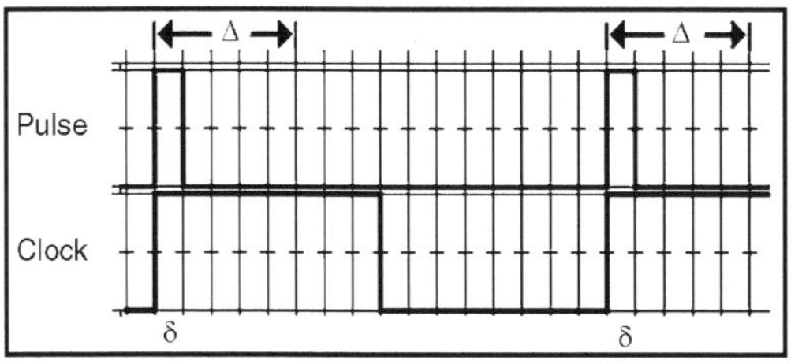

How can one insure that the relative timings of two circuits, the D flip-flop and the rest of the CPU circuitry, operate with the correct timings? This is one of the issues of central importance in the design of a CPU; since we have stumbled into it, let's talk about it. To be more precise, define two total gate delays: Δ_{MIN} and Δ_{MAX}. Δ_{MIN} is the total time delay for the fastest CPU operation and Δ_{MAX}. the delay for the slowest. We must have MIN >, or the circuit would occasionally display uncontrolled feedback. Conservatively, we might say Δ_{MIN} 1.5• δ. The next criterion is a bit more difficult to state precisely, but it might be stated something like $T \geq 1.5 \bullet \Delta_{MAX}$, where T denotes the clock period. What we say here is that the clock period must be long enough for the CPU output to"settle". Note, however, that a value of T much larger than MAX is just wasted time.

Put another way, the value of Δ_{MAX} determines the fastest clock that can reasonably be applied to the CPU. A good part of the art of CPU design is based on this issue. When we study the RISC (Reduced Instruction Set Computer) movement, we shall see that one of the issues was to remove the more complex instructions, thus reducing Δ_{MAX} and allowing for a faster clock. There is a trade-off here that we shall explore in later chapters. To be honest, the sum of CPU gate delays is not always the limiting factor in the clock speed. Some recent CPUs have been designed with a"hot clock" that is hot in both ways. It is very fast, being of the order of 4 to 5 GHz. It is also hot in the literal sense, in that the CPU, operating at that clock rate, emits so much heat that it overheats itself. The art of CPU design is always bumping up against those messy laws of physics.

The SR Flip-Flop

We have completely defined the SR flip-flop, based on the idea of an SR latch. While we could just leave the topic and proceed, it is appropriate at this time to review the subject and state, in one place, what the student is expected to know. We begin with a depiction of the SR flip-flop that will be used in all future discussions.

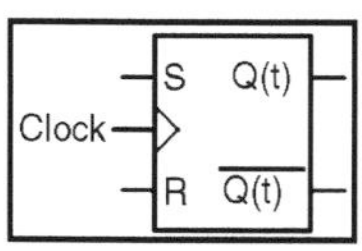

At this point we are no longer interested in the internal construction of the flip-flop, but on its operational characteristics. These are given in the characteristic table.

S	R	Q(t + 1)
0	0	Q(t)
0	1	0
1	0	1
1	1	ERROR

We next address an issue that commonly arises in the use of flip-flops in circuit design. We have a number of scenarios. For each, we know Q(t) and what Q(t + 1) should be. The question is how to achieve that change. For example, if Q(t) = 0 and we want Q(t + 1) = 0, we have two choices: either S = 0 and R = 0, or S = 0 and R = 1. The first option, keeps the state unchanged at 0; the second forces it to 0. As S = 0 is sufficient to do this without regard to the value of R, we say that the input is S = 0 and R = d; the d standing for"don't care".

On the other hand, if Q(t) = 0 and Q(t + 1) = 1, only S = 1 and R = 0 will do. This is the only combination that will give a next state of 1 when the present state is 0. If we have Q(t) = 1 and want Q(t + 1) = 0, then our choice is simple:

S = 0 and R = 1.

If we have Q(t) = 1 and want Q(t + 1) = 1, then we can choose either S = 0 and R = 0, or S = 1 and R = 0. This is denoted as S = d and R = 0. The above discussions lead to the excitation table for the SR flip-flop.

Q(t)	Q(t + 1)	S	R
0	0	0	d
0	1	1	0
1	0	0	1
1	1	d	0

The JK Flip-Flop: Enhancing the SR Flip-Flop

Recall the characteristic table of the SR flip-flop. We repeat the table here for emphasis.

S	R	Q(t + 1)
0	0	Q(t)
0	1	0
1	0	1
1	1	ERROR

The theoretician examining this table would note two facts immediately.

- The input S = 1 and R = 1 is disallowed; we would like to do something with it.
- The values for Q(t + 1) are three of the possible four Boolean functions of 1 variable.

Considering Q as a Boolean variable, we now show that there are exactly four Boolean functions of this Boolean variable. These are f(Q) = 0, f(Q) = 1, f(Q) = Q, and f(Q) = $\overline{Q}$. We do this by showing the truth table for each of these functions and noting that there are only four different ways to put 0's and 1's into the two row entries for a function..

Table. The Four Boolean Functions of Boolean Variable Q

Q	0	Q	$\overline{Q}$	1
0	0	0	1	1
1	0	1	0	1

Given this, our enhanced SR flip-flop would have Q(t + 1) = $\overline{Q}$ (t) as one possible output. For maximal compatibility with the existing SR, we would want to leave the existing valid inputs alone and just make good use of the invalid one. What we get is a JK flip-flop.

Recalling that an SR flip-flop is so called because it is a Set-Reset device, we may ask for the meaning of JK. One is tempted to make up some story related to names in German, but the basic answer is that"I don't know". In any case, we present the characteristic table for the JK flip-flop and then ask how one might modify an SR flip to achieve that goal.

Here is the desired characteristic table.

J	K	Q(t + 1)
0	0	Q(t)
0	1	0
1	0	1
1	1	$\overline{Q}$ (t)

Viewing this as a modification of the SR flip-flop, we ask how to generate each of S and R from the inputs J and K under the following constraints;

- Except when J = 1 and K = 1, we want to have S = J and R = K. Under these circumstances, the behaviour is identical.
- When J = 1, K = 1, and Q = 0, we want S = 1 and R = 0. This makes Q(t + 1) = 1.
- When J = 1, K = 1, and Q = 1, we want S = 0 and R = 1. This makes Q(t + 1) = 0.

When in doubt about how to create a circuit, we make a truth table. The inputs to the truth table are J, K, and Q (the present state). The outputs are S and R.

Row	Q	J	K	S	R
0	0	0	0	0	0
1	0	0	1	0	1
2	0	1	0	1	0
3	0	1	1	1	0
4	1	0	0	0	0
5	1	0	1	0	1
6	1	1	0	1	0
7	1	1	1	0	1

We have two patterns that almost work: $S = J \bullet \overline{Q}$ and $R = K \bullet Q$. Let's examine each case.

$S = J \bullet \overline{Q}$ produces the expected result for all rows except row 6. In that row we have,

- Q = 1, J = 1, and K = 0. We want Q(t + 1) to be 1. But S = 0 and R = 0 will cause.
- Q(t + 1) = Q(t) = 1, exactly what we want. So this simple formula causes no trouble.
- $R = K \bullet Q$ produces the expected result for all rows except row 1. In that row we have
- Q = 0, J = 0, and K = 1. We want Q(t + 1) to be 0. But S = 0 and R = 0 will cause
- Q(t + 1) = Q(t) = 0, exactly what we want. So again we have no trouble.

Here is the basic detailed circuit for the JK flip-flop.

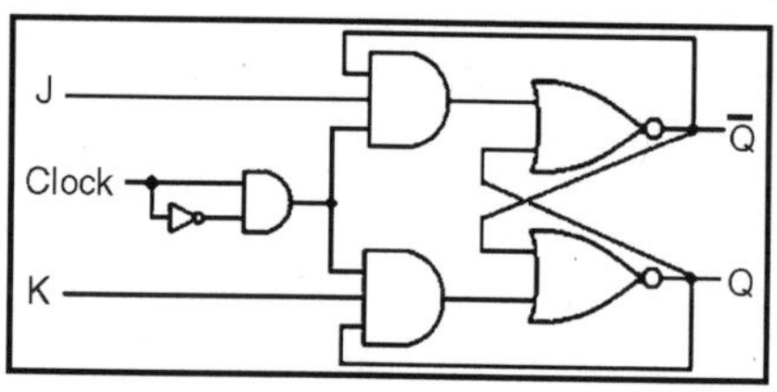

We now give the standard representation of the JK flip-flop as will be used in future discussions. Again, note the triangle symbol on the clock input, indicating edge triggering.

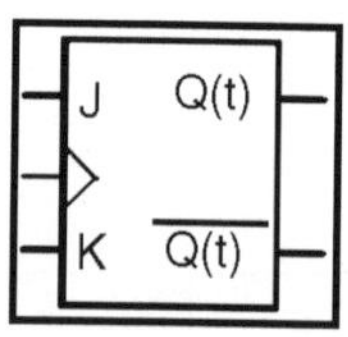

We have already presented the characteristic table for the JK flip-flop. Here it is again.

J	K	Q(t + 1)
0	0	Q(t)
0	1	0
1	0	1
1	1	$\overline{Q}$ (t)

We now create the excitation table for the JK.

- If Q(t) = 0 and Q(t + 1) is to be 0, we can use either J = 0 and K = 0, or J = 0 and K = 1.
- If Q(t) = 0 and Q(t + 1) is to be 1, we can use either J = 1 and K = 0, or J = 1 and K = 1.

Note that this is a new option, not available for an SR flip-flop.

- If Q(t) = 1 and Q(t + 1) is to be 0, we can use either J = 0 and K = 1, or J = 1 and K = 1.

Note that this also is a new option, not available for an SR flip-flop.

- If Q(t) = 1 and Q(t + 1) is to be 1, we can use either J = 0 and K = 0, or J = 1 and K = 0.

This gives the excitation table for the JK flip-flop.

Q(t)	Q(t + 1)	J	K
0	0	0	d
0	1	1	d
1	0	d	1
1	1	d	0

THE D FLIP-FLOP

We have already examined the D latch. The input is labeled"D" for"Data". The D flip-flop has a characteristic table identical to that of a D latch.

D	Q(t + 1)
0	0
1	1

The device is so simple that it does not require an excitation equation. We just use an excitation equation, which simply states"Give it what you want".

$$D = Q(t + 1)$$

Let's compare timing diagrams for a normal D latch versus one that is edge-triggered:

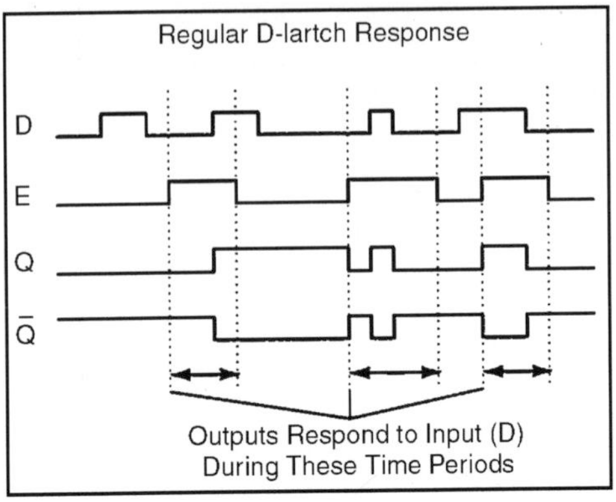

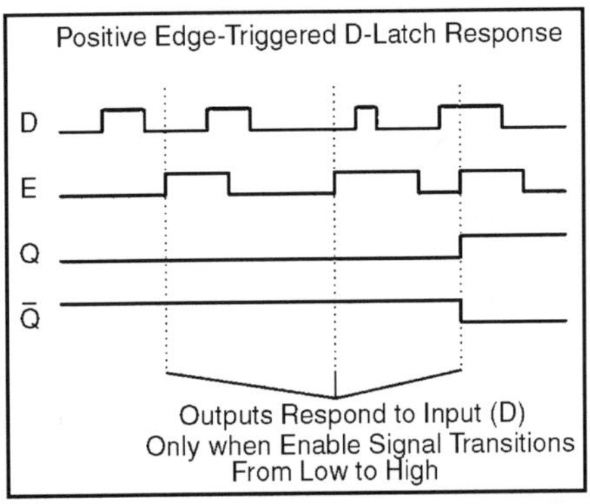

In the first timing diagram, the outputs respond to input D whenever the enable (E) input is high, for however long it remains high. When the enable signal falls back to a low state, the circuit remains latched. In the second timing diagram, we note a distinctly different response in the circuit output(s): it only responds to the D input during that brief moment of time when the enable signal *changes*, or *transitions*, from low to high. This is known as *positive* edge-triggering. There is such a thing as *negative* edge triggering as well, and it produces the following response to the same input signals:

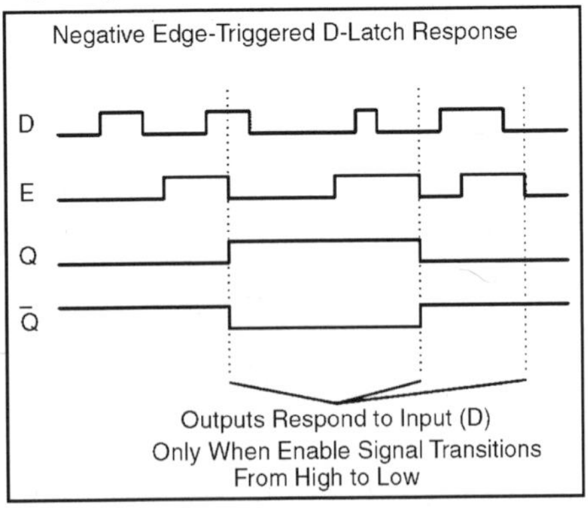

Whenever we enable a multivibrator circuit on the transitional edge of a square-wave enable signal, we call it a *flip-flop*instead of a *latch*. Consequently, and edge-triggered S-R circuit is more properly known as an S-R flip-flop, and an edge-triggered D circuit as a D flip-flop. The enable signal is renamed to be the *clock* signal.

Also, we refer to the data inputs (S, R, and D, respectively) of these flip-flops as *synchronous* inputs, because they have effect only at the time of the clock pulse edge (transition), thereby synchronizing any output changes with that clock pulse, rather than at the whim of the data inputs. But, how do we actually accomplish this edge-triggering? To create a "gated" S-R latch from a regular S-R latch is easy enough with a couple of AND gates, but how do we implement logic that only pays attention to the *rising or falling edge* of a changing digital signal?

What we need is a digital circuit that outputs a brief pulse whenever the input is activated for an arbitrary period of time, and we can use the output of this circuit to briefly enable the latch. We're getting a little ahead of ourselves here, but this is actually a kind of monostable multivibrator, which for now we'll call a *pulse detector*.

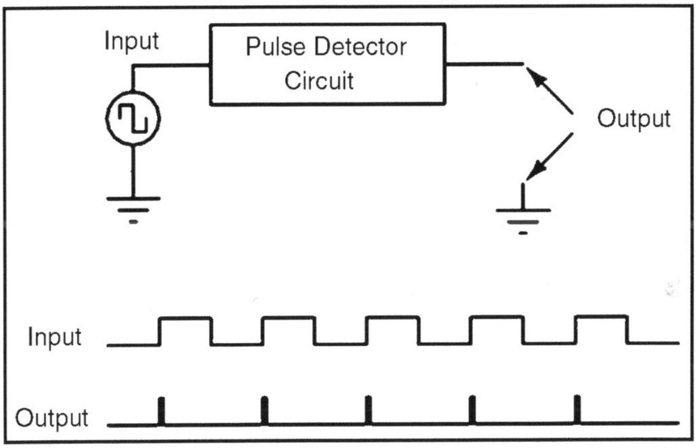

The duration of each output pulse is set by components in the pulse circuit itself. In ladder logic, this can be accomplished quite easily through the use of a time-delay relay with a very short delay time:

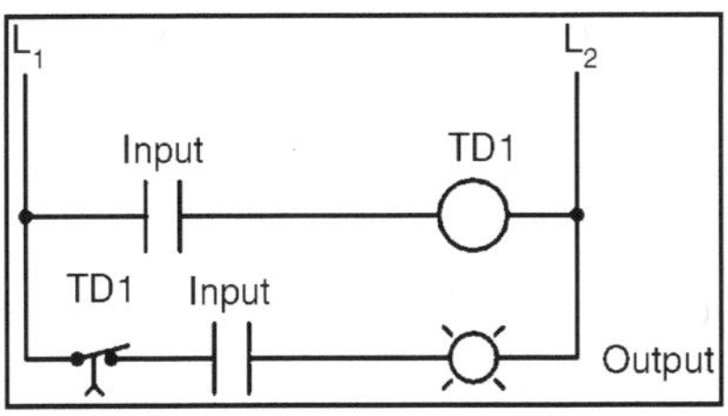

Implementing this timing function with semiconductor components is actually quite easy, as it exploits the inherent time delay within every logic gate (known as *propagation delay*). What we do is take an input signal and split it up two ways, then place a gate or a series of gates in one of those signal paths just to delay it a bit, then have both the original signal and its delayed counterpart enter into a two-input gate that outputs a high signal for the brief moment of time that the delayed signal has not yet caught up to the low-to-high change in the non-delayed signal. An example circuit for producing a clock pulse on a low-to-high input signal transition is shown here:

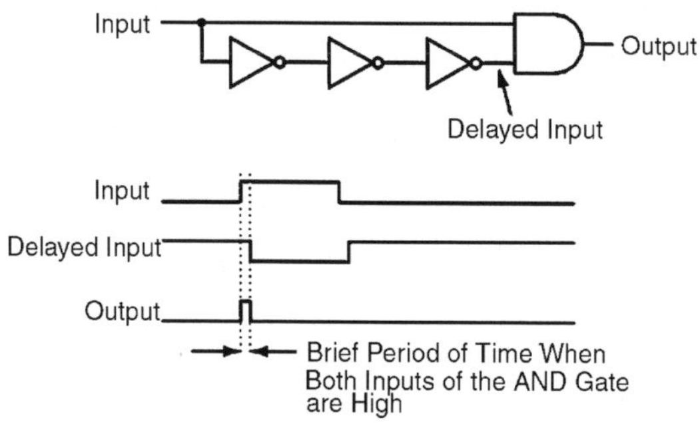

This circuit may be converted into a negative-edge pulse detector circuit with only a change of the final gate from AND to NOR:

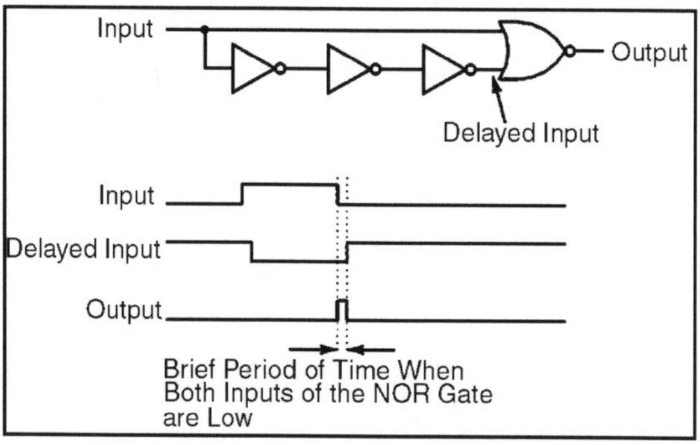

Now that we know how a pulse detector can be made, we can show it attached to the enable input of a latch to turn it into a flip-flop. In this case, the circuit is a S-R flip-flop:

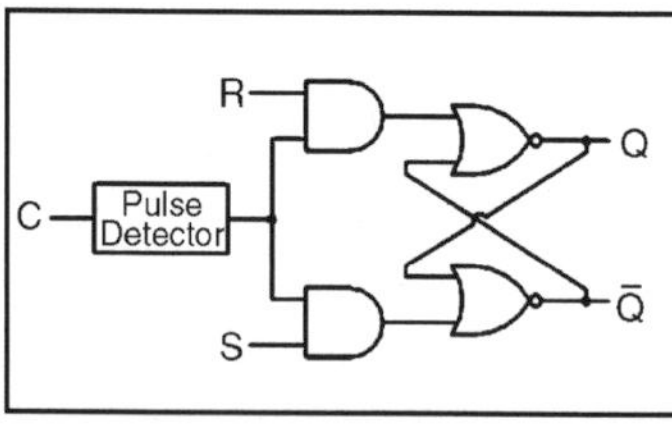

C	S	R	Q	$\bar{Q}$
↑	0	0	Latch	Latch
↑	0	1	0	1
↑	1	0	1	0
↑	1	1	0	0
X	0	0	Latch	Latch
X	0	1	Latch	Latch
X	1	0	Latch	Latch
X	1	1	Latch	Latch

Only when the clock signal (C) is transitioning from low to high is the circuit responsive to the S and R inputs. For any other condition of the clock signal ("x") the circuit will be latched.

A ladder logic version of the S-R flip-flop is shown here:

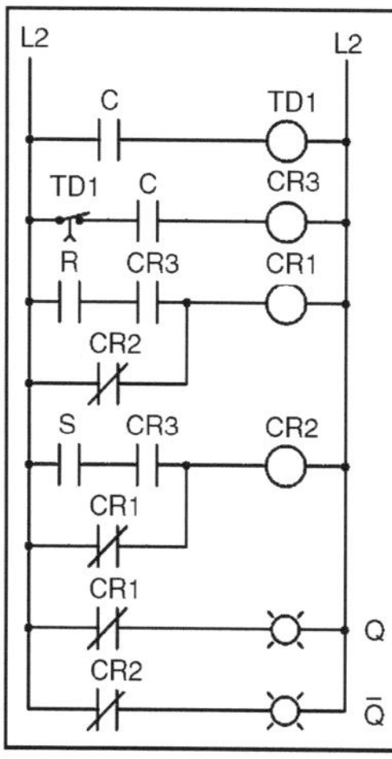

C	S	R	Q	Q̄
↑	0	0	Latch	Latch
↑	0	1	0	1
↑	1	0	1	0
↑	1	1	0	0
X	0	0	Latch	Latch
X	0	1	Latch	Latch
X	1	0	Latch	Latch
X	1	1	Latch	Latch

Relay contact CR_3 in the ladder diagram takes the place of the old E contact in the S-R latch circuit, and is closed only during the short time that both C is closed and time-delay contact TR_1 is closed. In either case (gate or ladder circuit), we see that the inputs S and R have no effect unless C is transitioning from a low (0) to a high (1) state. Otherwise, the flip-flop's outputs latch in their previous states.

It is important to note that the invalid state for the S-R flip-flop is maintained only for the short period of time that the pulse detector circuit allows the latch to be enabled. After that brief time period has elapsed, the outputs will latch into either the set or the reset state.

Once again, the problem of a *race condition* manifests itself. With no enable signal, an invalid output state cannot be maintained. However, the valid "latched" states of the multivibrator — set and reset — are mutually exclusive to one another. Therefore, the two gates of the multivibrator circuit will "race" each other for supremacy, and whichever one attains a high output state first will "win." The block symbols for flip-flops are slightly different from that of their respective latch counterparts:

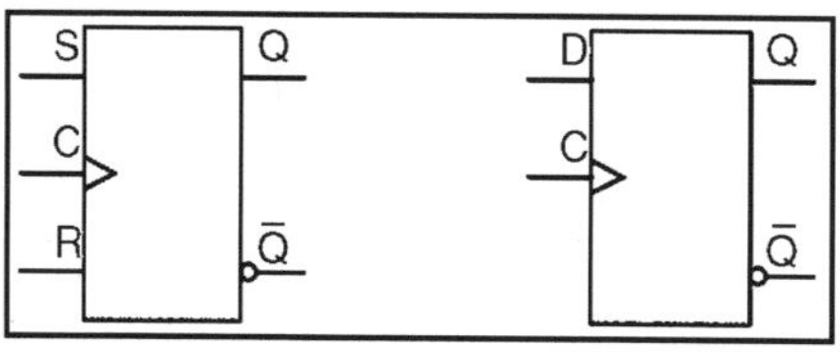

The triangle symbol next to the clock inputs tells us that these are edge-triggered devices, and consequently that these are flip-flops rather than latches. The symbols above are positive edge-triggered: that is, they "clock" on the rising edge (low-to-high transition) of the clock signal. Negative edge-triggered devices are symbolized with a bubble on the clock input line:

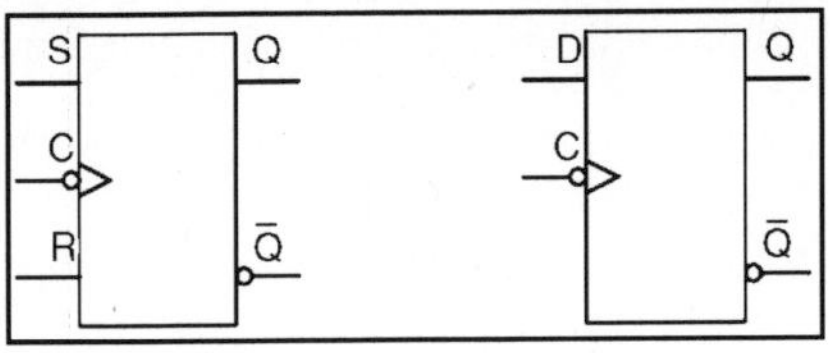

Both of the above flip-flops will "clock" on the falling edge (high-to-low transition) of the clock signal.

The T Flip-Flop

This is the fourth and last of the major types of flip-flops. The input to this flip-flop is labeled"T" for toggle. When T = 0, the state remains the same.

When T = 1, the flip-flop changes state. This gives rise to the following characteristic table.

T	**Q(t + 1)**
0	Q(t)
1	$\overline{Q}$ (t)

The excitation table for this flip-flop is almost obvious.

Q(t)	**Q(t + 1)**	**T**
0	0	0
0	1	1
1	0	1
1	1	0

This gives rise to an excitation equation.

$$T = Q(t) \oplus Q(t + 1)$$

THE JK AS A GENERAL FLIP-FLOP

We now take notice that the JK can be configured to function as any of the other 3 flip-flop types. In this, it is the most general type of flip-flop.

Another variation on a theme of bistable multivibrators is the J-K flip-flop. Essentially, this is a modified version of an S-R flip-flop with no "invalid" or "illegal" output state. Look closely at the following diagram to see how this is accomplished:

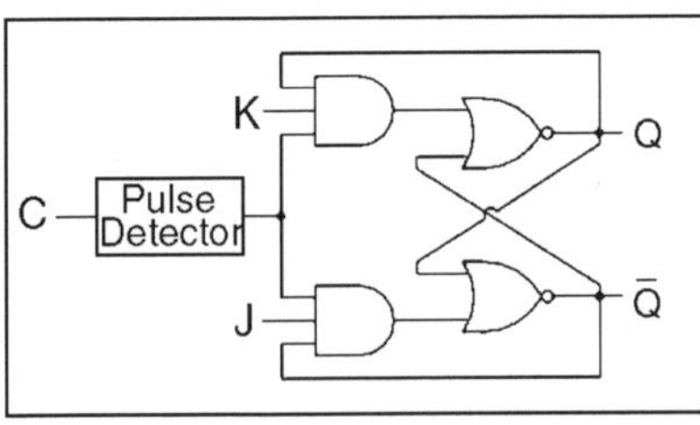

C	J	K	Q	$\overline{Q}$
↑	0	0	Latch	Latch
↑	0	1	0	1
↑	1	0	1	0
↑	1	1	Toggle	Toggle
X	0	0	Latch	Latch
X	0	1	Latch	Latch
X	1	0	Latch	Latch
X	1	1	Latch	Latch

What used to be the S and R inputs are now called the J and K inputs, respectively. The old two-input AND gates have been replaced with 3-input AND gates, and the third input of each gate receives feedback from the Q and not-Q outputs. What this does for us is permit the J input to have effect only when the circuit is reset, and permit the K input to have effect only when the circuit is set.

In other words, the two inputs are *interlocked,* to use a relay logic term, so that they cannot both be activated simultaneously. If the circuit is "set," the J input is inhibited by the 0 status of not-Q through the lower AND gate; if the circuit is "reset," the K input is inhibited by the 0 status of Q through the upper AND gate.

When both J and K inputs are 1, however, something unique happens. Because of the selective inhibiting action of those 3-input AND gates, a "set" state inhibits input J so that the flip-flop acts as if J=0 while K=1 when in fact both are 1. On the next clock pulse, the outputs will switch ("toggle") from set (Q=1 and not-Q=0) to reset (Q=0 and not-Q=1). Conversely, a "reset" state inhibits input K so that the flip-flop acts as if J=1 and K=0 when in fact both are 1. The next clock pulse toggles the circuit again from reset to set. See if you can follow this logical sequence with the ladder logic equivalent of the J-K flip-flop:

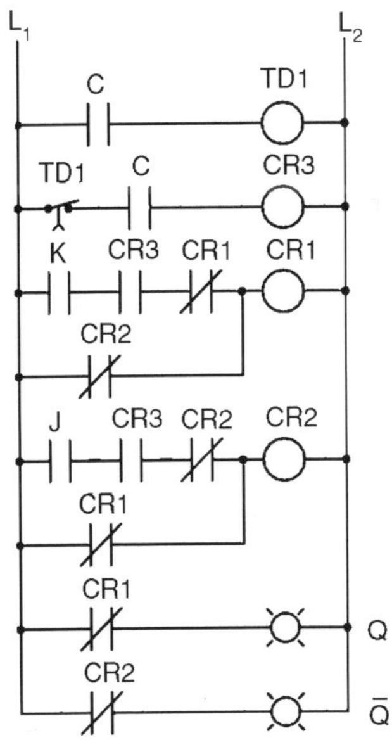

C	J	K	Q	$\bar{Q}$
↑	0	0	Latch	Latch
↑	0	1	0	1
↑	1	0	1	0
↑	1	1	Toggle	Toggle
X	0	0	Latch	Latch
X	0	1	Latch	Latch
X	1	0	Latch	Latch
X	1	1	Latch	Latch

The end result is that the S-R flip-flop's "invalid" state is eliminated (along with the race condition it engendered) and we get a useful feature as a bonus: the ability to toggle between the two (bistable) output states with every transition of the clock input signal. There is no such thing as a J-K latch, only J-K flip-flops. Without the edge-triggering of the clock input, the circuit would continuously toggle between its two output states when both J and K were held high (1), making it an astable device instead of a bistable device in that circumstance.

If we want to preserve bistable operation for all combinations of input states, we *must* use edge-triggering so that it toggles only when we tell it to, one step (clock pulse) at a time. The block symbol for a J-K flip-flop is a whole lot less frightening than its internal circuitry, and just like the S-R and D flip-flops, J-K flip-flops come in two clock varieties (negative and positive edge-triggered):

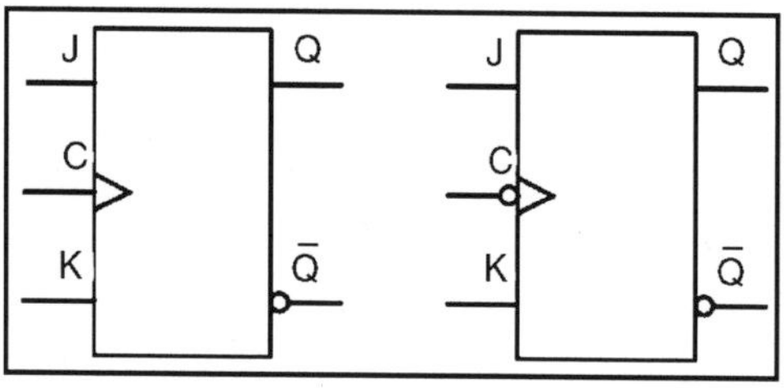

REVIEW

The JK as a D Flip-Flop

To convert a JK to a D flip-flop, connect the inputs as follows.

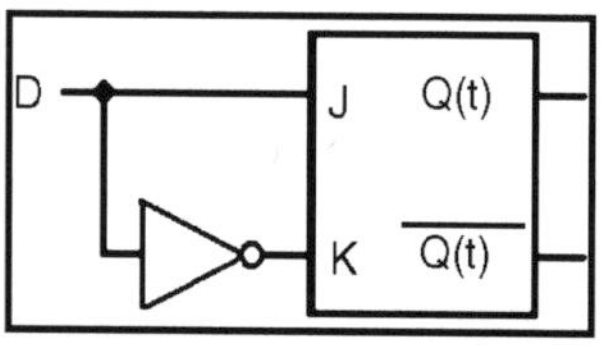

If D = 0, then J = 0, K = 1, and Q(t + 1) = 0, If D = 1, then J = 1, K = 0, and Q(t + 1) = 1. The JK As A T Flip-Flop. To convert a JK to a T flip-flop, connect the inputs as follows.

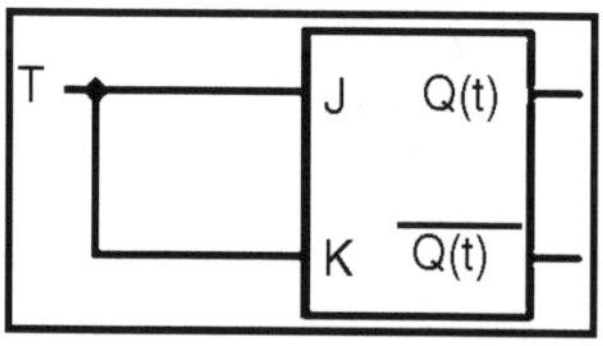

If T = 0, then J = 0, K = 0, and Q(t + 1) = Q(t).
If T = 1, then J = 1, K = 1, and Q(t + 1) = $\overline{Q}$ (t)

CIRCUIT ELEMENTS OF LATCHES

When showing either latches or flip-flops as circuit elements, it is undesirable to show the"internals" of the device.

Here are the symbols for SR and D latches.

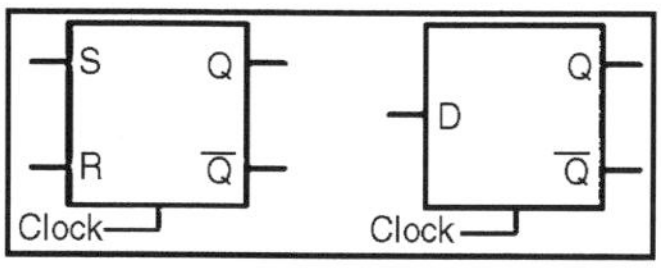

THE S-R LATCH

A bistable multivibrator has two stable states, as indicated by the prefix bi in its name. Typically, one state is referred to asset and the other as reset. The simplest bistable device, therefore, is known as a set-reset, or S-R, latch. To create an S-R latch, we can wire two NOR gates in such a way that the output of one feeds back to the input of another, and visa-versa, like this:

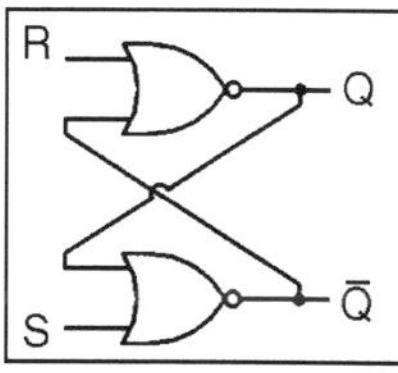

S	R	Q	$\overline{Q}$
0	0	Latch	Latch
0	1	0	1
1	0	1	0
1	1	0	0

The Q and not-Q outputs are supposed to be in opposite states. I say"supposed to" because making both the S and R inputs equal to 1 results in both Q and not-Q being 0. For this reason, having both S and R equal to 1 is called an invalid orillegal state for the S-R multivibrator. Otherwise, making S=1 and R=0"sets" the multivibrator so that Q=1 and not-Q=0. Conversely, making R=1 and S=0"resets" the multivibrator in the opposite state. When S and R are both equal to 0, the multivibrator's outputs"latch" in their prior states.

Note how the same multivibrator function can be implemented in ladder logic, with the same results:

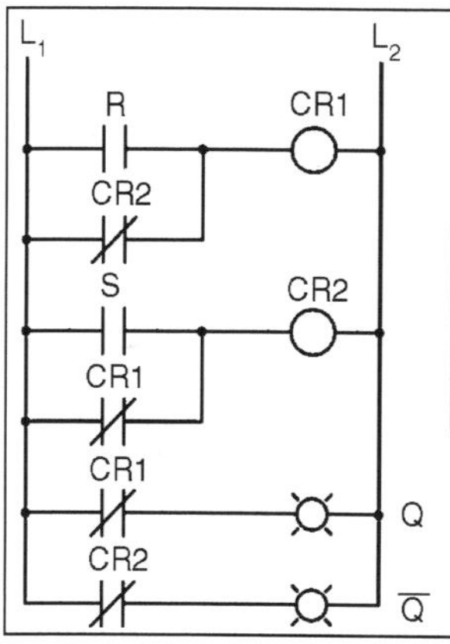

S	R	Q	$\overline{Q}$
0	0	Latch	Latch
0	1	0	1
1	0	1	0
1	1	0	0

By definition, a condition of Q=1 and not-Q=0 is set. A condition of Q=0 and not-Q=1 is reset. These terms are universal in describing the output states of any multivibrator circuit. The astute observer will note that the initial power-up condition of either the gate or ladder variety of S-R latch is such that both gates (coils) start in the de-energized mode. As such, one would expect that the circuit will start up in an invalid condition, with both Q and not-Q outputs being in the same state.

Actually, this is true! However, the invalid condition is unstable with both S and R inputs inactive, and the circuit will quickly stabilize in either the set or reset condition because one gate (or relay) is bound to react a little faster than the other. If both gates (or coils) were precisely identical, they would oscillate between high and low like an astable multivibrator upon power-up without ever reaching a point of stability! Fortunately for cases like this, such a precise match of components is a rare possibility. It must be noted that although an astable (continually oscillating) condition would be extremely rare, there will most likely be a cycle or two of oscillation in the above circuit, and the final state of the circuit (set or reset) after power-up would be unpredictable.

The root of the problem is a race condition between the two relays CR_1 and CR_2. A race condition occurs when two mutually-exclusive events are simultaneously initiated through different circuit elements by a single cause In this case, the circuit elements are relays CR_1 and CR_2, and their de-energized states are mutually exclusive due to the normally-closed interlocking contacts. If one relay coil is de-energized, its normally-closed contact will keep the other coil energized, thus maintaining the circuit in one of two states (set or reset). Interlocking prevents bothrelays from latching.

However, if both relay coils start in their de-energized states (such as after the whole circuit has been de-energized and is then powered up) both relays will"race" to become latched on as they receive power (the"single cause") through the normally-closed contact of the other relay. One of those relays will inevitably reach that condition before the other, thus opening its normally-closed interlocking contact and de-energizing the other relay coil. Which relay"wins" this race is dependent on the physical characteristics of the relays and not the circuit design, so the designer cannot ensure which state the circuit will fall into after power-up.

Race conditions should be avoided in circuit design primarily for the unpredictability that will be created. One way to avoid such a condition is to insert a time-delay relay into the circuit to disable one of the competing relays for a short time, giving the other one a clear advantage. In other words, by purposely slowing down the de-energization of one relay, we ensure that the other relay will always"win" and the race results will always be predictable. Here is an example of how a time-delay relay might be applied to the above circuit to avoid the race condition:

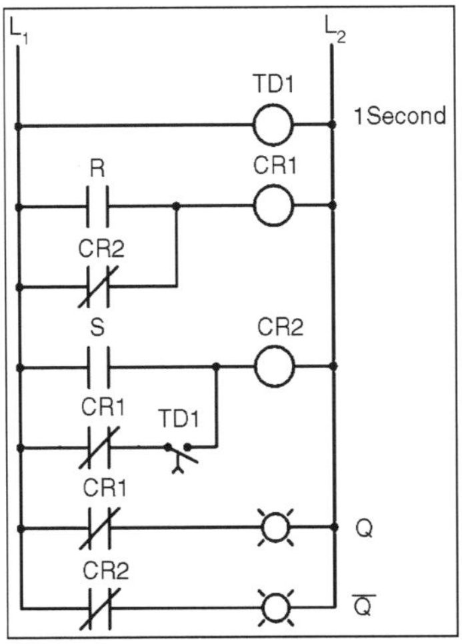

When the circuit powers up, time-delay relay contact TD1 in the fifth rung down will delay closing for 1 second. Having that contact open for 1 second prevents relay CR2 from energizing through contact CR1 in its normally-closed state after power-up. Therefore, relay CR1 will be allowed to energize first (with a 1-second head start), thus opening the normally-closed CR1contact in the fifth rung, preventing CR2 from being energized without the S input going active. The end result is that the circuit powers up cleanly and predictably in the reset state with S=0 and R=0.

It should be mentioned that race conditions are not restricted to relay circuits. Solid-state logic gate circuits may also suffer from the ill effects of race conditions if improperly designed. Complex computer programmes, for that matter, may also incur race problems if improperly designed. Race problems are a possibility for any sequential system, and may not be discovered until some time after initial testing of the system. They can be very difficult problems to detect and eliminate. A practical application of an S-R latch circuit might be for starting and stopping a motor, using normally-open, momentary pushbutton switch contacts for both start (S) and stop (R) switches, then energizing a motor contactor with either a CR1 or CR2 contact (or using a contactor in place of CR1 or CR2).

Normally, a much simpler ladder logic circuit is employed, such as this:

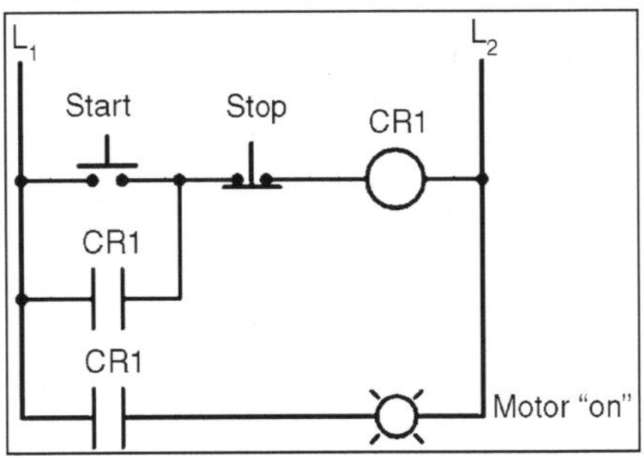

In the above motor start/stop circuit, the CR1 contact in parallel with the start switch contact is referred to as a"seal-in" contact, because it"seals" or latches control relay CR1 in the energized state after the start switch has been released. To break the"seal," or to"unlatch" or"reset" the circuit, the stop pushbutton is pressed, which de-energizes CR1 and restores the seal-in contact to its normally open status. Notice, however, that this circuit performs much the same function as the S-R latch. Also note that this circuit has no inherent instability problem (if even a remote possibility) as does the double-relay S-R latch design. In semiconductor form, S-R latches come in prepackaged units so that you don't have to build them from individual gates. They are symbolized as such:

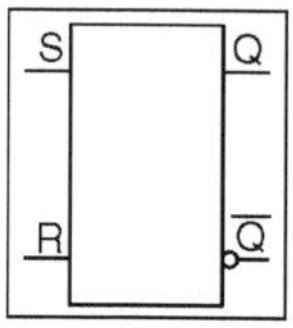

The gated S-R latch

It is sometimes useful in logic circuits to have a multivibrator which changes state only when certain conditions are met, regardless of its S and R input states. The conditional input is called the enable, and is symbolized by the letter E.

Study the following example to see how this works:

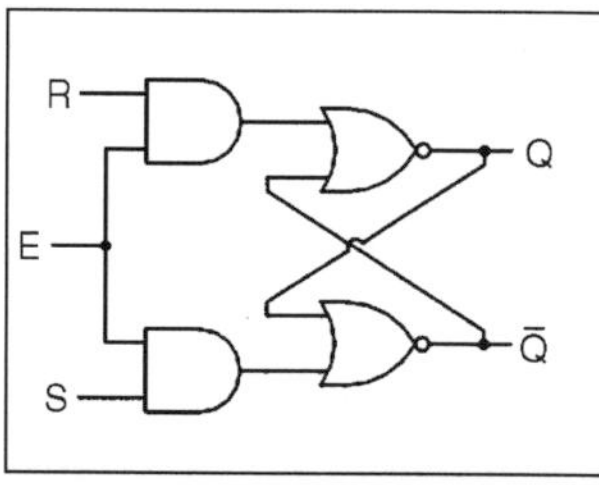

E	S	R	Q	$\bar{Q}$
0	0	0	Latch	Latch
0	0	1	Latch	Latch
0	1	0	Latch	Latch
0	1	1	Latch	Latch
1	0	0	Latch	Latch
1	0	1	0	1
1	1	0	1	0
1	1	1	0	0

When the E=0, the outputs of the two AND gates are forced to 0, regardless of the states of either S or R. Consequently, the circuit behaves as though S and R were both 0, latching the Q and not-Q outputs in their last states. Only when the enable input is activated (1) will the latch respond to the S and R inputs.

Note the identical function in ladder logic:

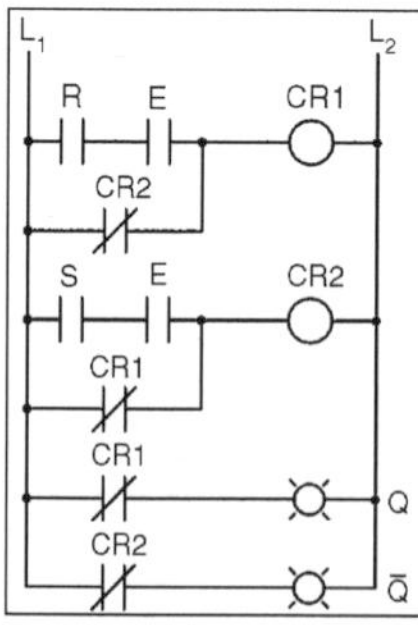

E	S	R	Q	$\bar{Q}$
0	0	0	Latch	Latch
0	0	1	Latch	Latch
0	1	0	Latch	Latch
0	1	1	Latch	Latch
1	0	0	Latch	Latch
1	0	1	0	1
1	1	0	1	0
1	1	1	0	0

A practical application of this might be the same motor control circuit, except with the addition of a master lockout input (E) that disables both pushbuttons from having control over the motor when it's low (0).

Once again, these multivibrator circuits are available as prepackaged semiconductor devices, and are symbolized as such:

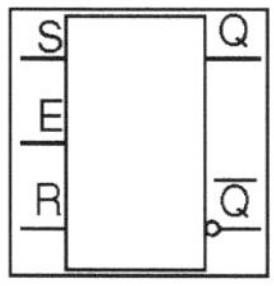

It is also common to see the enable input designated by the letters"EN" instead of just"E."

THE D LATCH

Since the enable input on a gated S-R latch provides a way to latch the Q and not-Q outputs without regard to the status of S or R, we can eliminate one of those inputs to create a multivibrator latch circuit with no"illegal" input states.

Such a circuit is called a D latch, and its internal logic looks like this:

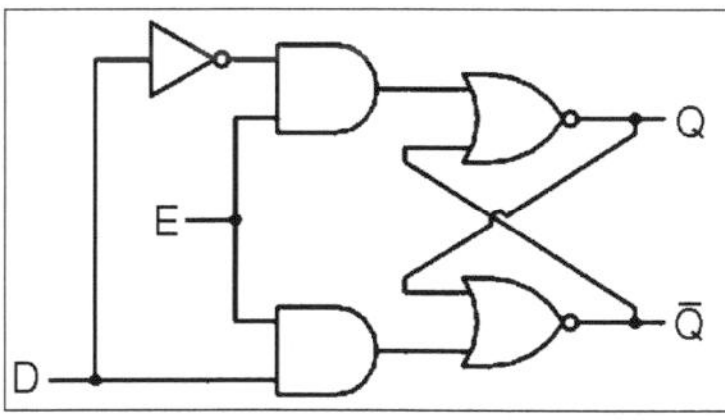

E	D	Q	$\overline{Q}$
0	0	Latch	Latch
0	1	Latch	Latch
1	0	0	1
1	1	1	0

Note that the R input has been replaced with the complement (inversion) of the old S input, and the S input has been renamed to D. As with the gated S-R latch, the D latch will not respond to a signal input if the enable input is 0 -- it simply stays latched in its last state. When the enable input is 1, however, the Q output follows the D input. Since the R input of the S-R circuitry has been done away with, this latch has no"invalid" or"illegal" state. Q and not-Q arealways opposite of one another.

If the above diagram is confusing at all, the next diagram should make the concept simpler:

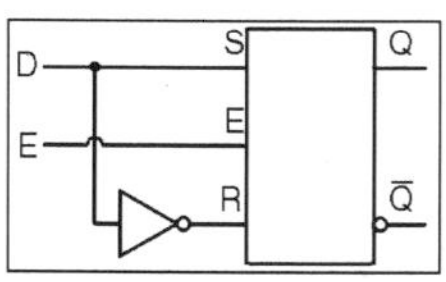

Like both the S-R and gated S-R latches, the D latch circuit may be found as its own prepackaged circuit, complete with a standard symbol:

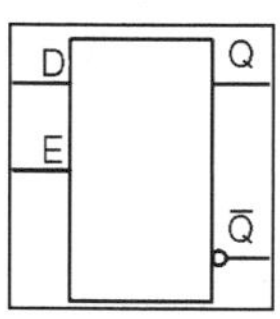

The D latch is nothing more than a gated S-R latch with an inverter added to make R the complement (inverse) of S. Let's explore the ladder logic equivalent of a D latch, modified from the basic ladder diagram of an S-R latch:

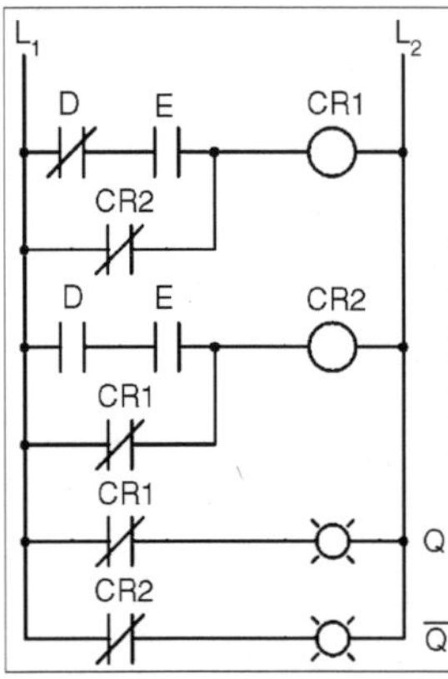

E	D	Q	$\overline{Q}$
0	0	Latch	Latch
0	1	Latch	Latch
1	0	0	1
1	1	1	0

An application for the D latch is a 1-bit memory circuit. You can"write" (store) a 0 or 1 bit in this latch circuit by making the enable input high (1) and setting D to whatever you want the stored bit to be. When the enable input is made low (0), the latch ignores the status of the D input and merrily holds the stored bit value, outputting at the stored value at Q, and its inverse on output not-Q.

10

Digital Signals and Gates

INTRODUCTION

While the binary numeration system is an interesting mathematical abstraction, we haven't yet seen its practical application to electronics. This chapter is devoted to just that: practically applying the concept of binary bits to circuits. What makes binary numeration so important to the application of digital electronics is the ease in which bits may be represented in physical terms. Because a binary bit can only have one of two different values, either 0 or 1, any physical medium capable of switching between two saturated states may be used to represent a bit. Consequently, any physical system capable of representing binary bits is able to represent numerical quantities, and potentially has the ability to manipulate those numbers. This is the basic concept underlying digital computing.

Electronic circuits are physical systems that lend themselves well to the representation of binary numbers. Transistors, when operated at their bias limits, may be in one of two different states: either cutoff (no controlled current) or saturation (maximum controlled current). If a transistor circuit is designed to maximize the probability of falling into either one of these states (and not operating in the linear, or *active*, mode), it can serve as a physical representation of a binary bit. A voltage signal measured at the output of such a circuit may also serve as a representation of a single bit, a low voltage representing a binary "0" and a (relatively) high voltage representing a binary "1."

Note the following transistor circuit:

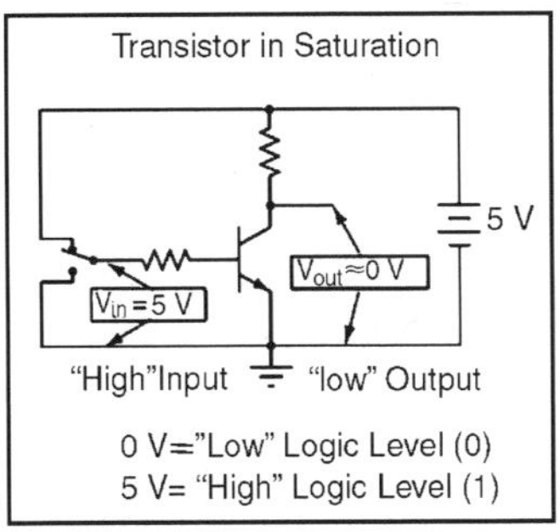

In this circuit, the transistor is in a state of saturation by virtue of the applied input voltage (5 volts) through the two-position switch. Because it's saturated, the transistor drops very little voltage between collector and emitter, resulting in an output voltage of (practically) 0 volts.

If we were using this circuit to represent binary bits, we would say that the input signal is a binary "1" and that the output signal is a binary "0." Any voltage close to full supply voltage (measured in reference to ground, of course) is considered a "1" and a lack of voltage is considered a "0." Alternative terms for these voltage levels are*high* (same as a binary "1") and *low* (same as a binary "0"). A general term for the representation of a binary bit by a circuit voltage is *logic level.*

Moving the switch to the other position, we apply a binary "0" to the input and receive a binary "1" at the output:

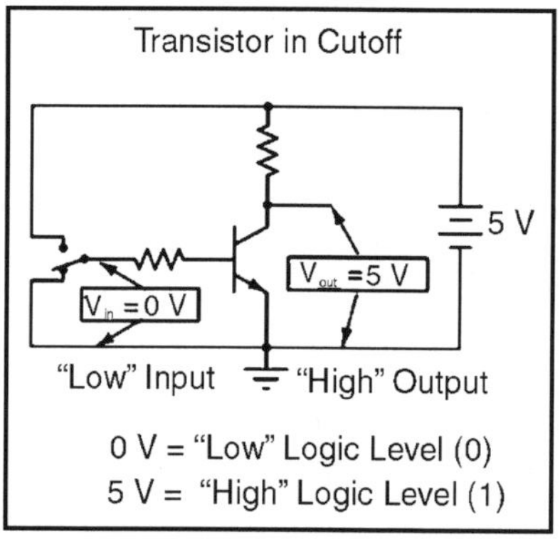

What we've created here with a single transistor is a circuit generally known as a *logic gate,* or simply *gate.* A gate is a special type of amplifier circuit designed to accept and generate voltage signals corresponding to binary 1's and 0's. As such, gates are not intended to be used for amplifying analog signals (voltage signals *between* 0 and full voltage).

Used together, multiple gates may be applied to the task of binary number storage (memory circuits) or manipulation (computing circuits), each gate's output representing one bit of a multi-bit binary number. Just how this is done is a subject for a later chapter. Right now it is important to focus on the operation of individual gates.

The gate shown here with the single transistor is known as an *inverter,* or NOT gate, because it outputs the exact opposite digital signal as what is input. For convenience, gate circuits are generally represented by their own symbols rather than by their constituent transistors and resistors.

The following is the symbol for an inverter:

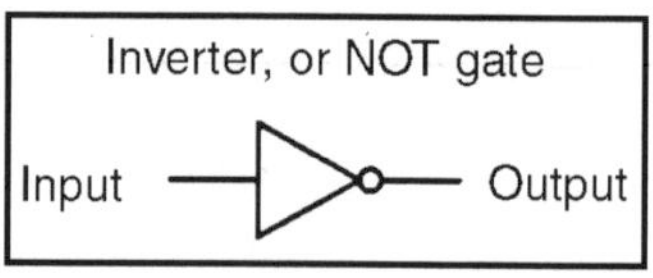

An alternative symbol for an inverter is shown here:

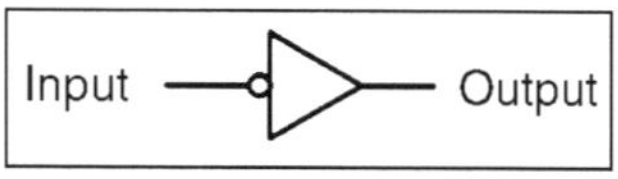

Notice the triangular shape of the gate symbol, much like that of an operational amplifier. As was stated before, gate circuits actually are amplifiers. The small circle, or "bubble" shown on either the input or output terminal is standard for representing the inversion function. As you might suspect, if we were to remove the bubble from the gate symbol, leaving only a triangle, the resulting symbol would no longer indicate inversion, but merely direct amplification. Such a symbol and such a gate actually do exist, and it is called a *buffer*, the subject of the next section.

Like an operational amplifier symbol, input and output connections are shown as single wires, the implied reference point for each voltage signal being "ground." In digital gate circuits, ground is almost always the negative connection of a single voltage source (power supply). Dual, or "split," power supplies are seldom used in gate circuitry. Because gate circuits are amplifiers, they require a source of power to operate. Like operational amplifiers, the power supply connections for digital gates are often omitted from the symbol for simplicity's sake. If we were to show *all* the necessary connections needed for operating this gate, the schematic would look something like this:

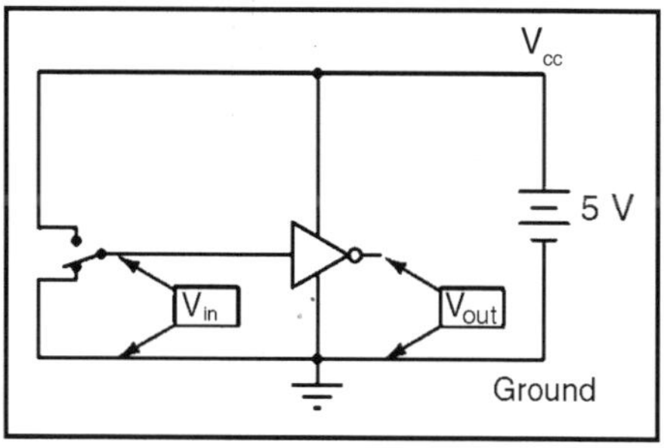

Power supply conductors are rarely shown in gate circuit schematics, even if the power supply connections at each gate are. *Minimizing lines in our schematic, we get this:*

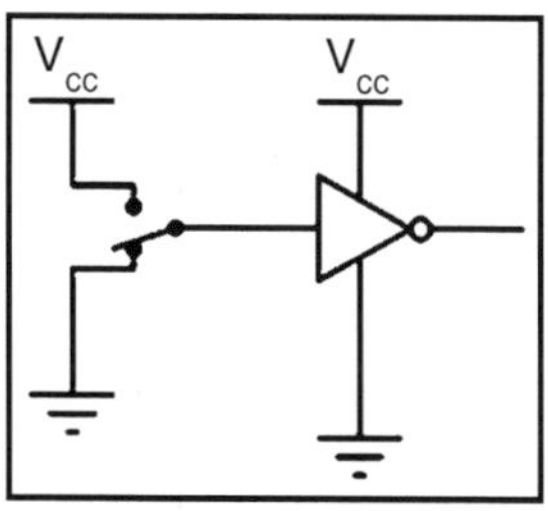

"V_{CC}" stands for the constant voltage supplied to the collector of a bipolar junction transistor circuit, in reference to ground. Those points in a gate circuit marked by the label "V_{cc}" are all connected to the same point, and that point is the positive terminal of a DC voltage source, usually 5 volts. As we will see in other sections of this chapter, there are quite a few different types of logic gates, most of which have multiple input terminals for accepting more than one signal. The output of any gate is dependent on the state of its input(s) and its logical function. One common way to express the particular function of a gate circuit is called a *truth table*. Truth tables show all combinations of input conditions in terms of logic level states (either "high" or "low," "1" or "0," for each input terminal of the gate), along with the corresponding output logic level, either "high" or "low." For the inverter, or NOT, circuit just illustrated, the truth table is very simple indeed:

NOT Gate Truth Table

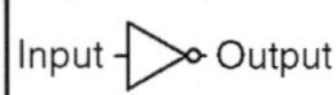

Input	Output
0	1
1	0

Truth tables for more complex gates are, of course, larger than the one shown for the NOT gate. A gate's truth table must have as many rows as there are possibilities for unique input combinations. For a single-input gate like the NOT gate, there are only two possibilities, 0 and 1. For a two input gate, there are *four* possibilities (00, 01, 10, and 11), and thus four rows to the corresponding truth table. For a three-input gate, there are *eight* possibilities (000, 001, 010, 011, 100, 101, 110, and 111), and thus a truth table with eight rows are needed. The mathematically inclined will realise that the number of truth table rows needed for a gate is equal to 2 raised to the power of the number of input terminals.

VARIATIONS OF THE EXCLUSIVE AND OR GATE

The last six gate types are all fairly direct variations on three basic functions: AND, OR, and NOT. The Exclusive-OR gate, however, is something quite different. Exclusive-OR gates output a "high" (1) logic level if the inputs are at *different* logic levels, either 0 and 1 or 1 and 0. Conversely, they output a "low" (0) logic level if the inputs are at the *same* logic levels. The Exclusive-OR (sometimes called XOR) gate has both a symbol and a truth table pattern that is unique:

Exclusive-OR Gate

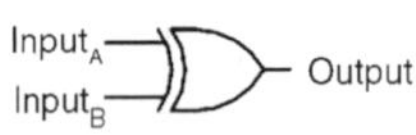

A	B	Output
0	0	0
0	1	1
1	0	1
1	1	0

There are equivalent circuits for an Exclusive-OR gate made up of AND, OR, and NOT gates, just as there were for NAND, NOR, and the negative-input gates. A rather direct approach to simulating an Exclusive-OR gate is to start with a regular OR gate, then add additional gates to inhibit the output from going "high" (1) when both inputs are "high" (1):

Exclusive OR Equivalent Circuit

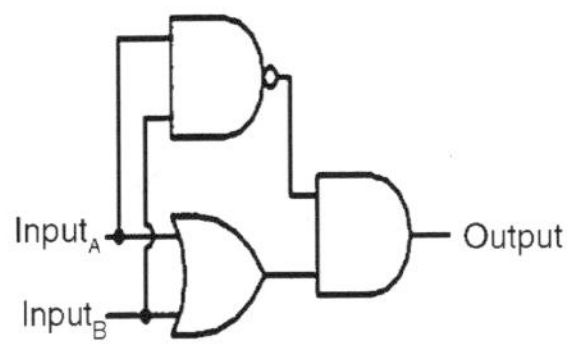

A	B	Output
0	0	0
0	1	1
1	0	1
1	1	0

In this circuit, the final AND gate acts as a buffer for the output of the OR gate whenever the NAND gate's output is high, which it is for the first three input state combinations (00, 01, and 10). However, when both inputs are "high" (1), the NAND gate outputs a "low" (0) logic level, which forces the final AND gate to produce a "low" (0) output. Another equivalent circuit for the Exclusive-OR gate uses a strategy of two AND gates with inverters, set up to generate "high" (1) outputs for input conditions 01 and 10. A final OR gate then allows either of the AND gates' "high" outputs to create a final "high" output:

Exclusive-OR Equivalent Circuit

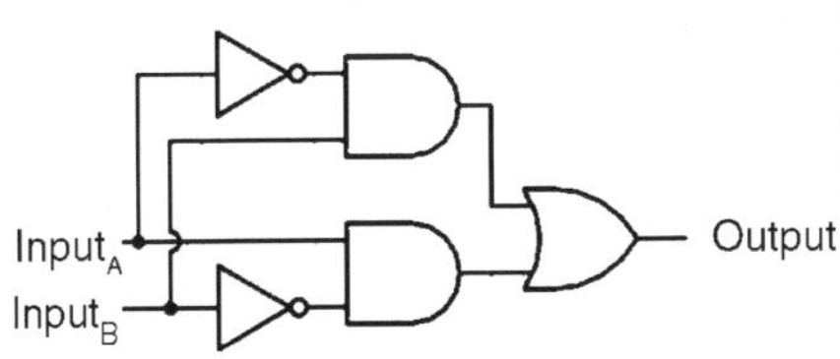

A	B	Output
0	0	0
0	1	1
1	0	1
1	1	0

Exclusive-OR gates are very useful for circuits where two or more binary numbers are to be compared bit-for-bit, and also for error detection (parity check) and code conversion (binary to Grey and visa-versa).

IMPLEMENTATION OF NAND AND NOR GATE

THE NAND

The NAND or Not AND function is a combination of two separate functions, the AND function and theNOT function connected together in series, and can be expressed by the Boolean expression of, $\overline{A.B}$

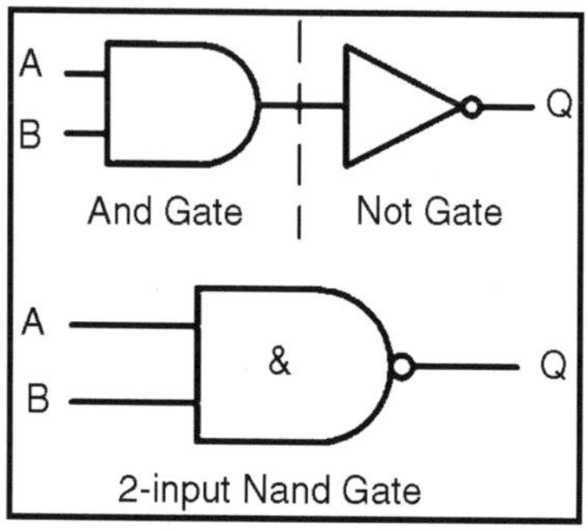

Switch Representation of the NAND Function

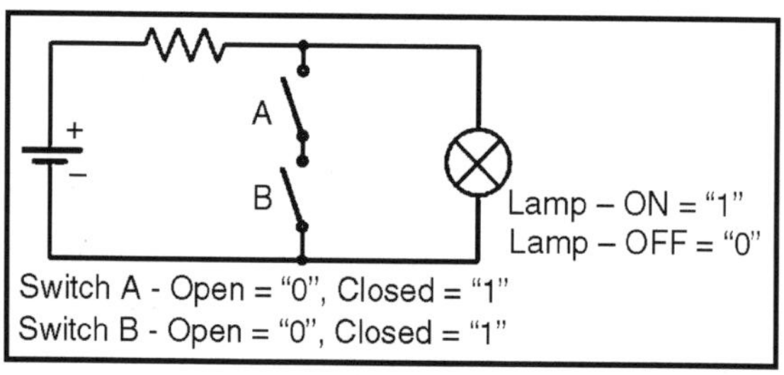

Truth Table

Switch A	Switch B	Output	Description
0	0	1	A and B are both open, lamp ON
0	1	1	A is open and B is closed, lamp ON
1	0	1	A is closed and B is open, lamp ON
1	1	0	A is closed and B is closed, lamp OFF

Boolean Expression ($\overline{A}$ AND $\overline{B}$) $\overline{A.B}$

The NAND Function is sometimes known as the Sheffer Stroke Function and is denoted by a vertical bar or upwards arrow operator, for example, A NAND B = A|B or A↑B.

NAND Gates are used as the basic"building blocks" to construct other logic gate functions and are available in standard i.c. packages such as the very common TTL 74LS00 Quadruple 2-input NANDGates, the TTL 74LS10

Triple 3-input NAND Gates or the 74LS20 Dual 4-input NAND Gates. There is even a single chip 74LS30 8-input NAND Gate.

THE NOR

Like the NAND Gate above, the NOR or Not OR Gate is also a combination of two separate functions, theOR function and the NOT function connected together in series and is expressed by the Boolean expression as, A + B

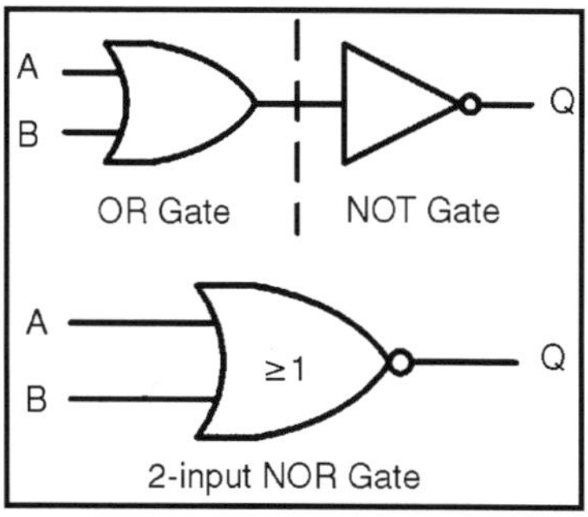

Switch Representation of the NOR Function

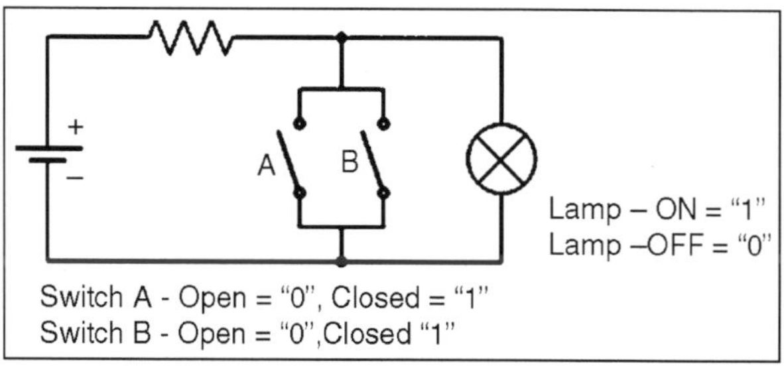

Truth Table

Switch A	Switch B	Output	Description
0	0	1	Both A and B are open, lamp ON
0	1	0	A is open and B is closed, lamp OFF
1	0	0	A is closed and B is open, lamp OFF
1	1	0	A is closed and B is closed, lamp OFF
Boolean Expression (A OR B)			A + B

The NOR Function is sometimes known as the Pierce Function and is denoted by a downwards arrow operator as shown, A NOR B = A↓B. NOR Gates are available as standard i.c. packages such as the TTL 74LS02 Quadruple 2-input NORGate, the TTL 74LS27 Triple 3-input NOR Gate or the 74LS260 Dual 5-input NOR Gate.

NAND and NOR Gates

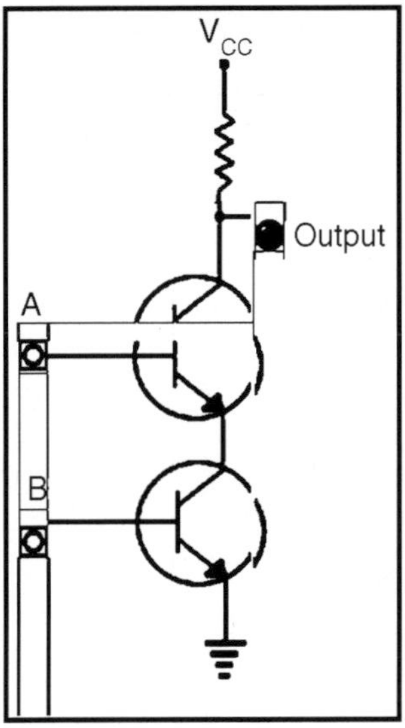

Fig. A NAND Gate.

The value of the output is controlled by the two inputs A and B.

The circuit of Figure illustrates some important concepts, but it isn't very interesting. We can do more if we build circuits with two or more inputs. Shows a NAND gate. The name NAND is a contraction of not-and. Current can flow, and produce a voltage drop across the resistor, only if both transistors are conducting. Having either transistor switched off is enough to block current flow and hold the output high.

For purposes of this lecture we are going to define a "high" voltage—a voltage near Vcc—to indicate a logical 1, or true. A low voltage, near zero will indicate a logical 0, or false. (It is possible to reverse those definitions so long as one is consistent. We will not studynegative logic circuits here.)

Table. NAND

A	B	X
0	0	1
0	1	1
1	0	1
1	1	0

Using 1 to represent a high voltage and 0 for low, we can write a truth table that describes the behaviour of the NAND gate. Columns A and B of the table represent the two inputs, A and B, of the NAND gate. The X column shows what the output will be for each combination of A and B. The truth table for the Boolean NAND function appears at the left. Experiment with the circuit in Figure and verify that it actually computes the NAND function. It is clear from the schematic diagram that we could build a NAND gate with more than two inputs. Adding a third transistor in series gives a three-input NAND. As an exercise, write the truth table for a three-input NAND gate. You will have inputs A, B, and C and output X.

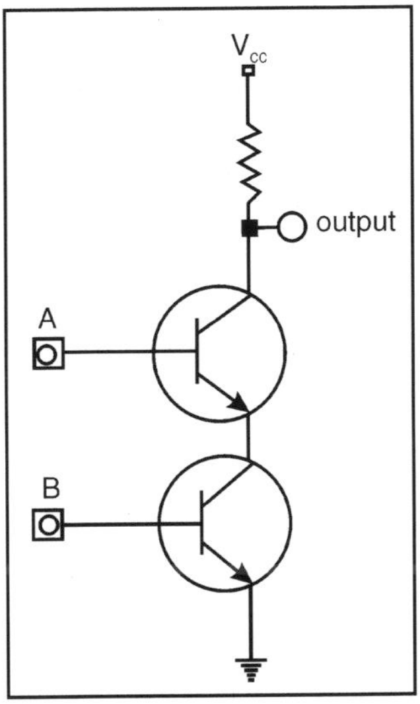

Fig. A NOR gate.

The transistors are connected in parallel. The NAND gate has its transistors connected in series. Recall from the Electric Circuits Web Lecture that switches can be connected in series or parallel. If we connect transistors in parallel as shown in Figure, applying a signal to the base of eithertransistor is sufficient to allow current to flow through the resistor and pull the output voltage to near zero. This is the NOR gate. The name NOR is a contraction of not-or.

Table. NOR

A	B	X
0	0	1
0	1	0
1	0	0
1	1	0

Let's look at the truth table for the NOR gate. Again we have inputs A and B and output X. This time, X is true, or 1, only when A and B are both 0. Another way of saying that is that X is 1 when neither A nor B is true. Experiment with the circuit to verify that it computes the function given in Table.

As with the NAND gate, the NOR gate can be extended to more than two inputs by adding more transistors, this time in parallel. Figure makes it obvious why the power supply voltage is called Vcc. It is connected in parallel, or in common, through the resistor to the collectors of both transistors. In a complex digital logic circuit, the same power supply voltage will be connected in common to all the gates. About now you may be wondering why we started with NAND and NOR gates instead of the more familiar AND and OR functions. There are two reasons, one founded in electrical engineering and one founded in logic. Although the gates shown here are simplified by comparison to the actual construction of integrated circuits, you could go to an electrical engineering lab and build the circuits of Figures. If you did, they would function just as the animations demonstrate. These three gates, NOT, NAND, and NOR are the simplest possible digital logic gates.

Each has only one transistor per input. Any other gate, and in particular the non-inverting gates AND and OR require more transistors. Even more important is the fact that NAND and NOR are complete. This means that any other digital logic gate can be constructed using only NAND gates or only NORgates. A manufacturer of integrated circuits can lay down a pattern of one type of gate, and then implement any digital logic function by modifying how the gates are connected.

THE EXCLUSIVE-NOR GATE

Finally, our last gate for analysis is the Exclusive-NOR gate, otherwise known as the XNOR gate. It is equivalent to an Exclusive-OR gate with an inverted output.

The truth table for this gate is exactly opposite as for the Exclusive-OR gate:

Exclusive-NOR Gate

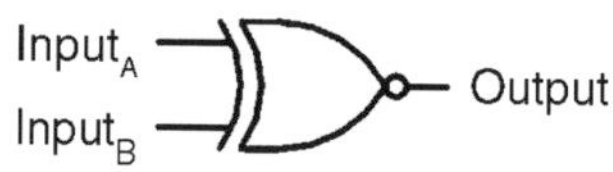

A	B	Output
0	0	1
0	1	0
1	0	0
1	1	1

Equivalent Gate Circuits

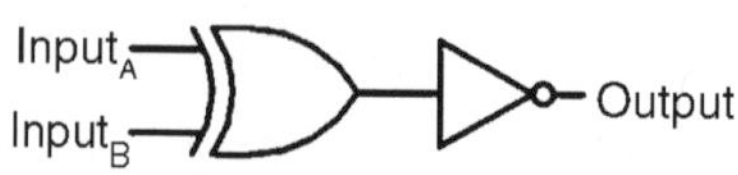

As indicated by the truth table, the purpose of an Exclusive-NOR gate is to output a "high" (1) logic level whenever both inputs are at the same logic levels (either 00 or 11).

TTL NAND GATES

Suppose we altered our basic open-collector inverter circuit, adding a second input terminal just like the first:

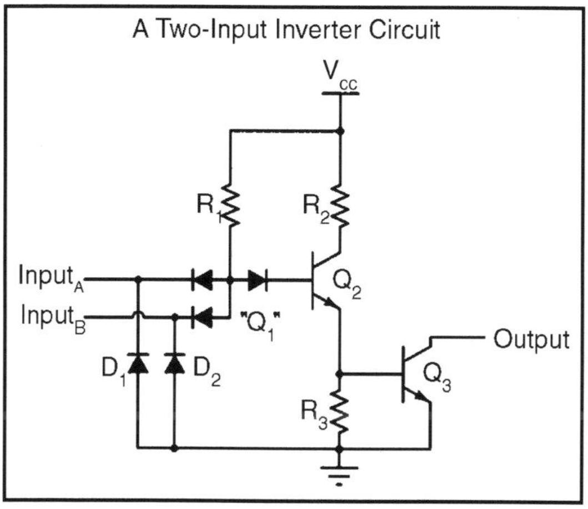

This schematic illustrates a real circuit, but it isn't called a "two-input inverter." Through analysis we will discover what this circuit's logic function is and correspondingly what it should be designated as.

Just as in the case of the inverter and buffer, the "steering" diode cluster marked "Q_1" is actually formed like a transistor, even though it isn't used in any amplifying capacity. Unfortunately, a simple NPN transistor structure is inadequate to simulate the *three* PN junctions necessary in this diode network, so a different transistor (and symbol) is needed. This transistor has one collector, one base, and *two* emitters, and in the circuit it looks like this:

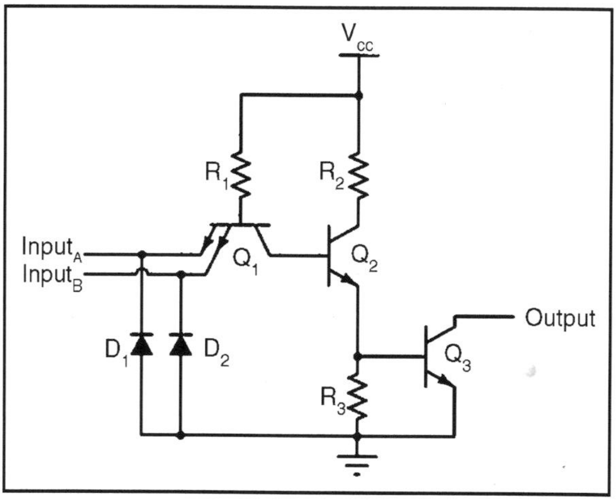

In the single-input (inverter) circuit, grounding the input resulted in an output that assumed the "high" (1) state. In the case of the open-collector output configuration, this "high" state was simply "floating." Allowing the input to float (or be connected to V_{cc}) resulted in the output becoming grounded, which is the "low" or 0 state. Thus, a 1 in resulted in a 0 out, and visa-versa.

Since this circuit bears so much resemblance to the simple inverter circuit, the only difference being a second input terminal connected in the same way to the base of transistor Q_2, we can say that each of the inputs will have the same effect on the output. Namely, if either of the inputs are grounded, transistor Q_2 will be forced into a condition of cutoff, thus turning Q_3 off and floating the output (output goes "high"). The following series of illustrations shows this for three input states (00, 01, and 10):

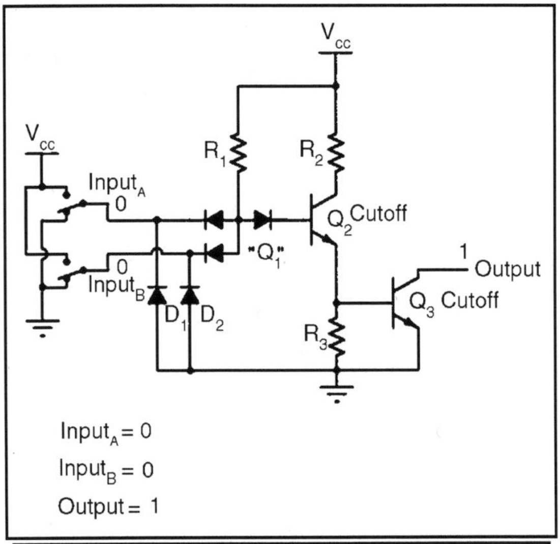

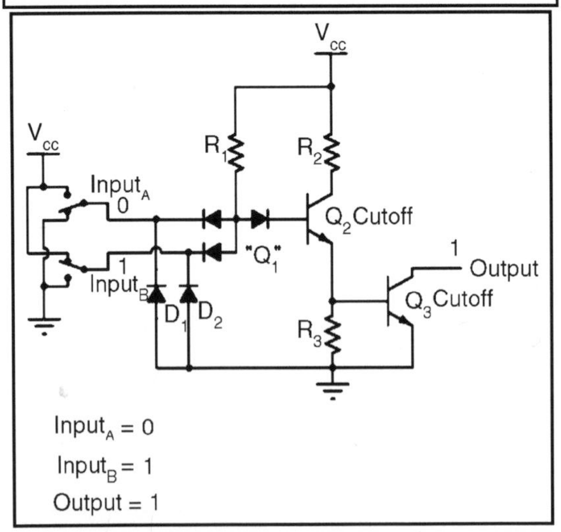

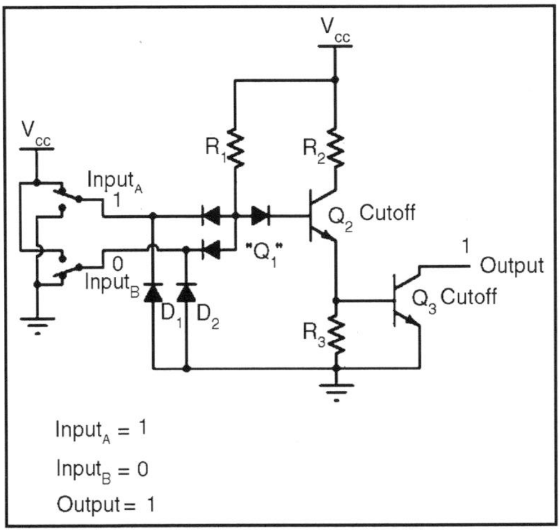

In any case where there is a grounded ("low") input, the output is guaranteed to be floating ("high"). Conversely, the only time the output will ever go "low" is if transistor Q_3 turns on, which means transistor Q_2 must be turned on (saturated), which means neither input can be diverting R_1 current away from the base of Q_2. The only condition that will satisfy this requirement is when both inputs are "high" (1):

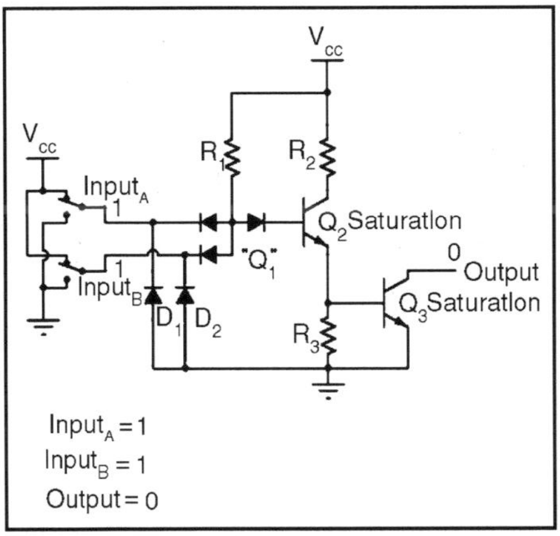

Collecting and tabulating these results into a truth table, we see that the pattern matches that of the NAND gate:

NAND Gate

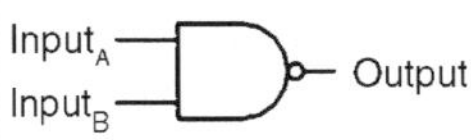

A	B	Output
0	0	1
0	1	1
1	0	1
1	1	0

In the earlier section on NAND gates, this type of gate was created by taking an AND gate and increasing its complexity by adding an inverter (NOT gate) to the output. However, when we examine this circuit, we see that the NAND function is actually the simplest, most natural mode of operation for this TTL design.

To create an AND function using TTL circuitry, we need to *increase* the complexity of this circuit by adding an inverter stage to the output, just like we had to add an additional transistor stage to the TTL inverter circuit to turn it into a buffer:

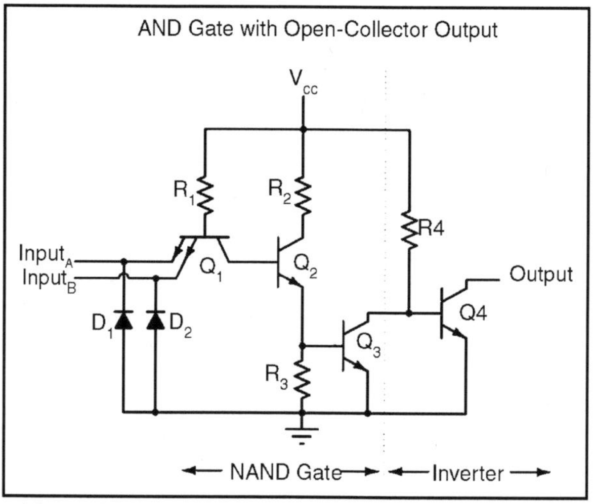

The truth table and equivalent gate circuit (an inverted-output NAND gate) are shown here:

AND Gate

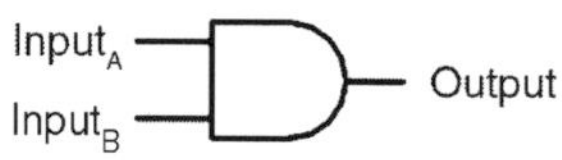

A	B	Output
0	0	0
0	1	0
1	0	0
1	1	1

Equivalent Circuit

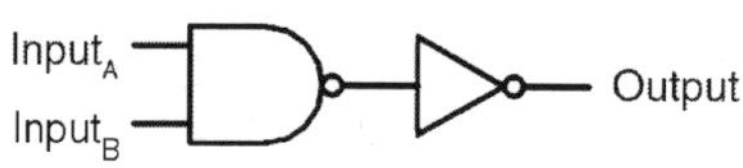

Of course, both NAND and AND gate circuits may be designed with totem-pole output stages rather than open-collector. I am opting to show the open-collector versions for the sake of simplicity.

TTL NOR AND OR GATES

Let's examine the following TTL circuit and analyse its operation:

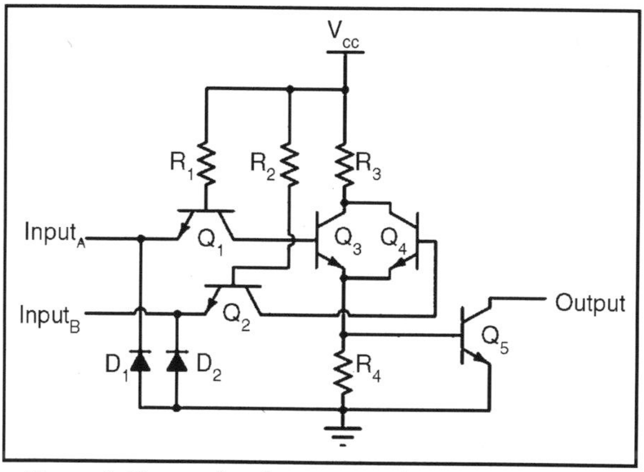

Transistors Q_1 and Q_2 are both arranged in the same manner that we've seen for transistor Q_1 in all the other TTL circuits.

Rather than functioning as amplifiers, Q_1 and Q_2 are both being used as two-diode "steering" networks.

We may replace Q_1 and Q_2 with diode sets to help illustrate:

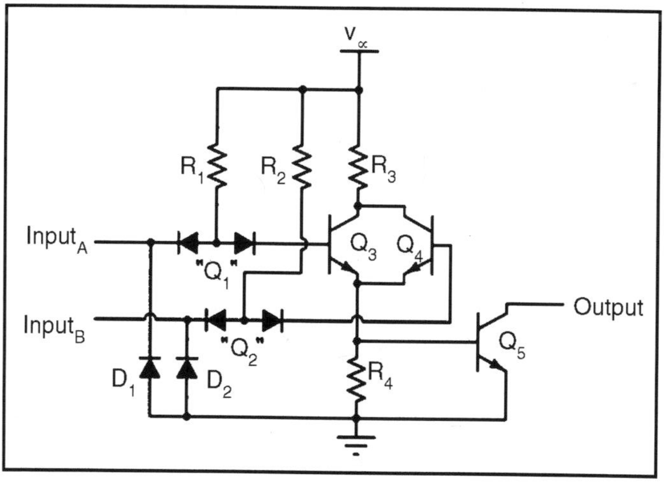

If input A is left floating (or connected to V_{cc}), current will go through the base of transistor Q_3, saturating it. If input A is grounded, that current is diverted away from Q_3's base through the left steering diode of "Q_1," thus forcing Q_3 into cutoff. The same can be said for input B and transistor Q_4: the logic level of input B determines Q_4's conduction: either saturated or cutoff.

Notice how transistors Q_3 and Q_4 are paralleled at their collector and emitter terminals. In essence, these two transistors are acting as paralleled switches, allowing current through resistors R_3 and R_4 according to the logic levels of inputs A and B.

If *any* input is at a "high" (1) level, then at least one of the two transistors (Q_3 and/or Q_4) will be saturated, allowing current through resistors R_3 and R_4, and turning on the final output transistor Q_5 for a "low" (0) logic level output.

The only way the output of this circuit can ever assume a "high" (1) state is if *both* Q_3 and Q_4 are cutoff, which means *both* inputs would have to be grounded, or "low" (0).

This circuit's truth table, then, is equivalent to that of the NOR gate:

NOR Gate

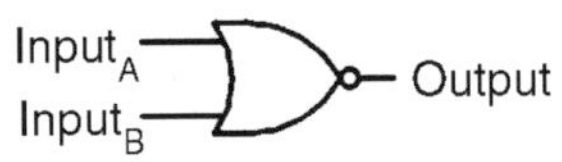

A	B	Output
0	0	1
0	1	0
1	0	0
1	1	0

In order to turn this NOR gate circuit into an OR gate, we would have to invert the output logic level with another transistor stage, just like we did with the NAND-to-AND gate example:

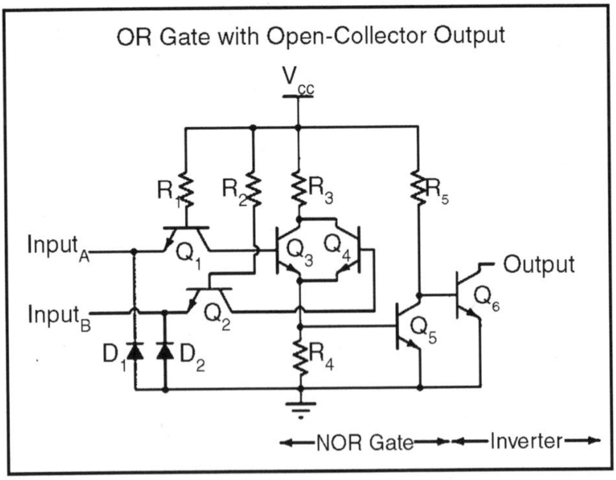

The truth table and equivalent gate circuit (an inverted-output NOR gate) are shown here:

OR Gate

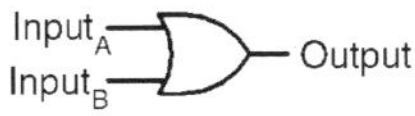

A	B	Output
0	0	0
0	1	1
1	0	1
1	1	1

Equivalent Circuit

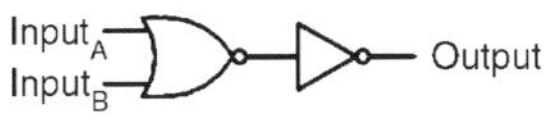

Of course, totem-pole output stages are also possible in both NOR and OR TTL logic circuits.

MULTIPLE LOGIC INPUT GATES

Inverters and buffers exhaust the possibilities for single-input gate circuits. What more can be done with a single logic signal but to buffer it or invert it? To explore more logic gate possibilities, we must add more input terminals to the circuit(s). Adding more input terminals to a logic gate increases the number of input state possibilities. With a single-input gate such as the inverter or buffer, there can only be two possible input states: either the input is "high" (1) or it is "low" (0). As was mentioned previously in this chapter, a two input gate has *four* possibilities (00, 01, 10, and 11). A three-input gate has*eight* possibilities (000, 001, 010, 011, 100, 101, 110, and 111) for input states. The number of possible input states is equal to two to the power of the number of inputs:

$$\text{Number of Possible Input States} = 2^n$$

Where: n = Number of Inputs

This increase in the number of possible input states obviously allows for more complex gate behaviour. Now, instead of merely inverting or amplifying (buffering) a single "high" or "low" logic level, the output of the gate will be determined by whatever *combination* of 1's and 0's is present at the input terminals.

Since so many combinations are possible with just a few input terminals, there are many different types of multiple-input gates, unlike single-input gates which can only be inverters or buffers. Each basic gate type will be presented in this section, showing its standard symbol, truth table, and practical operation. The actual TTL circuitry of these different gates will be explored in subsequent sections.

THE AND GATE

One of the easiest multiple-input gates to understand is the AND gate, so-called because the output of this gate will be "high" (1) if and only if *all* inputs (first input *and* the second input *and* ...) are "high" (1). If any input(s) are "low" (0), the output is guaranteed to be in a "low" state as well.

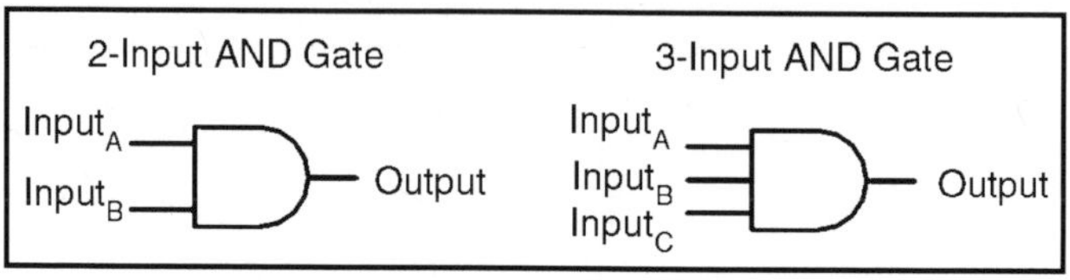

In case you might have been wondering, AND gates are made with more than three inputs, but this is less common than the simple two-input variety.

A two-input and Gate's Truth Table Looks Like this

2-Input AND Gate

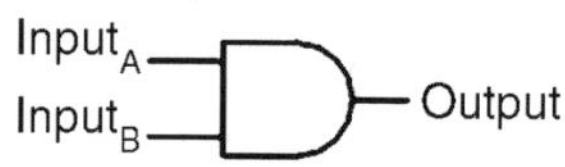

A	B	Output
0	0	0
0	1	0
1	0	0
1	1	1

What this truth table means in practical terms is shown in the following sequence of illustrations, with the 2-input AND gate subjected to all possibilities of input logic levels. An LED (Light-Emitting Diode) provides visual indication of the output logic level:

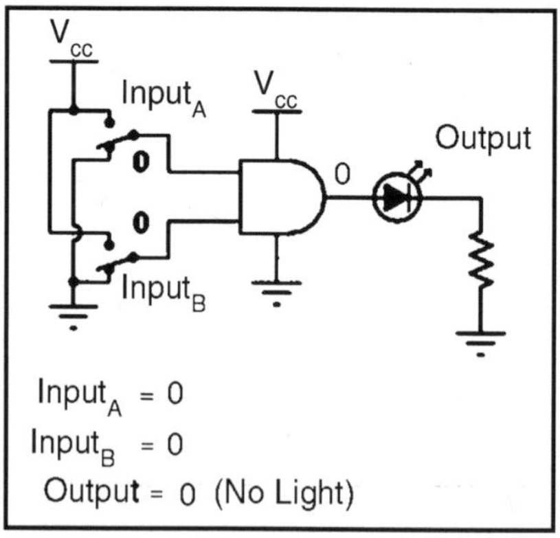

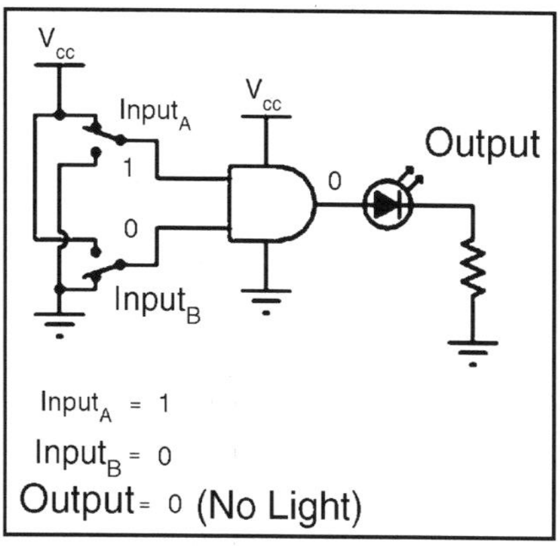

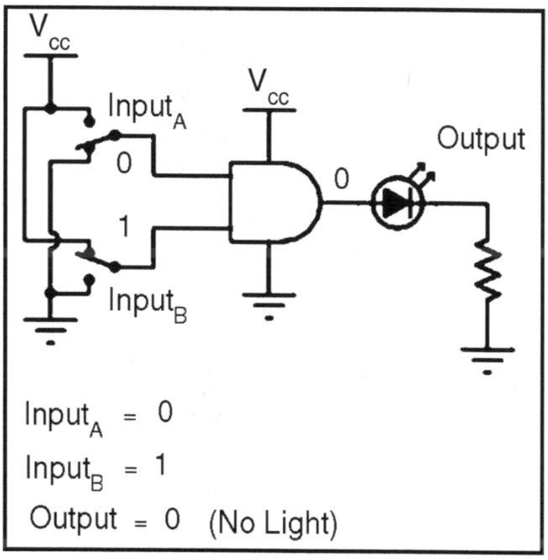

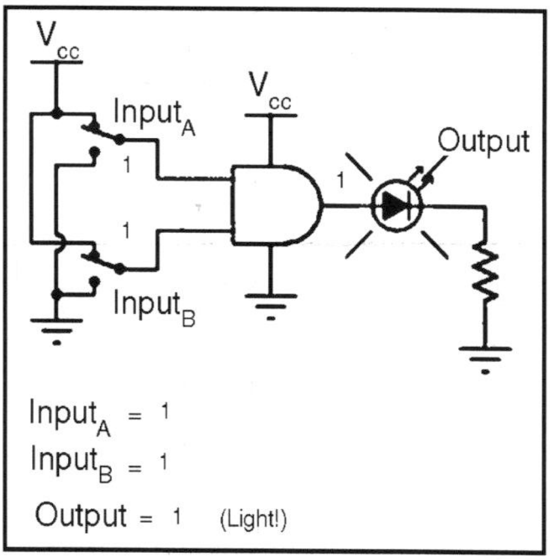

It is only with all inputs raised to "high" logic levels that the AND gate's output goes "high," thus energizing the LED for only one out of the four input combination states.

THE NAND GATE

A variation on the idea of the AND gate is called the NAND gate. The word "NAND" is a verbal contraction of the words NOT and AND. Essentially, a NAND gate behaves the same as an AND gate with a NOT (inverter) gate connected to the output terminal.

To symbolize this output signal inversion, the NAND gate symbol has a bubble on the output line. The truth table for a NAND gate is as one might expect, exactly opposite as that of an AND gate:

2-Input NAND Gate

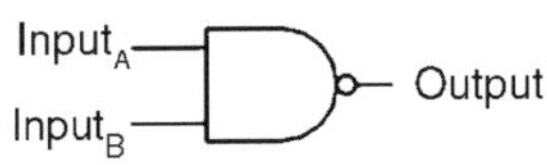

A	B	Output
0	0	1
0	1	1
1	0	1
1	1	0

Equivalent Gate Circuit

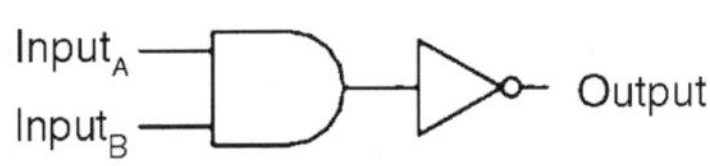

As with AND gates, NAND gates are made with more than two inputs. In such cases, the same general principle applies: the output will be "low" (0) if and only if all inputs are "high" (1). If any input is "low" (0), the output will go "high" (1).

THE OR GATE

Our next gate to investigate is the OR gate, so-called because the output of this gate will be "high" (1) if *any* of the inputs (first input *or* the second input *or* ...) are "high" (1). The output of an OR gate goes "low" (0) if and only if all inputs are "low" (0).

2-Input OR Gate

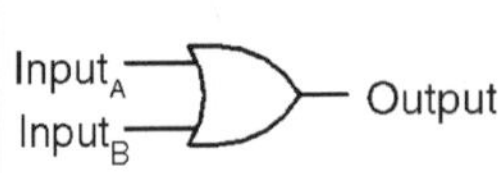

3-Input OR Gate

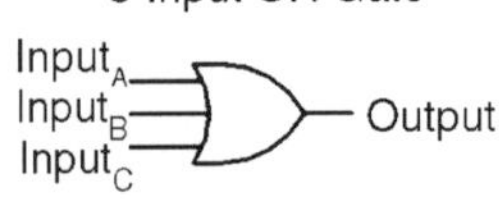

A two-input OR gate's truth table looks like this:

2-Input OR Gate

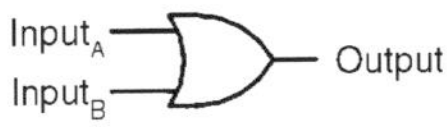

A	B	Output
0	0	0
0	1	1
1	0	1
1	1	1

The following sequence of illustrations demonstrates the OR gate's function, with the 2-inputs experiencing all possible logic levels. An LED (Light-Emitting Diode) provides visual indication of the gate's output logic level:

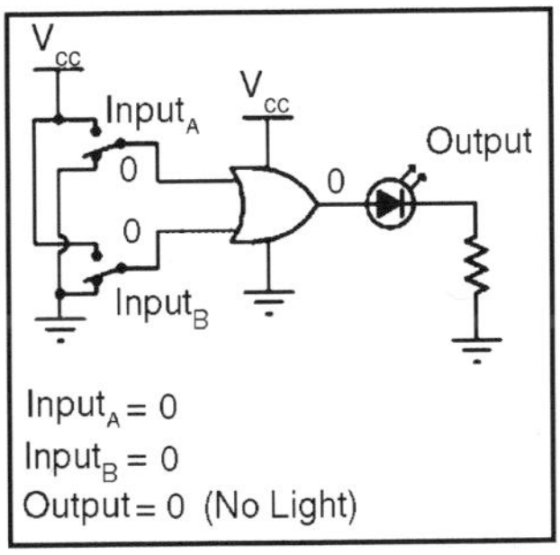

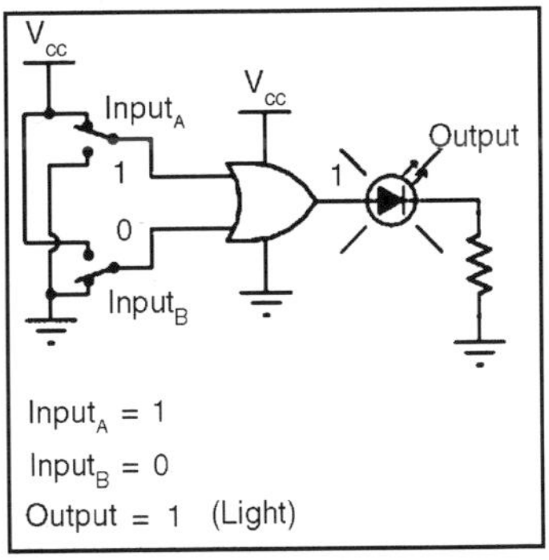

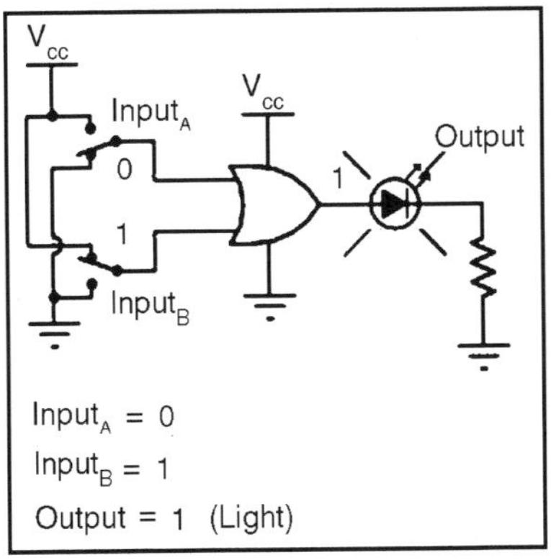

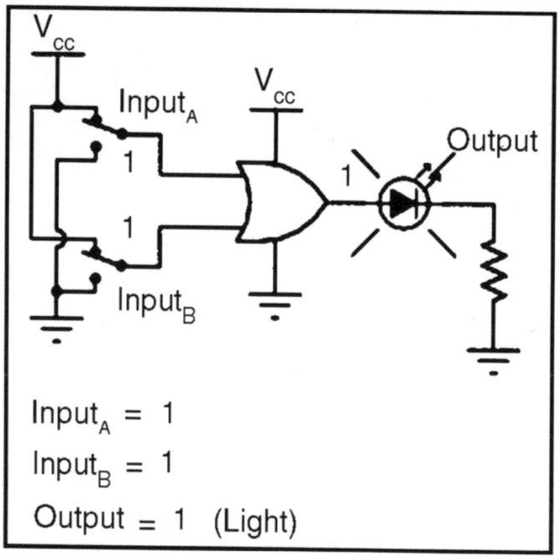

A condition of any input being raised to a "high" logic level makes the OR gate's output go "high," thus energizing the LED for three out of the four input combination states.

THE NOR GATE

As you might have suspected, the NOR gate is an OR gate with its output inverted, just like a NAND gate is an AND gate with an inverted output.

2-Input NOR Gate

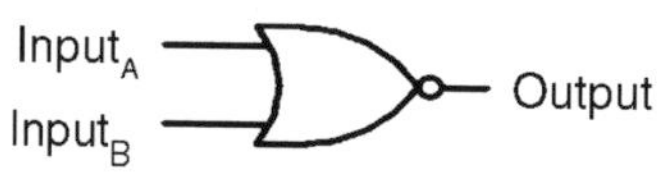

A	B	Output
0	0	1
0	1	0
1	0	0
1	1	0

Equivalent Gate Circuit

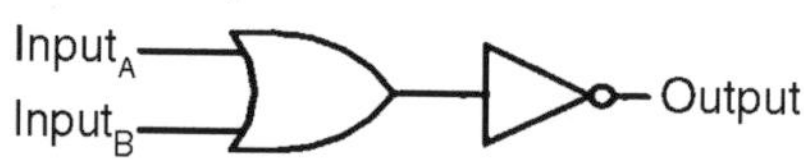

NOR gates, like all the other multiple-input gates seen thus far, can be manufactured with more than two inputs. Still, the same logical principle applies: the output goes "low" (0) if any of the inputs are made "high" (1). The output is "high" (1) only when all inputs are "low" (0).

THE NEGATIVE-AND GATE

A Negative-AND gate functions the same as an AND gate with all its inputs inverted (connected through NOT gates). In keeping with standard gate symbol convention, these inverted inputs are signified by bubbles. Contrary to most peoples' first instinct, the logical behaviour of a Negative-AND gate is *not* the same as a NAND gate.

Its truth table, actually, is identical to a NOR gate:

2- Input Negative-And Gate

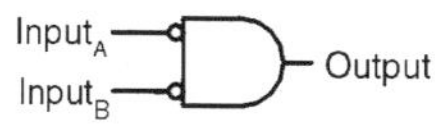

A	B	Output
0	0	1
0	1	0
1	0	0
1	1	0

Equivalent Gate Circuits

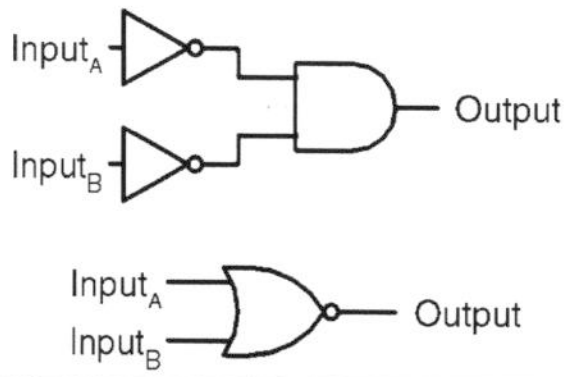

THE NEGATIVE-OR GATE

Following the same pattern, a Negative-OR gate functions the same as an OR gate with all its inputs inverted. In keeping with standard gate symbol convention, these inverted inputs are signified by bubbles. The behaviour and truth table of a Negative-OR gate is the same as for a NAND gate:

2-Input Negative-OR Gate

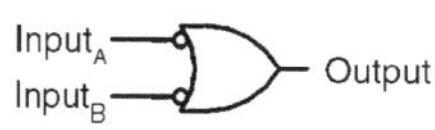

A	B	Output
0	0	1
0	1	1
1	0	1
1	1	0

Equivalent Gate Circuits

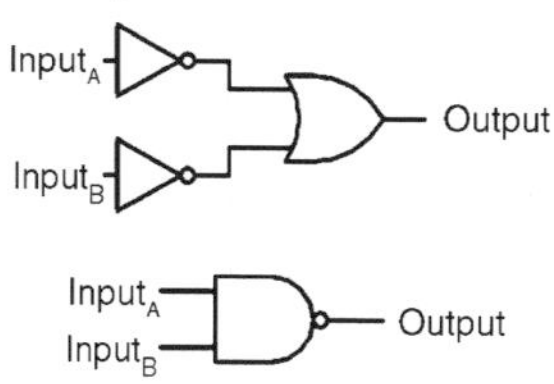

THE INVERTER AND "BUFFER" GATE

If we were to connect two inverter gates together so that the output of one fed into the input of another, the two inversion functions would "cancel" each other out so that there would be no inversion from input to final output:

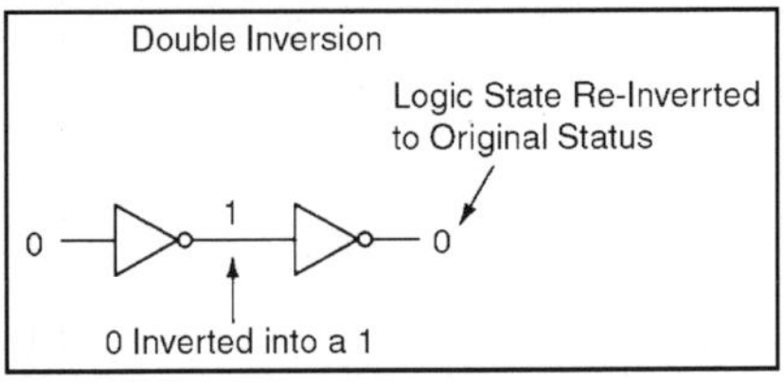

While this may seem like a pointless thing to do, it does have practical application. Remember that gate circuits are signal*amplifiers,* regardless of what logic function they may perform. A weak signal source (one that is not capable of sourcing or sinking very much current to a load) may be boosted by means of two inverters like the pair shown in the previous illustration. The logic level is unchanged, but the full current-sourcing or -sinking capabilities of the final inverter are available to drive a load resistance if needed.

For this purpose, a special logic gate called a *buffer* is manufactured to perform the same function as two inverters. *Its symbol is simply a triangle, with no inverting "bubble" on the output terminal*:

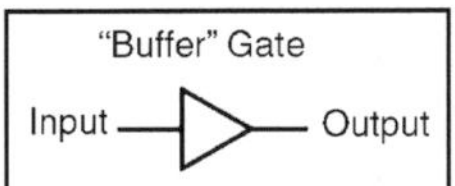

Input	Output
0	0
1	1

The internal schematic diagram for a typical open-collector buffer is not much different from that of a simple inverter: only one more common-emitter transistor stage is added to re-invert the output signal.

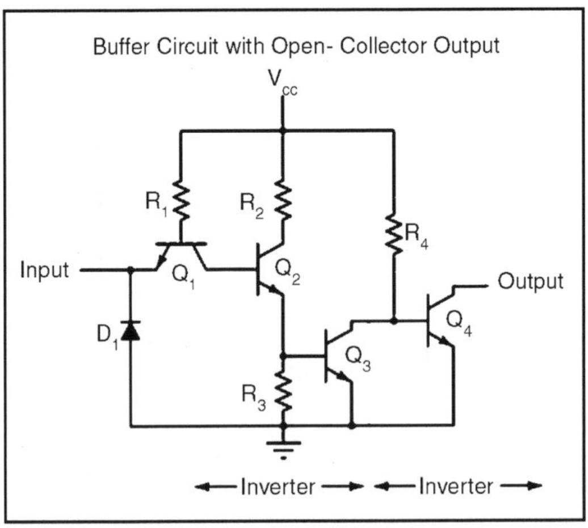

Let's analyse this circuit for two conditions: an input logic level of "1" and an input logic level of "0." First, a "high" (1) input:

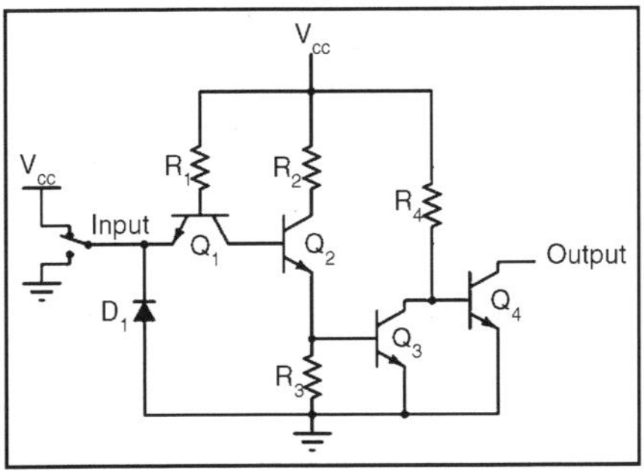

As before with the inverter circuit, the "high" input causes no conduction through the left steering diode of Q_1 (emitter-to-base PN junction). All of R_1's current goes through the base of transistor Q_2, saturating it:

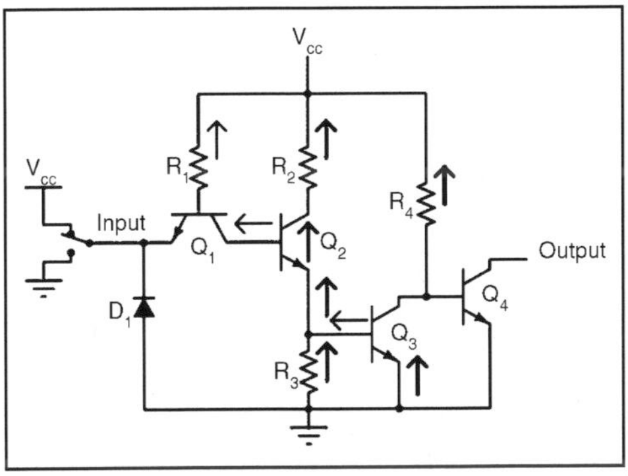

Having Q_2 saturated causes Q_3 to be saturated as well, resulting in very little voltage dropped between the base and emitter of the final output transistor Q_4. Thus, Q_4 will be in cutoff mode, conducting no current. The output terminal will be floating (neither connected to ground nor V_{cc}), and this will be equivalent to a "high" state on the input of the next TTL gate that this one feeds in to. Thus, a "high" input gives a "high" output.

With a "low" input signal (input terminal grounded), the analysis looks something like this:

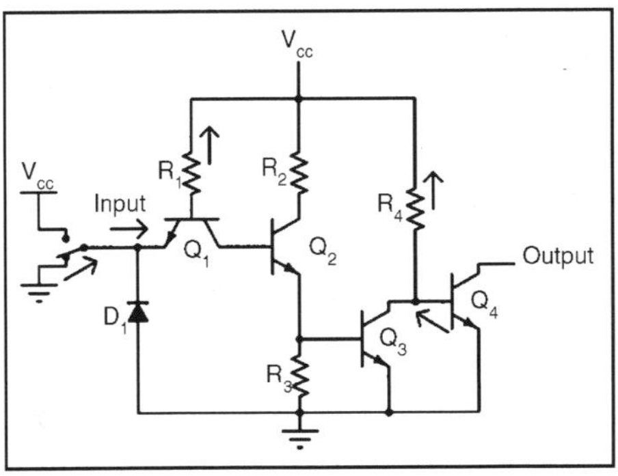

All of R_1's current is now diverted through the input switch, thus eliminating base current through Q_2. This forces transistor Q_2 into cutoff so that no base current goes through Q_3 either. With Q_3 cutoff as well, Q_4 is will be saturated by the current through resistor R_4, thus connecting the output terminal to ground, making it a "low" logic level. Thus, a "low" input gives a "low" output. The schematic diagram for a buffer circuit with totem pole output transistors is a bit more complex, but the basic principles, and certainly the truth table, are the same as for the open-collector circuit:

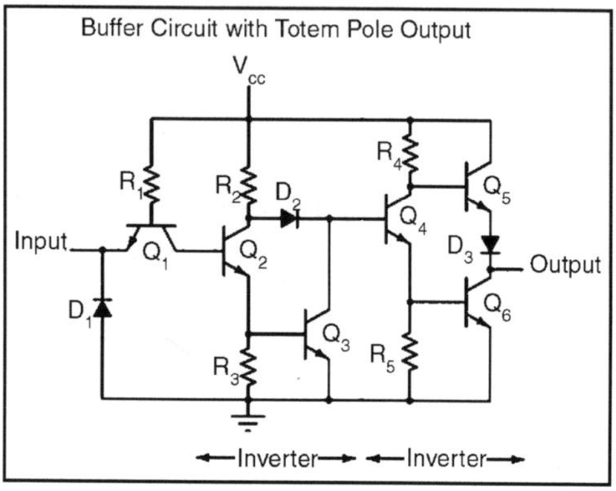

SINGLE-TRANSISTOR INVERTER CIRCUIT OF THE NOT GATE

The single-transistor inverter circuit illustrated earlier is actually too crude to be of practical use as a gate. Real inverter circuits contain more than one transistor to maximize voltage gain (so as to ensure that the final output transistor is either in full cutoff or full saturation), and other components designed to reduce the chance of accidental damage. Shown here is a schematic diagram for a real inverter circuit, complete with all necessary components for efficient and reliable operation:

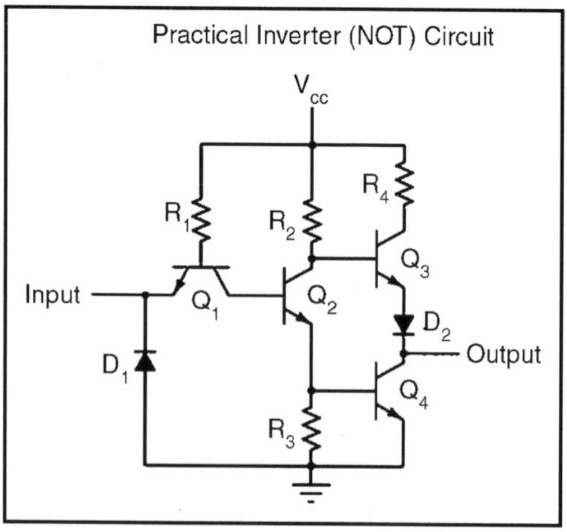

This circuit is composed exclusively of resistors and bipolar transistors. Bear in mind that other circuit designs are capable of performing the NOT gate function, including designs substituting field-effect transistors for bipolar (discussed later in this chapter).

Let's analyse this circuit for the condition where the input is "high," or in a binary "1" state. We can simulate this by showing the input terminal connected to V_{cc} through a switch:

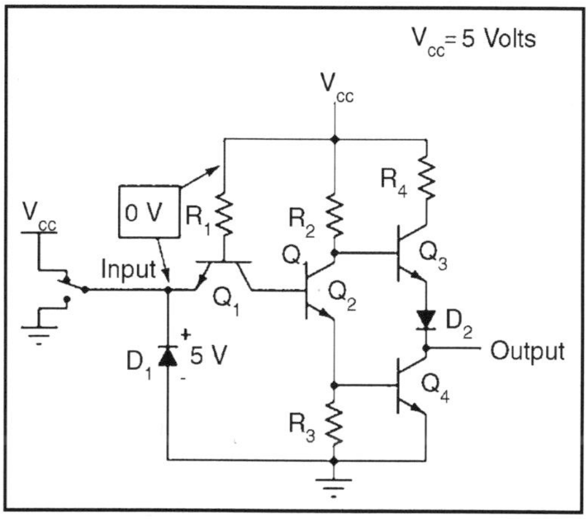

In this case, diode D_1 will be reverse-biased, and therefore not conduct any current. In fact, the only purpose for having D_1 in the circuit is to prevent transistor damage in the case of a *negative* voltage being impressed on the input (a voltage that is negative, rather than positive, with respect to ground). With no voltage between the base and emitter of transistor Q_1, we would expect no current through it, either. However, as strange as it may seem, transistor Q_1 is not being used as is customary for a transistor. In reality, Q_1 is being used in this circuit as nothing more than a back-to-back pair of diodes.

The following schematic shows the real function of Q_1:

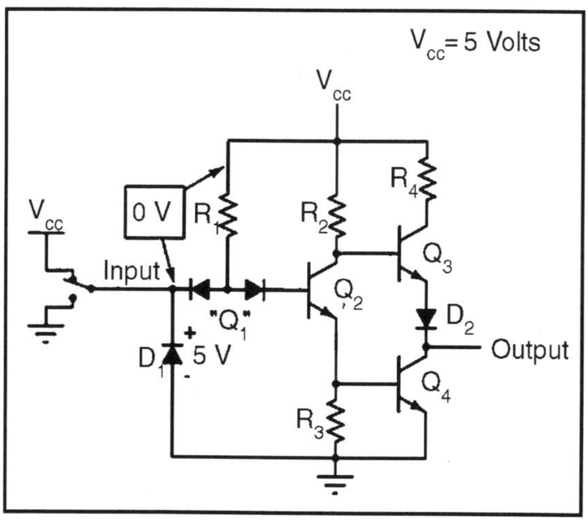

The purpose of these diodes is to "steer" current to or away from the base of transistor Q_2, depending on the logic level of the input. Exactly how these two diodes are able to "steer" current isn't exactly obvious at first inspection, so a short example may be necessary for understanding. Suppose we had the following diode/resistor circuit, representing the base-emitter junctions of transistors Q_2 and Q_4 as single diodes, stripping away all other portions of the circuit so that we can concentrate on the current "steered" through the two back-to-back diodes:

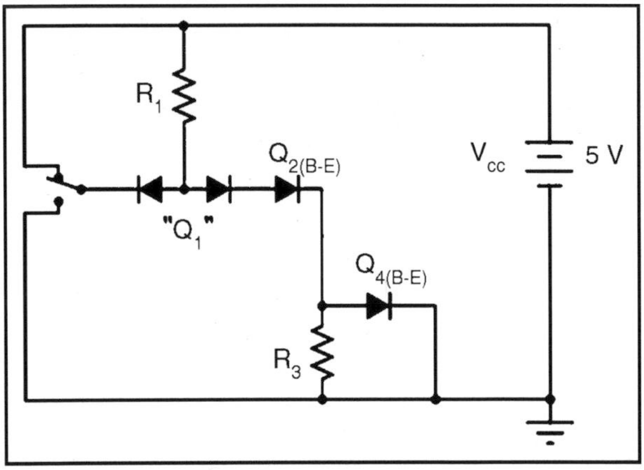

With the input switch in the "up" position (connected to V_{cc}), it should be obvious that there will be no current through the left steering diode of Q_1, because there isn't any voltage in the switch-diode-R_1-switch loop to motivate electrons to flow. However, there *will* be current through the right steering diode of Q_1, as well as through Q_2's base-emitter diode junction and Q_4's base-emitter diode junction:

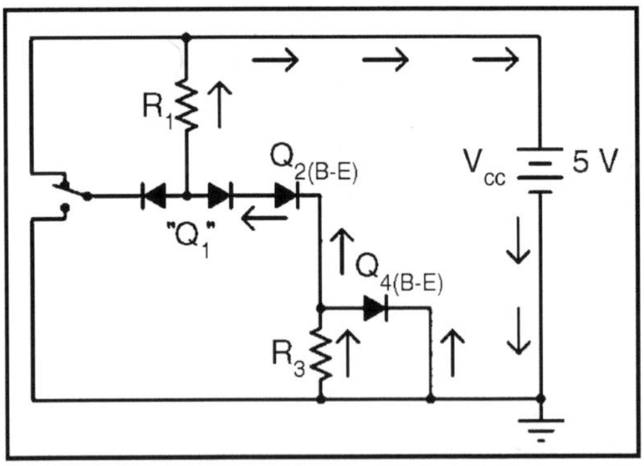

This tells us that in the real gate circuit, transistors Q_2 and Q_4 will have base current, which will turn them on to conduct collector current. The total voltage dropped between the base of Q_1 and ground will be about 2.1 volts, equal to the combined voltage drops of three PN junctions: the right steering diode, Q_2's base-emitter diode, and Q_4's base-emitter diode.

Now, let's move the input switch to the "down" position and see what happens:

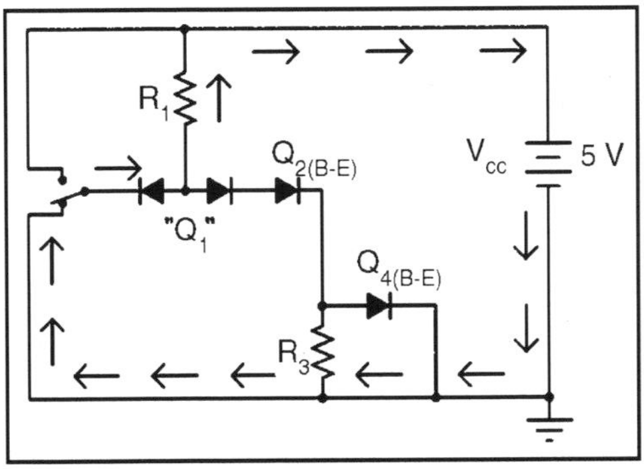

If we were to measure current in this circuit, we would find that *all* of the current goes through the left steering diode of Q_1 and *none* of it through the right diode. Why is this? It still appears as though there is a complete path for current through Q_4's diode, Q_2's diode, the right diode of the pair, and R_1, so why will there be no current through that path?

Remember that PN junction diodes are very nonlinear devices: they do not even begin to conduct current until the forward voltage applied across them reaches a certain minimum quantity, approximately 0.7 volts for silicon and 0.3 volts for germanium. And then when they begin to conduct current, they will not drop substantially more than 0.7 volts. When the switch in this circuit is in the "down" position, the left diode of the steering diode pair is fully conducting, and so it drops about 0.7 volts across it and no more.

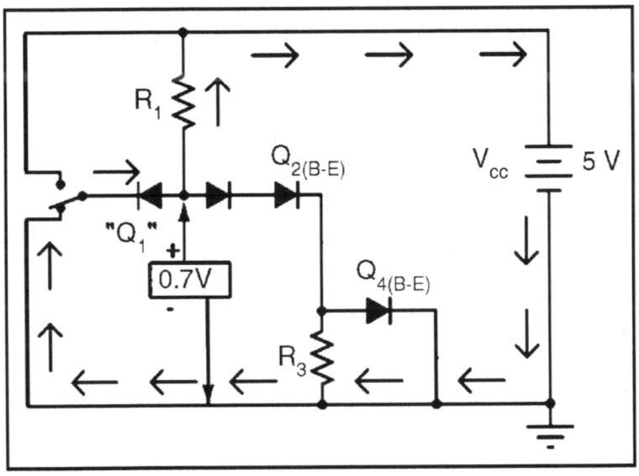

Recall that with the switch in the "up" position (transistors Q_2 and Q_4 conducting), there was about 2.1 volts dropped between those same two points (Q_1's base and ground), which also happens to be the *minimum* voltage necessary to forward-bias three series-connected silicon PN junctions into a state of conduction.

The 0.7 volts provided by the left diode's forward voltage drop is simply insufficient to allow any electron flow through the series string of the right diode, Q_2's diode, and the $R_3//Q_4$ diode parallel subcircuit, and so no electrons flow through that path. With no current through the bases of either transistor

Q_2 or Q_4, neither one will be able to conduct collector current: transistors Q_2 and Q_4 will both be in a state of cutoff. Consequently, this circuit configuration allows 100 per cent switching of Q_2 base current (and therefore control over the rest of the gate circuit, including voltage at the output) by diversion of current through the left steering diode.

In the case of our example gate circuit, the input is held "high" by the switch (connected to V_{cc}), making the left steering diode (zero voltage dropped across it). However, the right steering diode is conducting current through the base of Q_2, through resistor R_1:

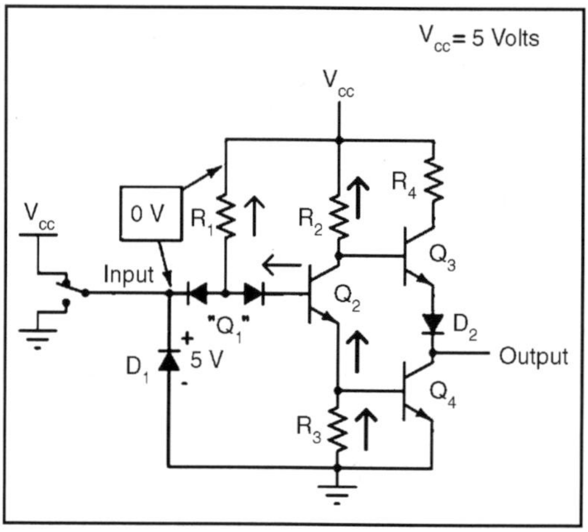

With base current provided, transistor Q_2 will be turned "on." More specifically, it will be *saturated* by virtue of the more-than-adequate current allowed by R_1 through the base.

With Q_2 saturated, resistor R_3 will be dropping enough voltage to forward-bias the base-emitter junction of transistor Q_4, thus saturating it as well:

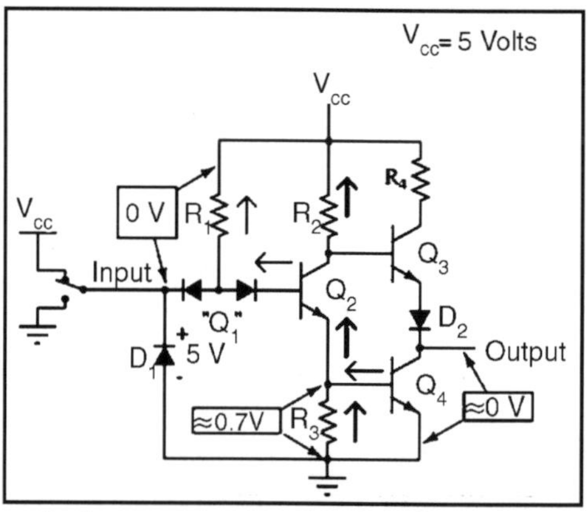

With Q_4 saturated, the output terminal will be almost directly shorted to ground, leaving the output terminal at a voltage (in reference to ground) of almost 0 volts, or a binary "0" ("low") logic level. Due to the presence of diode D_2, there will not be enough voltage between the base of Q_3 and its emitter to turn it on, so it remains in cutoff.

Let's see now what happens if we reverse the input's logic level to a binary "0" by actuating the input switch:

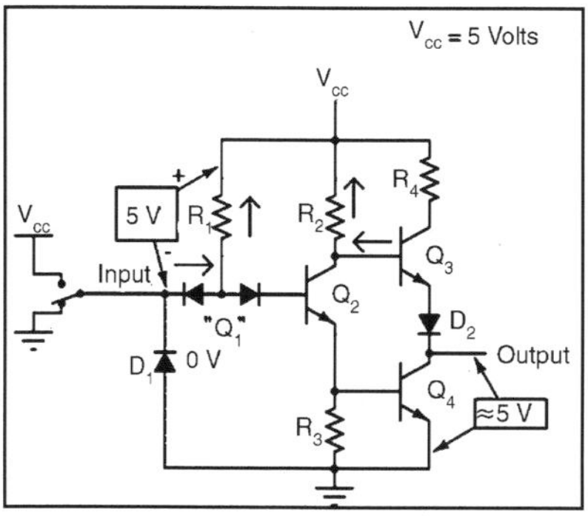

Now there will be current through the left steering diode of Q_1 and no current through the right steering diode. This eliminates current through the base of Q_2, thus turning it off. With Q_2 off, there is no longer a path for Q_4 base current, so Q_4 goes into cutoff as well. Q_3, on the other hand, now has sufficient voltage dropped between its base and ground to forward-bias its base-emitter junction and saturate it, thus raising the output terminal voltage to a "high" state. In actuality, the output voltage will be somewhere around 4 volts depending on the degree of saturation and any load current, but still high enough to be considered a "high" (1) logic level. *With this, our simulation of the inverter circuit is complete*: a "1" in gives a "0" out, and visa-versa. The astute observer will note that this inverter circuit's input will assume a "high" state of left floating (not connected to either V_{cc} or ground). With the input terminal left unconnected, there will be no current through the left steering diode of Q_1, leaving all of R_1's current to go through Q_2's base, thus saturating Q_2 and driving the circuit output to a "low" state:

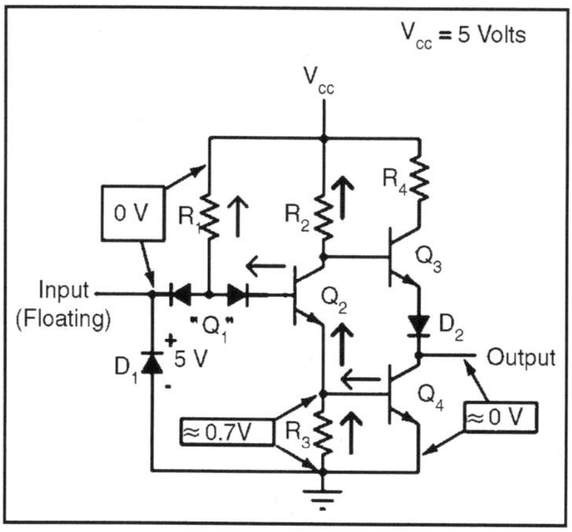

The tendency for such a circuit to assume a high input state if left floating is one shared by all gate circuits based on this type of design, known as Transistor-to-Transistor Logic, or *TTL*. This characteristic may be taken advantage of in simplifying the design of a gate's *output* circuitry, knowing that the outputs of gates typically drive the inputs of other gates. If the input of a TTL gate circuit assumes a high state when floating, then the output of any gate driving a TTL input need only provide a path to ground for a low state and be floating for a high state. This concept may require further elaboration for full understanding, so I will explore it in detail here.

A gate circuit as we have just analysed has the ability to handle output current in two directions: in and out. Technically, this is known as *sourcing* and *sinking* current, respectively. When the gate output is high, there is continuity from the output terminal to V_{cc} through the top output transistor (Q_3), allowing electrons to flow from ground, through a load, into the gate's output terminal, through the emitter of Q_3, and eventually up to the V_{cc} power terminal (positive side of the DC power supply):

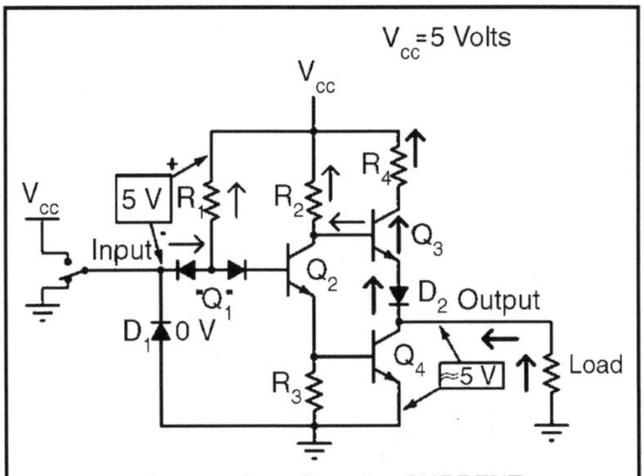

Inverter Gate Sourcing CURRENT

To simplify this concept, we may show the output of a gate circuit as being a double-throw switch, capable of connecting the output terminal either to V_{cc} or ground, depending on its state. For a gate outputting a "high" logic level, the combination of Q_3 saturated and Q_4 cutoff is analogous to a double-throw switch in the "V_{cc}" position, providing a path for current through a grounded load:

Simplified Gate Circuit Sourcing Current

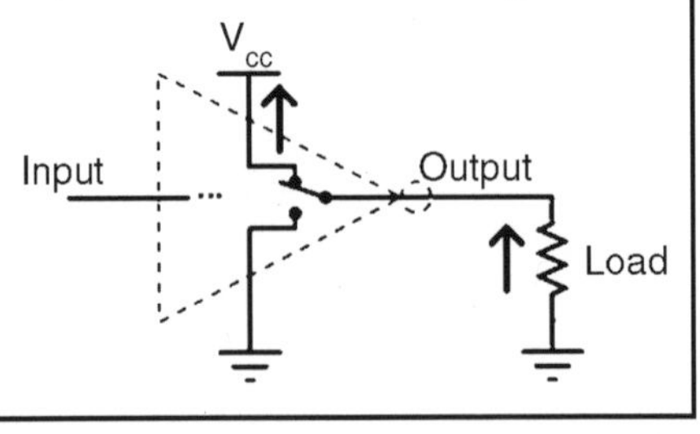

Please note that this two-position switch shown inside the gate symbol is representative of transistors Q_3 and Q_4alternately connecting the output terminal to V_{cc} or ground, *not* of the switch previously shown sending an input signal to the gate!

Conversely, when a gate circuit is outputting a "low" logic level to a load, it is analogous to the double-throw switch being set in the "ground" position. Current will then be going the other way if the load resistance connects to V_{cc}: from ground, through the emitter of Q_4, out the output terminal, through the load resistance, and back to V_{cc}. In this condition, the gate is said to be *sinking* current:

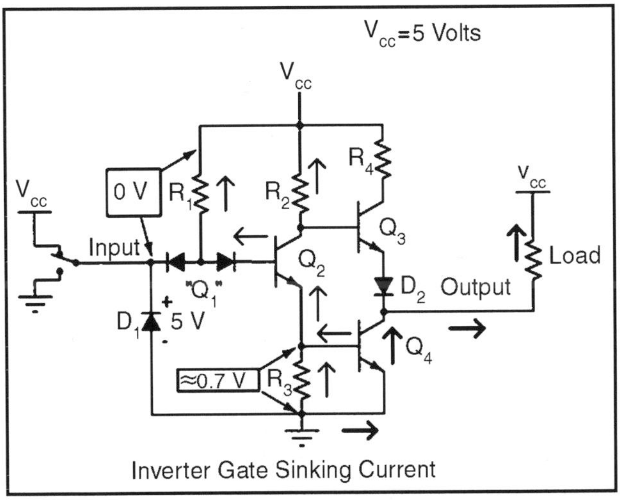

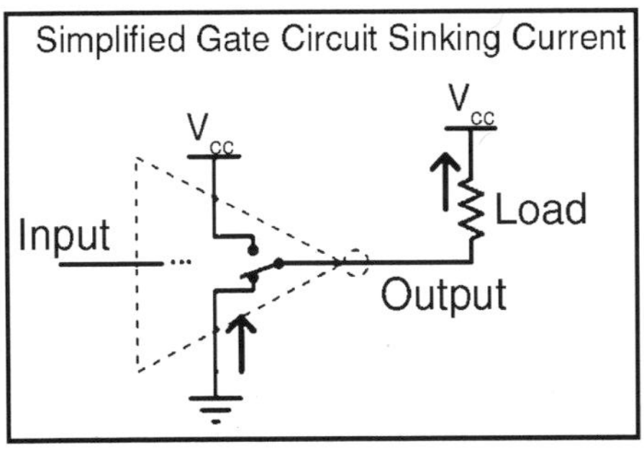

The combination of Q_3 and Q_4 working as a "push-pull" transistor pair (otherwise known as a *totem pole output*) has the ability to either source current (draw in current to V_{cc}) or sink current (output current from ground) to a load. However, a standard TTL gate *input* never needs current to be sourced, only sunk. That is, since a TTL gate input naturally assumes a high state if left floating, any gate output driving a TTL input need only sink current to provide a "0" or "low" input, and need not source current to provide a "1" or a "high" logic level at the input of the receiving gate.

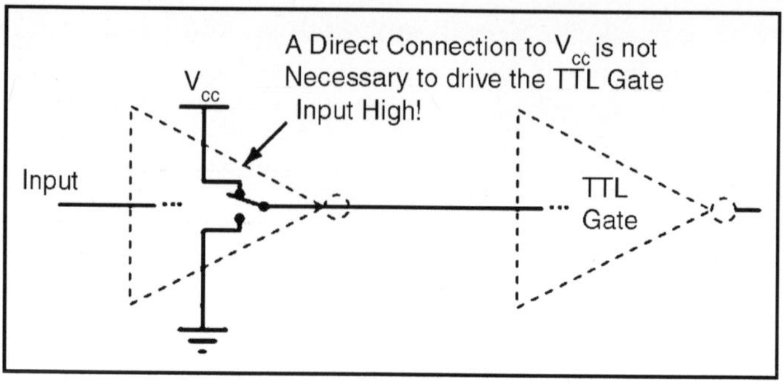

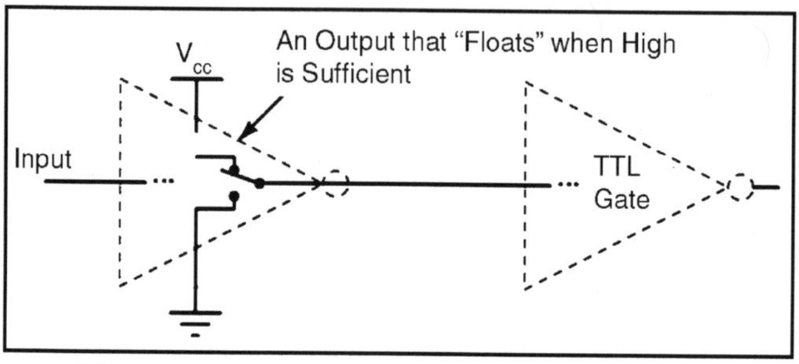

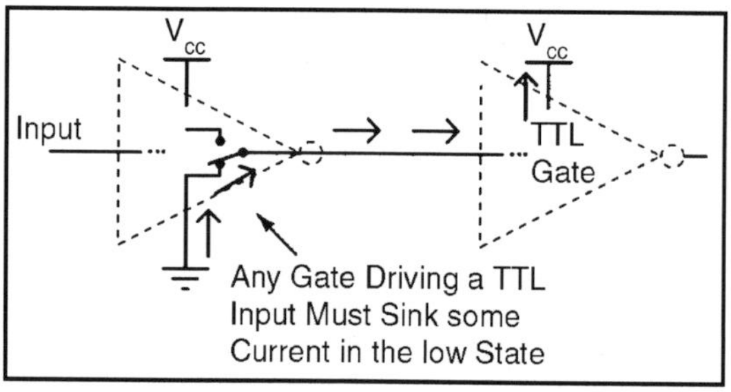

This means we have the option of simplifying the output stage of a gate circuit so as to eliminate Q_3 altogether.

The result is known as an open-collector output:

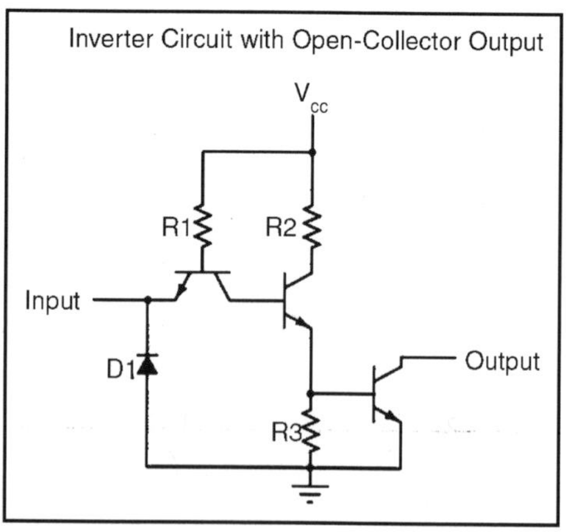

To designate open-collector output circuitry within a standard gate symbol, a special marker is used. Shown here is the symbol for an inverter gate with open-collector output:

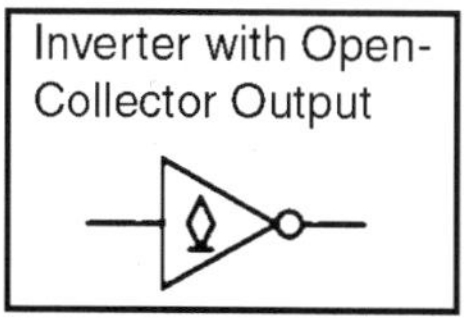

Please keep in mind that the "high" default condition of a floating gate input is only true for TTL circuitry, and not necessarily for other types, especially for logic gates constructed of field-effect transistors.

LOGIC OF OUTPUT GATES

It is sometimes desirable to have a logic gate that provides both inverted and non-inverted outputs. For example, a single-input gate that is both a buffer and an inverter, with a separate output terminal for each function. Or, a two-input gate that provides both the AND and the NAND functions in a single circuit. Such gates do exist and they are referred to as*complementary output* gates.

The general symbology for such a gate is the basic gate figure with a bar and two output lines protruding from it. An array of complementary gate symbols is shown in the following illustration:

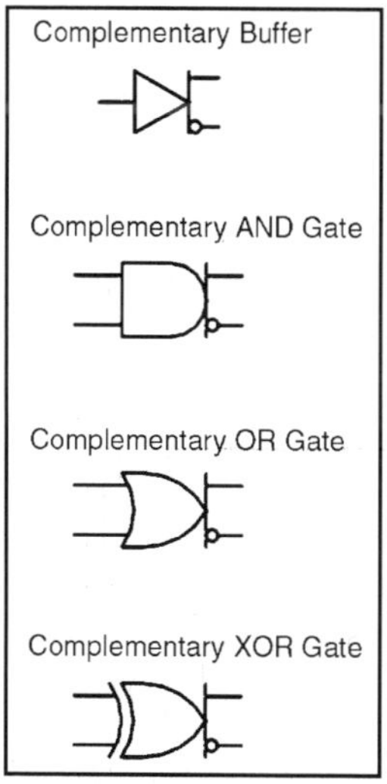

Complementary gates are especially useful in "crowded" circuits where there may not be enough physical room to mount the additional integrated circuit chips necessary to provide both inverted and noninverted outputs using standard gates and additional inverters. They are also useful in applications where a complementary output is necessary from a gate, but the addition of an inverter would introduce an unwanted time lag in the inverted output relative to the noninverted output. The internal circuitry of complemented gates is such that both inverted and noninverted outputs change state at almost exactly the same time:

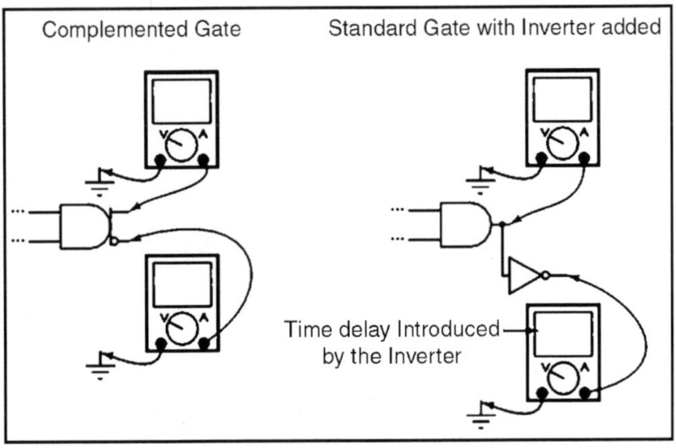

Another type of special gate output is called *tristate,* because it has the ability to provide three different output modes: current sinking ("low" logic level), current sourcing ("high"), and floating ("high-Z," or *high-impedance*). Tristate outputs are usually found as an optional feature on buffer gates. Such gates require an extra input terminal to control the "high-Z" mode, and this input is usually called the *enable.*

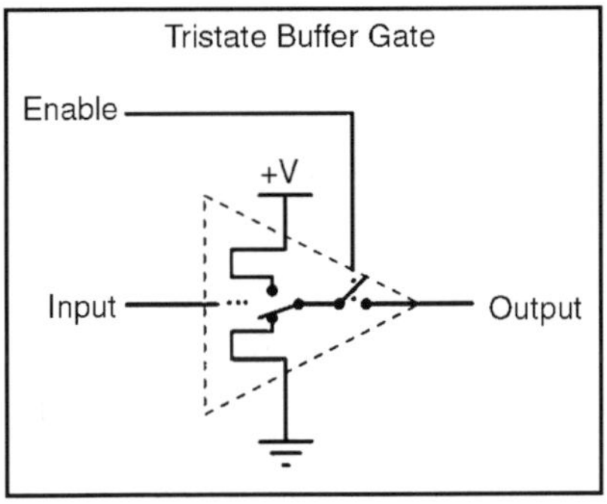

With the enable input held "high" (1), the buffer acts like an ordinary buffer with a totem pole output stage: it is capable of both sourcing and sinking current. However, the output terminal floats (goes into "high-Z" mode) if ever the enable input is grounded ("low"), regardless of the data signal's logic level. In other words, making the enable input terminal "low" (0) effectively *disconnects* the gate from whatever its output is wired to so that it can no longer have any effect.

Tristate buffers are marked in schematic diagrams by a triangle character within the gate symbol like this:

Tristate Buffer Symbol

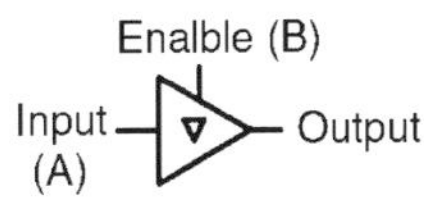

Truth Table

A	B	Output
0	0	High-Z
0	1	0
1	0	High-Z
1	1	1

Tristate buffers are also made with inverted enable inputs. Such a gate acts normal when the enable input is "low" (0) and goes into high-Z output mode when the enable input is "high" (1):

Tristate Buffer with Inverted Enable Input

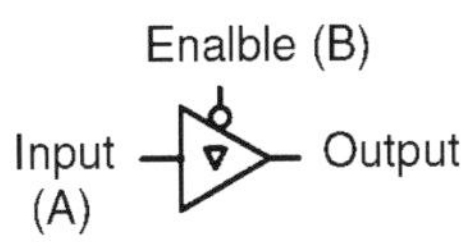

Truth Table

A	B	Output
0	0	0
0	1	High-Z
1	0	1
1	1	High-Z

One special type of gate known as the *bilateral switch* uses gate-controlled MOSFET transistors acting as on/off switches to switch electrical signals, analog or digital. The "on" resistance of such a switch is in the range of several hundred ohms, the "off" resistance being in the range of several hundred *mega*-ohms. Bilateral switches appear in schematics as SPST (Single-Pole, Single-Throw) switches inside of rectangular boxes, with a control terminal on one of the box's long sides:

CMOS Bilateral Switch

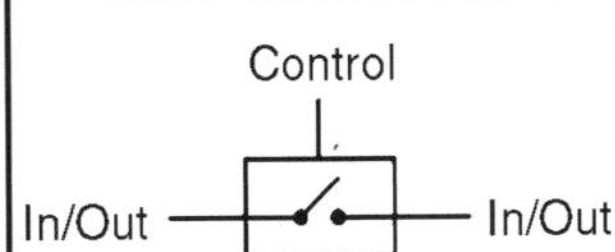

A bilateral switch might be best envisioned as a solid-state (semiconductor) version of an electromechanical relay: a signal-actuated switch contact that may be used to conduct virtually any type of electric signal. Of course, being solid-state, the bilateral switch has none of the undesirable characteristics of electromechanical relays, such as contact "bouncing," arcing, slow speed, or susceptibility to mechanical vibration.

Conversely, though, they are rather limited in their current-carrying ability. Additionally, the signal conducted by the "contact" must not exceed the power supply "rail" voltages powering the bilateral switch circuit.

BUFFER FUNCTION

Being that it is quite easy to employ NAND and NOR gates to perform the inverter (NOT) function, it stands to reason that two such stages of gates will result in a buffer function, where the output is the same logical state as the input.

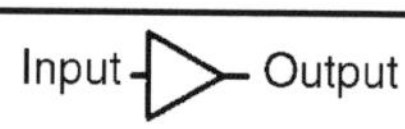

Input	Output
0	0
1	1

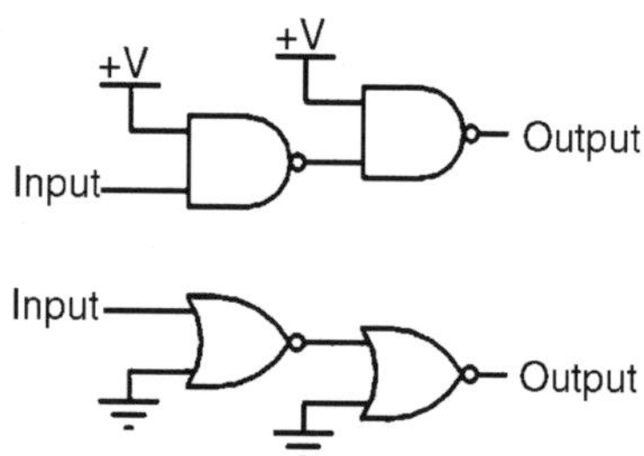

CONSTRUCTING THE AND FUNCTION

To make the AND function from NAND gates, all that is needed is an inverter (NOT) stage on the output of a NAND gate. This extra inversion "cancels out" the first *N* in *NAND*, leaving the AND function. It takes a little more work to wrestle the same functionality out of NOR gates, but it can be done by inverting ("NOT") all of the inputs to a NOR gate.

2-Input AND Gate

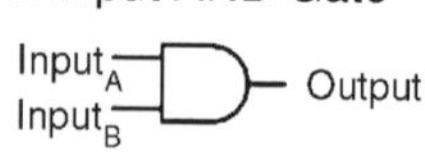

A	B	Output
0	0	0
0	1	0
1	0	0
1	1	1

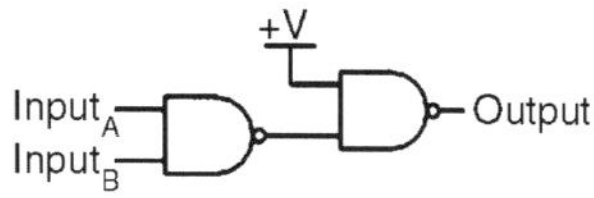

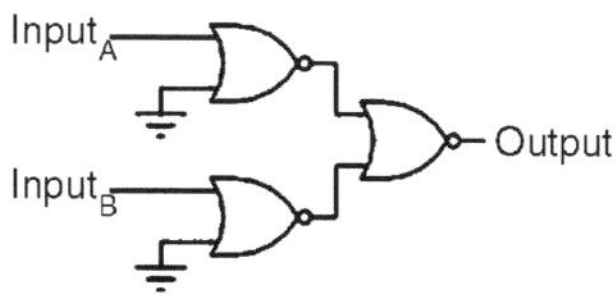

NAND FUNCTION

It would be pointless to show you how to "construct" the NAND function using a NAND gate, since there is nothing to do. To make a NOR gate perform the NAND function, we must invert all inputs to the NOR gate as well as the NOR gate's output. For a two-input gate, this requires three more NOR gates connected as inverters.

2-Input AND Gate

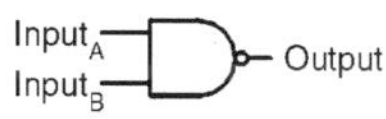

A	B	Output
0	0	1
0	1	1
1	0	1
1	1	0

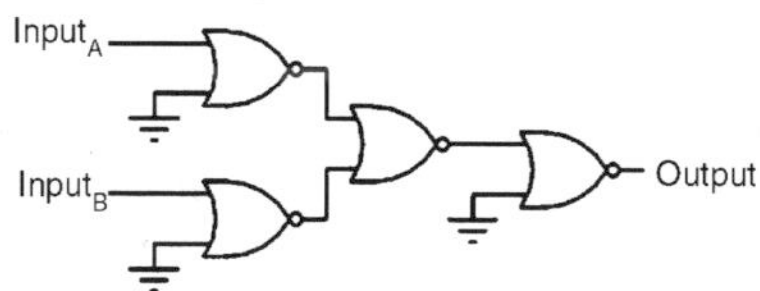

OR FUNCTION

Inverting the output of a NOR gate (with another NOR gate connected as an inverter) results in the OR function. The NAND gate, on the other hand, requires inversion of all inputs to mimic the OR function, just as we needed to invert all inputs of a NOR gate to obtain the AND function. Remember that inversion of all inputs to a gate results in changing that gate's essential function from AND to OR (or visa-versa), plus an inverted output. Thus, with all inputs inverted, a NAND behaves as an OR, a NOR behaves as an AND, an AND behaves as a NOR, and an OR behaves as a NAND. In Boolean algebra, this transformation is referred to as *DeMorgan's Theorem*, covered in more detail in a later chapter of this book.

2-Input OR Gate

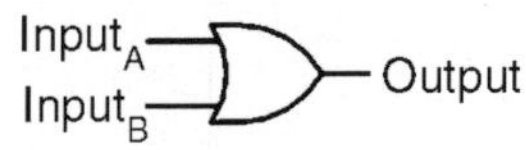

A	B	Output
0	0	0
0	1	1
1	0	1
1	1	1

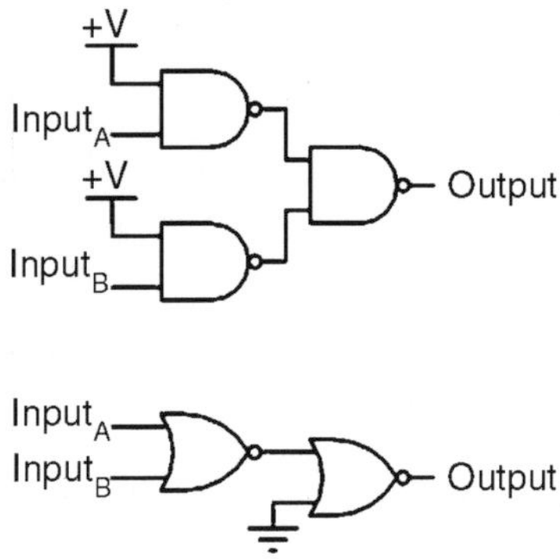

NOR FUNCTION

Much the same as the procedure for making a NOR gate behave as a NAND, we must invert all inputs and the output to make a NAND gate function as a NOR.

2-Input NOR Gate

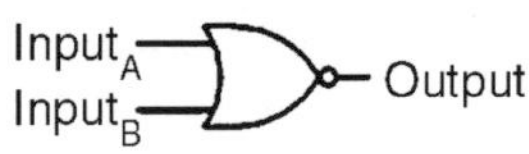

A	B	Output
0	0	1
0	1	0
1	0	0
1	1	0

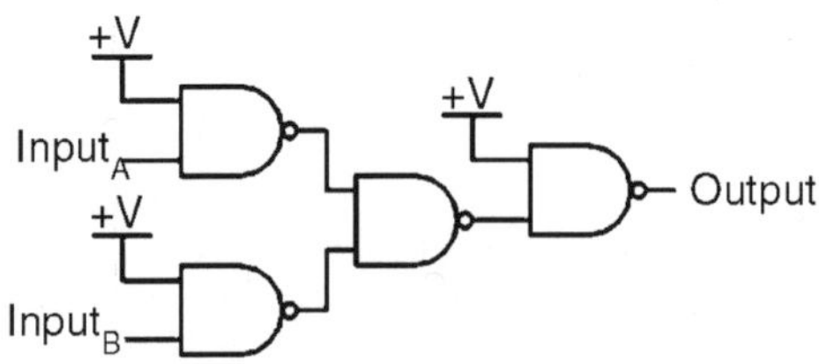

Logic Signal Voltage Levels

Logic gate circuits are designed to input and output only two types of signals: "high" (1) and "low" (0), as represented by a variable voltage: full power supply voltage for a "high" state and zero voltage for a "low" state. In a perfect world, all logic circuit signals would exist at these extreme voltage limits, and never deviate from them (*i.e.*, less than full voltage for a "high," or more than zero voltage for a "low").

However, in reality, logic signal voltage levels rarely attain these perfect limits due to stray voltage drops in the transistor circuitry, and so we must understand the signal level limitations of gate circuits as they try to interpret signal voltages lying somewhere *between* full supply voltage and zero. TTL gates operate on a nominal power supply voltage of 5 volts, +/- 0.25 volts. Ideally, a TTL "high" signal would be 5.00 volts exactly, and a TTL "low" signal 0.00 volts exactly.

However, real TTL gate circuits cannot output such perfect voltage levels, and are designed to accept "high" and "low" signals deviating substantially from these ideal values. "Acceptable" input signal voltages range from 0 volts to 0.8 volts for a "low" logic state, and 2 volts to 5 volts for a "high" logic state. "Acceptable" output signal voltages (voltage levels guaranteed by the gate manufacturer over a specified range of load conditions) range from 0 volts to 0.5 volts for a "low" logic state, and 2.7 volts to 5 volts for a "high" logic state:

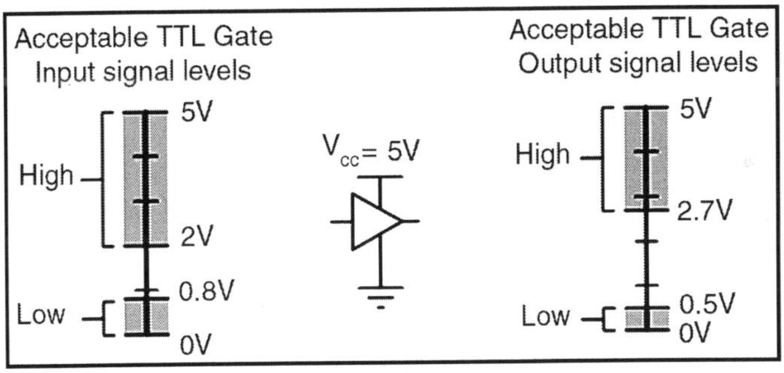

If a voltage signal ranging between 0.8 volts and 2 volts were to be sent into the input of a TTL gate, there would be no certain response from the gate. Such a signal would be considered *uncertain*, and no logic gate manufacturer would guarantee how their gate circuit would interpret such a signal.

As you can see, the tolerable ranges for output signal levels are narrower than for input signal levels, to ensure that any TTL gate outputting a digital signal into the input of another TTL gate will transmit voltages acceptable to the receiving gate. The difference between the tolerable output and input ranges is called the *noise margin* of the gate. For TTL gates, the low-level noise margin is the difference between 0.8 volts and 0.5 volts (0.3 volts), while the high-level noise margin is the difference between 2.7 volts and 2 volts (0.7 volts). Simply put, the noise margin is the peak amount of spurious or "noise" voltage that may be superimposed on a weak gate output voltage signal before the receiving gate might interpret it wrongly:

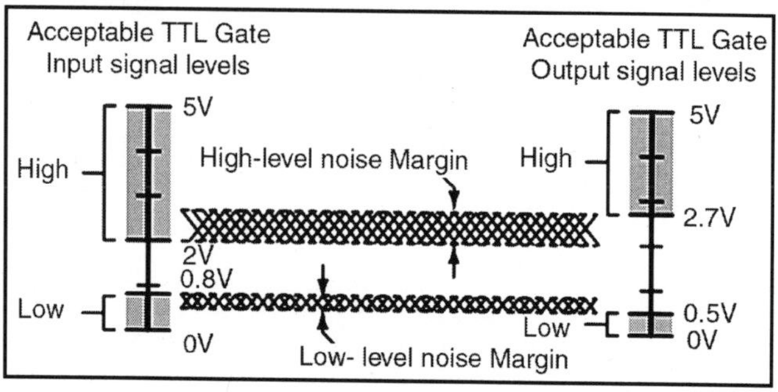

CMOS gate circuits have input and output signal specifications that are quite different from TTL. For a CMOS gate operating at a power supply voltage of 5 volts, the acceptable input signal voltages range from 0 volts to 1.5 volts for a "low" logic state, and 3.5 volts to 5 volts for a "high" logic state.

"Acceptable" output signal voltages (voltage levels guaranteed by the gate manufacturer over a specified range of load conditions) range from 0 volts to 0.05 volts for a "low" logic state, and 4.95 volts to 5 volts for a "high" logic state:

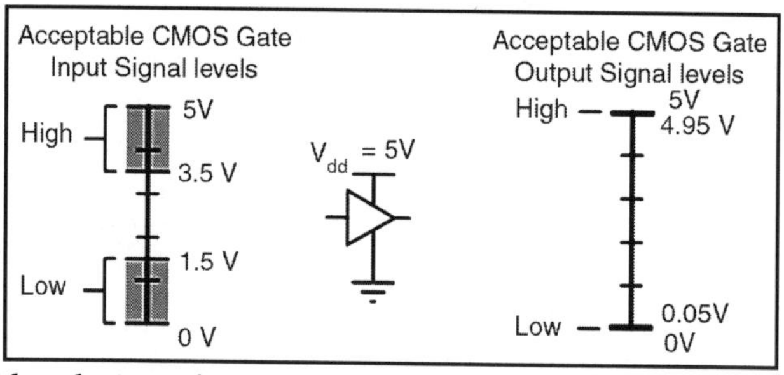

It should be obvious from these figures that CMOS gate circuits have far greater noise margins than TTL: 1.45 volts for CMOS low-level and high-level margins, versus a maximum of 0.7 volts for TTL. In other words, CMOS circuits can tolerate over twice the amount of superimposed "noise" voltage on their input lines before signal interpretation errors will result.

CMOS noise margins widen even further with higher operating voltages. Unlike TTL, which is restricted to a power supply voltage of 5 volts, CMOS may be powered by voltages as high as 15 volts (some CMOS circuits as high as 18 volts). Shown here are the acceptable "high" and "low" states, for both input and output, of CMOS integrated circuits operating at 10 volts and 15 volts, respectively: The margins for acceptable "high" and "low" signals may be greater than what is shown in the previous illustrations. What is shown represents "worst-case" input signal performance, based on manufacturer's specifications. In practice, it may be found that a gate circuit will tolerate "high" signals of considerably less voltage and "low" signals of considerably greater voltage than those specified here.

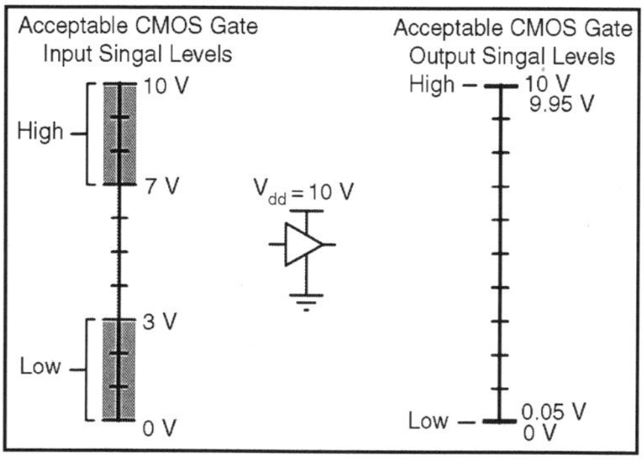

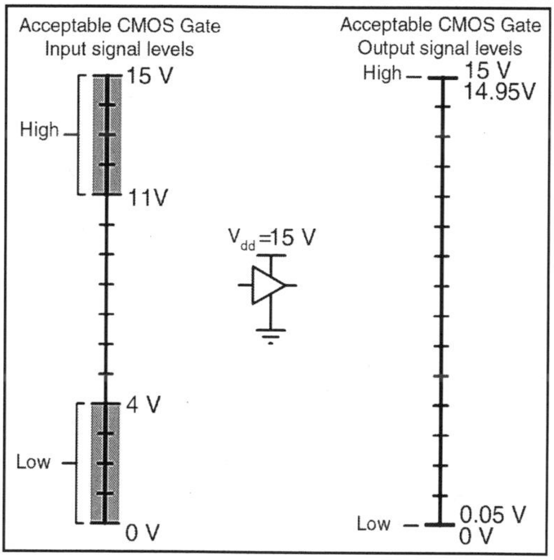

Conversely, the extremely small output margins shown — guaranteeing output states for "high" and "low" signals to within 0.05 volts of the power supply "rails" — are optimistic. Such "solid" output voltage levels will be true only for conditions of minimum loading. If the gate is sourcing or sinking substantial current to a load, the output voltage will not be able to maintain these optimum levels, due to internal channel resistance of the gate's final output MOSFETs. Within the "uncertain" range for any gate input, there will be some point of demarcation dividing the gate's actual "low" input signal range from its actual "high" input signal range.

That is, somewhere between the lowest "high" signal voltage level and the highest "low" signal voltage level guaranteed by the gate manufacturer, there is a threshold voltage at which the gate will*actually* switch its interpretation of a signal from "low" or "high" or visa-versa. For most gate circuits, this unspecified voltage is a single point:

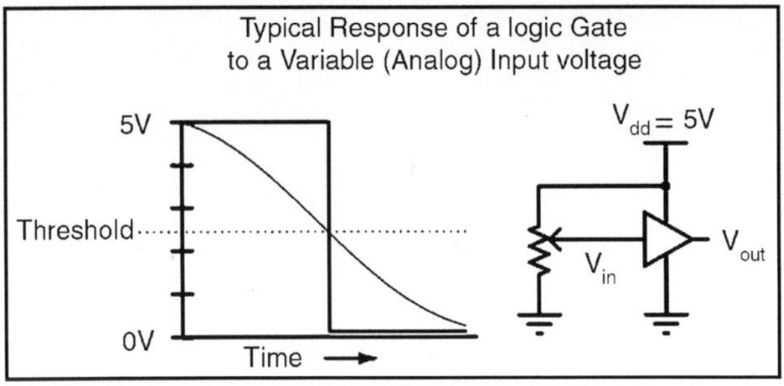

In the presence of AC "noise" voltage superimposed on the DC input signal, a single threshold point at which the gate alters its interpretation of logic level will result in an erratic output:

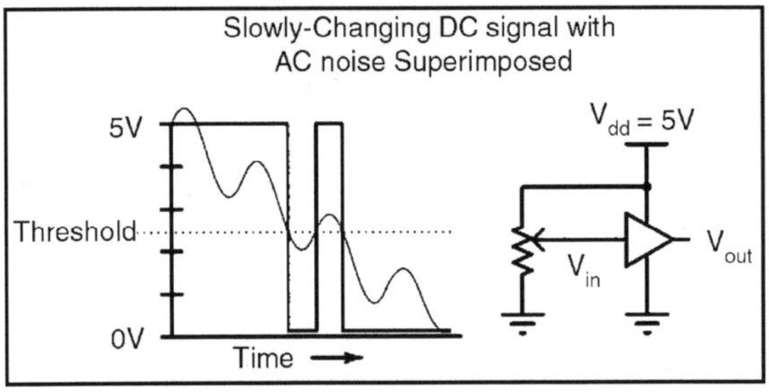

If this scenario looks familiar to you, it's because you remember a similar problem with (analog) voltage comparator op-amp circuits. With a single threshold point at which an input causes the output to switch between "high" and "low" states, the presence of significant noise will cause erratic changes in the output:

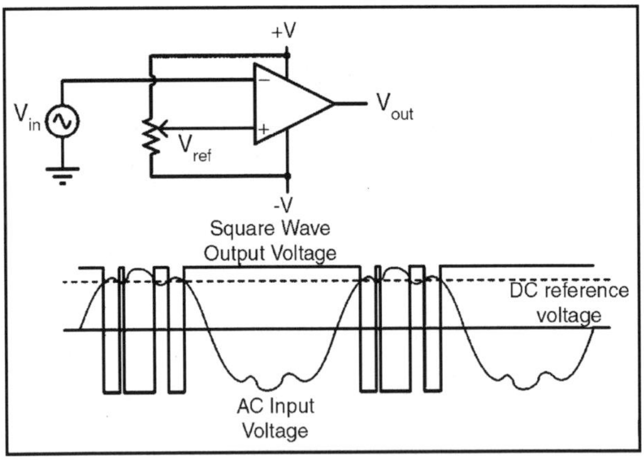

The solution to this problem is a bit of *positive feedback* introduced into the amplifier circuit. With an op-amp, this is done by connecting the output back around to the noninverting (+) input through a resistor. In a gate circuit, this entails redesigning the internal gate circuitry, establishing the feedback inside the gate package rather than through external connections. A gate so designed is called a *Schmitt trigger*. Schmitt triggers interpret varying input voltages according to*two* threshold voltages: a *positive-going* threshold (V_{T+}), and a *negative-going* threshold (V_{T-}):

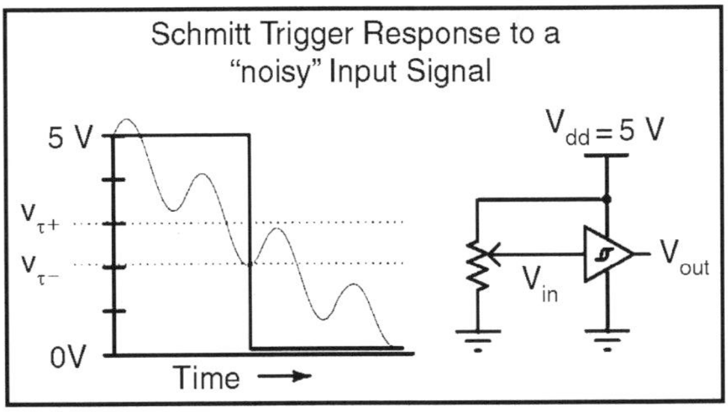

Schmitt trigger gates are distinguished in schematic diagrams by the small "hysteresis" symbol drawn within them, reminiscent of the B-H curve for a ferromagnetic material. Hysteresis engendered by positive feedback within the gate circuitry adds an additional level of noise immunity to the gate's performance. Schmitt trigger gates are frequently used in applications where noise is expected on the input signal line(s), and/or where an erratic output would be very detrimental to system performance.

The differing voltage level requirements of TTL and CMOS technology present problems when the two types of gates are used in the same system. Although operating CMOS gates on the same 5.00 volt power supply voltage required by the TTL gates is no problem, TTL output voltage levels will not be compatible with CMOS input voltage requirements. Take for instance a TTL NAND gate outputting a signal into the input of a CMOS inverter gate. Both gates are powered by the same 5.00 volt supply (V_{cc}). If the TTL gate outputs a "low" signal (guaranteed to be between 0 volts and 0.5 volts), it will be properly interpreted by the CMOS gate's input as a "low" (expecting a voltage between 0 volts and 1.5 volts):

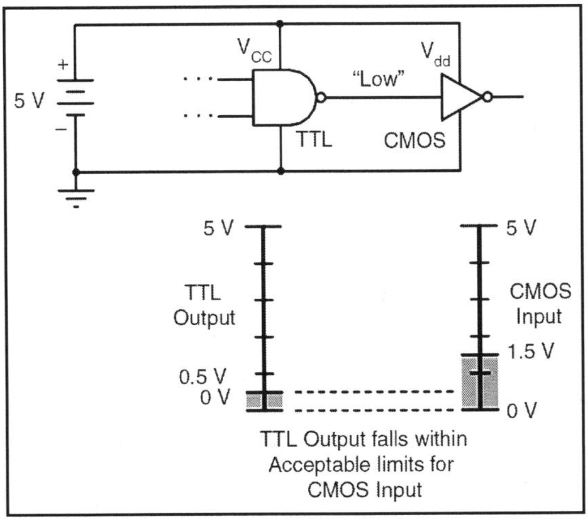

However, if the TTL gate outputs a "high" signal (guaranteed to be between 5 volts and 2.7 volts), it *might not* be properly interpreted by the CMOS gate's input as a "high" (expecting a voltage between 5 volts and *3.5* volts):

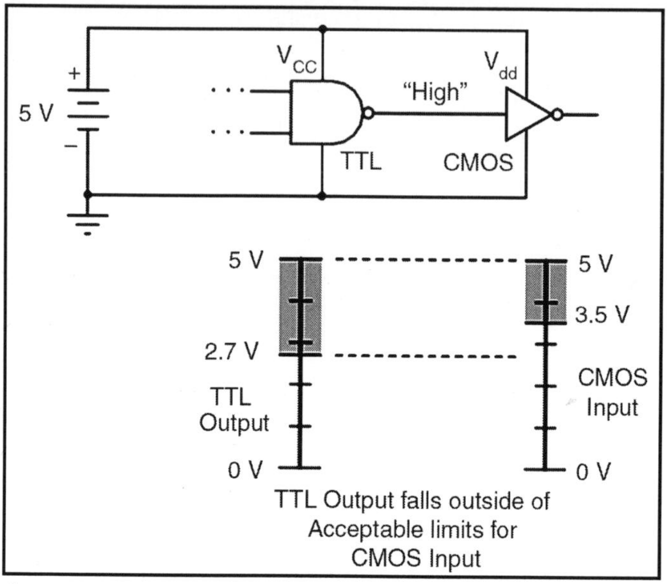

Given this mismatch, it is entirely possible for the TTL gate to output a valid "high" signal (valid, that is, according to the standards for TTL) that lies within the "uncertain" range for the CMOS input, and may be (falsely) interpreted as a "low" by the receiving gate. An easy "fix" for this problem is to augment the TTL gate's "high" signal voltage level by means of a pullup resistor:

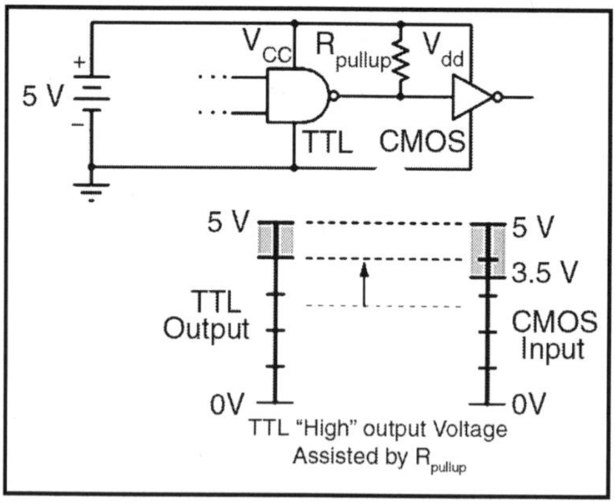

Something more than this, though, is required to interface a TTL output with a CMOS input, if the receiving CMOS gate is powered by a greater power supply voltage:

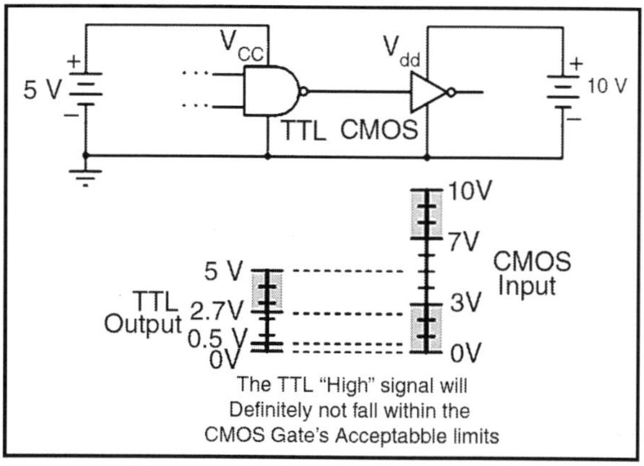

There will be no problem with the CMOS gate interpreting the TTL gate's "low" output, of course, but a "high" signal from the TTL gate is another matter entirely. The guaranteed output voltage range of 2.7 volts to 5 volts from the TTL gate output is nowhere near the CMOS gate's acceptable range of 7 volts to 10 volts for a "high" signal.

If we use an *open-collector* TTL gate instead of a totem-pole output gate, though, a pullup resistor to the 10 volt V_{dd} supply rail will raise the TTL gate's "high" output voltage to the full power supply voltage supplying the CMOS gate. Since an open-collector gate can only sink current, not source current, the "high" state voltage level is entirely determined by the power supply to which the pullup resistor is attached, thus neatly solving the mismatch problem:

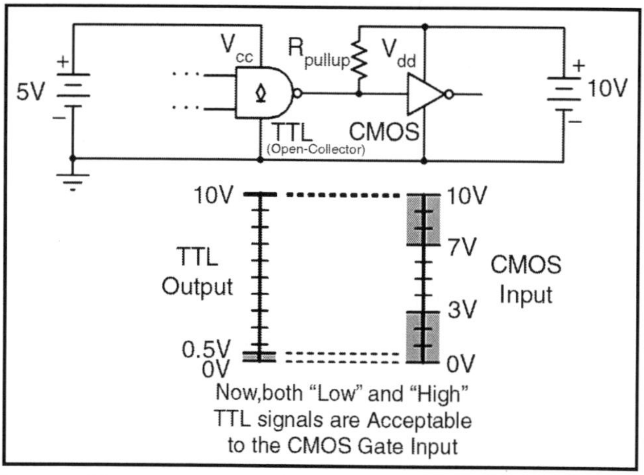

Due to the excellent output voltage characteristics of CMOS gates, there is typically no problem connecting a CMOS output to a TTL input. The only significant issue is the current loading presented by the TTL inputs, since the CMOS output must sink current for each of the TTL inputs while in the "low" state.

When the CMOS gate in question is powered by a voltage source in excess of 5 volts (V_{cc}), though, a problem will result. The "high" output state of the CMOS gate, being greater than 5 volts, will exceed the TTL gate's acceptable input limits for a "high" signal. A solution to this problem is to create an "open-collector" inverter circuit using a discrete NPN transistor, and use it to interface the two gates together:

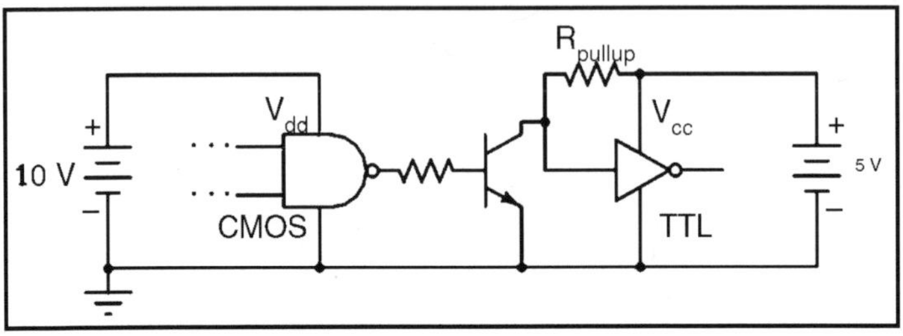

The "R_{pullup}" resistor is optional, since TTL inputs automatically assume a "high" state when left floating, which is what will happen when the CMOS gate output is "low" and the transistor cuts off. Of course, one very important consequence of implementing this solution is the logical inversion created by the transistor: when the CMOS gate outputs a "low" signal, the TTL gate sees a "high" input; and when the CMOS gate outputs a "high" signal, the transistor saturates and the TTL gate sees a "low" input. So long as this inversion is accounted for in the logical scheme of the system, all will be well.

11

Binary System

BASIC RULES OF BINARY SYSTEM

To understand binary numbers, begin by recalling elementary school math. When we first learned about numbers, we were taught that, in the decimal system, things are organized into columns:

H	T	O
1	9	3

Such that "H" is the hundreds column, "T" is the tens column, and "O" is the ones column. So the number "193" is 1-hundreds plus 9-tens plus 3-ones. later, we learned that the ones column meant 10^0, the tens column meant 10^1, the hundreds column 10^2 and so on, such that

10^2	10^1	10^0
1	9	3

The number 193 is really $\{(1*10^2)+(9*10^1)+(3*10^0)\}$.

As you know, the decimal system uses the digits 0—9 to represent numbers. If we wanted to put a larger number in column 10^n (*e.g.*, 10), we would have to multiply $10*10^n$, which would give $10^{(n+1)}$, and be carried a column to the left. For example, putting ten in the 10^0 column is impossible, so we put a 1 in the 10^1 column, and a 0 in the 10^0 column, thus using two columns. Twelve would be $12*10^0$, or $10^0(10+2)$, or $10^1 + 2*10^0$, which also uses an additional column to the left (12).The binary system works under the exact same principles as the decimal system, only it operates in base 2 rather than base 10. In other words, instead of columns being they are

10^2	10^1	10^0
2^2	2^1	2^0

Instead of using the digits 0-9, we only use 0-1 (again, if we used anything larger it would be like multiplying $2*2^n$ and getting 2^{n+1}, which would not fit in the 2^n column. Therefore, it would shift you one column to the left. For example, "3" in binary cannot be put into one column. The first column we fill is the right-most column, which is 2^0, or 1. Since 3>1, we need to use an extra column to the left, and indicate it as "11" in binary $(1*2^1) + (1*2^0)$.

BINARY NUMBERS

So far we have considered how computers can represent integers as unsigned quantities. It is more realistic and practical to represent them as signed integers having both positive and negative values. Let's consider how this can be done. First, it should be observed that we will still be restricted to a uniform (finite) precision for representing signed integers. Thus, the same number of bits will now have to serve for for both negative and positive values. A reasonable approach would be to assign half of the binary values to negative decimal values and half to positive decimal values. For example, suppose that we had a precision of only four bits. Figure 2 shows how these might be assigned in an orderly fashion.

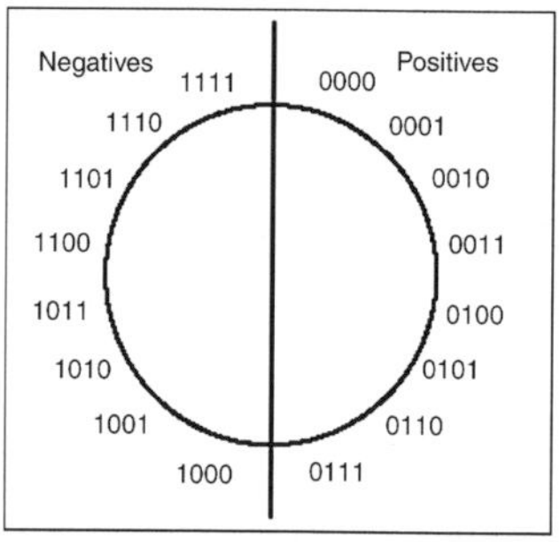

Fig. Dividing 4-bit Precision Binary into Positive and Negative Segments.

The binary values 0-7 could represent positive decimal values and the binary values 8-15 could signify negative decimal values. This divides the range into 8 values for positives and 8 values for negatives. Notice that the binary values 0–7 representing positives have the most significant bit (MSB) of 0. The binary values 8–15 representing negatives have a MSB of 1. Thus, we could use the MSB to denote the sign and the remaining bits to signify the quantity or magnitude as shown in Figure. This scheme is appropriately called sign and magnitude.

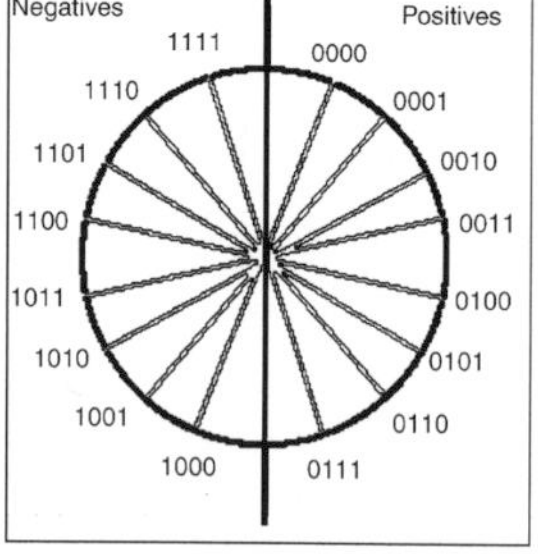

Fig. The Most Significant Bit Denotes the Sign and the Last Three Bits Signify the Magnitude.

As you can see in Figure 3, each positive has a corresponding negative value that differs only in the sign bit, *i.e.,* the MSB. With a 4-bit precision, our range is small, +7... –7. But, even if we extend the precision to 16 bits or 32 bits, there are other problems that remain. First, notice that there are codes for both +0 and –0; this is not convenient if, for example, we should have to decide whether a number is 0 or not. A more serious problem arises when doing arithmetic.

Recall that any binary integer can be represented by the sequence

+4 0100
+ -3 +1011
+1 1111
= –7

To do the arithmetic correctly, we have to consider the signs and the relative magnitudes of both numbers. It is much too complicated and therefore potentially expensive to implement as computer circuits. There is another approach: using Ns-complement. Blaise Pascal, for example, employed this technique for his decimal calculating machine later known as the Pascaline.

Suppose that we had a decimal precision of 4 digits. The range of values would be from 0000 to 9999. In 9s-complement (*i.e.,* N = 9), a negative value is determined by taking its additive inverse. This is the result of subtracting the magnitude from 9999. Here are some examples.

–11 9999
–0011
= 9988

–53 9999
–0053
= 9946

Simple addition operations can be used for both addition and subtraction. For example, adding a positive and negative number works provided that the carry-out value is added to adjust the sum.

+373 0373
+ –53 + 9946
+320 1 0319
(add carry) + 1
0320

Subtraction can also be solved using addition provided that the term subtracted is complemented and then added to the other term. The example illustrates.

2430 2430
–11 + 9988
2419 1 2418
(add carry) + 1
2419

Twos Complement

Most computer systems employ a variation of this method for representing signed integers called twos-complement. The procedures are similar.

Negative values are represented by:

1. Finding the complement (bit-value inverse) of the unsigned quantity.
2. The result is adjusted by adding +1.

Examples

Decimal Value	(Binary) Magnitude	(Binary) Inverse	Adjusted Result
-4	0100	1011	1100
		+1	
		1100	

Decimal Value	(Binary) Magnitude	(Binary) Inverse	Adjusted Result
-7	0111	1000	1001
		+1	
		1001	

One advantage of this scheme is that the MSB still serves to signify the sign of the number. In general, values for which the MSB = 1 are negative; values for which the MSB = 0 are positive. Addition and subtraction can also be handled by performing simple additions.

Examples

+7 0111

+ –4 +1100

+3 1 0011

(ignore carry out) = +3

+3 011

- -4(convert to comp) +0100

+7 0111

= +7

But, in some instances, we can produce a value that it too large for our precision. This causes an overflow error condition. The results are incorrect. For instance,

+7 0111

– –4 (convert to comp) +0100

+11 1011

(too big) = –5

In short, adding two numbers with the same sign (MSB) results in overflow when the sign (MSB) changes.

OCTAL NUMBER SYSTEM

Because binary numeration requires so many bits to represent relatively small numbers compared to the economy of the decimal system, analyzing the numerical states inside of digital electronic circuitry can be a tedious task. Computer programmers who design sequences of number codes instructing a computer what to do would have a very difficult task if they were forced to work with nothing but long strings of 1's and 0's, the "native language" of any digital circuit.

To make it easier for human engineers, technicians, and programmers to "speak" this language of the digital world, other systems of place-weighted numeration have been made which are very easy to convert to and from binary. One of those numeration systems is called octal, because it is a place-weighted system with a base of eight. Valid ciphers include the symbols 0, 1, 2, 3, 4, 5, 6, and 7. Each place weight differs from the one next to it by a factor of eight.

Another system is called hexadecimal, because it is a place-weighted system with a base of sixteen. Valid ciphers include the normal decimal symbols 0, 1, 2, 3, 4, 5, 6, 7, 8, and 9, plus six alphabetical characters A, B, C, D, E, and F, to make a total of sixteen.

As you might have guessed already, each place weight differs from the one before it by a factor of sixteen. Let's count again from zero to twenty using decimal, binary, octal, and hexadecimal to contrast these systems of numeration:

Number	Decimal	Binary	Octal	Hexadecimal
Zero	0	0	0	0
One	1	1	1	1
Two	2	10	2	2
Three	3	11	3	3
Four	4	100	4	4
Five	5	101	5	5
Six	6	110	6	6
Seven	7	111	7	7
Eight	8	1000	10	8
Nine	9	1001	11	9
Ten	10	1010	12	A
Eleven	11	1011	13	B
Twelve	12	1100	14	C
Thirteen	13	1101	15	D
Fourteen	14	1110	16	E
Fifteen	15	1111	17	F
Sixteen	16	10000	20	10
Seventeen	17	10001	21	11
Eighteen	18	10010	22	12
Nineteen	19	10011	23	13
Twenty	20	10100	24	14

Octal and hexadecimal numeration systems would be pointless if not for their ability to be easily converted to and from binary notation. Their primary purpose in being is to serve as a "shorthand" method of denoting a number represented electronically in binary form.

Because the bases of octal (eight) and hexadecimal (sixteen) are even multiples of binary's base (two), binary bits can be grouped together and directly converted to or from their respective octal or hexadecimal digits. With octal, the binary bits are grouped in three's (because $2^3 = 8$), and with hexadecimal, the binary bits are grouped in four's (because $2^4 = 16$):

BINARY TO OCTAL CONVERSION

Convert 10110111.1_2 to octal:

```
                    implied zero        implied zeros
                            |                 ||
                            010  110 111   100
Convert each group of      ### ### ###.  ###
bits
to its octal equivalent: 2    6    7    4
Answer: 10110111.1₂ = 267.4₈
```

We had to group the bits in three's, from the binary point left, and from the binary point right, adding (implied) zeros as necessary to make complete 3-bit groups. Each octal digit was translated from the 3-bit binary groups. Binary-to-Hexadecimal conversion is much the same:

BINARY TO HEXADECIMAL CONVERSION

Convert 10110111.1_2 to hexadecimal:

```
                                  implied zeros
                                         |||
                         1011 0111 1000
Convert each group       - - - -. - -
of bits to its
hexadecimal equivalent:  B    7    8
Answer: 10110111.1₂ = B7.8₁₆
```

Here we had to group the bits in four's, from the binary point left, and from the binary point right, adding (implied) zeros as necessary to make complete 4-bit groups:

Likewise, the conversion from either octal or hexadecimal to binary is done by taking each octal or hexadecimal digit and converting it to its equivalent binary (3 or 4 bit) group, then putting all the binary bit groups together. Incidentally, hexadecimal notation is more popular, because binary bit groupings in digital equipment are commonly multiples of eight (8, 16, 32, 64, and 128 bit), which are also multiples of 4. Octal, being based on binary bit groups of 3, doesn't work out evenly with those common bit group sizings.

HEXADECIMAL NUMBER SYSTEM

Although the prime intent of octal and hexadecimal numeration systems is for the "shorthand" representation of binary numbers in digital electronics, we sometimes have the need to convert from either of those systems to decimal form. Of course, we could simply convert the hexadecimal or octal format to binary, then convert from binary to decimal, since we already know how to do both, but we can also convert directly.

Because octal is a base-eight numeration system, each place-weight value differs from either adjacent place by a factor of eight. For example, the octal number 245.37 can be broken down into place values as such:

```
octal
digits =    2  4  5  .  3  7
.    -  -  -  -  -  -
weight =    6  8  1     1  1
(in deci-   4           /  /
mal notation)           8  6
.                    4
```

The decimal value of each octal place-weight times its respective cipher multiplier can be determined as follows:

$(2 \times 64_{10}) + (4 \times 8_{10}) + (5 \times 1_{10}) + (3 \times 0.125_{10}) + (7 \times 0.015625_{10}) = 165.484375_{10}$

The technique for converting hexadecimal notation to decimal is the same, except that each successive place-weight changes by a factor of sixteen. Simply denote each digit's weight, multiply each hexadecimal digit value by its respective weight (in decimal form), then add up all the decimal values to get a total. For example, the hexadecimal number $30F.A9_{16}$ can be converted like this:

```
hexadecimal
digits =     3   0   F   .   A   9
.            -   -   -   -   -   -
weight =     2   1   1       1   1
(in decimal  5   6           /   /
notation)    6               1   2
.                            6   5
.                                6
```

$(3 \times 256_{10}) + (0 \times 16_{10}) + (15 \times 1_{10}) + (10 \times 0.0625_{10}) + (9 \times 0.00390625_{10}) = 783.66015625_{10}$

These basic techniques may be used to convert a numerical notation of any base into decimal form, if you know the value of that numeration system's base.

CONVERSION FROM DECIMAL NUMERATION

Because octal and hexadecimal numeration systems have bases that are multiples of binary (base 2), conversion back and forth between either hexadecimal or octal and binary is very easy. Also, because we are so familiar with the decimal system, converting binary, octal, or hexadecimal to decimal form is relatively easy (simply add up the products of cipher values and place-weights). However, conversion from decimal to any of these "strange" numeration systems is a different matter.

The method which will probably make the most sense is the "trial-and-fit" method, where you try to "fit" the binary, octal, or hexadecimal notation to the desired value as represented in decimal form. For example, let's say that I wanted to represent the decimal value of 87 in binary form. Let's start by drawing a binary number field, complete with place-weight values:.

```
.               -   -   -   -   -   -    -   -
weight=         1   6   3   1   8   4    2   1
(in decimal 2   4   2   6
notation)       8
```

Well, we know that we won't have a "1" bit in the 128's place, because that would immediately give us a value greater than 87. However, since the next weight to the right (64) is less than 87, we know that we must have a "1" there.

```
. 1
. -  -  -   -   -   -   -   Decimal
value so
far = 64_10
weight =6   3   1   8   4   2   1
(in decimal notation)4  2   6
```

If we were to make the next place to the right a "1" as well, our total value would be $64_{10} + 32_{10}$, or 96_{10}. This is greater than 87_{10}, so we know that this bit must be a "0". If we make the next (16's) place bit equal to "1," this brings our total value to $64_{10} + 16_{10}$, or 80_{10}, which is closer to our desired value (87_{10}) without exceeding it:

```
.               1   0   1
. -  -  -   -   -   -   -   Decimal
value so
far = 80_10
weight =        6   3   1   8   4   2   1
(in decimal 4 2 6
notation)
```

By continuing in this progression, setting each lesser-weight bit as we need to come up to our desired total value without exceeding it, we will eventually arrive at the correct figure:

```
  .             1   0   1   0   1   1   1
  .             -   -   -   -   -   -   -   Decimal
                                value so
                    far = 87_10
  weight =          6   3   1   8   4   2   1
(in decimal 4   2   6
notation)
```

This trial-and-fit strategy will work with octal and hexadecimal conversions, too. Let's take the same decimal figure, 87_{10}, and convert it to octal numeration:.

```
.              -   -   -
weight  =      6   8   1
(in decimal    4
notation)
```

If we put a cipher of "1" in the 64's place, we would have a total value of 64_{10} (less than 87_{10}). If we put a cipher of "2" in the 64's place, we would have a total value of 128_{10} (greater than 87_{10}). This tells us that our octal numeration must start with a "1" in the 64's place:

```
.              1
.              -   -   -  Decimal value so far = 64₁₀
weight  =      6   8   1
(in decimal    4
notation)
```

Now, we need to experiment with cipher values in the 8's place to try and get a total (decimal) value as close to 87 as possible without exceeding it. Trying the first few cipher options, we get:

$$"1" = 64_{10} + 8_{10} = 72_{10}$$
$$"2" = 64_{10} + 16_{10} = 80_{10}$$
$$"3" = 64_{10} + 24_{10} = 88_{10}$$

A cipher value of "3" in the 8's place would put us over the desired total of 87_{10}, so "2" it is!

```
.              1   2
.              -   -   -  Decimal value so far = 80₁₀
weight  =      6   8   1
(in decimal    4
notation)
```

Now, all we need to make a total of 87 is a cipher of "7" in the 1's place:

```
.              1   2   7
.              -   -   -  Decimal value so far = 87₁₀
weight  =      6   8   1
(in decimal    4
notation)
```

Of course, if you were paying attention during the last section on octal/binary conversions, you will realize that we can take the binary representation of (decimal) 87_{10}, which we previously determined to be 1010111_2, and easily convert from that to octal to check our work:

```
.    Implied zeros
.         ||
.         001 010 111  Binary
.         ---  ---  ---
.          1   2   7   Octal
.
Answer:  1010111₂ = 127₈
```

Can we do decimal-to-hexadecimal conversion the same way? Sure, but who would want to? This method is simple to understand, but laborious to carry out. There is another way to do these conversions, which is essentially the same (mathematically), but easier to accomplish.

This other method uses repeated cycles of division (using decimal notation) to break the decimal numeration down into multiples of binary, octal, or hexadecimal place-weight values. In the first cycle of division, we take the original decimal number and divide it by the base of the numeration system that we're converting to (binary=2 octal=8, hex=16).

Then, we take the whole-number portion of division result (quotient) and divide it by the base value again, and so on, until we end up with a quotient of less than 1. The binary, octal, or hexadecimal digits are determined by the "remainders" left over by each division step. Let's see how this works for binary, with the decimal example of 87_{10}:

```
. 87        Divide 87 by 2, to get a quotient
  of 43.5
. — =       43.5 Division "remainder" = 1, or
  the < 1 portion
. 2         of the quotient times the divisor
  (0.5 x 2)
.
. 43        Take the whole-number portion of 43.5
     (43)
. — = 21.5  and divide it by 2 to get 21.5, or
     21 with
. 2         a remainder of 1
.
. 21        And so on... remainder = 1 (0.5
  x 2)
. — = 10.5
. 2
.
. 10        And so on... remainder = 0
. — = 5.0
. 2
.
. 5         And so on... remainder = 1 (0.5
  x 2)
. — = 2.5
. 2
.
. 2         And so on... remainder = 0
. — = 1.0
. 2
.
```

```
. 1          ... until we get a quotient of
less than 1
. — = 0.5   remainder = 1 (0.5 x 2)
. 2
```

The binary bits are assembled from the remainders of the successive division steps, beginning with the LSB and proceeding to the MSB. In this case, we arrive at a binary notation of 1010111_2. When we divide by 2, we will always get a quotient ending with either ".0" or ".5", i.e. a remainder of either 0 or 1. As was said before, this repeat-division technique for conversion will work for numeration systems other than binary. If we were to perform successive divisions using a different number, such as 8 for conversion to octal, we will necessarily get remainders between 0 and 7. Let's try this with the same decimal number, 87_{10}:

```
. 87 Divide 87 by 8, to get a quotient of 10.875
. — = 10.875 Division "remainder"
  = 7, or the < 1 portion
. 8 of the quotient times the divisor(.875 x 8)
.
. 10
. — = 1.25          Remainder = 2
. 8
.
. 1
. — = 0.125         Quotient is less than 1, so
  we'll stop here.
. 8 Remainder =     1
.
. RESULT: 87₁₀ =    127₈
```

We can use a similar technique for converting numeration systems dealing with quantities less than 1, as well. For converting a decimal number less than 1 into binary, octal, or hexadecimal, we use repeated multiplication, taking the integer portion of the product in each step as the next digit of our converted number. Let's use the decimal number 0.8125_{10} as an example, converting to binary:

```
. 0.8125 x 2 = 1.625   Integer portion of
           product = 1
.
. 0.625 x 2 = 1.25     Take < 1 portion of
           product and remultiply
.                      Integer portion of
           product = 1
.
. 0.25 x 2 = 0.5       Integer portion of
           product = 0
.
```

```
. 0.5 x 2 = 1.0          Integer portion of
            product = 1
.                        Stop when product is a
            pure integer
.                        (ends with.0)
.
```

. **RESULT:** 0.8125_{10} = 0.1101_2

As with the repeat-division process for integers, each step gives us the next digit (or bit) further away from the "point." With integer (division), we worked from the LSB to the MSB (right-to-left), but with repeated multiplication, we worked from the left to the right. To convert a decimal number greater than 1, with a < 1 component, we must use both techniques, one at a time. Take the decimal example of 54.40625_{10}, converting to binary:

REPEATED DIVISION FOR THE INTEGER PORTION:

$\frac{54}{2} = 27.0$ Remainder = 0

$\frac{27}{2} = 13.5$ Remainder = 1 (0.5 × 2)

$\frac{13}{2} = 6.5$ Remainder = 1 (0.5 × 2)

$\frac{6}{2} = 3.0$ Remainder = 0

$\frac{3}{2} = 1.5$ Remainder = 1 (0.5 × 2)

$\frac{1}{2} = 0.5$ Remainder = 1 (0.5 × 2)

PARTIAL ANSWER: 54_{10} = 110110_2

REPEATED MULTIPLICATION FOR THE < 1 PORTION:

```
.
. 0.40625 x 2 = 0.8125 Integer portion of product = 0
```

```
.
. 0.8125 x 2 = 1.625 Integer portion of product = 1
.
. 0.625 x 2 = 1.25 Integer portion of product = 1
.
. 0.25 x 2 = 0.5 Integer portion of product = 0
.
. 0.5 x 2 = 1.0 Integer portion of product = 1
.
. PARTIAL ANSWER: 0.40625_10 = 0.01101_2
.
. COMPLETE ANSWER: 54_10 + 0.40625_10 = 54.40625_10
.
.                 110110_2 + 0.01101_2 = 110110.01101_2
```

INTEGER NUMBER

If we are given an *m*-bit computer word B with bits $b_{m-1}, b_{m-2},\ldots, b_0$, we can interpret it as an unsigned number with value,

$$\text{unsigned}(B) = b_{m-1}{*}2^{m-1} + b_{m-2}{*}2^{m-2} + \ldots + b_0{*}2^0.$$

This gives us a representation for numbers from 0 to $2^m - 1$.

If we want to represent negative values as well, we can just change the sign of the high-order bit b_{m-1}, giving a signed number with value

$$\text{signed}(B) = -b_{m-1}{*}2^{m-1} + b_{m-2}{*}2^{m-2} + \ldots + b_0{*}2^0.$$

This is called the *m*-bit *2's complement* interpretation of B.

With $b_{m-1} = 0$, we get representations for numbers from 0 to $2^{m-1} - 1$. With $b_{m-1} = 1$, we get representations for numbers from -2^{m-1} to $-2^{m-1} + (2^{m-1} - 1) = -1$. Thus we have several important facts about the *m*-bit 2's complement representation.

- It represents numbers from -2^{m-1} to $2^{m-1} - 1$.
- If b_{m-1} is 1 then the value is negative; otherwise it is non-negative. Thus the high-order bit, b_{m-1} is called the *sign bit.*
- When the sign bit of B is 0, signed(B) = unsigned(B).
- When the sign bit of B is 1, signed(B) = unsigned(B) – 2^m.
- In either case, signed(B) — unsigned(B) is a multiple of 2^m.

The third fact tells you how to convert between a computer word with sign bit 0 and its 2's complement signed value, assuming you know how to convert between unsigned binary numbers and decimal. The fourth fact could be used to do the same when the sign bit is 1, but there is an alternative method described below that does not require that you remember powers of 2. The fifth fact can be used to determine when arithmetic with signed numbers fails.

Negation and the 2's Complement Operation

The one's complement operation is important bitwise operation for computer words. It converts each 0 bit in the word to 1 and each 1 bit in the word to 0. This operation is closely related to the negation operation for numbers. To see this, look at the follwing sum where B′ is the one's complement of B.

signed(B) + signed(B′) + 1 = $-b_{m-1}{*}2^{m-1} + b_{m-2}{*}2^{m-2} + ... + b_0{*}2^0 + -b'_{m-1}{*}2^{m-1} + b'_{m-2}{*}2^{m-2} + ... + b'_0{*}2^0 + 1 =$

$-b_{m-1}{*}2^{m-1} + -b'_{mû1}{*}2^{m-1} + b_{m-2}{*}2^{m-2} + b'_{m-2}{*}2^{m-2} + ... + b_0{*}2^0 + b'_0{*}2^0 + 1 =$

$-2^{m-1} + 2^{m-2} + ... + 2^0 + 1 =$

$-2^{m-1} + 2^{m-1} - 1 + 1 = 0$

The terms in the third line are just the terms in the second line, rearranged to bring together like powers of 2. Then the b_is and the b'_is drop out because one of them is always 0 and the other is always 1. The equality between the fourth and fifth lines follows from the formula for summing a geometric series. The above formulas show that the negative of signed(B) is signed(B′) + 1. To make computer arithmetic reflect our arithmetic with numbers, addition on computer words is defined so that,

signed(B + C) = signed(B) + signed(C) Thus we can write

–signed(B) = signed(B′ + 1)

The operation on the right-hand side—doing a one's complement and adding one - is called the two's complement operation (not to be confused with the two's complement number representation). It is the computer equivalent of negating a number. There is one case where the two's complement operation fails to give us the same result as negation. This is to be expected when our computer operations use limited size words. Since the range of integers represented by an *m*-bit two's complement representation is from, -2^{m-1} to $2^{m-1} - 1$, there is number, -2^{m-1}, whose negative is not even representable. In this case, the add one step fails to work correctly.

CONVERTING SIGNED DECIMAL NUMBERS TO *M*-BIT 2'S COMPLEMENT

As noted above, the signed and unsigned *m*-bit representations are the same for representable non-negative integers. The equivalence of negation and the two's complement operation gives us a quick way of finding the *m*-bit two's complement representation of a negative integer: find the unsigned representation of its absolute value, then do a two's complement operation.

Conversion in this direction fails whenever the decimal number is outside the range -2^{m-1} to $2^{m-1} - 1$.

Converting *m*-bit 2's Complement Numbers to Signed Decimal

To convert a *m*-bit two's complement number to decimal, you first look at the sign bit (the high order bit). If it is 0 the the number is non-negative and the determination of the decimal value is just an unsigned conversion from binary (or hexadecimal) to decimal. If the sign bit is 1, then do a two's complement operation, convert as an unsigned number, and affix a negative sign. Conversion in this direction never fails.

Signed Number Conversions in Hexadecimal

Since conversions are easier and more reliable in hexadecimal, it is useful to be able to to do the two's complement operation in hexadecimal.

To do this, you only need to be able to do the following:

- Recognize a negative number in hexadecimal
- Do a one's complement in hexadecimal
- Add one in hexadecimal

If the number of bits is a multiple of 4 then recognizing negative numbers in hexadecimal is easy: look at the high-order headecimal digit. If it is from 0 to 7 then the number is non-negative. If it is from 8 to F then the number is negative. The following table shows how to do the one's complement step. The two hexadecimal digits in a row of the table are one's complements of each other. You can do a one's complement operation on a multi-digit hexadecimal number by converting each of the hexadecimal digit to its one's complement.

Hex	Binary	Decimal	Hex	Binary	Decimal
0	0000	0	F	1111	15
1	0001	1	E	1110	14
2	0010	2	D	1101	13
3	0011	3	C	1100	12
4	0100	4	B	1011	11
5	0101	5	A	1010	10
6	0110	6	9	1001	9
7	0111	7	8	1000	8

FIXED-LENGTH REPRESENTATIONS

Computers generally use fixed length representations for numbers. For example, in C and C^{++}, there are three types for signed integers: int (usually 32 bits), short (usually 16 bits), and char (8 bits). Recent compilers also support long long (64 bits). At times, it is necessary to coerce a signed integer from one type to another, resulting in a change in the number of bits used to represent the number. When a signed integer is coerced from a larger length to a smaller length, high order (leftmost) bits are discarded. If any of the duscarded bits are 1 then the coerced value is incorrect. Compilers will generally warn you of this possibility. When a signed integer is coerced from a smaller length to a larger length the original bits are padded on the left with copies of the sign bit of the original number. This is called sign extension.

ADDITION OF LARGE BIT BINARY NUMBERE

Adding binary numbers is a very simple task, and very similar to the longhand addition of decimal numbers. As with decimal numbers, you start by adding the bits (digits) one column, or place weight, at a time, from right to left. Unlike decimal addition, there is little to memorize in the way of rules for the addition of binary bits:

$$0 + 0 = 0$$
$$1 + 0 = 1$$
$$0 + 1 = 1$$
$$1 + 1 = 10$$
$$1 + 1 + 1 = 11$$

Just as with decimal addition, when the sum in one column is a two-bit (two-digit) number, the least significant figure is written as part of the total sum and the most significant figure is "carried" to the next left column. Consider the following examples:

$$\begin{array}{ccc} & 11\,1 \leftarrow \text{Carry bits} \rightarrow 11 & \\ 1001101 & 1001001 & 1000111 \\ +0010010 & +0011001 & +0010110 \\ \hline 1011111 & 1100010 & 1011101 \end{array}$$

The addition problem on the left did not require any bits to be carried, since the sum of bits in each column was either 1 or 0, not 10 or 11. In the other two problems, there definitely were bits to be carried, but the process of addition is still quite simple.

As we'll see later, there are ways that electronic circuits can be built to perform this very task of addition, by representing each bit of each binary number as a voltage signal (either "high," for a 1; or "low" for a 0). This is the very foundation of all the arithmetic which modern digital computers perform.

Consider the addition of decimal numbers:

$$\begin{array}{r} 23 \\ +48 \\ \hline \end{array}$$

We begin by adding 3+8=11. Since 11 is greater than 10, a one is put into the 10's column (carried), and a 1 is recorded in the one's column of the sum. Next, add {(2+4) +1} (the one is from the carry)=7, which is put in the 10's column of the sum. Thus, the answer is 71.

WORKING

Binary addition works on the same principle, but the numerals are different. Begin with one-bit binary addition:

$$\begin{array}{ccc} 0 & 0 & 1 \\ +0 & +1 & +0 \\ \hline 0 & 1 & 1 \end{array}$$

1+1 carries us into the next column. In decimal form, 1+1=2. In binary, any digit higher than 1 puts us a column to the left (as would 10 in decimal notation). The decimal number "2" is written in binary notation as "10"

$(1*2^1)+(0*2^0)$. Record the 0 in the ones column, and carry the 1 to the twos column to get an answer of "10." In our vertical notation,

$$\begin{array}{r} 1 \\ +1 \\ \hline 10 \end{array}$$

The process is the same for multiple-bit binary numbers:

$$\begin{array}{r} 1010 \\ +1111 \\ \hline \end{array}$$

- *Step one*: Column 2^0: 0+1=1.
  Record the 1.
  Temporary Result: 1; Carry: 0
- *Step two*: Column 2^1: 1+1=10.
  Record the 0, carry the 1.
  Temporary Result: 01; Carry: 1
- *Step three*: Column 2^2: 1+0=1 Add 1 from carry: 1+1=10.
  Record the 0, carry the 1.
- *Step four*: Column 2^3: 1+1=10. Add 1 from carry: 10+1=11.
  Record the 11.
  Final result: 11001

Alternately

$$\begin{array}{l} 11(\text{carry}) \\ 1010 \\ +1111 \\ \hline \;\;11001 \end{array}$$

Always remember

- 0+0=0
- 1+0=1
- 1+1=10

Try a few examples of binary addition:

$$\begin{array}{rrr} 111 & 101 & 111 \\ +110 & +111 & +111 \\ \hline \end{array}$$

NUMBERS VERSUS NUMERATION

It is imperative to understand that the type of numeration system used to represent numbers has no impact upon the outcome of any arithmetical function (addition, subtraction, multiplication, division, roots, powers, or logarithms). A number is a number is a number; one plus one will always equal two (so long as we're dealing with real numbers), no matter how you symbolize one, one, and two. A prime number in decimal form is still prime if its shown in binary form, or octal, or hexadecimal. Π is still the ratio between the circumference and diameter of a circle, no matter what symbols you use to denote its value. The essential functions and interrelations of mathematics are unaffected by the particular system of symbols we might choose to represent quantities.

This distinction between numbers and systems of numeration is critical to understand. The essential distinction between the two is much like that between an object and the spoken word(s) we associate with it. A house is still a house regardless of whether we call it by its English name house or its Spanish name casa. The first is the actual thing, while the second is merely the symbol for the thing.

That being said, performing a simple arithmetic operation such as addition (longhand) in binary form can be confusing to a person accustomed to working with decimal numeration only. In this lesson, we'll explore the techniques used to perform simple arithmetic functions on binary numbers, since these techniques will be employed in the design of electronic circuits to do the same. You might take longhand addition and subtraction for granted, having used a calculator for so long, but deep inside that calculator's circuitry all those operations are performed "longhand," using binary numeration. To understand how that's accomplished, we need to review to the basics of arithmetic.

NEGATIVE BINARY NUMBERS

With addition being easily accomplished, we can perform the operation of subtraction with the same technique simply by making one of the numbers negative. For example, the subtraction problem of 7–5 is essentially the same as the addition problem 7 + (–5). Since we already know how to represent positive numbers in binary, all we need to know now is how to represent their negative counterparts and we'll be able to subtract. Usually we represent a negative decimal number by placing a minus sign directly to the left of the most significant digit, just as in the example above, with -5. However, the whole purpose of using binary notation is for constructing on/off circuits that can represent bit values in terms of voltage (2 alternative values: either "high" or "low"). In this context, we don't have the luxury of a third symbol such as a "minus" sign, since these circuits can only be on or off (two possible states).

One solution is to reserve a bit (circuit) that does nothing but represent the mathematical sign:

$$101_2 = 5_{10} \text{ (positive)}$$

Extra bit, representing sign (0=positive, 1=negative)

|

$$0101_2 = 5_{10} \text{ (positive)}$$

Extra bit, representing sign (0=positive, 1=negative)

|

$$1101_2 = -5_{10} \text{ (negative)}$$

As you can see, we have to be careful when we start using bits for any purpose other than standard place-weighted values. Otherwise, 1101_2 could be misinterpreted as the number thirteen when in fact we mean to represent negative five. To keep things straight here, we must first decide how many bits are going to be needed to represent the largest numbers we'll be dealing with, and then be sure not to exceed that bit field length in our arithmetic operations.

For the above example, I've limited myself to the representation of numbers from negative seven (1111_2) to positive seven (0111_2), and no more, by making the fourth bit the "sign" bit. Only by first establishing these limits can I avoid confusion of a negative number with a larger, positive number. Representing negative five as 1101_2 is an example of the sign-magnitude system of negative binary numeration. By using the leftmost bit as a sign indicator and not a place-weighted value, I am sacrificing the "pure" form of binary notation for something that gives me a practical advantage: the representation of negative numbers. The leftmost bit is read as the sign, either positive or negative, and the remaining bits are interpreted according to the standard binary notation: left to right, place weights in multiples of two. As simple as the sign-magnitude approach is, it is not very practical for arithmetic purposes.

There's another method for representing negative numbers which works with our familiar technique of longhand addition, and also happens to make more sense from a place-weighted numeration point of view, called complementation. With this strategy, we assign the leftmost bit to serve a special purpose, just as we did with the sign-magnitude approach, defining our number limits just as before. However, this time, the leftmost bit is more than just a sign bit; rather, it possesses a negative place-weight value.

For example, a value of negative five would be represented as such:

Extra bit, place weight = Negative eight

|

$$1011_2 = 5_{10}\,(\text{negative})$$

$$(1 \times -8_{10}) + (0 \times 4_{10}) + (1 \times 2_{10}) + (1 \times 1_{10}) = -5_{10}$$

With the right three bits being able to represent a magnitude from zero through seven, and the leftmost bit representing either zero or negative eight, we can successfully represent any integer number from negative seven ($1001_2 = -8_{10} + 1_{10} = -7_{10}$) to positive seven ($0111_2 = 0_{10} + 7_{10} = 7_{10}$).

Representing positive numbers in this scheme (with the fourth bit designated as the negative weight) is no different from that of ordinary binary notation. However, represent-ing negative numbers is not quite as straightforward:

```
zero              0000
positive one      0001          negative one 1111
positive two      0010          negative two 1110
```

```
positive three    0011         negative three  1101
positive four     0100         negative four   1100
positive five     0101         negative five   1011
positive six      0110         negative six    1010
positive seven    0111         negative seven  1001
.                               negative eight    1000
```

Note that the negative binary numbers in the right column, being the sum of the right three bits' total plus the negative eight of the leftmost bit, don't "count" in the same progression as the positive binary numbers in the left column. Rather, the right three bits have to be set at the proper value to equal the desired (negative) total when summed with the negative eight place value of the leftmost bit. Those right three bits are referred to as the two's complement of the corresponding positive number. Consider the following comparison:

Positive Number	Two's Complement
001	111
010	110
011	101
100	100
101	011
110	010
111	001

In this case, with the negative weight bit being the fourth bit (place value of negative eight), the two's complement for any positive number will be whatever value is needed to add to negative eight to make that positive value's negative equivalent.

Thankfully, there's an easy way to figure out the two's complement for any binary number: simply invert all the bits of that number, changing all 1's to 0's and vice versa (to arrive at what is called the one's complement) and then add one. For example, to obtain the two's complement of five (101_2), we would first invert all the bits to obtain 010_2 (the "one's complement"), then add one to obtain 011_2, or -5_{10} in three-bit, two's complement form.

Interestingly enough, generating the two's complement of a binary number works the same if you manipulate all the bits, including the leftmost (sign) bit at the same time as the magnitude bits. Let's try this with the former example, converting a positive five to a negative five, but performing the complementation process on all four bits.

We must be sure to include the 0 (positive) sign bit on the original number, five (0101_2). First, inverting all bits to obtain the one's complement: 1010_2. Then, adding one, we obtain the final answer: 1011_2, or -5_{10} expressed in four-bit, two's complement form. It is critically important to remember that the place of the negative-weight bit must be already determined before any two's complement conversions can be done. If our binary numeration field were such that the eighth bit was designated as the negative-weight bit (10000000_2), we'd have to determine the two's complement based on all seven of the other bits. Here, the two's complement of five (0000101_2) would be 1111011_2. A positive five in this system would be represented as 00000101_2, and a negative five as 11111011_2.

SUBTRACTION OF LARGE BIT BINARY NUMBERS

We can subtract one binary number from another by using the standard techniques adapted for decimal numbers (subtraction of each bit pair, right to left, "borrowing" as needed from bits to the left). However, if we can leverage the already familiar (and easier) technique of binary addition to subtract, that would be better. As we just learned, we can represent negative binary numbers by using the "two's complement" method and a negative place-weight bit. Here, we'll use those negative binary numbers to subtract through addition. Here's a sample problem:

CONCEPT

Subtraction: $7_{10} - 5_{10}$ Addition equivalent: $7_{10} + (-5_{10})$

If all we need to do is represent seven and negative five in binary (two's complemented) form, all we need is three bits plus the negative-weight bit:

Positive seven = 0111_2

Negative five = 1011_2

Now, let's add them together:

```
 1111 ←Carry bits
  0111
+1011
------
 10010
 |
```

Discard extra bit

Answer = 0010_2

Since we've already defined our number bit field as three bits plus the negative-weight bit, the fifth bit in the answer (1) will be discarded to give us a result of 0010_2, or positive two, which is the correct answer. Another way to understand why we discard that extra bit is to remember that the leftmost bit of the lower number possesses a negative weight, in this case equal to negative eight. When we add these two binary numbers together, what we're actually doing with the MSBs is subtracting the lower number's MSB from the upper number's MSB. In subtraction, one never "carries" a digit or bit on to the next left place-weight. Let's try another example, this time with larger numbers. If we want to add -25_{10} to 18_{10}, we must first decide how large our binary bit field must be. To represent the largest (absolute value) number in our problem, which is twenty-five, we need at least five bits, plus a sixth bit for the negative-weight bit. Let's start by representing positive twenty-five, then finding the two's complement and putting it all together into one numeration:

$+25_{10} = 011001_2$ (showing all six bits)

One's complement of $11001_2 = 100110_2$

One's complement + 1 = two's complement = 100111_2

$-25_{10} = 100111_2$

Essentially, we're representing negative twenty-five by using the negative-weight (sixth) bit with a value of negative thirty-two, plus positive seven (binary 111_2). Now, let's represent positive eighteen in binary form, showing all six bits:

$$18_{10} = 010010_2$$

Now, let's add them together and see what we get:

$$\begin{array}{l} 11 \leftarrow \text{Carry bits} \\ 1001111 \\ \underline{+010010} \\ 111001 \end{array}$$

Since there were no "extra" bits on the left, there are no bits to discard. The leftmost bit on the answer is a 1, which means that the answer is negative, in two's complement form, as it should be. Converting the answer to decimal form by summing all the bits times their respective weight values, we get:

$$(1 \times -32_{10}) + (1 \times 16_{10}) + (1 \times 8_{10}) + (1 \times 1_{10}) = -7_{10}$$

Indeed -7_{10} is the proper sum of -25_{10} and 18_{10}.

Overflow

One caveat with signed binary numbers is that of overflow, where the answer to an addition or subtraction problem exceeds the magnitude which can be represented with the alloted number of bits. Remember that the place of the sign bit is fixed from the beginning of the problem. With the last example problem, we used five binary bits to represent the magnitude of the number, and the left-most (sixth) bit as the negative-weight, or sign, bit. With five bits to represent magnitude, we have a representation range of 2^5, or thirty-two integer steps from 0 to maximum. This means that we can represent a number as high as $+31_{10}$ (011111_2), or as low as -32_{10} (100000_2). If we set up an addition problem with two binary numbers, the sixth bit used for sign, and the result either exceeds $+31_{10}$ or is less than -32_{10}, our answer will be incorrect. Let's try adding 17_{10} and 19_{10} to see how this overflow condition works for excessive positive numbers:

$17_{10} = 10001_2$ $\qquad\qquad$ $19_{10} = 10011_2$

$$\begin{array}{ll} & 111 \quad \leftarrow \text{Carry bits} \\ (\text{Showing sign bits}) & 010001 \\ & \underline{+1010011} \\ & 100100 \end{array}$$

The answer (100100_2), interpreted with the sixth bit as the -32_{10} place, is actually equal to -28_{10}, not $+36_{10}$ as we should get with $+17_{10}$ and $+19_{10}$ added together! Obviously, this is not correct. What went wrong? The answer lies in the restrictions of the six-bit number field within which we're working Since the magnitude of the true and proper sum (36_{10}) exceeds the allowable limit for our designated bit field, we have an overflow error.

Simply put, six places doesn't give enough bits to represent the correct sum, so whatever figure we obtain using the strategy of discarding the left-most "carry" bit will be incorrect. A similar error will occur if we add two negative numbers together to produce a sum that is too low for our six-bit binary field. Let's try adding -17_{10} and -19_{10} together to see how this works (or doesn't work, as the case may be!):

$-17_{10} = 10111_{12}$ $\qquad$ $-19_{10} = 101101_2$

```
                                    1 1111   ← Carry bits
      (Showing sign bits)              101111
                                    + 101101
                                    --------
                                    1011100
                                    |
                          Discard extra bit
```

Final Answer: $011100_2 = +28_{10}$

The (incorrect) answer is a positive twenty-eight. The fact that the real sum of negative seventeen and negative nineteen was too low to be properly represented with a five bit magnitude field and a sixth sign bit is the root cause of this difficulty. Let's try these two problems again, except this time using the seventh bit for a sign bit, and allowing the use of 6 bits for representing the magnitude:

$17_{10} + 19_{10}$ $\qquad$ $(-17_{10}) + (-19_{10})$

```
       1   11              11   1111
      0010001                1101111
    + 0010011            +   1101101
    ---------            ---------
      0100100(2)         11011100(2)
                         |
                Discard extra bit
```

Answers: $0100100_2 = +36_{10}$

$1011100_2 = -36_{10}$

By using bit fields sufficiently large to handle the magnitude of the sums, we arrive at the correct answers. In these sample problems we've been able to detect overflow errors by performing the addition problems in decimal form and comparing the results with the binary answers. For example, when adding $+17_{10}$ and $+19_{10}$ together, we knew that the answer was supposed to be $+36_{10}$, so when the binary sum checked out to be -28_{10}, we knew that something had to be wrong. Although this is a valid way of detecting overflow, it is not very efficient.

After all, the whole idea of complementation is to be able to reliably add binary numbers together and not have to double-check the result by adding the same numbers together in decimal form. This is especially true for the purpose of building electronic circuits to add binary quantities together: the circuit has to be able to check itself for overflow without the supervision of a human being who already knows what the correct answer is.

What we need is a simple error-detection method that doesn't require any additional arithmetic. Perhaps the most elegant solution is to check for the sign of the sum and compare it against the signs of the numbers added. Obviously, two positive numbers added together should give a positive result, and two negative numbers added together should give a negative result. Notice that whenever we had a condition of overflow in the example problems, the sign of the sum was always opposite of the two added numbers: $+17_{10}$ plus $+19_{10}$ giving -28_{10}, or -17_{10} plus -19_{10} giving $+28_{10}$.

By checking the signs alone we are able to tell that something is wrong. But what about cases where a positive number is added to a negative number? What sign should the sum be in order to be correct. Or, more precisely, what sign of sum would necessarily indicate an overflow error?

The answer to this is equally elegant: there will never be an overflow error when two numbers of opposite signs are added together! The reason for this is apparent when the nature of overflow is considered. Overflow occurs when the magnitude of a number exceeds the range allowed by the size of the bit field. The sum of two identically-signed numbers may very well exceed the range of the bit field of those two numbers, and so in this case overflow is a possibility. However, if a positive number is added to a negative number, the sum will always be closer to zero than either of the two added numbers: its magnitude must be less than the magnitude of either original number, and so overflow is impossible.Fortunately, this technique of overflow detection is easily implemented in electronic circuitry, and it is a standard feature in digital adder circuits: a subject for a later chapter.

Bit Groupings

The singular reason for learning and using the binary numeration system in electronics is to understand how to design, build, and troubleshoot circuits that represent and process numerical quantities in digital form. Since the bivalent (two-valued) system of binary bit numeration lends itself so easily to representation by "on" and "off" transistor states (saturation and cutoff, respectively), it makes sense to design and build circuits leveraging this principle to perform binary calculations. If we were to build a circuit to represent a binary number, we would have to allocate enough transistor circuits to represent as many bits as we desire. In other words, in designing a digital circuit, we must first decide how many bits (maximum) we would like to be able to represent, since each bit requires one on/off circuit to represent it. This is analogous to designing an abacus to digitally represent decimal numbers: we must decide how many digits we wish to handle in this primitive "calculator" device, for each digit requires a separate rod with its own beads.

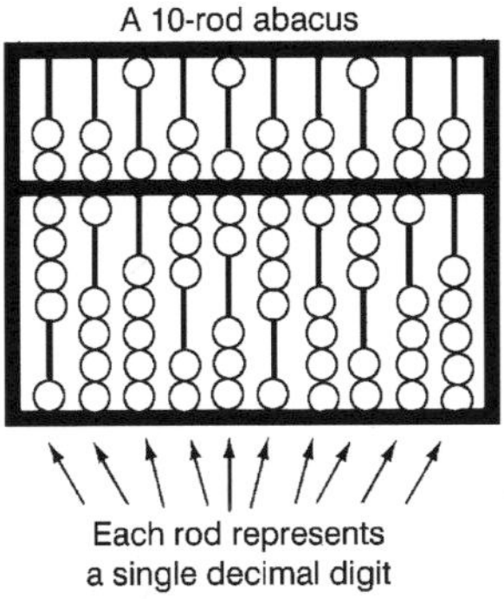

A ten-rod abacus would be able to represent a ten-digit decimal number, or a maximum value of 9,999,999,999. If we wished to represent a larger number on this abacus, we would be unable to, unless additional rods could be added to it. In digital, electronic computer design, it is common to design the system for a common "bit width:" a maximum number of bits allocated to represent numerical quantities. Early digital computers handled bits in groups of four or eight. More modern systems handle numbers in clusters of 32 bits or more.

To more conveniently express the "bit width" of such clusters in a digital computer, specific labels were applied to the more common groupings. Eight bits, grouped together to form a single binary quantity, is known as a byte. Four bits, grouped together as one binary number, is known by the humorous title of nibble, often spelled as nybble. A multitude of terms have followed byte and nibble for labeling specfiic groupings of binary bits. Most of the terms shown here are informal, and have not been made "authoritative" by any standards group or other sanctioning body.

However, their inclusion into this chapter is warranted by their occasional appearance in technical literature, as well as the levity they add to an otherwise dry subject:

- *Bit:* A single, bivalent unit of binary notation. Equivalent to a decimal "digit."
- *Crumb, Tydbit, or Tayste:* Two bits.
- *Nibble, or Nybble:* Four bits.
- *Nickle:* Five bits.

- *Byte:* Eight bits.
- *Deckle:* Ten bits.
- *Playte:* Sixteen bits.
- *Dynner:* Thirty-two bits.
- *Word:* (system dependent).

The most ambiguous term by far is word, referring to the standard bit-grouping within a particular digital system. For a computer system using a 32 bit-wide "data path," a "word" would mean 32 bits. If the system used 16 bits as the standard grouping for binary quantities, a "word" would mean 16 bits. The terms playte and dynner, by contrast, always refer to 16 and 32 bits, respectively, regardless of the system context in which they are used. Context dependence is likewise true for derivative terms of word, such as double word and longword (both meaning twice the standard bit-width), half-word (half the standard bit-width), and quad (meaning four times the standard bit-width). One humorous addition to this somewhat boring collection of word-derivatives is the term chawmp, which means the same as half-word. For example, a chawmp would be 16 bits in the context of a 32-bit digital system, and 18 bits in the context of a 36-bit system. Also, the term gawble is sometimes synonymous with word.

ADDITION USING 2 COMPLEMENT

Begin with the number in one's complement. Add 1 if the number is negative. Twelve would be represented as 00001100, and -12 as 11110100. To verify this, let's subtract 1 from 11110100, to get 11110011. If we flip the bits, we get 00001100, or 12 in decimal. In this notation, "m" indicates the total number of bits. For us (working with 8 bits), it would be excess 2^7. To represent a number (positive or negative) in excess 2^7, begin by taking the number in regular binary representation. Then add 2^7 (=128) to that number. For example, 7 would be 128 + 7=135, or $2^7+2^2+2^1+2^0$, and, in binary,10000111. We would represent –7 as 128–7=121, and, in binary, 01111001.

Unless you know which representation has been used, you cannot figure out the value of a number. A number in excess $2^{(m-1)}$ is the same as that number in two's complement with the leftmost bit flipped. To see the advantages and disadvantages of each method, let's try working with them. Using the regular algorithm for binary adition, add (5+12), (-5+12), (-12+-5), and (12+-12) in each system. Then convert back to decimal numbers.

What would the binary number 1011 be in decimal notation?

Answers: $1011 = (1*2^3)+(0*2^2)+(1*2^1)+(1*2^0)$

$= (1*8) + (0*4) + (1*2) + (1*1)$

= 11 (in decimal notation)

BINARY MULTIPLICATION

Multiplication in the binary system works the same way as in the decimal system:

- 1*1=1
- 1*0=0
- 0*1=0

$$\begin{array}{r} 101 \\ *\ 11 \\ \hline 101 \\ 1010 \\ \hline 1111 \end{array}$$

Note that multiplying by two is extremely easy. To multiply by two, just add a 0 on the end.

BINARY DIVISION

Follow the same rules as in decimal division. For the sake of simplicity, throw away the remainder.

For Example: 111011/11

$$\begin{array}{r} 10011\,r\,10 \\ 11\overline{)111011} \\ -11 \\ \hline 101 \\ -11 \\ \hline 101 \\ 11 \\ \hline 10 \end{array}$$

DECIMAL TO BINARY NOTATION

Converting from decimal to binary notation is slightly more difficult conceptually, but can easily be done once you know how through the use of algorithms. Begin by thinking of a few examples. We can easily see that the number 3= 2+1. and that this is equivalent to $(1*2^1)+(1*2^0)$.

This translates into putting a "1" in the 2^1 column and a "1" in the 2^0 column, to get "11". Almost as intuitive is the number 5: it is obviously 4+1, which is the same as saying [(2*2) +1], or 2^2+1. This can also be written as $[(1*2^2)+(1*2^0)]$. Looking at this in columns,

$$\begin{array}{c|c|c} 2^2 & 2^2 & 2^0 \\ 1 & 0 & 1 \end{array}$$

or 101.

What we're doing here is finding the largest power of two within the number ($2^2=4$ is the largest power of 2 in 5), subtracting that from the number (5–4=1), and finding the largest power of 2 in the remainder ($2^0=1$ is the largest power of 2 in 1). Then we just put this into columns. This process continues until we have a remainder of 0. Let's take a look at how it works. We know that:

2^0=1
2^1=2
2^2=4
2^3=8
2^4=16
2^5=32
2^6=64
2^7=128

and so on. To convert the decimal number 75 to binary, we would find the largest power of 2 less than 75, which is 64. Thus, we would put a 1 in the 2^6 column, and subtract 64 from 75, giving us 11. The largest power of 2 in 11 is 8, or 2^3. Put 1 in the 2^3 column, and 0 in 2^4 and 2^5. Subtract 8 from 11 to get 3. Put 1 in the 2^1 column, 0 in 2^2, and subtract 2 from 3. We're left with 1, which goes in 2^0, and we subtract one to get zero. Thus, our number is 1001011.

Making this algorithm a bit more formal gives us:

- Let D=number we wish to convert from decimal to binary
- Repeat until D=0
  - Find the largest power of two in D. Let this equal P.
  - Put a 1 in binary column P.
  - Subtract P from D.
- Put zeros in all columns which don't have ones.

This algorithm is a bit awkward. Particularly step 3, "filling in the zeros." Therefore, we should rewrite it such that we ascertain the value of each column individually, putting in 0's and 1's as we go:

- Let D= the number we wish to convert from decimal to binary
- Find P, such that 2^P is the largest power of two smaller than D.
- Repeat until P<0
  - If 2^P<=D then
    - a. put 1 into column P
    - b. subtract 2^P from D
- Else
  - a. put 0 into column P
- End if
- Subtract 1 from P

Now that we have an algorithm, we can use it to convert numbers from decimal to binary relatively painlessly. Let's try the number D=55.

- Our first step is to find P. We know that 2^4=16, 2^5=32, and 2^6=64. Therefore, P=5.
- $2^5 \leqslant$=55, so we put a 1 in the 2^5 column: 1———.
- Subtracting 55-32 leaves us with 23. Subtracting 1 from P gives us 4.
- Following step 3 again, $2^4 \leqslant$=23, so we put a 1 in the 2^4 column: 11——.

- Next, subtract 16 from 23, to get 7. Subtract 1 from P gives us 3.
- $2^3 > 7$, so we put a 0 in the 2^3 column: 110—-
- Next, subtract 1 from P, which gives us 2.
- $2^2 \leqslant = 7$, so we put a 1 in the 2^2 column: 1101—
- Subtract 4 from 7 to get 3. Subtract 1 from P to get 1.
- $2^1 \leqslant = 3$, so we put a 1 in the 2^1 column: 11011-
- Subtract 2 from 3 to get 1. Subtract 1 from P to get 0.
- $2^0 \leqslant = 1$, so we put a 1 in the 2^0 column: 110111
- Subtract 1 from 1 to get 0. Subtract 1 from P to get -1.
- P is now less than zero, so we stop.

Another algorithm for converting decimal to binary

However, this is not the only approach possible. We can start at the right, rather than the left.

All binary numbers are in the form

$$a[n]*2^n + a[n-1]*2^{(n-1)}+...+a[1]*2^1 + a[0]*2^0$$

where each a[i] is either a 1 or a 0 (the only possible digits for the binary system). The only way a number can be odd is if it has a 1 in the 2^0 column, because all powers of two greater than 0 are even numbers (2, 4, 8, 16...). This gives us the rightmost digit as a starting point.

Now we need to do the remaining digits. One idea is to "shift" them. It is also easy to see that multiplying and dividing by 2 shifts everything by one column: two in binary is 10, or $(1*2^1)$. Dividing $(1*2^1)$ by 2 gives us $(1*2^0)$, or just a 1 in binary. Similarly, multiplying by 2 shifts in the other direction: $(1*2^1)*2=(1*2^2)$ or 10 in binary. Therefore

$$\{a[n]*2^n + a[n-1]*2^{(n-1)} +... + a[1]*2^1 + a[0]*2^0\}/2$$

is equal to,

$$a[n]*2^{(n-1)} + a[n-1]*2^{(n-2)} +... + a[1]2^0$$

Let's look at how this can help us convert from decimal to binary. Take the number 163. We know that since it is odd, there must be a 1 in the 2^0 column (a[0]=1). We also know that it equals 162+1. If we put the 1 in the 2^0 column, we have 162 left, and have to decide how to translate the remaining digits.

Two's column: Dividing 162 by 2 gives 81. The number 81 in binary would also have a 1 in the 2^0 column. Since we divided the number by two, we "took out" one power of two.

Similarly, the statement $a[n-1]*2^{(n-1)} + a[n-2]*2^{(n-2)} +... + a[1]*2^0$ has a power of two removed. Our "new" 2^0 column now contains a1. We learned earlier that there is a 1 in the 2^0 column if the number is odd. Since 81 is odd, a[1]=1. Practically, we can simply keep a "running total", which now stands at 11 (a[1]=1 and a[0]=1). Also note that a1 is essentially "remultiplied" by two just by putting it in front of a[0], so it is automatically fit into the correct column.

Four's column: Now we can subtract 1 from 81 to see what remainder we still must place (80). Dividing 80 by 2 gives 40. Therefore, there must be a 0 in the 4's column, (because what we are actually placing is a 2^0 column, and the number is not odd). *Eight's column*: We can divide by two again to get 20. This is even, so we put a 0 in the 8's column. Our running total now stands at a[3]=0, a[2]=0, a[1]=1, and a[0]=1.

We can continue in this manner until there is no remainder to place.

Let's formalize this algorithm:

- Let D= the number we wish to convert from decimal to binary.
- Repeat until D=0:
  - If D is odd, put "1" in the leftmost open column, and subtract 1 from D.
  - If D is even, put "0" in the leftmost open column.
  - Divide D by 2.

  End Repeat

For the number 163, this works as follows:

- Let D=163
- D is odd, put a 1 in the 2^0 column.
  Subtract 1 from D to get 162.
- Divide D=162 by 2.
  Temporary Result: 01 New D=81
  D does not equal 0, so we repeat step 2.
- D is odd, put a 1 in the 2^1 column.
  Subtract 1 from D to get 80.
- Divide D=80 by 2.
  Temporary Result: 11 New D=40
  D does not equal 0, so we repeat step 2.
- D is even, put a 0 in the 2^2 column.
- Divide D by 2.
  Temporary Result: 011 New D=20
- D is even, put a 0 in the 2^3 column.
- Divide D by 2.
  Temporary Result: 0011 New D=10
- D is even, put a 0 in the 2^4 column.
- Divide D by 2.
  Temporary Result: 00011 New D=5
- D is odd, put a 1 in the 2^5 column.
  Subtract 1 from D to get 4.
- Divide D by 2.
  Temporary Result: 100011 New D=2
- D is even, put a 0 in the 2^6 column.
- Divide D by 2.
  Temporary Result: 0100011 New D=1

- D is odd, put a 1 in the 27 column.
  Subtract 1 from D to get D=0.
- Divide D by 2.
  Temporary Result: 10100011 New D=0

D=0, so we are done, and the decimal number 163 is equivalent to the binary number 10100011.

Since we already knew how to convert from binary to decimal, we can easily verify our result. 10100011 = $(1*2^0) + (1*2^1)+(1*2^5)+(1*2^7)$=1+2+32+128 = 163.

RIGHT SHIFT METHOD

The simplest way to indicate negation is signed magnitude. In signed magnitude, the left-most bit is not actually part of the number, but is just the equivalent of a +/- sign. "0" indicates that the number is positive, "1" indicates negative. In 8 bits, 00001100 would be 12 (break this down into $(1*2^3) + (1*2^2)$). To indicate -12, we would simply put a "1" rather than a "0" as the first bit: 10001100.

Index

A

Abrasion 84
Adder-subtractor 173
Amplifier 16, 17, 206, 207, 248
Amplitude 1, 2
Analog 11, 12, 13, 14, 206, 241
Analysis procedure 148, 180
Anisotropy 92
Arbitrary 6
Asynchronous 6, 7, 179, 185
Asynchronous Sequential 185

B

Barriers 81
Binary 2, 5, 6, 7, 8, 83, 84, 85, 86
Binary Codes 59, 60
Binary Counting 13, 27
Binary Decoder 143
Binary Multiplier 172
Binary Quantities 14
Binary System 26
Bit Magnitude Comparator 171
Boolean 4, 5
Briefly 93

C

Characteristics 13, 155, 242, 251
Circuit 11, 13, 14, 15, 16, 17, 18, 21, 22, 23, 143, 192, 193, 194, 195, 196, 197, 205, 206, 207, 208, 215, 216, 217, 218, 219, 220, 221, 222, 223, 225, 228, 229, 230, 231, 232, 233, 234, 235, 237, 238, 239, 240, 241, 242, 245, 246, 247, 248, 249, 250, 251
Circuitry 3, 4, 9, 81, 86
Combinational 147, 148, 149, 151, 170, 179, 182, 184
Combinational Circuits 147, 184
Constructing 22, 242
Contaminated 90
Correcting Codes 72, 73, 74, 79, 80

D

Decimal Decoder 143
Decoder Generation 167
Digital Techniques 13
Discrete 1, 2, 3, 81, 83, 84

E

Encoders 169
Energetic 93
Error Detecting 71, 72
Error-Correcting 73, 74, 77, 78, 80
Etching 90, 91, 92, 93

F

Fabrication 8, 90, 93
Federal 90
Flip-flop 151, 176, 177, 180, 181, 182, 183, 184, 185, 186, 187, 188, 189, 190, 191, 196, 198
Fragile 3, 82, 91
Fundamental Concepts 74

G

Germanium 82, 83
Gray Conversion 28

H

Hamming codes 67, 73
Hexadecimal 13, 15, 18, 20, 21
Hexadecimal Conversion 20
Hydrofluoric 93

I

Implementation 78, 130, 166, 180, 183
Infinite 2
Input Multiplexer 166
Integrated 3, 4, 5, 8, 10, 11, 81, 82, 83, 84, 93
Intermediate 93
Intermediate Explanation 61
Isotropic 93

L

Latches 198, 199, 202, 203
Limitations 13, 151, 245

M

Magnitude Comparator 171
Multivibrator 193, 195, 196

N

Nitride 92, 93

O

Octal System 15
Operational 16, 17, 207
Origin 82
Oxidation 93

P

Parity 209
Polysilicon 92

Q

Quantified 92

R

Reflective Code 27
Reverse of Binary 18, 19

S

Seldom 93
Sequential 5, 6, 7, 28, 88
Sequential Codes 28
Simulated 8
Sputtering 91
Steadily 2
Susceptible 81
Switches 241
Symbolic 88, 89

T

Taxonomy 84

U

Ubiquitous 83

V

Vacuum 11, 82, 83

W

Weighted 23, 27, 28